Crosstown Traffic

Charles Shaar Murray began his career in 1970 as one of the participants in the *OZ* schoolkids' issue, joining *New Musical Express* two years later and eventually becoming *NME*'s Associate Editor before returning to a freelance career. He is the author of *Boogie Man: The Adventures of John Lee Hooker in the American Twentieth Century*, *Shots from the Hip: The Essential Guide to Blues on CD* and the co-author (with Roy Carr) of *David Bowie: An Illustrated Record*. His journalism and criticism have appeared in *Vogue*, *Rolling Stone*, *Q* , *Mojo*, the *Times Literary Supplement*, the *Literary Review*, the *Daily Telegraph*, *The Face*, the *Observer* and the *Independent*.

CROSSTOWN TRAFFIC

Jimi Hendrix and Post-war Pop

Charles Shaar Murray

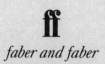

faber and faber

This book is dedicated to the memory of
Elizabeth de Gaster (1929–87)

and to Vernon Reid, Living Colour and
the Black Rock Coalition

First published in 1989
by Faber and Faber Limited
3 Queen Square London WCIN 3AU
This edition published in 2005

Photoset by Faber and Faber Ltd
Printed in the UK by CPI Bookmarque, Croydon

A CIP record for this book
is available from the British Library

ISBN 0–571–22722–8

2 4 6 8 10 9 7 5 3

Contents

Acknowledgements

'Yeah, uh, dig, brother . . . it's rilly outasite to be here . . .'

Jimi Hendrix, Monterey Pop Festival (18 June 1967)

Despite a sentimental fondness for the venerable 'solitary genius' theory and a well-nigh overwhelming temptation to grab this opportunity to deliver a quick chorus of 'I did it myyyyyy waaaayyyyyyy', such a fraudulent claim would stick in my throat. *Crosstown Traffic* is undoubtedly all my own fault, but it wouldn't be here at all, in this or any other form, without the contributions of a small army of people who, doubtless against their own better judgement, pitched in to help me transform a grab-bag of disconnected ideas and vague theories into what I hope is a coherent whole.

My largest debt of honour I owe to my wife, Ruth King, who provided unstinting spiritual, logistic and financial support throughout the entire process, despite the fact that she can't stand Jimi Hendrix and considered it an act of near-suicidal foolishness for me to devote thousands of hours to something like this when I could instead have been earning something vaguely resembling a living by maintaining my regular critical and journalistic practice. What can I say except – now the book's finished I promise to tidy up my study, Ruthie . . . first thing tomorrow morning.

Tom Paley, Nigel Levy (who also helped to transcribe the Pete Townshend interview) and Igor Goldkind unhesitatingly volunteered to endure the disruption of their personal and professional lives by offering temporary accommodation and work-space, thereby enabling work on *Crosstown Traffic* to continue during the Great Redecoration of 1988. Steve Sparks introduced me to the wonderful world of word-processing, while Su Small, Steve Wallington and Andy Oldfield accepted panicky phone calls at unsocial hours, provided Flying Programmer services and generally soothed a highly non-technical two-finger typist through the early stages of Computer Trauma.

My good friend Peter Hogan originally commissioned the book – in vastly different form – during his days as an editor at the now-defunct Eel

Pie Publishing. Later, as my agent, he fearlessly steered it on the storm-tossed course which eventually ended up at Faber and Faber, where Chris Barstow and Tracey Scoffield not only beat the manuscript – and, for that matter, the author – into shape, but protected me from the righteous wrath thundering about my ears through a succession of perforated deadlines.

John Berry, a tireless collector of Hendrix memorabilia, virtually adopted the project as his own during the extensive period of pre-production, and enthusiastically ransacked his vast archives for rare, unreleased tapes of Hendrix's 'secret music', and obscure quotes and anecdotes, thereby providing insights into my subject's musical subconscious which it would have been near-impossible for me to have obtained any other way. And my mother, Agnes Schaar Murray, helped me to realize that I was on to something worthwhile back in 1970, when – as a messianic young hippie – I dragged her to a local cinema to see *Woodstock*. She sat through the whole thing with a pained expression of someone stoically enduring a bad smell until Hendrix came on to play 'The Star Spangled Banner' for the grand finale. 'Now *that*,' she said, 'was *marvellous*.' Sean Hogan (brother of the aforementioned Peter) assembled the photo section with commendable elegance and efficiency.

More people than I can ever hope – or afford – to thank adequately provided anecdotes, interviews, insights, opinions and plain old ordinary encouragement over the years since this book (or something like it) was first contemplated. Some loaned records, tapes, books and clippings, some organized interviews or opened their address books, and some told me what I needed to know about things I knew little or nothing about. Others shot holes in my dumber ideas or honed and refined my brighter ones. Others still simply dragged me out for a drink when I was feeling mildly hysterical and desperately needed one.

They are not all quoted directly in the text, but all of them contributed materially to making this book what(ever) it is. In alphabetical order, then, can we please have some of that o-o-old soul clappin' for Keith Altham, Alan Balfour, J. G. Ballard, John Bauldie, Alfreda Benge, Larry Blackmon, Peter Boe, Steve Boon, David Bowie, Lloyd Bradley, Felicity Brooks, Tony Brown, Joanna Burn, Will Calhoun, Roy Carr, Stuart Cohn, Richard Cousins, Robert Cray, Johnny Guitar Crippen, Miles Davis, Bernard 'Papa Doc' Doherty, Paul DuNoyer, Mark Ellen, Pete Frame, Debbie Geller, Andy Gill, Corey Glover, Daryl Hall, Barney Hoskyns, Ernie Isley, Wilko Johnson, Nick Jones, Dik Jude, Peter Kameron, Nick

Kent, B. B. King, Garrie J. Lammin, Herman Leonard, Ian MacDonald, Tom McGuinness, George McManus, Phil Manzanera, Michael Moorcock, Alan Moore, Bill Nitopi, Rob Partridge, Little Richard Penniman, Noel Redding, Vernon Reid, Marsha Rowe, Vermilion Sands, Jon Savage, Harry Shapiro, David Sinclair, Mark Sinker, Neil Slaven, Mat Snow, Neil Spencer, T. M. Stevens, Barnaby Thompson, Pete Townshend, Tina Turner, Ed Ward, Harold Waterman, the late Muddy Waters, Cliff White, T-Bone Wolk, Bobby Womack, Robin Wood, Ron Wood (no relation), Robert Wyatt and Elizabeth J. Young.

Crosstown Traffic was originally written on an Amstrad PCW 8512 with NewWord 1.4 word-processing software. Author's cigarettes by Lambert & Butler, lighters by Zippo, guitars by Fender, jeans by Levi's, boots by Hi-Tec, overdraft by NatWest.

Now – move over, Rover, and let Jimi take over . . .

Acknowledgements to the Revised Edition
Needless to say, anyone who got thanked the first time round in the original edition stays thanked. Big ups to the following for contributing materially to the production of this one:

A gleaming 'Major Player Award' to my agent, Antony Harwood, for doing whatever it is that agents do with as much style and sympathy as any author, however flaky and insecure, could possibly desire. One just like it goes to Lee Brackstone at Faber & Faber in London, who steered the book through revision, redesign and republication.

Portions of the new material in this edition first appeared, sometimes in radically different form, in *Mojo*, *Guitarist*, *Guitar World*, *Revolver* and the *Daily Telegraph*; my thanks to commissioning editors Mat Snow, Paul Trynka, Neville Marten, Brad Tolinski, Tim Rostron and Caspar Llewellyn-Smith for enabling me to pursue the topic beyond the confines of the book. The short story *1963* was commissioned for, and originally appeared in, the anthology *Jimi Hendrix: The Ultimate Experience* (Boxtree, 1995), edited by Chris Salewicz and Adrian Boot.

Major thanks for the platform and the hospitality to everyone at the Experience Music Project in Seattle, especially Chief Curators Peter Blecha and Jim Fricke. A special shout-out to Alan 'Jah Worf' Mitchell: 'You are, and will always be, my friend.' And, once again, to the world's top girlfriend, my beloved comrade Anna Chen.

Introduction to the Original Edition:
The English and American
Combined Anthem

There comes a screaming across the sky. It has happened before, but there is nothing to compare it to now . . .

Thomas Pynchon, *Gravity's Rainbow* (1973)

1987: a British television arts series called *Equinox* is featuring a documentary history of the electric guitar under the splendidly onomatopoeic title *Twang Bang Kerrang*. After the obligatory nods to Charlie Christian and Les Paul, we are introduced to a couple of hopeful semi-pros, invited to marvel at the clean-cut chicken-pickin' wizardry of country cousins Jerry McGee and Jerry Donahue, reverently permitted to inspect the antiquarian wonders of Steve Howe's guitar collection and the technological sorcery of Andy Summers' effects rack, and vouchsafed a searing glimpse of the hotwired, hyperthyroid freneticism of Chicago bluesman Buddy Guy.

Somewhere along the line, Jimi Hendrix appears, briefly captured in that oft-quoted clip from the Monterey Pop Festival film where he out-Visigoths The Who – who had preceded him onstage – by not only smashing a guitar but igniting it with lighter fluid. Cut to Dr Glenn Wilson, a visiting psychoanalyst, who explains, in a tone so exquisitely condescending that it must have been rented from Margaret Thatcher, that pyromaniacs often attain orgasm at the moment of conflagration. Exit Jimi Hendrix, his place in the history of his instrument, his music and his times neatly encapsulated for posterity, his legacy reduced to a pile of trashed speaker cabinets, a Stratocaster served *flambé* and a soiled headband. Later on, the programme lovingly devotes a full ten minutes to the spectacle of a toweringly uninteresting corporate rock band at work on their next album. It is this kind of dismissive relegation of Hendrix to curio status – a loony black man peddling sex and violence, just another rocking Elephant Man from the sixties freakshow – which helped remind me why I was writing this book.

Like rock music itself, nostalgia is governed by a simple, straightforward principle: First Simplify, Then Exaggerate. Nostalgia is a filter for history operated partially by the unconscious and partially by the architects and gardeners who tend what J. G. Ballard calls The Media Landscape. It is designed to remove history's nasty, inconvenient lumps, and it trawls the resulting soup for raw materials – images of sufficient resonance to solidify into symbols. When these nuggets surface, they can then serve double duty: they can function as comforting, reassuring landmarks, enabling us to navigate in a general consensus of everyday reality, and – since symbols are infinitely more mobile and flexible than our use of them can ever acknowledge – they can be rearranged into an ever-changing kaleidoscope of values and imperatives. Just as the term 'traditional values' can mean anything which a conservative politician wants it to when he or she is about to announce something not in your best interests, so the sights and sounds of the past can be endlessly shuffled into 'proof' of virtually any contention or interest. Nostalgia makes good Stalinists of us all, as that which it is inconvenient or unpopular to remember becomes progressively less real, fading to a grey rendered ever more muzzy by the bold tones and snappy graphics of the authorized version.

The 'authorized version' of the Jimi Hendrix experience (*sic*) is that Hendrix was a crazy black man who did funny things with a guitar, had thousands of women and eventually died of drugs, which was a shame because he was a really good guitarist, and he could play it with his teeth, too. (Like David Bowie's Ziggy Stardust, 'he took it all too far/but boy, could he play guitar'.) He is a convenient focus for cosy generalizations about the innate phallocentricity of hard rock, the evils of drug use and the reactionary tedium of the extended guitar solo; and equally for mawkish or cautionary homilies on the destructive potential of stardom, the naïve futility of sixties idealism and how terrible it is that gifted people sometimes die young. All this has been digested; Hendrix is as serviceable as a symbol of the excesses, indulgences and pretensions of his era, as he is of its aspirations and vaulting imagination. His death, like the final collapse of The Beatles, is a handy cultural marker for that moment when (depending on your personal view of these matters) the surge towards the millennium was ambushed in its prime, or – thankfully – everybody came to their senses and resumed business as usual.

Yet once we haul ourselves out of our comfortable bath of body-temperature privatized history, we rediscover that solid skeleton which the filter won't pass, that which refuses to be reduced to sampleable cliché, reproducible mannerism and a tidy package of greatest hits. His entire career – from his days as a hired guitarist in scuzzy clubs and bars to his peak as an international celebrity – was a ceaseless struggle against racial and cultural stereotyping; he was trapped first by unthinking reaction and rejection, and then by unthinking acceptance of what were originally intended simply as attention-getting devices to attract an audience to his music. His innovations were developed as a means of creating a personal vocabulary; he found himself lionized as a stuntman while he saw himself as a poet.

Stated at its simplest, he was the most eloquent instrumentalist ever to work in rock. I once asked B. B. King if he considered Jimi Hendrix to be a bluesman; he gazed at me pityingly and replied, 'I consider him to be a *musician*; a great, *great* musician.' Since 'rock criticism' has generally been practised by drop-outs from literature classes, discussion of music *as music* has generally been subordinated to textual analysis of lyrics, with their musical settings given only minimal consideration (a critical method which, incidentally, has generally served black musicians poorly, since the verbal content of blues and soul music is an inextricable part of the whole, and therefore dependent on musical context and vocal intonation to communicate most fully). Hendrix himself was a composer and lyricist of considerable gifts, but his songwriting talents have been largely overshadowed by his achievements as a showman and an instrumentalist. Nevertheless, he developed a more personal 'voice' through his instrument than most popular musicians could do with their words. *Crosstown Traffic* is about that 'voice', and about some of what I hear it saying.

1988: Vernon Reid, founder of the Black Rock Coalition and guitarist/leader of Living Colour, is describing to me his indignation at the rock establishment's co-option of Jimi Hendrix as an 'honorary white'. 'The first thing that made me aware of race in music and the role it plays,' he recalled, not without considerable bitterness, 'was when I was in high school. There was a local rock radio station I used to listen to all the time, and late at night on the anniversary of Hendrix's death they were playing some Hendrix music and the deejay said that Hendrix was black, but that the music didn't sound very black to him. Yeah, it was a white deejay . . . and I flipped out. At the time I was very culturally aware of the race issues because of Martin Luther King and Malcolm X and all the ferment that was happening in the Black Power movement. I didn't really connect it all so much to *music*, but that really threw it in my face. It was a phone-in show, and I spent all night trying to call in. I fell *asleep* with the phone in my hand . . .

3

'It was not only an insult to his music, but I took it as an affront to me personally. Because if what the deejay said was true, what is he saying about me as a listener who loves Hendrix *as a black artist*? That started my awareness of these things in music . . .'

Guitarist Alvin Lee, whose band Ten Years After co-starred with Hendrix at the Woodstock Festival in 1969, once commented, 'Hendrix wasn't black or white. Hendrix was Hendrix.' Remarks like this from whites often simply translate as 'He wasn't one of us, but he wasn't really one of *them* either – and anyway he liked us best.' However, Lee has hit on that aspect of Jimi Hendrix which created the tortured dichotomy that so infuriated Vernon Reid; his frustration with received ideas of what a black performer was or was not allowed to do and be. His 'discovery' by British rock musician Chas Chandler enabled him to gatecrash the white boys' 'come as a black man' fancy-dress party, and walk off with the most glittering prizes; but his death – coming at a pivotal point in his musical development and aborting what would have been a fully-fledged artistic rebirth – left him forever identified with hard rock, a style of music in which black musicians have since been historically unwelcome. It also left his reputation helplessly vulnerable to the maudlin hagiography of popular culture's martyr syndrome; conveniently defenceless against the notion that he was simply a shooting star, screaming across the sky, a fabulous monster whose music came from nowhere and went nowhere, with neither ancestors nor offspring. In his 1961 essay, 'The Retreat from the Word', George Steiner wrote of James Joyce, 'There have been no successors to Joyce in English; perhaps there can be none to a talent so exhaustive of its own potential.' Is this, then, also the final judgement on the legacy of Jimi Hendrix?

It is undoubtedly flattering to Hendrix to suggest that everything he used he created from scratch, and also that his work was so idiosyncratic and personal that it could not be absorbed, only mimicked. However, such hagiography rebounds unpleasantly upon its subject: his mystique thus assumes such intimidating proportions that his music survives in lonely majesty, a magnificent irrelevance looming atop a pedestal in its own revered annexe in the Great Rock Museum's 'Psychedelic' Wing, rejected by a callous and insensitive black community and adored by imaginative, understanding whites. (We can almost hear, over hidden speakers, Steve Martin's narration from *The Jerk*: 'I was born a poor black child . . .')

User-friendly though this pat little myth may be (just *how* friendly depends, of course, on the user), it does serious disservice not only to the man and his music but, as Vernon Reid suggests, to the roots and branches alike of the black American musical traditions from which – this book contends – Hendrix's art drank so thirstily, and to which it gave so generously in return. Ultimately, it is a deeply racist myth, one which surgically amputates Hendrix from the broad swathe of black culture; he has become, effectively, colonized territory. Rather than being recognized as a proud, shining link in the chain of great black American improvising musicians, he has been enshrined as a magnificent aberration, his genius – for that it was, insomuch as anything in popular music can be so described – magically transferred from the black page of the ledger to the white. To put it mildly, this is the cultural equivalent of a mugging on a crowded street in broad daylight. In this respect, *Crosstown Traffic*, therefore, is an attempt at a citizen's arrest.

'If I'm free,' Hendrix once said, 'it's because I'm always running,' and he did indeed spend his whole life running. If there is an experiential core to his music, it is about the interlocking terrors of rootlessness and of feeling trapped. 'There must be some kind of way out of here,' he sang in Bob Dylan's 'All Along the Watchtower', and it requires no great powers of empathy to sense the intensity of his identification with that line. In his life as in his songs, he was forever searching for a place of his own; he escaped Seattle and school by joining the army; he escaped from the army into the world of the road musicians, perpetually shifting from group to group; he escaped from Harlem by moving to Greenwich Village; by relocating to London he escaped the codes of black showbiz and their attendant rules as to what a black entertainer could be, only, finally, to be ensnared by the more insidious webs of expectation and assumption spun by his well-meaning new admirers. *Crosstown Traffic* sets out to chart the routes along which Jimi Hendrix ran. In 'trying to get to the other side of town', he transgressed many boundaries; both arbitrary musical definitions separating blues and soul or jazz and rock, and also those more fundamental divides between the archaic and the avant-garde, between individualist and collectivist philosophies, between blacks and whites, between America and Britain, between passive acquiescence and furious resistance, between lust for life and obsession with death.

Like Robert Johnson, the haunted Delta bluesman whose slavering demons never let him rest, Hendrix never did quite 'get to the other side of town'. Wherever he was, people always assumed his 'real' home was somewhere else. Bobby Womack, the self-styled 'Last Soul Man' who knew Hendrix when he was a penniless hired guitarist touring at the bottom of the bill on the soul revues, believes, 'He was tryin' to fit in on his side of town, but it wasn't his side of town. He needed to be in another place . . . when he got to Europe, he got with people that was like him, and I was glad that he found a place.' But to 'those people that was like him', the story seemed very different. Pete Townshend suggests, '[In London] Hendrix must've thought he was in a madhouse, but one that was great fun, sort of like going to Hong Kong. I can't imagine what it was like for him: the idea of him feeling *comfortable* is pretty preposterous. He might've been happy to find himself, like the eternal hippies always talk about "finding themselves" in India.' Robert Wyatt – the former Soft Machine drummer/vocalist who shared management with the Jimi Hendrix Experience and toured America and Europe with them for more than a year – recalls, 'The nearest I ever saw to him looking at home was the closest I ever saw him *to* home, which was going up to Seattle and there was this huge family at the airport. What a wonderful sight! There was the history of America in the airport, almost. My initial impression was a lot of black men and a lot of Native American women. What a lovely bloke his dad looked with that lovely smile, and Hendrix seemed such a proud boy-come-home . . .

Except, of course, that you can't go home.

'Keep a foot in each camp long enough, Johnnie,' I said, 'and they'll build the barbed wire right through you,' and Johnnie nodded and the rain dripped from his face.

Len Deighton, Funeral in Berlin (1964)

The important part of Alvin Lee's comment is not his contention that Hendrix was not 'black or white', but that 'Hendrix was Hendrix'. We are all of us formed not only by the major landmarks of our culture, but by our private and personal experiences, and one central and singular aspect of Jimi Hendrix which is inexplicable in terms of the broad swathes of black American culture is his devotion to older forms of music which most blacks of his generation considered obsolete. Generally speaking, and prior to the emergence of younger black classicists like Wynton Marsalis and Robert Cray, black musicians have utilized the music of the present as a basis on which to build a music of the future; the past has been – to say the least – unpleasant, and the future can only be better. Robert Wyatt points out that 'black musicians tend not to play trad versions of older things; they're normally like Miles Davis, who just wants to keep moving ahead . . . it was extraordinary that [Hendrix] would have used [rural blues] the most primitive form of electric rock as a basis for his stuff.' This cannot indeed be explained in broad terms, but in personal terms it possibly can: the jazz and blues of the forties and early fifties was the music Hendrix heard in his childhood, when he was happiest, when his mother was still alive and his parents were still together. Much of the rock of the sixties can be explained in terms of childhood history and fantasy – the ghosts of British music-hall songs which haunt the music of The Beatles, The Kinks and The Who; the TV-derived cowboys-and-indians frontier imagery which shadows San Francisco psychedelia – so why should Hendrix be so different?

He was unquestionably a man of his times, formed by his environment and his era, but his unique musical formulation – that 'jazz', 'blues', 'rock' and 'soul' were not distinct musics which needed to be combined through fusions and hyphenations, but one music seen from different perspectives – was utterly his own. He was not a hyphenated man; he did not play hyphenated music. Like most interesting people, he embodied paradox and contradiction. A supreme individualist (by nature, if not by choice), he hungered for community, acceptance, belonging. Pacifist by philosophy and shy and quiet-spoken by upbringing, he was capable of extraordinary, terrifying violence; both in the stylized form of his performances and in sudden, unexpected private eruptions. He was a fervent iconoclast with a deep, abiding respect for tradition; a symbol of rampant maleness whose earliest supporters and closest confidantes were women; an American artist transplanted to Britain and then sold American as a British act; a musical rootsman pioneering new technology; a black man who borrowed from whites who had stolen from blacks; a supremely gifted improvising instrumentalist working in a genre built around the three-minute song; the committed pessimist who never ceased to crave salvation; the guitarist who wanted to be an orchestra.

Once given the freedom to pursue his own vision, his impact was stunning. I remember seeing him, for the first time, performing 'Hey Joe' one Friday evening on a British TV rock show called *Ready Steady Go!*: it seemed to be what I had been waiting all my life to hear. His music had the wayward adventurousness and sheer sensory overload I loved in the loud, weird rock of those immediately pre-psychedelic times, but it was weighted with the solid humanity and emotional authenticity I'd found only in soul music and the blues. Hendrix was hugely and quixotically *himself*; he was everything which the Townshends and Mayalls and Jaggers and Claptons had only pretended to be. At the same time he seemed contemporary and modern in a way that Muddy Waters, Howlin' Wolf, Bo Diddley and Chuck Berry could never be; intense, direct and forthright where the Motown stars seemed glitzy and restrained; as nakedly spontaneous as Otis Redding and as colourfully surreal as The Beatles. Where The Rolling Stones had artfully and ironically demonstrated both their *aficionados'* knowledge of black music and their awareness of their own distance from the worlds of hidden experience it contained, Hendrix acknowledged no such barriers. He was subverting both the black codes in which he was schooled, and the British Invasion which had adapted those codes for its own purposes. Right then, I started working on this book (and still finished it late).

His impact on those more knowledgeable and sophisticated than myself was equally traumatic. Pete Townshend recalls it thus: 'It's the most psychedelic experience I ever had, going to see Hendrix play. When he started to play, something changed: colours changed, everything changed. The sound changed. In those days they were using shitty little club PAs and a single Marshall stack. The drums would be heard straight with no microphones. Noel [Redding] was just a very basic bass player. It was just so superbly psychedelic . . . I didn't know what I'd heard and I didn't know what I'd seen. I was never a heavy psychedelics user and I certainly wasn't using them on that occasion. I didn't smoke that much pot. I didn't even drink very much.

'But I remember flames and water dripping out of the ends of his hands. I remember him playing [trills] and doing something with his tongue and things happening around him in the air. He was such a manipulator, such a magician to me, such a charismatic figure that my intimidation turned into complete and total shock that I didn't recover from until his death.'

More prosaically, but no less eloquently, Robert Wyatt has a similar testament. 'They weren't a pub-rock band, you know what I mean? You walked in and you suddenly noticed that the room seemed a bit small and inadequate while they played. I'm not talking about volume, because all kinds of people were playing loud by then, but it really did seem as if there was something *large* going on. By contrast, even the best of the London bands were stodgy. I would say that it was as dramatic as the sudden use of Technicolor after X years of black-and-white films. It was as clear as that.'

I never met Jimi Hendrix, or spoke to him. He died more than a year before I became a music-business professional, thereby acquiring a legitimate licence to meet famous people and be either rude or sycophantic towards them. I saw him twice in concert: once at the tail end of 1967 at an all-night event called 'Christmas on Earth Continued', where he headed a bill which included Pink Floyd, Traffic, Soft Machine, The Move, Tomorrow and assorted others. Then he was exuberant, saucer-eyed, extrovert, seemingly pulling the most outrageous and extraordinary sounds out of the very molecules of the air; a funky conjurer who seemed as surprised and delighted by his feats as anyone in the audience. He had just returned to Britain after taking his homeland by storm, his second album was about to be released; he was surfing his moment with the euphoric incredulity of a poor kid suddenly let loose in a toyshop.

The second and last time was at the Isle of Wight Pop Festival at the end of August 1970: an event racked by running battles between the organizers and a loose grouping of anarchists and bikers who wanted to 'liberate' the show and turn it into a free festival. Hendrix hadn't performed in Britain for almost a year and a half, and, despite the presence of Miles Davis, The Doors, Joni Mitchell, Sly & the Family Stone and – you should pardon the expression – Emerson, Lake and Palmer, he was unquestionably the main event. After an unconscionably protracted delay, he sauntered on stage and grimly muscled his way through a set of his best-known tunes, padded out with meandering jams. Hendrix and his accompanists – bassist Billy Cox, drummer Mitch Mitchell – seemed to be operating in parallel but separate universes, never meshing, only sporadically catching fire. The electronic demons, once so effortlessly summoned from his wall of Marshall amplifiers and controlled and tamed with his guitar, now mocked and evaded him. Even on his slow blues 'Red House', the musical refuge to which he could always retreat for shelter when things weren't going right, the guitar fought him, betrayed him; strings tauntingly slipping from beneath unaccountably numb fingers. Shivering in the damp chill night, the crowd willed him on – he was, after all, the reason they were there – but to no avail. He seemed exhausted, tormented, trapped. His death, less than three weeks later, seemed hideously appropriate. On the festival stage, Hendrix had already seemed three parts dead.

Of course, what none of us in that audience could possibly know was that Hendrix was bored to death with power-trio hard rock; that economic pressures caused by financial mismanagement had forced him back out on the road to play a tour in which he had no artistic interest whatsoever, that he was not so much a burned-out case as an artist still lumbered with devices he felt he had outgrown, and which his audiences were reluctant to see him abandon.

> I got stoned and I can't go home
> I'm callin' long distance on a public saxophone . . .
> Feel like I got run over
> By public opinion and the past . . .
>> Jimi Hendrix, 'Midnight Lightning' (Isle of Wight, 1970)

'Y'all wanna hear all those *old* songs, man? Damn, everybody's tryin' to get some *other* things together . . .'
>> Jimi Hendrix (Isle of Wight, 1970)

Jimi Hendrix was, by all accounts, an exceptionally private man. His privacy did not derive from isolation – it is difficult to imagine him living like Elvis Presley, walled up in a mansion surrounded by stooges and bodyguards – and whenever he was in London, Los Angeles or New York he could generally be found toting a guitar and a pair of Revox tape recorders from club to club, sitting in with whichever musicians happened to be in town that night, whether it was Stephen Stills or Roland Kirk, Howlin' Wolf or Johnny Winter. He created that privacy with his own reticence, his half-mocking, half-shy demeanour; he had many acquaintances, but few friends. His girlfriends – Monika Danneman, Kathy Etchingham, Fayne Pridgeon, the late Devon Wilson – certainly knew him well, as did his colleagues – Billy Cox, Chas Chandler, Mitch Mitchell, Noel Redding, Eddie Kramer, Alan Douglas – but all of these and more have their own versions of history, their own perspectives, and their own business interests.

Since *Crosstown Traffic* is not a biography of Jimi Hendrix – there have been five so far, with more on the way – I have chosen to search for Jimi Hendrix and to explore his world through the medium where his innermost feelings were most thoroughly exposed: in the body of work which was the most important entity in his life. If Jimi Hendrix is to be found, it is in his music; and in the music from which he learned and which learned from him, and also in the climate in which his music was made. This book is about music; it is also about what the music is about.

And I hope it does that music justice.

Charles Shaar Murray
London, March 1989

Introduction to the Revised Edition:
Still Reigning, Still Dreaming

The original introduction may help to explain why much of the text of this book may seem like the work of an author frenziedly kicking an open door. When *Crosstown Traffic* was originally written at the butt-end of the 1980s, with the twentieth anniversary of Jimi Hendrix's death fast approaching, he seemed to be primarily represented in the mass consciousness as a caricature, a stereotype, a clown, a 'psychedelic Uncle Tom'. To punks, his protracted guitar soloing and oblique lyrics seemed overly redolent of the obsolete and discredited tropes of hippie. To rap's black nationalists, his sound, style and working environment seemed tainted by the tropes of 'white' rock. For the rigidly beats-per-minute-conscious dance-music scene, his music was rhythmically too fussy and turbulent. His lionization by guitar fetishists was only a small counterweight: indeed, the heavy-metal hordes clustering around his banner contributed materially to keeping civilians at a distance.

Even his record company didn't seem to care. As if the release of increasingly weird Alan Douglas productions hadn't been bad enough – radically distorting as they did the public perception of Hendrix's later music and strengthening the contention that he had 'lost it' or 'burnt out' after the release of *Electric Ladyland*, his relocation to the US and the departure of key 'British contingent' players like Chas Chandler and Noel Redding – even the primary texts released in his lifetime were shoddily handled in the CD era. My first CD copy of *Ladyland* arrived as a two–disc boxed set which appeared to have been directly mastered from the original vinyl double-album which, dating as it did from the era of 'autochange' turntables, backed sides 1 and 4 on to one disc and sides 2 and 3 on to the other. The CD package mimicked this arrangement, which meant that if you wanted to hear the entire work as God and Jimi Hendrix originally intended, you had to play the first half of CD 1, take it off, put on CD 2, play it all the way through, and then finally return to the second half of CD 1. Madness. Or, if you prefer, a really bad joke with Hendrix and you as its joint butts.

Now, of course, you can indeed listen to *Electric Ladyland* in a single sitting, and it sounds better than ever. Not surprisingly, since the current editions of Hendrix's albums have been repackaged, remastered, redesigned and reannotated to within an inch of their lives. Which in turn is not surprising: after a morass of lawsuits, accusations and counter-accusations, Hendrix's surviving family, primarily his father Al and half-sister Janie, wrested control of Hendrix's musical legacy from producer/administrator Alan Douglas and attorney Leo Branton following the 1993 sale of the Hendrix catalogue, previously represented by Polydor Records in Europe and Warner/Reprise in the US, to MCA/Universal. Under the estate's supervision, the entire Hendrix *oeuvre* is being methodically restored to the public domain.

This is definitely not the time and place for an exhaustive account of the legal proceedings that changed the game: as Alan DiPerna pointed out in a 1995 *Guitar World* cover story flashed as 'The Battle for Jimi's Soul: Who Owns Hendrix's Music?', such an account would require an entire book all of its own. Nevertheless, for our current purposes it should be sufficient to state that, thanks to a combination of historical circumstances, shifting perspectives of public taste and the policies of the Hendrix estate, Jimi's gotten his props at last. (I hope the original edition of this book helped a little, too.)

Henderix songs have featured in movies like *Withnail and I* and *In the Name of the Father*, though not in Dave Stewart's giddyingly awful *Honest*, starring three-quarters of All Saints. Apparently the estate refused permission for Stewart to feature 'Purple Haze' in an orgy scene because they didn't want Hendrix's music to be associated with sex and drugs. It's probably a bit late to start worrying about that. His music has also been heard in commercials for jeans and cars (though in a recent car ad Hendrix's 'Voodoo Chile' was replicated by a session guitarist who did such a good job that I thought it was Stevie Ray Vaughan's version). Fender still proudly showcase him in ads for their guitars (as well they might). TV documentaries are still made about his life and work, the most recent being an edition of BBC2's *Reputations* series. Hendrix websites, official and unofficial, star-spangle cyberspace. He's been sampled by hip-hoppers like Digital Underground and Chuck D. He was the subject of an all-star, all-original tribute album featuring his former 'competitors' like Eric Clapton and Jeff Beck (respectively teamed with Chic and Seal) alongside 'descendants' like Living Colour and Body Count and even an 'ancestor' in the form of Buddy Guy, as well as 'grandchildren' like The Cure, The Pretenders and PM Dawn, and the black sheep of the classical family, violinist Nigel Kennedy, who has issued his own all-Hendrix album, *The Kennedy Experience.*

Most spectacular of all, his hometown has honoured him with the construction of the Experience Music Project, a massive $240 million avant-garde building initiated and sponsored by Microsoft billionaire Paul Allen and designed by the distinguished architect Frank O. Gehry. Hendrix's main London girlfriend Kathy Etchingham, who hung on to Hendrix's record collection, ended up auctioning it off at Sotheby's of London in 1991, and the EMP purchased it for the knockdown price of £2,420. Some of the EMP's merchandising may seem a little iffy – I must confess to a major double-take when I heard about the Jimi Hendrix signature golf-balls; I mean, *huh?* – but it still represents the highest acknowledgement that our society can offer any artist.

So that's what's happened to Hendrix's music, and to his reputation. What of the values that he represented? How would he have felt about the state of the Western world three decades after he left the set? Would he have felt at home in a world where, even if late capitalism cannot quite be said to have won its final victory, it is – as soccer fans would say – four-nil up with five minutes left to play?

The 'Hendrix era' was – let's be blunt about this – the most progressive period of recent times. Hendrix made his contribution to social transformation through his music, and through simply being who he was. 'You don't have to go round making political statements on top of that,' opines Robert Wyatt, an intimate of Hendrix's and the most politically literate musician of his generation, in an interview conducted specifically for the first edition of this book. 'He was *living* a political life of great importance.'

A man with the vision, courage and artistry to deliver a performance like 'The Star Spangled Banner' in a context like Woodstock was indubitably politically involved whether or not he made any overt political speeches or toed any particular party line. Whether Hendrix was a revolutionary in terms of the classic formal political definitions is highly debatable. To state that, with his 1969 performance of 'The Star Spangled Banner' and, later that same year, with 'Machine Gun', he was making revolutionary art, is not. West Coast contemporaries like Jefferson Airplane or Country Joe & the Fish certainly outdid Hendrix when it came to flourishes of radical rhetoric in their lyrics, but they never came anywhere near to challenging the social and cultural status quo as profoundly as Hendrix did.

Nowadays, pop stars are not required to put themselves 'on the line' for their beliefs. Indeed, it's difficult to tell if anybody in the music business *has* any beliefs or not these days: the silence of rock's lambs during the Gulf War and the Kosovo conflict was positively deafening. During the sixties, and during punk, such cop-outs would have been considered inexcusable: even if artists weren't required to put their bodies where their lyrics were, they were cheerleaders for change. The catalyst was Bob Dylan, who entered the rock world from the folk scene, bringing with him the folk world's tradition of topical left polemic; and Dylan – albeit in his later 'symbolist poet' phase, his Rimbaud rather than Guthrie period – was Hendrix's primary influence as a lyricist.

Vanessa Redgrave and Chrissie Hynde notwithstanding, even the most radical of artists tend to be artists first and activists second, as the likes of Country Joe and David Crosby have cheerfully admitted. The likes of Joe Strummer, punk's leading political loudmouth during the heyday of The Clash, steered extremely clear of signing any party's dotted line. 'We were guitar-playing drug addicts,' he acknowledged in a 1999 interview to launch his long-delayed comeback. 'It's seen as completely non-revolutionary, having a spliff. There was no way we were going to put the Rizlas away and start marching up and down. We were just going, "Fuck off, man! Smoke a bloody joint!" I'd like to think The Clash were revolutionaries, but we loved a bit of posing as well. Where's the hair gel? We can't start the revolution 'til someone finds the hair gel! And I *mean* that!' I think Hendrix would have smiled at that.

So here we are, on the 'other' side of the millennial divide. Hendrix has now been dead for longer than he was alive. Have we managed yet to build a categorical box big enough, wide enough and deep enough to accommodate him? Thankfully, we haven't. Any category to which one assigns Jimi Hendrix turns into an obscene 'Bed of Procrustes': some aspect of Hendrix, some part of the man and his music, always seems to be arbitrarily lopped off. Whether it's a musical classification (blues, soul, rock, jazz) or a national boundary (British, American), a political division (left or right, revolutionary or reformist, radical or conservative) or a racial definition (black, white), it never seems to be big enough for him. We can argue all we want about where he fits in, or how appropriate each description seems to be, but ultimately what it comes down to is this: both implicitly and explicitly, in art and utterance, Hendrix was playing and working towards a world and a society in which such distinctions and classifications and separations are obsolete, where they no longer matter. A world without hatred, a world without fear, a world without inequality, a society where everybody is valued and no one is excluded, where all of this planet can provide a warm and safe home to all of its people.

You want to honour Jimi Hendrix, to pursue the spirit of his life and work and take it for your own? Then – as we used to say in the sixties – tear down the walls, motherfucker.

Charles Shaar Murray
London, September 2000

I

The We Decade

The sixties as a state of mind, and how the Anglo-American
cultural continuum got here from there

'Wee-e-e-e shall overco-o-o-o-ome . . .'

> Pete Seeger's adaptation of a traditional gospel song; beloved of union
> activists and mandatory at sixties demonstrations

'If you can remember the sixties, you weren't really there.'

> Robin Williams

'Hi, I'm Bob Dylan. Remember those fabulous sixties? The marches, the be-ins,
the draft-card burnings and best of all – the music. Now Apple House has collected
the best of those songs on one album called *Golden Protest* . . . and if you order now
you'll also receive *A Treasury of Acid Rock* and *The Best of the Supergroups*. Yes, it's
a collector's dream: *Golden Protest* and two fabulous sixties albums for only $3.95.
If you were to purchase these selections separately they'd cost you many hundreds
of dollars, and many cannot be found today at any price . . .'

> The Dummy Bob Dylan on National Lampoon's *Radio Dinner* (1972)

'The tragedy of our generation is that we will *always* be "the kids".'

> The only perceptive line ever heard in *Thirtysomething* (1989)

The passing of time flattens everything: the altered perspective thus created annihilates the sequence of events and replaces it with the illusion of
simultaneity, an illusion reinforced by the convenient habit of slicing history into neat, decade-sized chunks. The notion of 'the sixties' as a clear-
cut, homogeneous blob of time is an exceptionally persuasive one,
creating as it does the myth of some strange, warped period – turn left at
the end of 'the fifties' and emerge dazed, confused and peculiarly-dressed
in time to turn right at the beginning of 'the seventies' – where Mersey-
beat and Macmillan, the Vietcong and Vidal Sassoon, James Bond and
Jack Kennedy, Andy Warhol and Harold Wilson, Danny the Red and
David Frost, Martin Luther King and Mandy Rice-Davies all somehow
rub shoulders, fellow-guests at the longest cocktail party, fellow-extras in
the ultimate rock video.

The correct response to the question 'What *really* happened in the sixties?' is *'When* in the sixties? And *where?'* Even the most widespread cul-

tural phenomena – the totemization of Youth, the public fascination with sexuality, the mass acceptance of rock music, the popular adoption of anti-establishment rhetoric as conversational small change – erupted in different settings at different times, and for vastly different reasons. Britain and America had travelled highly dissimilar paths to reach their common eventual cultural destination; as one contracted, the other expanded. Britain had ended the Second World War as one of the nominal victors, but the nation was near-destitute, exhausted, bloody and bruised. Its cities were ruined, its casualties – both military and civilian – enormous, its industries in tatters, its debts were immense, and every erg of energy was needed to heal its wounds and to commence the daunting task of national reconstruction and renewal. America, on the other hand, emerged from the conflict as the dominant military and economic power (of all the allies, it had given least, suffered least and gained most), and it had the highest standard of living in the world. While Britain began the painful process of divesting itself of an empire it could no longer justify on moral, political or practical grounds, America set about acquiring one.

And, of course, in terms of popular culture, Britain became part of that empire. As little Brits struggled with the remains of rationing and swilled National Health orange juice, they gazed across the Atlantic, and saw televisions in (seemingly) every home, huge gas-guzzling cars with chrome trimmings, beautiful clothes, and money everywhere; all the signs of wealth, power, status and conspicuous consumption. They watched American movies and TV shows, read American comic books and listened to American music. America was heaven, specifically *kids'* heaven: America was where the money was, it was where the fun came from. American kids had everything; at a time when British families were grubbing away to acquire the new basics of life – cars, TV sets, washing machines, refrigerators – it seemed as if nearly every American teenager already had his or her own car and TV. They also had Elvis and Superman, Levi jeans and Fender guitars.

Then as now, this colonization of taste met with some disapproval, but in those days it was the political Right who were frowning. As much as anything else, America represented the future to Brits; in the fifties and early sixties, it was the Right which feared and distrusted the future, suspecting – quite correctly – that they were the ones who were threatened by what was coming their way: an explicit challenge to hierarchy, and a celebration of youth and energy. Then, the subtext of American pop culture in general (and its most overtly black-derived aspects, at that) was the opportunity and wherewithal to make loud noises, look flash, act ridiculous and scandalize one's elders, an abandonment of the need for hypocritical deference and feigned respect. Nowadays, the ethos of America's cultural exports simply and complacently celebrates wealth and power without considering (let alone understanding) the implications of either.

Of course, British kids didn't have the whole story: they were too young to know or care about such things. They failed to see that while America had material prosperity, it was as conformist a culture as our own. The Conservative gerontocracy which governed Britain between 1951 and 1964 was matched in its odd mixture of complacency and paranoia by the Republican gerontocracy of the US, eventually blown away by the hairs-breadth Kennedy victory of 1960. The American rock and roll which young Brits devoured so hungrily – Elvis! Little Richard! Jerry Lee Lewis! – was the voice of a Southern underclass both black and white which hadn't shared in the mass prosperity of the Eisenhower era. For different reasons, it spoke at least as eloquently to the British youth of the fifties as it did to the American middle-class kids who took it up so speedily. For Americans, it may have been the hitherto suppressed voice of blacks and 'billies; in damp, grey Britain, it was simply the voice of America.

In 1957, the Conservative Prime Minister Harold Macmillan announced that mass prosperity on something approaching American lines had finally arrived in Britain. His statement has gone down in popular mythology as 'We've never had it so good', though what he actually said was 'Let's be frank about it. The majority of our people have never had it so good.' Still, the principle remained the same: Britain had more or less recovered from the debilitations of the war and the inglorious post-colonial retreat, and was now once again open for business. In one important sense, that was when the fifties finally began in Britain, only three years before the election of John F. Kennedy introduced the sixties in the USA. What Macmillan was saying, with the simultaneous self-deprecation and self-congratulation which was his personal hallmark, was that Britain at last had jobs and money, and was therefore ready to start consuming with the best of 'em.

The early sixties in Britain bore a certain resemblance, then, to the American fifties: it was a time to celebrate consumerism and the power of money, to bury austerity, to acquire possessions and go on holidays. American youth, in the meantime, had begun to grow bored with consumerism and to discover that particular strain of bourgeois idealism which despises prosperity but cannot exist without it. Kennedy was young, handsome and crusading: his domestic policy was courageously egalitarian and anti-racist, but his foreign policy applied that same crusading spirit to an extension of the international commie-bashing inherited from his Republican predecessors, and the propping-up of the same old dictators. That, at least, was inevitable: as demonstrated by Richard Nixon's Chinese initiative and Ronald Reagan's Mutt and Jeff routines with Mikhail Gorbachev, only Republican presidents and administrations could do business with Communist powers while remaining safe from accusations of crypto-Communist sympathies. Democrats, in effect, are lumbered with Republican foreign policy; Democratic foreign policies can only be carried out by Republicans. Which means, considering the current state of the Republican Party, that they won't be carried out at all, if indeed the Democrats still have anything identifiable as distinctive foreign policies, which is in itself highly debatable.

In the aftermath of the Bay of Pigs catastrophe, Kennedy began to realize that the army and the CIA had grievously misled him in the interests of their own ideological agenda, and determined to introduce a drastic rethink. It is conceivable that had he escaped assassination, he would have pulled back from the brink of the abyss of the Vietnam war; it is also conceivable that this proposed shifting of outlook was a contributory factor to the events of 22 November 1963. That, however, is the kind of speculation which can safely be left in the capable hands of professional conspiracy buffs.

At home, though, the Kennedy White House was admiringly dubbed Camelot; America had a beautiful, gifted king and queen, and a court which recognized culture and invited new and adventurous thought. 'Just think of going to a party given by Eisenhower as opposed to a party thrown by Kennedy,' wrote Norman Mailer. 'Do you have to wonder at which party you'd have the better time?' Suddenly, the White House – which had been an old folks' home for so many years – seemed fertile and sexy, and a palpable spring was in the air. Indeed, sex had been off the agenda for years in all but the most stylized and sublimated forms: the giant, pod-like bosoms and blinding blonde bleaches of the Monroes and Mansfields were fleshly analogues of the bulgy chrome excrescences on dreamboat Cadillacs, triumphs of American engineering. Now came the definitive proof that sex was back in America: the President and the First Lady (not to mention a cast of thousands) were doing it! In the White House!

British politicians had been doing it as well, but in circumstances rather less likely to provoke admiration or approval. To the accompaniment of massed and stentorian harrumphing from a British Establishment too embarrassed to know where to put its face, it was revealed that the Right Honourable John Profumo, Her Majesty's Secretary of State for Defence, had not only 'shared' a 'girlfriend' with the Soviet Naval Attache, but had lied about the matter to Parliament. It would be a palpable exaggeration to suggest that the Profumo affair brought down the Government, or even precipitated the fall of Macmillan – the Conservatives had, after all, been trailing Labour in the opinion polls for quite some time – but it certainly didn't help matters much.

In terms of political history, the central aspect of the Profumo affair was the hushing-up of the fact that the Soviet Naval Attaché in question had only been involved because MI5 had pimped him with a view to arranging his defection, but its cultural significance lay in the revelation that so many rigidly separated strata of British society – West Indian dope dealers from Notting Hill, senior politicos, and 'my dear, some of the *best families*' – had been rubbing up against each other for mutual fun and *frisson*. Modern Britain had been moving for some time towards mimicking the American model of straightforward division by race and money; the Britain of Macmillan was divided along far more traditional lines. The British system of social class is frequently confused with the Marxist analysis of economic class, which is not surprising because both discourses share a similar vocabulary: the expression 'working class' means something different in each even though both may be referring to many of the same people. It would be more accurate to refer to it as 'caste', because it stratified the nation according to a social origin detectable by accent, education and cultural choice. It was a system that depended on everyone knowing their place and meeting only under circumstances controlled by the 'better' participant (i.e. 'slumming'). For the middle and upper classes, the rock boom started out as 'slumming', but the slummees soon took the upper hand.

By a wonderful irony, the Crown's case against Stephen Ward, the young artist, osteopath and scene-maker who had introduced Profumo to his nemesis, Christine Keeler, was prosecuted by Mervyn Griffith-Jones QC, who had fulfilled a similar function when, in 1960, Penguin Books were hauled over the coals for publishing D. H. Lawrence's *Lady Chatterley's Lover*. 'Is it a book you would even want your wives and servants to read?' he asked in a rumble of rhetorical thunder, but the jury's response

– and that of the nation – was not quite what this distinguished advocate might have hoped. Griffith-Jones was inviting jury and nation to see the world in terms of the Right Sort of Chap taking decisions on behalf of everybody else, but public faith in the Right Sort of Chap was rapidly declining.

The wave of spy scandals which followed the Profumo affair – Vassall, Blake, Lonsdale *et al.* – demonstrated that the most likely person to sell the nation out to the Reds was not a trade unionist or a Labour left-winger, but a Right Sort of Chap who had, unfortunately, Gorn Orf the Rails. The combination of sexual hypocrisy and political incompetence reflected poorly on Macmillan's Right Sort of Chap government, which – despite having delivered the economic goods – seemed utterly anachronistic, increasingly out of touch with a newly frisky and inquisitive Britain. The media grew less and less deferential: the BBC screened *That Was the Week That Was*, in which cheeky young snots like David Frost enjoyed themselves hugely by baiting the crusty old molluscs in the government at every possible opportunity, and a new magazine called *Private Eye* enthusiastically did likewise. This was known as the Great Satire Boom.

Harold Macmillan was a sufficiently canny political operator to know when jigs were finally up, and he celebrated this realization by opting for retirement. Through the time-honoured and labyrinthine processes of the Conservative Party, a new Prime Minister 'emerged': the Foreign Secretary Lord Home (pronounced 'Hume') vanished from sight and was magically transformed into Sir Alec Douglas-Home, now eligible to sit in the House of Commons and serve as Prime Minister. The spectacle of this amiably desiccated aristo being railroaded to the top was the final demonstration that the Conservative Party was unfit to lead the kind of nation Britain needed to become. Harold Wilson was swept to power on a wave of buzzwords – 'classless', 'thrusting', 'the white heat of technology' and so forth – and it became vaguely fashionable to be young, working-class or 'provincial'; that is, from somewhere other than London or the Home Counties. My arrival at grammar school coincided with the release of the first Beatles single; by the following summer, most of my classmates had perfected what we fondly imagined to be 'authentic' Liverpool accents.

The Beatles were fortunate enough to arrive at exactly the right time for all concerned. They were the perfect news story for British editors to wheel on in order to take everybody's mind off the Profumo affair, and Beatlemania was unleashed in the US almost before the reverberations of Lee Harvey Oswald's gunshot had died away. They were young, they were talented, they were funny, they were working-class-kids-made-good, and they couldn't have been better mascots for the New Britain if Harold Wilson had personally invented them. They became, if not the world's idols, then the world's pets and finally the world's holy fools.

The end of the sixties was – in pop-cultural terms, anyway – like some unimaginably wild, extravagant and glamorous party where everybody is brave and beautiful and witty and charismatically strange and wonderful until the overhead lights are switched on. Some brazened it out, repeating their stylized gestures and daring anyone to challenge them. Others drifted away, beating their retreat with varying degrees of elegance and dignity, to be replaced by new arrivals who knew what time it was. The Beatles and Jimi Hendrix were the quintessential sixties pop stars, and it is somehow fitting that neither survived to see 1971. The Beatles broke up and collapsed into their component parts, the sum of which was shockingly less than the whole, and Jimi Hendrix, one of the few sixties icons with both the sensitivity to realize that repetition was not enough and the courage to plan the necessary public transformation, missed that opportunity by expiring quietly in the rented apartment of the woman who later claimed he was intending to marry her. He died of an overdose of barbiturates, though anyone with a fondness for metaphor could claim that he died of an overdose of the sixties, or an overdose of fame, or an overdose of rock and roll, or a combination of all of these. His death was a tragedy for many reasons, but most of all because it was so undignified and unnecessary: choking on one's own vomit is such an ugly, stupid, gross and degrading way to die. It was as gruesomely symbolic an end to the woozily utopian sixties as any ironist could desire.

It is difficult to imagine how Jimi Hendrix could have been improved upon as a cultural hero for the wild youth of the late sixties. At a time when sexual freedom – specifically, *male* sexual freedom – was high on the agenda, he established himself as King Stud, both with the most explicitly erotic performances any rock audience had seen for a while, and an off-stage reputation as a wildly promiscuous ladies' man. When the guitar became fetishized as penis-surrogate, Hendrix was the guitarist's guitarist; the man who reinvented both its vocabulary and its symbolism. When 'hip' and 'radical' white youth sought a musical and political *rapprochement* with black culture but found the problem of relating to real live black people virtually insuperable, Hendrix was there; a black man of their own generation who understood them, shared their rhetoric and, indeed, actively courted their favour.

Playing on their fantasies as well as initiating them into his own, he would mau-mau them half to death, and then giggle and say 'Peace'. When 'far out' became the password and audiences craved the 'mind-blowing', Hendrix's act – initially, anyway – was the loudest and most sensationalistic around, and he was the most spectacular dandy on the music scene. His music was obviously derived from the same rhythm and blues as the musics of the ruling white-rock 'geniuses', but it retained the unmistakable feel of the original prototypes, even when it was blown up to eardrum-vibrating volume and garnished with extravagant, hallucinatory production devices derived from The Beatles. Moreover, the lyrics of his songs were transparent testament to his admiration for Bob Dylan, though he was clearly more familiar with pulp science fiction than with French symbolist poets. Furthermore, he personified Anglo-American dialogue; he brought the unique inimitable flavour of black American music into British rock, and arrived back in the USA as the spearhead of the British avant-garde.

Even his politics were those of the Love Generation, rather than of the New Left or Malcolm X and the rising generation of black militants; he stood *for* music, freedom and brotherhood, *against* war, hatred, racism and petty-bourgeois 'straight' propriety. In other words, the hippie equivalent of standing up for God, America, Mom and apple pie; just as vague and platitudinous as that. Opinions differ as to whether these were strategic concessions to the attitudes of his putative audience or his own deeply-felt beliefs: some suggest that beneath his freak-flag exterior Hendrix was actually quite a conventional soul, while others insist that he was a hippie through and through, and had been one even before the existence of such creatures had been formally logged and ratified. Nevertheless, it was fortunate for all concerned that Hendrix existed: if he hadn't, who would have had the foresight to invent *him*?

> White collared conservative flashing down the street
> Pointing their plastic finger at me
> They're hoping soon my kind will drop and die
> But I'm gonna wave my freak flag high
> High!
>
> Jimi Hendrix, 'If 6 Was 9' (1967)
>
> Something is happening but you don't know what it is,
> Do you, Mr Jones?
>
> Bob Dylan, 'Ballad of a Thin Man' (1965)

I fought the law and the law won
The Bobby Fuller Four, 'I Fought the Law' (1966)

If the sixties were truly 'about' anything, it was the notion of a decisive shift of power away from its traditional centres and towards people who had been historically excluded from any significant degree of control over their own circumstances and history. From the rich to the poor, from the old to the young, from the Right to the Left, from whites to blacks. As a result, there emerged a peculiar coalition of groups that had been scarcely aware of each other's existence before: lefties, beats and folkies collided with snappy, status-conscious city kids and debauched art students with heads full of weird ideas. Individualist and collectivist philosophies were reconciled as if by magic; consumerism and anti-materialism were simultaneously celebrated. Most of all, it was a time for adventure.

'A modern democracy', wrote Norman Mailer in the introduction to his 1964 collection, *The Presidential Papers*, 'is a tyranny whose borders are undefined; one discovers how far one can go only by travelling in a straight line until one is stopped.' This aphorism will do at least as well as any other to describe (however broadly and loosely) 'what happened in the sixties'. Be the path political, cultural, behavioural, entrepreneurial or whatever, in the sixties, a lot of people set out to do just that: to travel in a straight line until they were stopped. Under the shadow of the bomb, in the aftermath of the Cuban missile crisis – when the world came as near to ending as it has done at any time in recorded history – the brightest and the bravest set about testing the absolute limits of the societies in which they found themselves.

Some struggles were in deadly earnest, with real prizes and real penalties – the Civil Rights movement in the USA, the Vietnamese battle against America and its puppets, the African National Congress's mobilization against apartheid in South Africa – while others, like the 'underground' in Britain, were, despite their credibility-by-association, lip-service allegiance to actual liberation and revolutionary movements, pure hedonistic pranksterism. Whether the various Establishments really were in actual danger from the hippies, yippies and rockers is debatable: that they felt as if they were and acted accordingly is not. Apart from the routine stuff like cops and soldiers pulping people at demonstrations (which culminated in American National Guardsmen actually shooting four students dead at Kent State University in 1970), the FBI considered John Lennon and Yoko Ono a sufficient threat to US security to maintain surveillance on them, and some sophisticated conspiracy-theorists have evolved a reasonably seductive claim that Jimi Hendrix's death was no accident, but a covert CIA assassination. (Beat that, paranoia buffs!)

What linked the radicals with those who simply regarded the revolution as an excuse not to tidy up their rooms was a sense of possibility; a notion that anything could happen, that the ogres of oppression weren't so big – they were just tall, that's all. The rockers had their symbolic roles to play in all this: The Beatles were lovably cheeky to authority; The Rolling Stones slouched and sneered at it; Bob Dylan first accused and then baffled it; Hendrix simply acted as if it wasn't there.

The central facts of American public life in the sixties were the black struggle – expressed first through Dr Martin Luther King Jr and the Civil Rights movement, and later through Huey P. Newton and Bobby Seale's paramilitary Black Panther Party – and the Vietnam war; both indicators of the limitations of US power. 'No Vietnamese ever called me nigger,' said Muhammad Ali as he was stripped of his World Heavyweight Championship title for refusing to be inducted into the armed forces, but it certainly wasn't young black Americans who were escaping the draft through student deferments or parental influence. A wholly disproportionate number of blacks fought in Vietnam, theoretically defending – just as they had in two World Wars and in Korea – an American Way in which they were still not guaranteed first-class citizenship. Much of the massive political discontent of the sixties was directly attributable to institutionalized racism and to the war: almost 50 per cent of the American public disapproved of the war, but neither of America's two political parties (or, to be more precise, neither of the two tendencies in America's one-party state) was prepared to run for election in 1968 on a platform of ending the war. The political establishment thus closed ranks; US citizens opposing the war were effectively disenfranchised on the nation's most pressing international issue.

In Britain, Harold Wilson's Labour Party infuriated many of its supporters by refusing to condemn US policy in South-East Asia (though his lukewarm verbal endorsement fell far short of the degree of involvement sought by President Lyndon B. Johnson, who had requested actual British military participation). On a more trivial level, the 'youth vote' was singularly unimpressed with the way Wilson's government dealt with the pirate offshore radio stations which challenged the BBC's paternalistic monopoly by pumping out wall-to-wall pop music; under Anthony Wedgwood Benn (not yet the born-again neo-proletarian Tony Benn), the lot of them were closed down, and the best (or the most manageable) of their disc-jockeys were hired by the BBC, who ironed out their unorthodoxies and installed them at a new all-pop service called Radio One. The pirate stations had blithely combined the crass and the avant-garde in a manner which made for genuinely unpredictable pop radio. Listening to them (which was theoretically illegal) was also a protest vote against a BBC which played only a few hours of pop each week.

This point cannot be emphasized too strongly: if you lived in Britain in the early sixties, it was almost impossible to hear any pop with some bite to it on the radio. Television was scarcely more helpful. The stuff was *rare*; you had to *chase* it. You'd listen to a half-hour of tedious radio comedy to get one guest appearance by a group halfway through. 'Children' were catered to; so were adults. If you were an adolescent, though, with all the fears and curiosities and energies of adolescence, you listened to Radio Luxembourg or the pirates, chasing a fluctuating signal around the dial. It wasn't exactly the French Resistance – not for nothing did The Clash use *London Calling* as an album title – but the records seemed to be dispatches from somewhere more colourful and enticing, somewhere more challenging and exhilarating than a suburb with a well-cut lawn.

In America – or so British kids had heard – there were thousands of radio stations, and some of them played pop or soul or country or jazz *all day and all night*. All young Brits had were a few hours on the BBC Light Programme. Then there were the pirates; then there they weren't. Benn's action was the equivalent of a grown-up confiscating a wonderful toy and then telling you that you could have it back occasionally, but only under supervision and with the proviso that you had to play with it *nicely*, dear. Paternalism? It just made you want to *spit*.

In terms of going with the *Zeitgeist*, the government couldn't have made a worse move. Wilson had tried so hard to be a young person's Prime Minister, reminding everybody that he and The Beatles were all from Liverpool, and now here he was behaving just like those stuffy old Tories. The Tories would have disliked the pirates on the grounds that they were vulgar and common and out of control; Labour disliked them for impeccable socialist reasons. Acting from straightforward practicality (the frequencies used by the pirates were playing hell with shipping and with official European broadcasting), political orthodoxy (broadcasting was a state monopoly) and sheer inertia (broadcasting was a state monopoly), they clobbered this raggedy manifestation of youth-cultural autonomy and dishevelled capitalism with the heavy hand of The State.

It was a ludicrous little episode, emphasizing the intense circumstantial differences between the British 'underground' and its US equivalent. Broadly speaking, the Americans had *politics* and Brits had *behaviour*, and each borrowed freely from the other. American youth, after all, had to deal with the omnipresent spectre of the Vietnam war and the seismic shifts of the black upheaval; their Limey cousins were playing around with the aesthetics of style and rubbishing the notion that good children should be seen and not heard. It was – in quintessentially British fashion – essentially a class conflict: the rock scene and the 'underground' were places where refugees from all classes could escape the constriction of designated hierarchies and prescribed modes of conduct. Renegade Old Etonians and yobbos from Shepherds Bush or Tyneside rubbed shoulders – not without a certain amount of mutual suspicion – in the relative equality of a buffer zone between the upwardly and downwardly mobile, each faction fascinated with the other's behaviour and style. Without the grim context provided by the genuine social upheavals in the US, the British Underground was simply a gorgeously playful and decadent exercise in lifestyle.

The continuum of those who paid lip service to the Movement stretched from committed urban guerillas like Europe's Angry Brigade and America's Weathermen (who went around blowing up buildings) to grey-haired record company executives who sprouted bushy sideburns, kitted themselves out with Nehru jackets and medallions, started keeping joints in their office humidors and trained themselves to greet favoured acts with clenched-fist salutes and a murmured 'Right on'. It was, I suppose, inevitable that talk would shift from blowing up the Bank of America to blowing up CBS Records, especially after the latter organization sought to capitalize on the inflammable political climate of 1968 – the police riot at the Democratic Convention, the King and Kennedy assassinations, *et al.* – with the now infamous 'The Man Can't Bust Our Music' campaign, in which a squad of defiantly hirsute types were seen grimly waving placards (based on CBS album covers) from behind bars, presumably with porcine Chicago cops lurking just out of shot clutching billy clubs from which the last layer of blood and hair had only just been cleansed. This equated buying a Big Brother, Electric Flag or Moby Grape album with burning a draft card, marching in solidarity with the Black Panthers or demonstrating against the cynical decision of the Democratic Party to withhold political legitimacy from opponents of the Vietnam war. It was – to say the least – a somewhat disingenuous piece of marketing: sleazy, corrupt and condescending. It exploited the most urgent social and political issues of the time simply in order to shift units, and no matter how much the underground press raged about 'ripping off the people's culture' or 'diversion of revolutionary energies', it enabled large numbers of American kids to get as close to the Revolution as they wanted to be: a chance to bug their parents, a little sex, a joint or a tab of acid and a *bitchin'* new album.

It's very easy to be cynical about those times, to skewer the pretensions of the era, to recite the litany of failures and naïveties and hypocrisies, or gleefully anatomize the opportunism, the incoherence and the internal contradictions of the social and political ideologies of the late sixties. Yet during those years Britain liberalized its reactionary homosexuality and abortion laws – much to the continuing dismay of conservative politicians and leader-writers – and the American protest movement stopped the Vietnam war and brought down a President in the process (even though the end result was simply to replace him with a worse one). In doing so, they gave sterling service to both their nation and the world: simultaneously better patriots and better internationalists than the bulk of their elected representatives.

In crude terms, it was a clear 'us' against a clear 'them'; even if most of 'us' had much less in common than could ever have been acknowledged. Tom Wolfe skewered the seventies as 'the Me Decade' (correctly, of course); what made his observation so penetrating was its admission of the extent of the retreat from the broken sixties promise that 'we' would overcome. The sixties were, by this token, the We Decade – the era in which a new consensus would form and undo the iniquities of the past. But in the end, 'we' met the enemy, and it was 'us'.

> They got the guns but
> We got the numbers
> Gonna win, babe, we're
> Takin' OVAH . . .
> Jim Morrison for The Doors, 'Five to One' (1968)

Even the ones who went to the demonstrations for no better reasons than to get stoned, fight cops, hear bands or pick someone up – or because of simple boredom or peer pressure – made a contribution. Simply by being there, they helped remind the world that not all Americans supported the war. At the time, that was important. There were, after all, seemingly two Americas. The dominant one was as casually brutal and suffocatingly bureaucratic as the Soviet Union, and, simultaneously, as relentlessly superficial and hysterically greedy as a low-budget afternoon game show. At once, it waged vicious and unjust war both against a distant, inoffensive little country and against those of its own people who refused to accept second-class citizenship. This America was a blinded monster – go, Norman Mailer, *go!* – thrashing in a feverish indiscriminately destructive rage. It loved, protected and defended the Vietnam war.

The other America, by contrast, had laughter and love, imagination and style. It believed in peace, freedom, justice and brotherhood at home and abroad, for one and all, and in everybody's right to be exactly who *they* wanted to be. (It also gave the best parties.) Most important, it loathed, derided and attacked the Vietnam war. Essentially, the issue of Vietnam defined who was who, albeit hastily and not always accurately. For example, the soldiers who fought the war were then simplistically cast as baby-slaughtering sadists, when for the most part their sin was simply to be either ill-informed about the genuine purpose and conduct of the war, or else insufficiently resourceful or influential to escape the draft. Inevitably, the shadow of Vietnam overhangs much of the most urgent pop of the time; no aspect of American life (and, by proxy, the cultural and political life of much of the world) could hope to be entirely free of it.

'I'd like to dedicate this one to all the soldiers that are fightin' in Chicago, Milwaukee and New York . . . oh yes, and all the soldiers fightin' in Vietnam. Like to do a thing called "Machine Gun" . . .'

Jimi Hendrix, Fillmore East, New York City, New Year's Eve (1969)

One day I went out with the ARVN on an operation in the rice paddies above Vinh Long, forty terrified Vietnamese troops and five Americans, all packed in three Hueys that dropped us up to our knees in paddy muck. I had never been in a rice paddy before. We spread out and moved towards the marshy swale that led to the jungle. We were still twenty feet from the first cover, a low paddy wall, when we took fire from the treeline. It was probably the working half of a crossfire that had somehow gone wrong. It caught one of the ARVN in the head, and he dropped back into the water and disappeared. We made it to the wall with two casualties. There was no way of stopping their fire, no room to send in a flanking party, so gunships were called and we crouched behind the wall and waited. There was a lot of fire coming down from the trees, but we were all right as long as we kept down. And I was thinking, Oh man, so this is a rice paddy, yes, wow! when I suddenly heard an electric guitar shooting right up in my ear and a mean, rapturous black voice singing, coaxing, 'Now c'mon baby, stop actin' so crazy' and when I got it all together I turned to see a grinning black corporal hunched over a cassette recorder. 'Might's well,' he said. 'We ain't going nowhere till them gunships come.'

That's the story of the first time I ever heard Jimi Hendrix, but in a war where a lot of people talked about Aretha's 'Satisfaction' the way other people speak of Brahms' Fourth, it was more than a story; it was Credentials. 'Say, that Jimi Hendrix is my main man,' someone would say. 'He has *def*initely got his shit together.' Hendrix had once been in the 101st Airborne, and the Airborne in Vietnam was fill of wiggy-brilliant spades like him, really mean and really good, guys who would always take care of you when things got bad. That music meant a lot to them. I never once heard it over the Armed Forces Radio Network.

Michael Herr, *Dispatches* (1977)

Jimi Hendrix's old regiment, the 101st Airborne Division (a.k.a. 'Screaming Eagles'), was assigned to Vietnam in early 1965. By this time, Hendrix himself was long gone – he was honourably discharged following a training injury in the autumn of 1962 – and was kicking around Harlem almost a year away from being scooped up by Chas Chandler and swept to London. If he had been a few years younger, or had not already done armed service by the time the draft was introduced, he might well have had to take Uncle Sam's free ticket to what had once been French Indo-China. As it was, men he knew, and with whom he had trained, went to Vietnam to contain the spread of Marxism-Leninism – and to save the political ass of a hard-bitten old wheeler-dealer of a President seeking to appease a right wing deeply suspicious of Civil Rights, Welfare and the Great Society. Hendrix knew the score as far as the position of the black GI was concerned: in 'Nam they represented 2 per cent of the officers and were assigned 28 per cent of the combat missions. When he dedicated 'Machine Gun' to 'all the soldiers fighting in Vietnam', he was neither jiving his audience nor indulging in cheap irony. Hendrix knew *exactly* who was paying the price of the politicians' games, and when he used the uncanny onomatopoeic power of his guitar to evoke the sounds of urban riots and jungle fire-fights – as he did in 'Machine Gun' and 'The Star Spangled Banner' – he used every atom of that knowledge.

The authenticity of these performances was such that Vernon Reid, the avant-metal guitarist who formed and led Living Colour and helped found the Black Rock Coalition, at one point firmly believed that Hendrix himself was a Vietnam vet. Reid knows Hendrix's music intimately and his personal history (at the time, anyway) rather less so, but his error nevertheless contains a profound psychological truth. Hendrix, said

Reid, 'tapped into the whole Vietnam experience. He is *in* it, completely immersed, and it is *beyond playing*. Even the feedback sounds like people crying and it sounds like napalmed villages . . . he plugged into something *deep*, beyond good or bad.'

Hendrix performed 'The Star Spangled Banner' on a number of occasions, but his best-known rendition of his country's national anthem is the one he played as the climax of his set at the Woodstock Festival ('Three days of peace and music') in August 1969. The ironies were murderous: a black man with a white guitar; a massive, almost exclusively white audience wallowing in a paddy field of its own making; the clear, pure, trumpet-like notes of the familiar melody struggling to pierce through clouds of tear-gas, the explosions of cluster-bombs, the screams of the dying, the crackle of the flames, the heavy palls of smoke stinking with human grease, the hovering chatter of helicopters . . . It is utterly appropriate that Francis Ford Coppola hired Randy Hansen, a young guitarist whose act used to consist of note-for-note Hendrix reproductions in full wig and make-up, to contribute sedulously Hendrix-derived guitar overkill to the soundtrack of an ambush scene in his 1979 Vietnam exorcism *Apocalypse Now*.

'The Star Spangled Banner' is probably the most complex and powerful work of American art to deal with the Vietnam war and its corrupting, distorting effect on successive generations of the American psyche. One man with one guitar said more in three and a half minutes about that peculiarly disgusting war and its reverberations than all the novels, memoirs and movies put together. It is an interpretation of history which permits no space for either the gung-ho revisionism of Sylvester Stallone and Chuck Norris or the solipsistic angst of Coppola and Oliver Stone; it depicts, as graphically as a piece of music can possibly do, both what the Americans did to the Vietnamese and what they did to themselves.

And it won't go away, either: in 1988, the Irish rock messiahs U2 used a snatch of 'The Star Spangled Banner' to preface a live performance of 'Bullet the Blue Sky', a savage critique of the US-sponsored Contra terrorism in Nicaragua. And – moving from tragedy to farce – Stevie Ray Vaughan, who for a time was, amongst many other things, Hendrix's greatest living imitator, performed 'The Star Spangled Banner' to open the 1985 baseball season at the Houston Astrodome. Vaughan indignantly rejected any suggestion that the occasion deserved comment. 'Why do people make it out to be more than it is?' he asked, somewhat disingenuously. 'I can't stand these comparisons.'

Hendrix would probably have greeted the spectacle of 'his' version of the national anthem opening the baseball season with a certain amount of wry amusement. In an age when art exists primarily in commodity form, the artist has ultimately very little say in what kinds of commodity his or her art becomes. After all, while political establishments regarded sixties counterculture as a threat, the music industry simply treated it as a market, and even when the perceived threat evaporated, the market remained.

And it remains to this day: sixties kids turned sober, turned responsible, turned Conservative, turned Republican. The Days of Rage are long gone: a veteran sixties student radical like David Stockman ended up as Ronald Reagan's Budget Director, ramming unreconstructed monetarism down the throats of the long-suffering American public, while Jonathan Aitken, a former signatory of the 1967 Legalise Marijuana advertisement in *The Times* financed by Paul McCartney, was – before his momentous fall from grace in the late nineties – comfortably and seamlessly reincarnated as a Tory MP, running on Margaret Thatcher's Victorian Values ticket. The strange trajectory of Yippie figurehead Jerry Rubin, one of the heroes of the great 1968 demonstration at the Democratic convention in Chicago, led him to Wall Street; having failed to burn down the Bank of America during his revolutionary phase, he ended his days presumably bent on buying it. By contrast, Abbie Hoffman, Rubin's old partner in yippie mischief, committed suicide in 1989; his last major public act was to get arrested alongside Amy Carter in a demonstration. Even Neil Young, composer of the Kent State eulogy 'Ohio' ('Tin soldiers and Nixon coming/we're finally on our own'), temporarily succumbed to a terror of diseased faggots and crazed Eye-ranians, and spent a few months on the Reagan booster squad before regaining his lucidity and fire, returning to his time-honoured oppositional stance. Reagan's successor, the first George Bush, maintained the bandwagon's momentum with a campaign which played freely on Middle America's racial nightmares and used 'Liberal' the way Joe McCarthy used 'Commie'; it was run by the late Lee Atwater, a one-time Southern soul-rocker. When a host of R&B and rock stars showed up to jam at a Bush inauguration party, Ron Wood presented Atwater with his guitar. (*Rolling Stone*'s correspondence column subsequently carried a tart communiqué from one Mike Woodard of Phoenix, Arizona, pointing out that 'by embracing blues music, the [Republican] party hopes to attract many of the people to whom it gave the blues in the first place with its repressive élitist policies.') For a while, America's best-loved contemporary humorist was right-wing ex-hippie P. J. O'Rourke, who represents an updated, upmarket, literate version of the conservative anarchism that once led the Hell's Angels to break up anti-war demonstrations. O'Rourke's best-known public forum is, naturally enough, *Rolling Stone*, which came out in a rash of US Army ads bearing the mystic, new-age slogan BE ALL YOU CAN BE. Cat Stevens, in what was possibly the most extreme case of sixties rejection, metamorphosed into Muslim community leader Yusuf Islam, who endorsed and supported the *fatwa* against Salman Rushdie.

Both Britain and America saw in the millennium with superannuated rockers at their respective helms. Whilst running for election as President, Bill Clinton clamped on a pair of shades, blew his tenor sax on Arsenio Hall's late-night chat show and did his campaign no harm at all. The former lead singer of seventies college-rock band Ugly Rumours, Tony Blair, whose speciality used to be a bare-chested rendition of The Rolling Stones' 'Brown Sugar', now poses for pictures strumming his Stratocaster and fatuously declares himself to be a 'modern man' because he comes from the era of 'The Beatles and colour television'. (Remarkably, no one bothered to point out that, since The Beatles had broken up in 1970, they were 'history' – in both the literal and colloquial senses of the term – to all voters below the age of thirty-five, none of whom can remember black-and-white TV either.) Clinton adopted Fleetwood Mac's 'Don't Stop (Thinking about Tomorrow)' as his campaign song and his inaugurations boasted more stars than there were in heaven; Blair attempted to co-opt a shortlived 'Britpop' boom by cosying up to Oasis head honcho and one-man Lennon-and-McCartney wannabe Noel Gallagher, a short-lived liaison which resulted in tears before bedtime as Gallagher and his label boss Alan McGee acrimoniously bailed out of New Labour's 'Cool Britannia' project.

Both men paid voter-friendly lip-service to the music and ideals of their youth. And neither led a government that seemed remotely progressive except by direct comparison with their atavistic and even more reactionary counterparts. So it goes. And – this side of the revolution, anyway – so it will continue.

Much of this is simply due to the craving for stability and common sense that comes with the passing of thirtieth birthdays, but there is also the simple urge to be seen to be backing winners. (The notion of the 'beautiful loser' – immortalized in the title of a Leonard Cohen novel – is *very* sixties. Despite the nineties punk-style 'dramatization of alienation' of the post-Nirvana grunge merchants, there's nothing beautiful about being a loser nowadays, and the pose is more likely to be adapted ironically, as in *wunderkind* Beck's introductory hit.) George Orwell ascribed the fascination which Stalin's Russia held for Western intellectuals to 'power worship' – the irresistible urge to huddle around the nearest immovable object – and a very similar motive has helped to lead many of their eighties equivalents to the Right. In the sixties, Kennedy Democrats and Wilson Socialists felt that the tide of history was with them – just as, later in the decade, the New Left surfed what seemed like a rising moment – and the appropriate rhetorical and behavioural veneers were routinely applied to all manner of smooth blank surfaces. As easily and unthinkingly, indeed, as the economic liberalism and social conservatism of the eighties were twenty years later. And despite a cursory airbrushing of 'kinder, gentler' social concern, that holds as true this side of the millennium as it did on the other.

But – *hey! phew!* – the baby boomers still go for their rock and roll. It is undoubtedly what they loved most about their wild years: it is what they have hung on to. 'Freedom' is still treasured, but it is interpreted almost exclusively in terms of freedom *to* as opposed to freedom *from*. P. J. O'Rourke, for example, was for a while perhaps the most articulate and vociferous spokesman for the oldest of all Western freedoms: that of the well-off white male to do just about anything he wants, anywhere in the world. The notion of freedom *from* (poverty, racism, illness, pollution, homelessness, unemployment, war) is honoured mostly in the breach; after all, whilst everybody is expected to claim to care about that stuff and advocate the occasional minor reform, no one but a fool or a troublemaker would seriously challenge the essential rightness of a social system under which they have personally profited. At their most inspired, the political and theoretical branches of hippie transcended the clichés of both left- and right-wing political discourse by demanding both freedom *from* and freedom *to*, but once the economic pressure was on, the two freedoms proved distinctly unequal. It turned out to be the kind of fight that the referee stops in the fifth round.

Anti-racism, once proudly professed, has proved no match for the more urgent imperative of protecting real-estate prices; AIDS, rampant homophobia and the critiques marshalled by the women's movement have between them trashed the sixties notion of 'sexual freedom'; and the battle for the environment has already been lost. The Grateful Dead were doing booming business right up until the death of Jerry Garcia; Crosby, Stills, Nash & Young still get together once in a while; Stevie Winwood and celeb Alcoholics Anonymous member Eric Clapton appeared in beer commercials; The Beatles' albums became best-sellers all over again the moment they were reincarnated as compact discs; and all of a sudden movies about Vietnam became almost unavoidable. The era of Thatcher and Reagan reinstated fifties values, but it also stimulated a resurgence of sixties tastes, however incongruous this may seem to anybody who remembers them first time round. The sixties, brothers and sisters, are here to stay. In fact, they're on continuous rotation – but the tape deteriorates each time.

There's a song that I sing, and I believe that if *everybody* was to sing this song we could save the whole world. *Listen* to me!

Solomon Burke, 'Everybody Needs Somebody to Love' (1964)

Fast forward: imagine a more or less typical rock fan being kidnapped by a UFO sometime around mid-1970 and dumped back in what we laughingly refer to as the Real World in 1985 next to a news-stand displaying the special Live Aid edition of *Rolling Stone*. He or she would find a comforting array of familiar faces staring back: Mick Jagger, Bob Dylan, Paul McCartney, Pete Townshend, Eric Clapton, Robert Plant and Tina Turner (plus, as a slightly longer shot, David Bowie, whom our specimen might possibly know from his 1969 'Space Oddity' hit). Now toss the victim back into the UFO, along with a 1985 equivalent, and fast forward yet another fifteen years, to the Top 50 of 'The Virgin All Time Top 1000 Albums', as reported in the 3 September 2000 edition of London's *Independent on Sunday*. The 1985er would find a few unfamiliar names – Radiohead? Stone Roses? Nirvana? Oasis? Massive Attack? Portishead? – but also plenty of the then-usual suspects: REM, U2, The Smiths, Prince, Bruce Springsteen, The Sex Pistols, The Clash. For the 1970-naut, though, a whole herd of the old lags would still be there: The Beatles, Bob Dylan, Pink Floyd, The Velvet Underground, Love, Van Morrison, The Beach Boys, David Bowie, Joni Mitchell, Fleetwood Mac (albeit a radically different group from the blues-powered Peter Green-led Mac our time-traveller would remember), Hendrix, of course, the Stones, The Who, The Band, The Doors, Captain Beefheart, Paul Simon, Led Zeppelin, Marvin Gaye. Just like old times, innit? And, more to the point, comparatively few of the new(er) names would provide any serious sonic challenges to the kidnapees' notions of what 'rock' or 'pop' were supposed to sound like.

However, if our UFO had commenced its fan-napping project in 1960, its first bemused victim would search in vain for a recognizable name or countenance. True enough, Elvis Presley, Rick(y) Nelson, Eddie Cochran, Gene Vincent and Buddy Holly are dead, and Chuck Berry, being famous enough for his own purposes but not nearly wealthy enough, has never done anything for free in his entire life, but what about Little Richard? What about Jerry Lee Lewis? What about Bo Diddley?

The answer is relatively straightforward. That illustrious trio – and all other functioning performers from that era – are 'oldies acts'. For the generation who organized and participated in Live Aid, 'contemporary pop' began roughly when The Beatles and The Rolling Stones became public property, and it's still going on. Everybody from before then is prehistoric: the dinosaurs that rocked like men. About the only performer who had hits in the fifties who's still having them now is James Brown (Dan Hartman, Full Force and PCP notwithstanding), though the late Roy Orbison seemed on the verge of a major comeback at the time of his death in December 1988, thanks partially to his highly successful involvement in The Traveling Wilburys, a joint project with Bob Dylan, George Harrison, Jeff Lynne and Tom Petty. *Their* collective age I haven't even dared to add up.

Still, old is beautiful. Old groups come back, suitably contrite about their political extremism, sexual excesses and history of near-fatal substance abuse. Old songs come back, performed by young artists who are infinitely more sensible and professional than their predecessors. Sometimes, if the new artists are feeling exceptionally generous, they will wheel on the original for a cameo duet; if they are in a hurry, they'll use a 'sample'. Radio stations churn out old songs non-stop, with the result that most new performers seem like the younger siblings, or even the children, of their predecessors. (In some cases – Julian Lennon, Ziggy Marley, Dweezil Zappa, Zak Starkey, Jakob Dylan – they are.) The arrival of the compact disc weighted the scales even further in favour of the past, as – in a classic demonstration of the conservative urge – thousands of people (including the present writer, naturally) rushed out to divest themselves of serious proportions of their total disposable income in order to buy an improved version of something they already had.

I've alluded specifically to pop music, but the same applies to the manic recycling which dominates the ecology of most of the popular arts: sequels, remakes, genre pieces, reruns of all descriptions, ranging from the simple regurgitations of the populists to the artful skeins of ironic variation knitted around our favourite clichés by the more consciously media-literate. And just as the new records and movies are more and more like the old ones, so technological advance enables the old ones to become more like the new ones. For a while, media mogul Ted Turner was threatening to 'colorize' (that's 'computerized tinting' to jargophobes) old MGM black-and-white movies like *Casablanca* as a concession to those who find black-and-white's intimations of antiquity too alienating; and there is a profitable trade in renovating old records whose absence of a drum-machine beat confuses today's pop-kids. An ''88 remix' of The Temptations' 'Papa Was a Rolling Stone' managed to destroy utterly all traces of the original's knife-edge tension by slapping a big, heavy *boof-baff* electrobeat behind all the quiet bits; nevertheless, it made Top 30, so it was obviously a good decision. Curiously enough, one of the first victims of this kind of overdub revisionism was Sly Stone, whose original sixties hits were tarted up and 'discofied' on the album *Ten Years Too Soon*. Unfortunately, 1979 was ten years too soon for this now-commonplace process to be acceptable, and the album died a horrible death. Maybe someone should take the *Ten Years Too Soon* album and update *that*. Of course, Motown owns 'Papa Was a Rolling Stone' and Ted Turner owns *Casablanca*, so the original work is simply a piece of raw material to be moulded and reshaped according to any entrepreneurial imperative which may present itself.

The traditional answer to the question 'Who owns history?' has always been 'the victors', though the USA 'owns' the history of the Vietnamese war despite losing the conflict itself. The answer to the question 'Who owns culture?' has always been more complex: one set of ideologues would claim the 'owners' to be the artists, another the audience. The eighties tell us that the *real* answer is none of the above: culture and history are simply commodities which can (and should) be treated as such. However, in one important respect, the audiences can 'own' the commodity in a more intimate sense than ever before; viewers operating a TV/video remote control can zap in and out of programmes at a dizzying velocity, giving each item encountered as few seconds as they choose to make an impact before it is zapped in favour of something else. A taped item can be put on pause, reversed, replayed in slow-motion, backed up or fast-forwarded to the viewer's heart's content. There is no reason for any viewer ever to be bored; they can cut straight to the 'good part'. It is scarcely surprising how many contemporary movies simply consist of 'good parts'. It is supremely appropriate that one of the best-named bands of the late eighties called themselves Pop Will Eat Itself; if it was only pop which was eating itself, there might be more cause for optimism. Having eaten itself, popular culture is now excreting itself. Mostly undigested, more's the pity.

> Is this tomorrow, or just the end of time?
>
> Jimi Hendrix, 'Purple Haze' (1967)

'. . . I feel that one needs a non-linear technique simply because our lives are not conducted in linear terms. They are much more quantified; a whole stream of random events is taking place . . . we switch on television sets, switch them off half an hour later, read magazines, dream, and so forth. We don't live our lives in linear terms the way the Victorians did.'

> J. G. Ballard, BBC Radio Three (1969)

If Tony Blair's fatuous 'Beatles and colour television' line has any resonance whatsoever, it is this: that, thanks to endless syndicated TV reruns, reissued records and so forth, we exist in a grotesquely distended cultural now which stretches back from here (wherever here may be when you're reading this) back to the early sixties. I've been avoiding for as long as possible any mention of the 'p' word (oh, all right: P*ST-M*D*RN*SM) both because it is a buzzword whose battery has run down, and because it is so thoroughly inadequate to describe a decontextualized cultural world which is simultaneously infantile and senile. To have lost all sense of history whilst remaining mired in the past is a dubious achievement of some considerable magnitude, but it is an entirely logical consequence of the coincidence of conservative ideology and technological advance; the inevitable result of applying advanced methods to antiquated goals.

'See those assholes? *Ordinary* people. AH HATE 'EM.'

> Harry Dean Stanton in Alex Cox's *Repo Man* (1984)

'It's real hard to be free when you are bought and sold in the marketplace. 'Course don't ever tell anybody that they're not free, 'cause then they're gonna get real busy killin' and maimin' to prove to you that they are . . .'

> Jack Nicholson in Dennis Hopper and Peter Fonda's *Easy Rider* (1969)

It is a Conservative truism – if not *the* Conservative truism – that competition inevitably stimulates both excellence and innovation. In practice, it encourages the former and discourages the latter, defining 'excellence' in the most conventional possible sense of the word: as doing what everybody else does, except louder, longer, heavier, bigger, faster, stronger, more profitably. It is, basically, the application of the notion of constant technological progress (with its omnipresent sub-text of planned obsolescence) to human beings, who are encouraged to think of themselves either as products, which need to incorporate the full range of industry-standard features in order to survive in the market, or as machines, which must be constantly upgraded or else be traded in for newer and more competitive models. Unfortunately, a purely technical criterion of excellence soon degenerates into stuntmanship and can-you-top-this contests; endless cavalcades of musicians and movie-makers all trampling each other to death as they stampede down the same cul-de-sac. Innovation in the popular arts is far too easily mistaken for incompetence, degeneracy or mischief for many to contemplate it as a realistic option; the chance of defeat, loss or humiliation is far too great. Thus do cultures which totemize 'individuality' set the agenda in such terms as to produce the ultimate conformist: the 'ordinary person' whose sense of self is most strongly felt and expressed when running with the herd.

Of course, it works: our athletes are bigger – faster – stronger, our heavy-metal guitarists play more and more notes, our movies routinely pull in more money faster than ever before. We get what we want: more of the same, only with better special effects. This presents the inevitable theoretical and ideological problem facing a conservative age nostalgically yearning for a turbulent one; how – bearing in mind that *Rollerball*, *The Running Man* and all the real-life gladiators-type game-shows face the insuperable practical problem that, at the time of writing, it's not actually permissible to kill the participants . . . yet – to reconcile the need for stability with the demand for excitement?

The eventual solution has proved classically neat; the sixties return defanged, deodorized, deconstructed and – best of all – over. It's a very exciting story, full of important things like wars and assassinations and insurrections, with Presidents and Prime Ministers crashing like timbers all over the place. The story overflows with weird and bizarre phenomena, such as large sections of the youthful population suddenly opting for systematic irrationality: insulting their parents, marching against the government, ingesting vast quantities of dangerous drugs, fucking anything that moved, hitch-hiking barefoot halfway across the country and – most troubling of all – showing insufficient respect for the absolute priorities of material security and private property. (They were, needless to say, the children of those who'd grown up in the Depression, which helps to explain why this particular generation gap seemed so huge.) The tale of the sixties also has plenty of light relief. There is something irresistibly comic about an era in which *Easy Rider* could be mistaken for a good movie (let alone a masterpiece), and *Hair* described as 'one of the most important developments in modern American theater' (thank you and goodnight, the *LA Times*). The former is incoherent, platitudinous and sags dangerously whenever Jack Nicholson is not on-camera, while the latter seems like the ultimate right-wing satire on the fatuity, indolence and depravity of all hippies. (I keenly await its revival, preferably financed by the Young Conservatives.) And what decade ever had a better sound-track? Why, most of the stars are still popular today!

Yep, it's a wonderful story, and it's blessed with the most basic require-ment of any good story: it has a happy ending. A few prominent hippies died (dirty white boys Brian Jones and Jim Morrison, loud-mouthed slut Janis Joplin, uppity nigger Jimi Hendrix), one of those big festivals in California went sour when Hell's Angels killed a young black man who was waving a gun at Mick Jagger, and gradually almost everybody drifted back into the fold nursing their hangovers as the eternal verities reasserted themselves. Or – to be more accurate – the struggle proved not only wearisome, not only boring, but actually terrifying. After all, what kind of society would they have had if they'd won?

I couldn't stay a Maoist forever. I got too fat to wear bell-bottoms. And I realized that communism meant giving my golf clubs to a family in Zaire.

P. J. O'Rourke, introduction to *Republican Party Reptile* (1986)

The most dispiriting aspect of the whole thing is that the offspring of the people who were behaving badly in the sixties did exactly what their par-ents did not do: take on a previous generation's tastes. 'Classic rock' radio stations – blasting out post-hippie pre-punk retreads based on the propo-sition that Led Zeppelin were both the last rock band of the sixties and the first rock band of the seventies – are as popular with teenagers as with thirtysomethingers or (godelpus) forty- or fiftysomethingers; a show by Eric Clapton or, whilst they were still with us, The Grateful Dead, can be a family affair. In the eighties, a full quarter of all albums sold in the US were by big-hair heavy-metal bands who served mainly to demonstrate (by omission) how delicate, sensitive and texturally varied Led Zeppelin's music had sometimes been. Traditional heavy metal was, thank whatever gods there may be, eventually displaced in the affections of young Amer-ica by what became known as 'grunge', with Nirvana as its most powerful, distinctive and affecting standard-bearers, The shade of Hendrix would probably permit itself a wry smile at the notion that the greatest American rock band of the nineties was led by a left-handed guitarist and came from Seattle. And even though metal has, once again, resurfaced, it has been indelibly altered by its encounters with punk and hip-hop, and – as led at the smart end by Rage Against the Machine and the Beavis and Butt-Head end by Limp Bizkit and Korn – nowadays practically qualifies as an entirely new subgenre: nu-metal.

The consensus still lingers: the sixties represented the Golden Age of pop, a notion that was taken to farcical extremes when a 1988 *Rolling Stone* critics' poll decided that no less than sixty-nine of the 100 Best Singles of the Last Twenty-Five Years (including sixteen of the Top 20) had been recorded before the end of 1970.* This seems to be a fairly conclusive vote of no confidence in popular music's ability to renew and reinvent itself, but is the result a reflection of the hollowness of contemporary pop, or of the rigid sixties-fetishism of the critics whose collective view it represents? Neither conclusion is particularly encouraging (though both are plausible). The implication is that post-rock popular culture has soaked so deeply into the fibres of the social fabric that it can never again mean as much as it did back then. Or that rock is a 'youth' music defined in perpetuity according to the terms of those who had their 'youth' in the sixties.

The sixties are thus comfortably institutionalized as an era of adventurousness and commitment; a time when great things were possible because people didn't have to be *sensible* all the time the way they do now. Simultaneously, right-wing politicians rail at the 'permissive society', and the resulting near-collapse of moral standards and public order; blaming all contemporary ills on the laxity and indiscipline engendered by John Lennon and Dr Benjamin Spock. Pop culture, magically, fuses these seemingly irreconcilable viewpoints; it understands that what they have in common is an obsession with power. The eighties were a decade in which power was all – who had it, who didn't – and the significant rock of the period put the music's power at the service of those against whom it had, in the sixties, been implicitly directed. In triumphalist movies like *Top Gun*, the bombast of stadium rock reinforced the bombast of gung-ho militarism, where heavy metal pumps iron and bombs Libya. *Hey! Rock and ROLL!*

---

*By contrast, 'classic soul' stations worked from the notion that an unbroken continuum stretches from Ray Charles and Jackie Wilson straight through to Alexander O'Neal, Anita Baker and beyond.

The We Decade

Everywhere I hear the sound of marchin', chargin' feet, boy . . .
Mick Jagger & Keith Richards, 'Street Fighting Man' (1969)

'The sixties was hashish and Hendrix, the seventies was cocaine and herpes, and the eighties are Perrier and push-ups.'
Michael Des Barres, singer with a vast number of groups you haven't heard of (1984)

Vote for something weak and to the point.
Paul Haines & Carla Bley, *Escalator Over the Hill* (1972)

The notion that artists are simply reflections of their audiences is flawed and incomplete, but it contains one kernel of truth: that a conservative, conformist audience will demand, and will – through the magic of the market – receive conservative, conformist entertainment. When cultural revisionism implies that The Beatles, The Rolling Stones, Jimi Hendrix or Bob Dylan *et al.* were the pied pipers leading sixties youth either forward or astray, the fact of the matter was that it was the audiences who were leading the artists. They were the ones who were 'far out', not Mick Jagger: during the heyday of Hippie (and again during punk, and yet again with hip-hop) bands were, as Robert Wyatt puts it, 'dragged along in the wake of the audiences' expectations', whereas in the eighties those audiences' expectations, being intrinsically conservative, dragged the artists back rather than forward. Prince, the only major eighties star to mount a serious challenge to his audience's adaptability, paid a heavy price for his presumption. By early 1989 his record sales were slumping, and his hits throughout the subsequent decade were few and far between.

'Music', says Wyatt, 'isn't about finished results; it's about trying things out.' That, in a nutshell, is the difference between the We Decade and the Power Decade, between the eras of Hippie and Yuppie. 'Finished results' are precisely what the eighties were about, and the eighties fascination with the sixties demonstrates the extent to which all the freewheeling bullshit of the sixties has become a 'finished result'. In the eighties it became safe to make movies about right-on sixties topics like Vietnam and Civil Rights; if anybody had had the nerve to make them at the time, they might actually have been useful. 'The good old days', as Loudon Wainwright III used to sing, 'are good because they're gone.'

And that is why a simple recycling of the stylistic devices of the sixties – either as nostalgic kitsch or wittily decontextualized scratch-mix – is a cop-out. The sixties questions haven't gone away simply because there is a consensus in favour of sweeping them under the carpet. What responsibilities do free individuals and a free society owe to each other? What do racial minorities and majorities have to say to each other in openly or covertly racist societies? What is the nature of the transaction between artists and their audiences? Does the term 'popular culture' ultimately mean the culture created by a people, or simply a leisure service provided for them by professionals? When a nation demands that an individual cooperates in something (s)he finds manifestly repulsive, does the higher patriotism lie in acquiescence or refusal? Does the person who dies with the most toys really win? Is, finally, popular culture part of the solution or – as it seems today – part of the problem?

The current answers to such questions are those of the fifties rather than the sixties: in the meantime, sixties culture, and those aspects of it which were institutionalized in the seventies, rules the roost. Removed from the hubbub of the times, the old songs and film clips continue to resonate; not for what they signify or even for what they once signified, but simply because of the residual power that those sounds and images still retain; the magical aura they possess because they once signified something. It's just that very few people are willing to remember what it was.

2

Highway Chile

The facts in the case of Jimi Hendrix

'We just want the facts, ma'am.'

Jack Webb as Sgt Joe Friday in Jack Webb's *Dragnet* (1954)

'Facts, sir, are nothing without their nuance.'

Norman Mailer testifying at the Chicago Conspiracy Trial (1970)

The facts in the case of Jimi Hendrix are as follows.

He was born in Seattle General Hospital, Washington, on 27 November 1942, of black, white and Cherokee blood: a real American, with the entire history of his nation imprinted in his genes. His father, James Allen (Al) Hendrix was away in the army; his mother, the former Lucille Jeter, named her baby John Allen Hendrix. Lucille was frail and tubercular, and the baby was farmed out to various relatives. When Al returned from the army in 1945, he trekked out to Berkeley to find the boy and bring him back to Seattle, where he was legally renamed James Marshall Hendrix. Al and Lucille, who had briefly separated, reunited long enough to have another son – Leon, who was born in 1948 – but by 1950 the marriage was over for good, and they were divorced. Al, who had been a gifted semi-professional jazz dancer in the pre-war years, was essentially unskilled, and found the going hard: while he struggled to find work as a gardener and handyman, the boys were sent to live with their aunt Patricia in Vancouver, where they stayed for the next two years. Some of Jimmy's happiest memories of that period were of the times he and Leon spent with their maternal grandmother, who was half Cherokee and lived on the local reservation. From her he learned the history of native Americans and their sufferings at the hands of the settlers who had displaced them, and was taught an intense pride in the Cherokee side of his heritage.

The young Jimmy Hendrix was an exceptionally shy and introverted child; sufficiently quiet and withdrawn to draw comment (often derisive) from friends, neighbours and relatives. In later years, he would remember his father as stern, authoritarian and hard-working, his mother as loud, fun-loving and fond of a drink and a good time. But his few school-friends would recall his continual worries about Lucille – her depressions, her poor health. After her final separation from Al, she had remarried up in Canada, but her partying and drinking soon put her back in hospital. She died in 1958, and Al refused to allow either of his sons to attend her funeral. Subsequently, Hendrix told interviewers that his mother had died when he was ten.

He found his refuge in music. He had always enjoyed church – the hand-clapping choral transcendence of the black Baptist church, where the spirit came down and the people got happy – but at the age of eight he'd been sent home from service because of his scruffy, raggedy clothes. He never forgot the humiliation, and he never went back to church. Instead, there was rock and roll music on the radio, and a new lover, companion and confidante: the guitar. When Jimmy was thirteen, Al had found his son holding the broom like a guitar, strumming away and making guitar noises with his mouth, and so he'd brought Jimmy a broken-down ukulele he'd found in the basement of some folks he'd been working for. The refurbished ukulele was replaced by an equally unprepossessing $5 acoustic guitar, and later still by a Silvertone electric, the cheapest model you could buy. (That Silvertone – actually a Danelectro 'badged' as a Silvertone – was, according to Harry Shapiro and Caesar Glebeek, sold in Nashville in 1962 and subsequently became the proud possession of soul man Bobby Womack; cleaned, reworked and polished to a blinding sheen, it occupied pride of place among the instruments in the music room of Womack's Los Angeles home.) And in 1957, when Jimmy was fifteen, Elvis Presley played Seattle. Guess who was in the audience.

Even the grasping of this psychic life-line was something of a struggle. Jimmy was left-handed, and left-handed guitars are both more expensive and harder to come by than their right-handed counterparts. For the right-handed player, life is considerably simpler: most instruments you find are right-handed and therefore accessible, and it is far easier to learn by grabbing the nearest guitar in order to experiment. A left-handed player, by contrast, needs to reverse the strings before playing. Even restrung, a right-handed guitar requires modification: the nut and bridge over which the strings pass at each end of their vibrating length must be cut and adjusted for the differing thickness of the strings. Some left-handed players (like Bobby Womack, Defunkt guitarist Ronnie Drayton and bluesmen Otis Rush and Albert King) learned to play 'backwards', with instruments set up and strung for a right-handed player: Jimmy decided early on to take the more trouble-some route of reversing the strings, performing on modified right-handed instruments long after he was able to afford the left-handed variety.

From then on, Jimmy spent virtually all his spare time with his guitar. He learned from anybody who could show him anything at all – Al's tight budget did not allow for anything like regular, formal tuition – and from the radio, pumping out all the rock and roll and R&B hits of the time. While Elvis Presley, Chuck Berry, Ray Charles, James Brown, Buddy Holly, Little Richard, Fats Domino, Bill Haley, Big Joe Turner, The Moonglows, Muddy Waters, Bo Diddley and all the other hit-makers of the time rampaged across the airwaves night after night, Jimmy Hendrix was closeted in his room with his radio and his guitar, soaking it all in. He was still terribly introverted and withdrawn, but the guitar brought him out, and he began playing with local bands here and there. Gradually, he started to get good. He settled into a high school band called The Rock-ing Kings, and it became apparent that the stage was his natural territory. Up there with the band, his awkwardness and shyness no longer mat-tered. It was as if he was a different person: the guitar completed him, gave him the confidence and strength to rock out, boogie down and show off. To become somebody.

This side of him went down great with audiences, particularly girls: it didn't go down so great with a few of his fellow band members. Young girls love boys who are shy and pretty; boys hate boys who are shy and pretty, particularly if they're popular with girls. A pre-gig fist-fight with a Rocking King who wasn't amused by his girlfriend's reaction to Jimmy's stage show ended with the break-up of the band, a process already set in motion by bandleader Fred Rollins' decision to enlist in the paratroopers. School had not gone well for Jimmy: in 1959, he dropped out and less than two years later followed Rollins into the 101st Airborne. Al attempted to dissuade his son, but to no avail. Jimmy had his heart set on the military: he was so determined to change his life that he didn't even take his guitar.

He hadn't been there long, though, before he wrote to his father, who sent the guitar winging its way to him. Stationed in Fort Campbell, Ken-tucky, it was Jimmy's first time down South. For the first time also, he was exposed to a deeper, richer musical tradition than that of the mainstream pop, rock and R&B they played on the Seattle radio stations, which had no significant black population to please. In Kentucky, he discovered the blues.

He didn't have a much better time in the army that he did in high school. His fellow paras found him weird and spacey, and when he started sleeping with his guitar they decided he was *definitely* nuts. He would talk about using his guitar to capture the sounds of the horn players in the swing and jump bands his father loved, and the rushing wind he heard when he made his parachute jumps. He was regularly mocked, harassed and beaten up; his guitar stolen and hidden until he would get down on his knees and plead for its return. He spent more and more of his time off-base in nearby Nashville, hanging out in Music City, the nation's capital of country music. He ricked his back on his twenty-sixth jump, and received his discharge papers in the summer of 1962. By all accounts, the army was almost as glad to be rid of Jimmy Hendrix as he was to be free of them.

It was in late 1961 that he made the acquaintance of the musician with whom he probably felt the greatest affinity. Billy Cox, a young Pennsylvanian, came from a highly musical family: his mother was a classical pianist, and his saxophonist uncle an alumnus of the Duke Ellington band. Cox himself was a multi-instrumentalist with both jazz and classical training, but his favoured instrument was the bass, and his hero Charles Mingus. Sheltering from the rain outside a service club, he heard some guitar-playing that sounded like 'a mixture of John Lee Hooker and Beethoven'. He rushed inside, checked out a bass from the club's stock of instruments, and the two of them sat down to jam. Soon, Hendrix and Cox had their own band, The Casuals (later re-named The King Kasuals), who entertained in the service clubs and soon expanded to work off-base, playing local lounges with a repertoire that included everything from Jimmy's favourite Chuck Berry and Albert King songs to standards like 'Misty', 'Harlem Nocturne' and 'Moonlight in Vermont'.

Cox's discharge came through a couple of months after Hendrix's, and they settled in Nashville. Cox, cautious by nature, was happy to live and work around Music City until a plausible opportunity to do otherwise presented itself, but Hendrix was considerably less patient: he would join virtually any touring band which passed through town, often getting stranded somewhere and having to dodge motel bills he couldn't pay before hitching his way back to Nashville. Over the next three years, Hendrix learned what professional show business was all about, studying in the hard school of what used to be known as the chitlin circuit.*

Being a freelance sideman in the R&B world was no picnic, whether the leader was an authentic hit-maker with an identity and repertoire of his own, or simply the front-man of a 'cover band'. While not every leader was as much of a perfectionist as James Brown (who would fine his musicians for missed dance steps, slovenly stage costumes or wrong notes, and who had a sufficiently acute musical ear to tell which of three trumpet players was sharp even while in the middle of a kick-microphone-full-spin-drop-splits-come-up-and-catch-microphone routine at stage front), they all knew exactly what they did and didn't want to hear, and they knew who was supposed to be the star of the show and who wasn't. In other words, upstaging (or even distracting) the star was *out*. Green young guitar players from the sticks weren't paid to have opinions; they were paid to stand where they were supposed to stand moving how they were supposed to move wearing what they were supposed to wear and playing the part they were supposed to play. They were also supposed to turn up on time, be sober enough to perform, and not bitch too loudly when they were booked into twenty-fourth rate motels or left unpaid for days at a time. Those were the rules. Some leaders enforced them more rigorously than others, but the ultimate enforcement was provided by cruel market forces. It was no big deal to dump an over-ambitious young musician: there were potential replacements in every town, and the repertoire of leading R&B stars were such common currency that most young players already knew them.

Hendrix got dumped plenty of times. He would behave for as long as he could, but after a while he would either upstage the star or miss the tour bus. He was often massively unpopular with his fellow musicians, some of whom would bully him as unmercifully as his school-mates or fellow paratroopers had. Touring the South in the backing band of Gorgeous George, the MC on a Sam Cooke/Jackie Wilson tour, he fell foul of

*B. B. King, for one, considers the term 'chitlin circuit' – commonly used to describe the network of black clubs, bars and theatres which pre-dated the 'integration' of show business, and still provides venues today for black artists with no substantial white audience – to be unacceptably derogatory: 'I still play a lot of those places, and some of those that can't afford me I wish I could still play.' 'Chitlin' is a contraction of 'chitterling', meaning the pigs' intestines which were a staple delicacy of 'soul food', the traditional Southern rural black cuisine based on the cheapest cuts of meat; the ones that the white folks didn't want, and therefore – in plantation days – generously donated to their slaves. Beneath the phrase 'chitlin circuit' lurks a massive historical subtext.

the late Harry Womack, Bobby's brother and one of Cooke's protégés, The Valentinos. Bobby himself – also a Valentino as well as playing guitar in Cooke's show – remembers those events in some detail. 'My brother Harry was in the dressing room with Jimi, and he'd rolled his money up and slid it inside his shoe . . . he left, and when he came back, the money was gone and Jimi's sittin' there playing his git-tar with his ear all down on it, 'cause without an amp you can't hear no electric git-tar. Harry said, "You took my money," and Jimi say, "I wouldn't take anything from any-body, I don't know where your money was." But Jimi had a couple of guys from that band with him, Billy Cox and another guy, and they all looked like him, real skinny. So I say, *"Damn*, maybe they take it, because *anybody* could have come in that dressing room," but Harry say when he left, Jimi was the only one there.

'Now Jimi was asleep one night, and Harry say, "I'm gonna get him," because Harry was broke that whole week. So he took Jimi's git-tar to the bus window, and he threw it out. I heard it hit the ground and Jimi was laying there asleep. Boy, he got up to play his git-tar – because he play it all night long, all day long, every day, that's all he did – and he looked for it and boy, he cried, he got upset, he didn't know *what* happen. At first I thought it was kinda funny, too, but then I thought *man*, I'm a guitar player too. I said, *"God*, James . . ."' Bobby ended up loaning Hendrix the money to buy a new guitar.

Occasionally, Hendrix's employers would leave him behind on pur-pose, and another guitarist would be taken on in the next town. Hendrix would hit the local clubs and bars looking for a new job, or else hitch to another town where the prospects might be better. It was the kind of hands-on training in practical performance which none of the rock stars with whom he would later compete had ever received. Between his dis-charge from the army in 1962 and his arrival in New York City in 1964, he had put in lengthy stints with Little Richard and worked in ensembles touring alongside everybody from Sam Cooke, Jackie Wilson and B. B. King to The Supremes, Chuck Jackson and Solomon Burke.

Many of these jobs didn't last long, but he learned from all of them. In his roamings, he dropped into the Stax studios in Memphis to chew the fat and swap some licks with Steve Cropper, the guitarist with Booker T & the MGs and linch-pin of the Memphis-based Stax Records operation, and auditioned for the Ike & Tina Turner Revue, though it's still a moot point whether or not he actually gigged with them: he claims he did, Tina Turner swears he didn't. He certainly claimed to have performed with

Cooke, Wilson and others; though he had certainly toured with them and learned a considerable amount of stage-craft from the experience, he never performed with them or was a member of their bands. Along the line, he received both a pointed but not unfriendly lecture on finer points of the blues from Muddy Waters, the Godfather of Chicago blues, and informal tuition from the left-handed guitarist Albert King. It certainly beat sitting around in Home Counties bedrooms learning songs off records.

His best-known professional association during those years was undoubtedly his stint with Little Richard. Hendrix met Little Richard in 1962 during a stay in Vancouver, when he was playing with a popular local outfit called The Vancouvers, led by one Bobby Taylor. Taylor was to brush against major success three times in his career without ever attaining it for himself. His partner in The Vancouvers was a Chinese-American singer named Tommy Chong, who later dumped music for comedy and teamed up with 'Cheech' Marin as the surprisingly durable duo Cheech & Chong. He also discovered a sensational Indiana-based family vocal group called The Jackson 5 and raved about them to Gladys Knight, who passed the word on to her bosses at Motown, only to find their début album released under the superbly mendacious title *Diana Ross Presents The Jackson 5*. Jimmy Hendrix played most weekends with Taylor and The Vancouvers until Little Richard Penniman – the most flamboyant and hysterically exciting of all the fifties rockers – passed through town looking for musicians. In the end, he scooped up half of Bobby Taylor's band, including the lead guitarist. (Little Richard has remembered events slightly differently; in Charles White's *The Life and Times of Little Richard: the Quasar of Rock*, he recalls Hendrix – then calling himself Maurice James – joining him after being stranded by Gorgeous George in Atlanta, Georgia.)

It is almost impossible to overestimate the importance of Little Richard as a formative influence on Jimi Hendrix. On his arrival in England, Hendrix told interviewers, 'I want to do with my guitar what Little Richard does with his voice.' Richard himself told Charles White that Hendrix 'just loved the way I wore those headbands round my hair and how wild I dressed . . . he wasn't playing my kind of music, though. He was playing like B. B. King, blues. He started rocking, though, and he was a good guy. He began to dress like me and he even grew a little moustache like mine.' According to one of Richard's road managers of the time, '[Hendrix] wasn't flamboyant or anything then . . . Richard brought Hendrix out. Helped him a lot to be what he became.' 'Maurice James' can be heard on a few of Little Richard's records from this period; his solo on a 1963 cover of Jerry Lee Lewis's 'Whole Lotta Shakin' Goin' on', which is as sloppy in its execution as it is ambitious in its intention, provides more than a hint of how hard Hendrix had to work to 'be what he became'.

Inevitably, Richard and Hendrix fell out. Hendrix later claimed that Richard had given him a hard time for wearing a ruffled shirt on stage, and had fired him by announcing, '*I'm* the only one allowed to dress pretty'. Richard, much incensed, insists that Hendrix was fired for persistent lateness after missing one bus too many. Whatever the cause, the upshot was that 'Maurice' returned to the itinerant freelance life. Periodically, Jimmy returned to Nashville, attempting to lure Billy Cox out on the road. Once he had even brought Little Richard with him, but Cox stayed put. They stayed in touch until Hendrix moved to New York City in 1964.

In New York, Hendrix set about scouring Harlem for work, trying to find someone willing to pay him for sounding like himself. There was definitely no room at the inn until he was taken on by The Isley Brothers, a young vocal group who already qualified as veterans thanks to late fifties smashes with 'Twist and Shout' and 'Shout'. He had been recommended by one of Ronnie Isley's friends who had seen him alienate the house band at one of his endless string of humiliating auditions, and even though he was so broke that Ronnie had to buy him strings for his guitar before he could audition, he got the job. The Isley Brothers took him on tour, recorded him on a few tunes and let him loose for a few brief but spectacular solos, which gave him considerably more scope than he'd had with most of his previous employers. He was even beginning to make something of a reputation: when the Isleys shared a bill with the wicked Wilson Pickett – still riding high with his international hit 'In the Midnight Hour' – he made an ineradicable impression on Pickett's drummer, a massive sixteen-year-old kid named Buddy Miles. However, he was still a hired hand, renting out his skills for thirty dollars a night, getting frustrated and bored, playing occasional low-budget recording sessions which invariably turned out to be duds. After eight months, he quit.

Possibly because he could get a little more space for himself playing in an unknown band alongside someone who wasn't an established star with a fixed way of doing things, Hendrix ended up with a hard-working club band called Curtis Knight & the Squires. They played a standard repertoire of soul, rock and blues hits, arranged to feature Hendrix almost as much as the leader. Curtis Knight himself was by no means a great singer or guitarist, but he was smart enough to know why his band was becoming a solid attraction in down-town rock clubs. So was Knight's manager, Ed Chalpin, who signed Hendrix to an exclusive recording deal. The advance paid on signature was one dollar.

Hendrix played with Curtis Knight on and off for almost a year. The recording deal signed with Chalpin resulted only in a few sporadic sessions, mostly rushed and poorly organized, and other outside studio work was scarcely more impressive. Hendrix and Knight got on well, though, and they had some good times: it was with Knight that Hendrix first started to hang out in Greenwich Village. There he discovered new musical worlds: the feedback-riddled avant-garde English blues-rock of The Who and The Yardbirds, the extravagant word-play of Bob Dylan – whose voice was (in conventional terms) so unattractive that Hendrix, for the first time, considered the possibility that *he* might be able to sing too – and the galvanic, unfettered expression of the New Jazz, created by John Coltrane, Ornette Coleman, Roland Kirk and those who followed in their wake. Each of these new influences closed a gap in Hendrix's musical jigsaw puzzle. He was beginning to click. He was also beginning to investigate the wonderful world of dope, experimenting more and more often with marijuana and this new thing they called *acid*: listening to music under this stuff put all the pieces together in different combinations. At the end of 1965, he took another money gig: a tour with Joey Dee & the Starliters. They'd had one huge hit – 'Peppermint Twist' – during the twist craze of a few years before, and strictly speaking they were has-beens, but outside the sophisticated city centres they still got the people up and moving.

In early 1966 came the apogee of Hendrix's career as an R&B sideman. An emergency vacancy came up in King Curtis's band The Kingpins, and Hendrix found himself playing alongside some of the greats of the New York R&B session scene. King Curtis (Curtis Ousley to the taxman) was a Texan saxophonist who'd contributed some of the most memorable tenor breaks in all of fifties rock to the celebrated Coasters hits, and his band was later used on most of Aretha Franklin's New York sessions. Here, too, Hendrix's woozy, abstracted manner, dishevelled appearance and wildly unorthodox playing brought him into conflict with the fiercely orthodox Curtis. The dissatisfaction was mutual, and from the King Curtis band there was nowhere for Hendrix to go but down – or sideways. So he moved downtown for good, and started looking for work in the Village.

For the first time, he formed his own band and started singing.

Fronting a motley team of white kids – including Randy California, later lead guitarist with psychedelic cult band Spirit – he led Jimmy James & the Blue Flames, playing the Café Wha?, the scuzziest and worst-paying dive in the Village, but he was soon moonlighting as lead guitarist for John Hammond Jr. Namesake son of the producer/entrepreneur who had sponsored the careers of everyone from Bessie Smith, Billie Holiday and Benny Goodman to Bob Dylan and Aretha Franklin, Hammond was a fanatical devotee of country blues who had just released *So Many Roads*, which formalized the folkies' fascination with urban blues by showcasing Hammond's interpretation of songs from the repertoires of Howlin' Wolf, Muddy Waters, Bo Diddley, Robert Johnson, Otis Rush, Jimmy Reed and others. A few of Hendrix's musicians were familiar with the album, so it was a simple matter for Hendrix to base much of The Blue Flames' repertoire on Hammond's.* As a result, when Hammond required a backing band who knew the songs on his album to accompany him for two weeks at the Café Au Go Go – a far more prestigious joint than the Wha? – he hired Hendrix's entire group.

And word started to spread. Hendrix would back Hammond up all night, displaying his hard-earned mastery of contemporary blues guitar, but in the last set of each night, Hammond would turn the spotlight over to his lead guitarist, who would perform Bo Diddley's 'I'm a Man' – his solo feature since the days of Curtis Knight & the Squires. Out would come every trick Hendrix had ever learned in his five years on the R&B scene and yearned to have the freedom to use: he played the guitar behind his neck or back, between his legs or with his teeth. And the instrument would squeal, roar and chuckle at its master's most casual gesture. Every night, audiences were in shock.

Even when the Hammond stint was over and Jimmy James & the Blue Flames returned to the Wha?, the famous and successful made a point of checking out this amazing young black guitarist who played with his teeth. Bob Dylan, Miles Davis, The Rolling Stones, Mike Bloomfield and Al Kooper, Micky Dolenz from The Monkees, John Phillips from The Mamas and the Papas: they all showed up, and they told *their* friends. By now, Hendrix's confidence had increased considerably; he was receiving professional acclaim, if not financial success. As Bloomfield, then at the

---

*In the studio, Hammond had been backed by, amongst others, Robbie Robertson, Eric 'Garth' Hudson and Levon Helm, all three of them a few months away from starting work with Bob Dylan and laying the foundations for their own subsequent career as The Band.

peak of his popularity with Paul Butterfield's Blues Band and fresh from his studio triumphs with Bob Dylan, later told Ed Ward, 'I went over there one night, and man, he wouldn't even shake hands. I mean, he knew how bad he was. He got up there . . . and there were jets taking off. There were nuclear explosions and buildings collapsing. I never heard anything like it in my life. I was sitting in the front row, and he was doing it right to me, like a machine gun. "You like this, man?" B–bb–bbb–room! He was just mowing me down. *Oh!* Talk about burning! *Oh!*'

One of Hendrix's most outspoken admirers was Linda Keith, who'd gone to see him with her boyfriend, Rolling Stones guitarist Keith Richards. A few days later, she button–holed a friend of hers named Chas Chandler. He had played bass for The Animals, one of the most genuinely soulful British Invasion bands, but the group was on the verge of break-ing up and Chandler, sick of the musician's life (and, possibly more to the point, the musician s economic lot), had decided to go into management in partnership with Mike Jeffery, who had managed The Animals. Linda Keith suggested to Chandler that if he was looking for acts to manage, she knew someone who might fit the bill. She also suggested to Hendrix that he might like to move into the hotel suite in which Keith Richards had established her.

Chandler went down to the Wha? with Linda Keith and experienced managerial epiphany. Whether or not he understood in one single, blazing flash of inspiration that the man on stage before him could not only tear up the British rock scene but then re–export himself back to the USA as a British sensation, he certainly displayed infinitely more acumen than any other music business professional who'd seen Hendrix thus far. As soon as the set was over, he offered Hendrix a management contract and invited him to London. Not the band, just Hendrix. It didn't take Hen-drix more than a few hours to make the most important decision of his life. He'd learned his craft the hard way, worked non–stop for five years, and it was about time he got a break. He agreed.

There then followed a few frustrating weeks while Chandler set off on his final tour as a member of The Animals. On his return, he went through the drudgery of obtaining Hendrix a passport and a work per-mit. He also did his best to make sure that his new client was free of any previous and outstanding contracts and professional agreements, but somehow Hendrix never got around to telling Chandler about the Ed Chalpin deal. One thing Hendrix *did* do was to call Billy Cox in Nashville and invite him along for the ride, but Cox was broke: he didn't even have a full set of strings on his bass or an amplifier of his own, let alone bus fare to New York City. Eventually, everything was – to the best of Chandler's knowledge and ability – straightened out. Hendrix and Chandler flew out of Kennedy Airport, and during the flight, they decided – in order to make it more memorable – to alter the spelling of Hendrix's first name. As far as the crowd at the Café Wha? were concerned, Hendrix had just plain vanished. Some of them thought he'd been busted or something. It wasn't until a few months later, when one of them spotted a spread on Hendrix in the British teen mag *Rave*, that they realized what had actually happened.

In the early morning of 21 September 1966, carrying only a suitcase an a guitar, Jimi Hendrix arrived in London, the city in which the ugly duckling of the chitlin circuit would become a gorgeous, psychedelic swan, and in which he would die a little more than four years later. He was almost twenty-four.

The London rock scene of late 1966 had its own established hierarchies. The Beatles and The Rolling Stones were the big boys, Eric Clapton and Jeff Beck were the guitar heroes, The Who had the most exciting and spectacular stage act. Clapton's newly-formed Cream – including drummer Ginger Baker and bassist/vocalist Jack Bruce – were the most fashionable new band, Baker and The Who's Keith Moon the top drummers. Bob Dylan was easily the most influential lyricist and songwriter, Phil Spector's record productions – especially 'River Deep Mountain High', sung by Tina Turner – were regarded with nothing short of awe, and everybody admired and collected American soul records from Stax, Atlantic and Tamla-Motown. Hip taste was rigidly stratified, and everybody knew their place. Chas Chandler knew that Hendrix was his secret weapon to demolish the caste structure of London's hipoisie. He installed his charge in a modest London hotel and proceeded to mobilize every contact he had.

Like a débutante, Hendrix spent the next few weeks being introduced to society. Chandler took him everywhere: dropped into a Who recording session to have his boy shake hands, did the round of all the clubs to see as many bands as possible, and finally accomplished the ultimate in audacity by having Hendrix head-hunt Eric Clapton himself at a Cream gig. At the time, Clapton was 'God', and *nobody* duelled with God. Hendrix hammered into Howlin' Wolf's 'Killing Floor', and committed deicide that night, earning Clapton's devoted friendship. Jamming, a few nights later, in a less competitive environment (with the Brian Auger Trinity), he was spotted by French star Johnny Hallyday, who immediately booked him as an opening act at the Paris Olympia. Chandler and Hendrix had two weeks in which to find and rehearse a band.

Auditions commenced immediately. A young guitarist from Folkestone who had dropped into Chandler's office to audition for an already-filled lead guitar vacancy in Eric Burdon's New Animals, was loaned a bass and sent in to jam with Hendrix, who was intrigued by his frizzed-out red hair and impressed by his ability to learn songs quickly. His name was Noel Redding; he was invited to return the following day and join the team. Various drummers tried their luck, including the veteran Aynesley Dunbar, who had played with Liverpool one-hit wonders The Mojos as well as John Mayall's deeply serious and highly respected Bluesbreakers, and a cocky kid named John 'Mitch' Mitchell, a former child actor temporarily at liberty following Georgie Fame's dissolution of his band, ironically also named The Blue Flames. In the end, Hendrix and Chandler flipped a coin, and Mitchell won the toss. He, too, was in. During the auditions, they had experimented briefly with keyboard players, but finally they decided to keep things simple and stay a trio. It was, after all, a fashionable configuration: The Who and Cream – the bands with which the newly-formed Jimi Hendrix Experience was most explicitly designed to compete – were both three-instrument outfits (the tambourine and harmonica played by The Who's vocalist, Roger Daltrey, didn't really count), and Mitch Mitchell's frenzied, Elvin Jones-derived drum style certainly stood comparison with the more established Moon and Baker. All that remained was to get some work and organize a record deal.

They had barely three days to rehearse for the Paris shows, and as a result, the repertoire consisted principally of stretched-out versions of soul standards like 'Respect', 'Land of 1000 Dances' and 'Mercy Mercy Mercy' almost as familiar to Redding from the US army bases he'd played in Germany as they were to Hendrix from his days on the chitlin circuit. They did sufficiently well at the Olympia for Hallyday to add them to his show for a few German dates before they returned to London to cut their début recording. Again, Chandler was ahead of his time: he and Mike Jeffery put up the money for the session themselves, with the intention of leasing the finished recording to a record company as an independent production. As a member of The Animals, he had learned at first hand how helpless an act could be when their studio decisions were taken for them by an autocratic producer. Chandler himself served as

Hendrix's producer on behalf of Jeffery's Yameta organization: he, Hendrix and engineer Eddie Kramer acted as a tight little collective for the next couple of years.

The first couple of tunes they recorded were 'Hey Joe' and 'Stone Free': the latter a Hendrix composition which fused blues chord-changes, a soul-revue beat and an incendiary guitar solo, and the former a US pop-folk hit which had been the sole Top-40 appearance for a group called The Leaves. It had also been recorded by The Byrds, but Hendrix's version was based on that of folk-rock cult figure Tim Rose, who had slowed the song's jaunty pace down to an anguished crawl. ('Hey Joe' had been composed by one Billy Roberts, but here the credit read 'Trad. arr. J. Hendrix': in English, this means a traditional song arranged by somebody-or-other. Arrangements of traditional songs could be lucrative: Chandler's former colleague Alan Price had raked in a tidy sum for the arrangement of The Animals' first international hit, 'House of the Rising Sun'.)

The single cut, Chandler set about hustling a record deal. Decca Records, in a spectacular display of the kind of music-business acumen which had led them to reject The Beatles four years earlier, turned him down. The band embarked on a series of showcase gigs in London's most fashionable rock *boîtes*; attendance was mandatory for anybody in town who was even remotely connected with the rock business. Journalists emerged sputtering superlatives (Chris Welch of *Melody Maker* and Keith Altham from *New Musical Express* were among his earliest and most vociferous admirers), top guitarists were both dazzled and threatened, and a lot of women fancied him like mad. 'Jimi Hendrix, a fantastic American guitarist, blew the minds of the star-packed crowd,' enthused Welch after one club gig. 'Jimi's trio blasted through some beautiful sounds . . . Jimi has great stage presence and exceptional guitar technique, which involves playing with his teeth on some occasions and no hands on others! Jimi looks like becoming one of the big club names of '67.'

The Who's management team, Kit Lambert and Chris Stamp, were interested in signing Hendrix for their new label, Track Records, but they weren't planning to launch until the following spring. The national daily tabloids treated him like a freakshow, dubbed him 'the Wild Man of Pop', and generally trotted out the would-you-let-your-sister-marry-this-man ritual greeting with which new pop phenomena have traditionally been welcomed since the invention of Elvis Presley in the fifties. Everything was going according to plan, except that no one wanted to release 'Hey

Joe', no one wanted to book the band for any shows, and Chandler and Jeffery were about to run out of money.

Or, to be precise, Chandler was. Jeffery was generally elsewhere when the bills fell due, and Chandler was reduced to financing the band by selling off his collection of bass guitars. He was down to his last one before Polydor Records, the distributors for Robert Stigwood's Reaction label, which had previously issued The Who's records, reluctantly agreed to release 'Hey Joe'.

For the princely sum of £25, the Experience opened for Eric Burdon's New Animals at a Croydon club, a show which established beyond a shadow of a doubt that Hendrix was a natural bill-topper and that anybody who wanted to follow his act did so at their own peril. Then came another show at London's Round House, at which Hendrix's guitar was stolen; Chandler had to part with his last bass in order to pay for a new one. A lucky break followed: the release of 'Hey Joe' was marked by a spot on *Ready Steady Go!*, the most forward-looking, trend-wise TV show in the country. As soon as the nation's record shops reopened for business after New Year, 'Hey Joe' was clambering its way up the Top 50. The bookings were coming in thick and fast, and by February it was in the Top Five. London was the unquestioned centre of the pop universe in that immediately pre-psychedelic era, and Hendrix, like some improbable blend of Julius Caesar and Cinderella, had come, seen, conquered and then promptly become the belle of the ball as well as the hero of the hour.

It must have seemed like a dream come true: as if Chas Chandler had waved a magic wand and, like some towering Fairy Godmother from Newcastle, had magically transported Hendrix to his *real* home, the place where he had belonged all along, the place where he always *should* have been. Everywhere, he was lionized; he padded in and out of the most exclusive clubs and parties clad in his newly-acquired finery, while the biggest names in British rock either queued up to accept his studiedly limp handshake or muttered angrily in corners about how he'd better stay away from *their* girlfriends. Hendrix formed one of his few firm London friendships with Brian Jones, the spoiled prince of The Rolling Stones, whose long decline into substance-addled paranoia and musical impotence had already begun. Mick Jagger and Keith Richards were treating Jones like an outsider, and none of them had much personal affection for Hendrix. Richards had not forgotten what had happened in New York with Linda Keith, and Jagger was smarting over an encounter between his girlfriend Marianne Faithfull and Hendrix which had almost resulted in a public humiliation for the King Stone, rock's supposed reigning bad boy and sex god. Jones's self-respect had been so thoroughly eroded by his colleagues that he had nothing left to protect from Hendrix, who in turn respected Jones's talents and felt a certain amount of empathy for a man treated so cavalierly by those around him. Together, they would skip the regular round of rock night life and visit London's jazz clubs instead.

Hendrix threw himself into frantic bouts of writing and recording: Track Records was finally due to commence operations in March, and enough new music for an album and a new single were urgently required. The band ended up stockpiling enough material for two singles, their first album and much of its successor. The first two were reserved for the single 'Purple Haze'/'51st Anniversary', which was to be the inaugural release on Track. The Who, whose managers owned and ran the label, felt some-what slighted, but their sales were faltering and Hendrix was the man of the moment. According to Pete Townshend, 'Kit Lambert, who was The Who's manager and my Svengali, was the person who first introduced me to Hendrix, the person that first told me about him, first told me how big he was going to be . . . and then he told me that he'd got him on Track. Kit had a terrific entrepreneurial gift. He couldn't be wrong. I felt threatened, because I thought, "Oh God, Kit Lambert has found another guitar player." He was my Svengali, and he'd found someone else.'

Booked – more than slightly incongruously – on a tour with The Walker Brothers and Engelbert Humperdinck, Hendrix, Chandler and Keith Altham cooked up the perfect headline-grabbing stunt. In a packed London theatre, Hendrix ended his performance by burning his guitar. Even Pete Townshend had never done *that!* Instant chaos, uproar, front-page is-this-the-end-of-civilization-as-we-know-it coverage, and an excel-lent send-off for 'Purple Haze'. Around the country, audiences went nuts, parents complained and wrote angry letters to newspapers and promot-ers. The other acts on the bill might as well not have bothered to show up.

By the middle of May, 'Purple Haze' was a bigger hit than 'Hey Joe' had been, and a third single, 'The Wind Cries Mary'/'Highway Chile', was rushed out in its wake. The word about Hendrix was spreading to the States, and the first company to act on the increasing swell of tantalizing rumour was Reprise – a subsidiary of Warner Bros founded by Frank Sinatra – who paid $120,000 for the band's US rights. They demon-strated commendable acuity by doing so; less than a month later, those rights would have cost them considerably more.

June 1967 was the date chosen for the Monterey International Pop Festival, Hippie's coming-out party and the official launch for the Summer of Love. The brainchild of four men – Los Angeles music-business hustler Alan Pariser, producer/entrepreneur Lou Adler, The Mamas and The Papas' leader John Phillips, and expatriate British publicist and on-and-off Beatles aide Derek Taylor – it was designed as a non-profit showcase for the New Pop. The 'International' part of the billing was provided by Indian sitar master Ravi Shankar and South African jazz trumpeter Hugh Masekela, hit-single clout by The Byrds, The Association, Simon and Garfunkel, and The Mamas and The Papas themselves. There was a sizeable San Francisco contingent including Big Brother and the Holding Company (starring Janis Joplin), the Steve Miller Band, The Grateful Dead, Jefferson Airplane, Mike Bloomfield's Electric Flag (including Buddy Miles on drums), Country Joe and the Fish, and Quicksilver Messenger Service. Otis Redding, backed by Booker T & the MGs (with Steve Cropper on guitar) and the Memphis Horns, was soul music's only representative, despite the presence of Smokey Robinson on the Festival's board. On the recommendation of Paul McCartney – who had been persuaded by Phillips and Taylor to take up a nominal position on the board – the British contingent consisted of Eric Burdon & The Animals, The Who and The Jimi Hendrix Experience.

At Monterey, Hippie made the transition from an eccentric West-Coast boho cult to a primary national pastime for white Western youth. That month, The Beatles released *Sgt Pepper's Lonely Hearts Club Band*, and both The Doors' 'Light My Fire' and Procol Harum's 'A Whiter Shade of Pale' entered the US best-seller list. Phillips and Adler's sugary production of the Festival's theme song 'San Francisco (Wear Some Flowers in Your Hair)', sung by journeyman folkie Scott McKenzie, became an 'anthem' and eventually resulted in San Francisco being swamped by thousands of stoned teenage runaways in search of nirvana. It was the prototype for a decade's worth of rock festivals.

The three days of Monterey produced four major débuts, each of whom could claim to be 'the' hit of the festival. Otis Redding, an R&B veteran beloved of soul folks and English mods alike, galvanized what he described as 'the love crowd' in a breakthrough rendered all the more poignant by his death in a plane crash six months later. Janis Joplin, backed by the ludicrously ramshackle Big Brother, became an international star in approximately the length of time it took her to sing 'Ball and Chain'. And after a rather messy back-stage altercation as to who was going to follow Who – a mirror-image of the standard rockbiz squabble in which the victor generally ends the show, and the result of an intense desire on The Who's part to avoid a repetition of a London Savile Theatre show where Hendrix had wiped them out before they even got on stage – The Who tore up the house and made the transition from a cult band for Anglophiles to a major rock-circuit draw. But Hendrix literally burned the house down.

Wired on acid and introduced by Brian Jones, who had flown over for that express purpose and had spent most of the Festival drifting around backstage in a benign haze, Hendrix ran through his UK hits, adapted songs by Howlin' Wolf and Bob Dylan into his own canon, threw in every scene-stealing stage trick he'd ever learned, chatted to the audience between songs in a gentle, stoned, soft-voiced patter which almost defused the aggression and sexual assertiveness of the music, and finished off his set by setting fire to his guitar before smashing it to pieces. Instant wipe-out. The night belonged to Hendrix: he was now officially the toast of rock's global village. He was invited to Los Angeles to jam and party-down at the home of Buffalo Springfield's Stephen Stills, and he, Stills, Neil Young, David Crosby, Buddy Miles, Hugh Masekela and assorted others got high and made loud noises for two full days. Hendrix ended up as house guest to Peter Tork of The Monkees, who had been using the Monterey backstage area as a backdrop for endless photo opportunities with anyone more prestigious than he was.

Meanwhile, Chandler and Jeffery were raking in the bookings. Hendrix was eagerly sought by all of the hippest halls and clubs on both coasts, by new-age entrepreneurs like Bill Graham (of the Fillmore Auditorium) and Steve Paul (of The Scene club). It therefore came as something of a shock to both Hendrix and Chandler that Jeffery had booked the band on to a tour with The Monkees. The combination of the Wild Man of Pop and the Prefab Four came as such an acute mutual culture shock that Chandler cooked up a cover story alleging that the right-wing Daughters of the American Revolution pressure group had engineered Hendrix's removal from the tour. This face-saving device enabled everybody to proceed with dignity and credibility more or less intact, and the band embarked on a whirlwind series of showcase gigs in California and New York, spreading the word. In New York, Hendrix had a brief reunion with Curtis Knight, jamming briefly in a recording studio and using the opportunity to explore the possibilities of the wah-wah pedal, a new guitar toy he had purchased earlier that day after seeing one being used by a strange California band called the Mothers of Invention.

It had not escaped Ed Chalpin's notice that the contract he had signed with Hendrix two years earlier was still technically valid, that it had been Hendrix who had breached it when he signed with Chandler, Polydor, Track and Reprise, and that it was now worth considerably more than the one-dollar advance Chalpin had paid out to the artist. Chalpin, who was still Knight's manager, speedily sold the jams, together with earlier pre-Experience Hendrix/Knight recordings, to Capitol Records, who issued them that November under the title *Get That Feeling (Jimi Hendrix Plays and Curtis Knight Sings)*, complete with a cover photograph shot during the Monterey performance. Chandler, Jeffery, Polydor, Track and Reprise were distinctly unamused: even though a British court threw out Chalpin's claim, they knew that it would stick in America, which was ultimately where it counted.

Back in England, they toured remorselessly (twenty-seven dates – two shows a night at many of them – including forays to Paris and Rotterdam) while putting the finishing touches to their second album, *Axis: Bold as Love*, the bulk of which had already been recorded during the same sessions which produced *Are You Experienced*. Straight after Hendrix's second Christmas and New Year away from home, they were rushed straight back out on tour, this time in Scandinavia. On 4 January 1968, Hendrix's quiet, affable façade cracked. He had for some time been eating enough LSD on a sufficiently regular basis to excite the concern of even his less abstemious colleagues, but this time, in Gothenburg, he topped it up with enough booze to get serious, mean drunk. Gripped by a berserk fury so intense that he smashed up most of his hotel room before bassist Noel Redding and roadie Gerry Stickells managed to restrain him, Hendrix was marched, handcuffed, to a cell, where he woke up the next morning confused, contrite and with absolutely no memory of the previous night's events.

No matter how intense the pressures on Hendrix were at this point, there was no respite from touring. By February, the band was back in the USA, this time headlining a package of British bands (not a few of whom – Eric Burdon & The Animals, Soft Machine, and The Alan Price Set – were clients of Jeffery and Chandler's Yameta company) trekking a circuit of arenas and large halls, playing to audiences of 20,000 or more. He even managed a triumphant return to Seattle, packing the city's Center Arena while Al Hendrix beamed proudly from the centre of the front row. The previous night, father and son had met for the first time in seven years.

The tour rolled on, smashing attendance record after attendance record. Chandler and Jeffery were delighted: they were on percentages rather than fixed fees, and they were pulling in astounding amounts of money. *Are You Experienced* had sold over a million copies and the 'Purple Haze' single 100,000; now *Axis: Bold as Love* was safely ensconced in the Top 20. Even Ed Chalpin's Curtis Knight sessions had sold 100,000 copies – though Hendrix wasn't receiving any royalties on that.

By the spring, the Hendrix operation had based itself in New York City as work commenced on the third Experience album. The problem was that everyone concerned had different ideas of what that work was going to be. Hendrix was becoming more and more frustrated within the tight structure of the Experience set-up: Noel on the bass, Mitch on the drums and Chas Chandler behind the control board. He was growing increasingly bored with the format of those endless shows, as well: the emphasis on showmanship, the same old Greatest Hits (though the *Axis* album had added a few welcome new songs to their repertoire) and the demands of an audience which would rather see him enact wild-black-stud routines and photogenic guitar stunts than listen to him tell them his story through the instrument. All those attention-grabbing stage tricks which had served him so well in the past were becoming his own private ball and chain. More and more, he wanted to produce his own records; he wanted to play with musicians other than – or, at least, in addition to – Mitch Mitchell and Noel Redding, and he wanted to take his music into areas more challenging than three-chord, three-instrument rock. On the other hand, Redding, Mitchell and Chandler – and probably the majority of Hendrix's fans – liked things fine the way they were, and couldn't see any reason why Hendrix wanted to change a winning formula.

Hendrix and his team grew further and further apart. His social life consisted of an endless round of nightclubs and studios, listening to his fellow musicians and as like as not sitting in with them. Everywhere he went, people would want to be his friends. He had more friends than he knew what to do with. They would give him dope (occasionally in a spiked drink when he wasn't expecting it; the assumption was that he wanted to be high as a kite *all* the time), trinkets and clothes. He would buy them cars and guitars, and give near-strangers thousands of dollars in cash. His recording sessions grew more and more unmanageable: he would suddenly show up at The Record Plant (at the time New York City's most expensive and sophisticated studio) with half a dozen musicians and all *their* friends in tow and start recording lengthy jams that lasted all night. He quarrelled more and more frequently with his English personnel: they felt themselves increasingly marginalized, and with good reason.

Hendrix had become steadily more and more impatient with Noel Redding, and they had come to blows on more than one occasion. Redding resented having his bass lines fed to him note for note, and occasionally Hendrix had overdubbed the bass on to certain tunes himself. The eventual double-album *Electric Ladyland* featured Jefferson Airplane's Jack Casady playing bass on one track, and the ever-more-ubiquitous Buddy Miles occupying Mitchell's drum stool on another, as well as an assortment of other 'friends and passengers' on various instruments – including Stevie Winwood, Dave Mason and Chris Wood of Traffic, and Al Kooper. Halfway through the recording, Hendrix suddenly took off for Los Angeles, where he hung out a lot with Buddy Miles (who was cutting an album with his own band, Buddy Miles Express), mixed and overdubbed parts of *Electric Ladyland* in local studios, indulged in highly uncharacteristic public drunkenness, bought expensive cars (which as like or not, he crashed a few days later) and had to pay out a substantial sum of hush money – something in the region of $10,000 – to buy off a girl whom he'd beaten to the point where hospitalization was necessary. This was certainly not the shy, placid, amenable Jimi Hendrix his English friends knew.

Eventually, it all got to be too much for Chas Chandler: he quit as both Hendrix's producer and manager. Jeffery bought him out for the more than respectable sum of $300,000, and *Electric Ladyland* appeared with the credit line 'Produced and Directed by Jimi Hendrix', even though several tracks had been recorded in London and produced by Chandler during that feverish burst of studio activity the previous year. It was Hendrix's most successful album – his first and only chart-topping long-player – and it gave him his biggest-selling US single: his epochal version of Bob Dylan's 'All Along the Watchtower' reached Number 20 in the pop charts. In terms of commercial success, it represented the peak of his career.

Yet to say that all was not well is something of an understatement. The Experience was on the verge of breaking up, and Ed Chalpin had by now parlayed his Hendrix/Knight tapes into no fewer than four albums. He and his one-dollar contract were certainly not going to go away, even though the US courts had dismissed his claim to Hendrix's management and recording rights. The resulting litigation went on for almost the next year.

By a judicious combination of coercion, threats and special pleading, Jeffery persuaded Hendrix, Mitchell and Redding to stay together long enough to fulfil existing commitments for their 1969 tour dates in Britain, Europe and the USA. Redding had, in the interim, formed his own group, Fat Mattress, in which he returned to his original vocation as a guitarist, and his precondition for participating in the Experience tour was that Fat Mattress would open the show for Hendrix. They slugged their way around Scandinavia and Europe with a film crew in attendance, gave their last British performance at the Royal Albert Hall on 24 February and returned to the US in March. By now, Hendrix was the highest-paid act on the circuit, never grossing less than $50,000 for a show and often, in the larger venues, $100,000 or more. Personal animosity within the Experience was running high, and the shows were notable for the lack of empathy between the three musicians; but the crowds were flocking in, and every show was a sell-out. The only real shock came when Jeffery – attracted by the notion of an extra $110,000 – booked an extra date in at the Maple Leaf Gardens in Toronto. Canadian customs are notoriously hard-assed about drugs; they shook the band down very thoroughly at the border, and in one of Hendrix's bags they found a small vial of heroin.

It was unquestionably a set-up: Hendrix indulged freely in psyche-delics and marijuana, and was not averse to an occasional spoon of cocaine, but heroin was a vice which – at that time, at least – he was happy to do without. Bail was swiftly arranged and the tour continued – with even a break permitted for a brief holiday in Morocco – but the event did nothing whatsoever for Hendrix's increasingly fragile peace of mind. In the eyes of his audience, though, a major drug bust simply added to his rebel-chic status: for his appearance at the Devonshire Downs festival on the West Coast, the Experience were paid a record-breaking $125,000. It was their penultimate performance; after one more open-air show in Denver, Noel Redding and Mitch Mitchell left for London and announced the break-up of The Jimi Hendrix Experience. Redding kept his word; Mitchell soon returned to the USA and became part of the loose circle of musicians who assembled around Hendrix's rented home in Boiseville, near Woodstock in upstate New York. But most important of all, Billy Cox had finally allowed himself to be persuaded to leave Nashville and join his old army buddy as Noel Redding's replacement. Hendrix trusted Cox implicitly: Cox had been a loyal friend to him at a time when he had really needed one, before the madness began. Further-more, Cox's funky, uncluttered bass style would give Hendrix's new music a more solid, less frenetic underpinning. In every way, Cox's function would be to provide the steadiness Hendrix so urgently required.

Theoretically, it could have been a time of tranquillity and regeneration; a chance for Hendrix to recover from the non-stop activity and craziness of the past three years. Unfortunately, it was nothing of the sort. His friend Brian Jones had recently died in England, drowned in his own swimming pool. The Toronto heroin charge was still hanging over his head, as was Ed Chalpin's law-suit, which had resulted in all Hendrix's royalty payments from Reprise Records being frozen until a legal solution was found. Worse, Hendrix was still spending a fortune in recording costs at The Record Plant in New York, jamming with Buddy Miles and members of John McLaughlin's studio band, laying down endless tracks for a planned double album. In an attempt to keep Hendrix's recording expenses under control, Mike Jeffery had decided – with considerable foresight – that Hendrix needed his own studio, a state-of-the-art workplace where he could record whenever he wanted, and which could be rented out to other performers when Hendrix himself wasn't using it. The trouble was that the construction of this new studio – known, naturally enough, as Electric Lady – kept running into serious problems. The site on West 8th Street was dangerously close to a subway tunnel, necessitating a fearsome amount of additional soundproofing, and things got worse still when excavation workers hit an underground stream, causing massive flooding. All this was costing a fortune, which – thanks to Chalpin – the organization no longer had. An extra advance of $250,000 had to be negotiated with Reprise just to keep everybody afloat.

As if all this wasn't enough, Jeffery was not pleased with the direction of Hendrix's musical experiments. He was socializing and jamming more and more with the jazz musicians to whom a new friend, producer Alan Douglas, was introducing him, and showing decreasing enthusiasm for the tried-and-trusted hard rock with which he had established himself. Douglas was trying to set up a joint session with Hendrix and Miles Davis – whose newest music clearly betrayed the influences of James Brown, Sly Stone and Hendrix himself – but it collapsed at the last minute when Miles demanded a $50,000 advance before entering the studio. John McLaughlin, a former colleague of Jack Bruce, Ginger Baker, Graham Bond and other early London jazz-rock fusionists, had Buddy Miles playing drums on the material he was recording for Douglas's label, and McLaughlin himself was a key figure in the development of Miles Davis's new sound. New alliances were being formed, new music was being played, and all of this seemed considerably more interesting to Hendrix than going out and playing 'Purple Haze' all over again.

Meanwhile, all of the upstate New York rock grapevines were abuzz with talk of a forthcoming rock festival that was supposed to be the biggest ever. Subtitled 'Three days of peace and music', the Woodstock Music and Arts Fair was planned to be the ultimate celebration of the counter-culture, and Hendrix was naturally invited to close the final night. He was to be the Festival's highest-paid performer, even though the fee was substantially lower than was his norm. For the occasion, he chose an expanded line-up, combining Mitch Mitchell and Billy Cox with rhythm guitarist Larry Lee and two percussionists. Cox was certainly receiving a baptism of fire: as well as being filmed and recorded, his first performance with Hendrix was to be in front of an audience originally estimated at a potential 100,000. In the event, it didn't turn out quite like that. Almost 300,000 people turned up to wallow in the mud, babble euphorically at each other and get tripped out of their skulls, but the programme overran so drastically that Hendrix's group – named 'Sky Church' for the occasion – was unable to take the stage until the morning after the festival had nominally ended, by which time only 30,000 or so of that massive crowd remained to hear them. Nevertheless, even if the audience had straggled wearily back to civilization, the tape machines and the cameras were still rolling, and what they captured was an epochal performance that provided the climax of the feature film and three-record album which defined what *Woodstock* was about for the rest of the world. Hendrix's most eloquent statement was wordless: an epic deconstruction of 'The Star Spangled Banner' for guitar and indifferently-recorded drums and percussion which recalled nothing so much as the sonic hurricanes which John Coltrane had built around the melodies of innocuous show tunes like 'Chim Chim Cheree' and 'My Favourite Things'. A sonic portrait of a land in turmoil, a nation in danger of tumbling into the abyss cracked open by the contradictions between its ideals and aspirations and its reality, it was both a performance which no other living musician would have been capable of conceiving or executing, and a graphic demonstration that Hendrix's artistic ambitions had grown in proportion to – but in a radically different direction from – his immense popularity.

It was time, next, to do battle with the courts: to get Ed Chalpin out of his hair and to face up to the Toronto heroin charges. Jeffery and Chalpin had finally found a solution: Chalpin would receive 2 per cent of the royalties from *Are You Experienced*, *Axis: Bold as Love* and *Electric Ladyland*, and an entirely new Hendrix album would be delivered to Chalpin's production company to be released by whichever record company turned out to be the highest bidder. Since Hendrix had already agreed to play a New Year's Eve concert at New York's Fillmore East, it was arranged for the concert to be recorded for a live album. This meant that Chalpin wouldn't get his hands on any of Hendrix's current batch of studio recordings, but it still rankled: Hendrix felt that if Jeffery and Reprise had fought the case as conscientiously as they should have done, he wouldn't have had to give Chalpin anything at all.

Much to his relief, he was acquitted in Toronto. Hendrix testified that he was always being given presents and on this occasion he had simply tossed the package into his bag without examining it, and he promised to be more careful in future. This argument – reinforced by a highly disingenuous and wholly untruthful claim to have given up drugs – proved acceptable to the judge and jury. Hendrix was unconditionally discharged; free to return to New York, where he, Billy Cox and Buddy Miles – Mitch Mitchell was on sabbatical, touring with Jack Bruce – were ready to go into intensive rehearsals for the Fillmore show. The new trio – to be known as Band of Gypsys (*sic*) – retained the format of the old Experience, but it transformed an English group with a black American frontman into three black Americans, and this prospect did not in any way appeal to Michael Jeffery. The overwhelming bulk of Hendrix's support, Jeffery felt, came from young whites, and for symbolic at least as much as musical reasons, they preferred to see Hendrix with Redding and Mitchell. The lyrical content of one of the songs performed at the Fillmore pleased Jeffery even less.

Hendrix was always ambivalent about the resulting album, *Band of Gypsys* – his guitar drifted out of tune too often for his liking – but it contained the towering, explicitly anti-war 'Machine Gun'. To one of Jeffery's conservative politics, it must have seemed as if Hendrix was about to sign up with the Black Panther Party. When Band of Gypsys agreed to headline a massive concert/rally for the Vietnam Moratorium Committee at Madison Square Garden, Jeffery's fury knew no bounds, but – strangely enough – fate played smoothly into his hands. Before the concert, Hendrix was given (by a person, or persons unknown, though Buddy Miles has claimed that it was Jeffery himself) some exceptionally vicious LSD, which almost immediately induced cramps and vomiting. The performance was a disaster: a spooked, shivering Hendrix dropped his guitar and walked off after the second number. Buddy Miles was fired the very next day, and barely a week later, Jeffery proudly announced the reunion of the original Experience. For one reason or another, however, Noel Redding didn't stay around, opting to sign up instead for a putative tour with Jeff Beck (which, in the event, never took place). Billy Cox thus held on to his job, though unlike Mitchell, he remained a salaried employee.

Jeffery speedily signed Hendrix up for a couple of movies: one a more or less straightforward concert film entitled *Jimi Plays Berkeley* and the other – considerably closer to his heart – an incoherent farrago of dope and mysticism shot on the Hawaiian island of Maui by a former Andy Warhol protégé named Chuck Wein. The latter project, *Rainbow Bridge*, was cross-financed with Warner-Reprise in exchange for the rights to the inevitable soundtrack album. Interspersed with feverish bouts of recording at the still-uncompleted Electric Lady studio, Hendrix, Mitchell and Cox set off on another round of touring, playing a mixture of old standbys and newer songs, but – much to Hendrix's disgust and despair – the fresh material seemed to be merely tolerated by the audiences, who reserved their most enthusiastic applause for the traditional crowd-pleasers. Both his management and his audiences seemed determined that Hendrix should be content with simply repeating his former triumphs, and it was observed that Hendrix's dope consumption, which was fairly monstrous even at the best of times, was escalating dramatically; not exactly a sign of great contentment and tranquillity. He began consulting independent lawyers and accountants with a view to sorting out his tangled finances and freeing himself from Mike Jeffery.

And he kept recording, recording, recording: he planned to release a double album with the working title of *First Rays of the New Rising Sun* at the end of the year, a record which would both summarize the work he had done in the sixties and point the way forward to the new music he intended to play when he had gained control of his own life and work. To this end, he had approached both Alan Douglas and Chas Chandler to take over his career, though how he had planned to reconcile their very different approaches to both music and business is still a mystery. The most ambitious of the plans he and Douglas had concocted was a collaboration with the great jazz arranger Gil Evans, best-known for his work with Miles Davis. It was arranged that Hendrix and Evans's orchestra would commence rehearsals for an album and concert of Evans's arrangements of Hendrix's compositions – with Hendrix himself as featured soloist – when the guitarist returned from his forthcoming European tour.

By the end of August, the studio was complete, and the album required only a few more weeks' work. Hendrix and the band flew straight from a gala launch-party to Europe, where their tour was planned to commence with the giant three-day Isle of Wight Festival. The festival had been marked by considerable conflict between the organizers and various groups – ranging from French anarchists led by one Jean-Jacques Lebel to Hell's Angels –who believed that the event should be transformed into a free concert. There was considerable tension in the air by the time Hendrix took the stage: the show had been running late, the temperature had dropped, and most of the audience were curled up in their sleeping bags, huddled around camp fires and trying to keep warm. The sound quality was wretched, the crowd's response was damp and fitful, walkie-talkie radio communications between the Festival's security corps kept crackling through the band's amps, and Hendrix himself was both stoned and exhausted. It was not an auspicious occasion for Hendrix's first British performance for a year and a half.

Things got worse as the tour progressed. Another festival, this time in Germany, was broken up by bikers and anarchists, and backstage, Billy Cox was handed a drink spiked with LSD. Steady, easy-going Cox was – unusually for an intimate of Hendrix's – totally averse to drugs, and the unwitting ingestion of a powerful dose of acid sent him whirling to the brink of a near-breakdown. At a local hospital, he was 'brought down' from the trip with a massive shot of the tranquillizer Thorazine, which left him near-catatonic. The next two shows were cancelled, and the troupe returned, in disarray, to London. Hendrix holed up at the home of his girlfriend Monika Danneman, where he could nurse the ailing Cox: he still maintained a suite at the Cumberland Hotel, but it was impossible for him to stay there, because – since the Ed Chalpin lawsuit had yet to be settled in the British courts – he was being sought by various process servers and bearers of subpoenas. He still made his social rounds – jamming with Eric Burdon and his new band War at Ronnie Scott's jazz club; making tentative arrangements to jam with Mitch Mitchell, Ginger Baker and Sly Stone when the latter arrived for a concert with Sly & the Family Stone; attending a dinner party hosted by ex-Monkee Mike Nesmith; even giving interviews – but basically he was lying low. A telegram had been dispatched to Noel Redding requesting him to sit in with the band so that the tour could go ahead; until then, he would hide out in London. Sometime during the night of 17 September, he decided to knock himself out with some of Monika Danneman's sleeping pills: he would sleep through the 18th and leave London at the weekend, return to New York to finish work on the album, pick up the tapes of his work-in-progress and then get together again with Chas Chandler.

It never happened. According to Monika Danneman, she had noticed early the next morning that Hendrix had thrown up during the night, but since he seemed to be breathing and sleeping normally, she popped out to the corner shop for cigarettes. When she returned, she was unable to wake him. Panicking, she phoned Eric Burdon, who screamed at her to call an ambulance. An ambulance duly arrived, but somehow, Hendrix was loaded into it lying on his back, and since his system was so paralysed by the pills that he was unable to spit out or cough up his vomit, he simply suffocated. She claimed that the ambulance crew had reassured her that Hendrix was going to be all right.

However, the story isn't remotely that clear-cut. Danneman herself told the story several different ways, and the records of the hospital to which Hendrix was rushed also challenge her account(s). Hendrix was pronounced dead on arrival, but this still begs the question of whether he died in the ambulance or earlier, in Danneman's apartment at the Samarkand Hotel.

Much of what happened that night had to wait for its final unravelling until the publication in 1997 of Hendrix researcher Tony Brown's *Hendrix: The Final Days*, which comprehensively demolishes Monika Danneman's testimony. If Danneman hadn't committed suicide whilst Brown's book was in its final stages, she would have had some fairly tough questions to answer following its publication.

What is beyond dispute is that on the morning of 18 September 1970, Jimi Hendrix died without regaining consciousness, in the city to which he had travelled with so much hope and optimism a little over four years earlier. He was twenty-seven years old.

These are the facts in the case of Jimi Hendrix. It is now time to explore some of their nuances.

3

I'm a Man (At Least I'm Trying to Be)

So was Jimi Hendrix a sexist pig or what?

'Niggers be holdin' them dicks too, Jack . . . white folks say, "Why do you guys hold your things?" 'Cause you done *took* everything else, motherfucker . . .'

Richard Pryor, *Is It Something I Said* (1975)

'Oh, but black guys are SO SEXIST . . .'

Conventional plaint frequently heard at liberal dinner parties

'The only position for women in SNCC [Student Non-violent Co-ordinating Committee] is *prone.*'

Civil Rights activist Stokeley Carmichael (1964)

When I was a young boy,
At the age of five,
I had sump'n in my pocket,
Keep a lot of folks alive,
Now I'm a man,
Way past twenty-one,
I tell you baby,
I have lots of fun,
I'm a man . . .
I spell M . . . A . . . N
Now ain't that a man?

Bo Diddley and Muddy Waters, 'I'm a Man'/'Manish Boy' (1955)

Back in the days when Jimi Hendrix was a backing guitarist for Curtis Knight and John Hammond, he would generally be featured as a vocalist on one song: Bo Diddley's 'I'm a Man'. Basically a declamatory vamp over an endlessly repeated single riff derived from the signature motif of Muddy Waters' classic brag song 'Hoochie Coochie Man' (written by Willie Dixon), it was almost instantly annexed by Waters himself, who retitled it 'Man(n)ish Boy'. Both versions were immensely popular among Britain's fledgling blues buffs, one young band (led by a certain David Jones, who later did quite well for himself under the name of David Bowie) going so far as to name themselves The Manish Boys. The Yardbirds made it one of the centrepieces of their stage show, and

recorded it twice: once in 1964, when Eric Clapton was their lead guitarist, and again the following year when Clapton had been replaced by
Jeff Beck. It also showed up on The Who's first album.

'I'm a Man' fitted in perfectly with the needs and preoccupations of
the young groovers who made up and listened to the British R&B groups
of the early sixties, although the song's phallocentric bluster seemed
faintly comical when delivered by spotty, reedy-voiced youths like The
Yardbirds' singer Keith Relf, and only slightly less so in Roger Daltrey's
mannered growl. The lyrics may have boasted of an extraordinary sexual
potency which served as a *de facto* badge of maturity, but their voices suggested otherwise: that here was a bunch of young boys laying claim to an
adulthood to which they were less than absolutely certain that they were
entitled, but which they desperately craved.

No such doubts afflicted Muddy Waters and Bo Diddley, which is one
reason why they were such appealing role-models for their young British
admirers; another is that as blacks they were perceived as being men
almost by definition. Both men recorded the song in 1955, when Bo was
twenty-seven and Muddy forty; it would seem that by no stretch of the
imagination could either of them have been considered anything other
than full-grown men. The difference was, of course, that racist whites of
whatever age had traditionally referred to black men of any age as 'boys'.
The subtext of the white versions of the songs was 'I'm a Man (and
you're a girl, so get 'em off)'; the subtext of Muddy's and Bo's was 'I'm a
Man (don't *ever* call me a boy).'

'I find coloured boys seem to be able to come out of the closet easier and sing
exactly what they're thinking about, rather than do a cosmetic job like your Span-
dau Ballets and so forth.'

David Coverdale, vocalist of Whitesnake, interviewed in *New Musical Express* (1984)

The story of how the sexuality expressed through the blues gradually
mutated into the penile dementia of heavy-metal rock and hardcore rap is
a long and curious one. Disingenuous 'hard' rockers like David Coverdale
(whose band's name is a rather over-literal nod to the lyrical content of
songs like Blind Lemon Jefferson's 'Black Snake Moan' or John Lee
Hooker's 'Crawling King Snake') legitimize their sexist bombast by citing bluesy precedents: well, all them old blues geezers sang about birds
an' booze an' that, didn't they? The answer is that yes, of course they did
– there are more blues songs about women than about anything else, with
alcohol and money as obvious runners-up – but sadly, life isn't that sim-

ple; those songs are considerably more eloquent than a simple transcript of their lyrics (or even a cover version by a white band) could possibly suggest. Traditionally, white power structures have found blacks least threatening when they are singing either about Jesus or about sex and dancing. As a result, such songs have ended up, to a greater or lesser extent, as codes for singing about virtually every subject under the sun, and the ultimate import of a blues, soul or gospel tune is, as likely as not, communicated as much through the nuances of rhythmic emphasis or vocal tone and melisma as through the overt content of a lyric. The best and finest moments of blues-based white rock have arrived through creative misunderstandings of the subtexts of the music which provided the inspirational spark; the worst have come through crass exaggeration of surface impressions, and the intoxicated egos of posturing ninnies who appear not to realize that they have someone else's dick stuffed down their trousers.

Let's take another specific example: Muddy Waters' 1963 recording of 'You Need Love' as transformed, a mere six years later, into Led Zeppelin's 'Whole Lotta Love' (with Willie Dixon's composing credit somehow going AWOL in the process). The former is a seduction, and its most heinous crime, even in terms of present-day sexual politics, is that it could be considered mildly condescending and vaguely paternalistic, though 'avuncular' is probably a more appropriate adjective. Muddy's tone is warm and solicitous: he suggests that the woman to whom he is singing is both sexually inexperienced and starved of affection, and volunteers to remedy both conditions. The music to which 'You Need Love' is set echoes Muddy's warmth with an intricate guitar figure and a Hammond organ that seeps into the tune like a measure of fine brandy; the total effect is intimate, relaxed, utterly sensual.

Led Zeppelin, by contrast, come on like thermonuclear gang rape. The woman – who, in Muddy Waters' song, is evoked as a real person with real emotions in a real situation – is here reduced to a mere receptacle; an entirely passive presence whose sole function is to receive the Great Zeppelin (as depicted on the group's first two album covers: lumbering facetiousness posing as irony) with a suitable degree of veneration and gratitude. Even her response is superfluous: Zeppelin's vocalist Robert Plant virtually has her orgasm for her. After all, the satisfaction of the woman in the case is not intended for her benefit, but for his: it is the validation of his masculine prowess and the price of his admission to the alpha-male society. The stud-strut of heavy metal is a ritual by which men celebrate each other; it is not primarily intended for women, who – at British metal shows, if not at their American counterparts – demonstrate their understanding of the nature of the event by not showing up. The woman is strictly an abstract, faceless presence; she is essential as a part of the intercourse kit, but not as an individual. 'Love', in this context, is a euphemism for something measurable with a ruler; when Plant howls, 'I'm gonna give you every inch of MAH LURVE', the term 'imply' is too mild for the intensity he brings to the suggestion that his love is, quite literally, his penis.

> Death and my cock are the world.
>
> Jim Morrison, 'An American Prayer'

The technical term for this stuff is 'cock rock': the good-humoured carnality and rueful social realism of the blues translated into the florid indulgence of male adolescent power fantasies. The women whom bluesmen from Robert Johnson to Robert Cray simultaneously pursue and contend with are strong palpable presences: they are at least the men's equals and often their superiors. Ultimately, the men need the women more than vice versa, and everybody knows it; the men also resent the hell out of the women for precisely this reason, and everybody knows *that*, too.

That said, no one would dispute that a considerable proportion of blues lyrics is, indeed, deeply sexist (no one, at least, except those committed chauvinists who consider the very notion of sexism fictitious). Why this *should be* so, however, is far less clear-cut.

First of all, the life of a working male entertainer (of any race, style or degree of eminence and financial success) was never particularly conducive to domestic stability. Long periods of absence from home made separation from wives, girlfriends and families inevitable, creating plenty of scope for sexual dalliances by both parties *and* inducing a considerable degree of cynicism about the durability of relationships. More relevantly, in any kind of racist society, members of racial out-groups have always laboured under severe economic disadvantages, creating additional familial stresses. In many cases, black women were far more likely to find employment (albeit poorly-paid and demeaning or degrading employment) than their men, which often made the women the likely breadwinners. In the process, feelings of inadequacy developed, which in turn demanded a higher degree of domestic self-assertion from the men, who wanted at least one place in their world where they could be treated with some respect: the outside (read 'white') world was treating them like shit.

The bluesman frequently stresses the urgency of his need to be treated like the head of his household, and the efforts he makes to function as a good provider. (B. B. King's 'Paying the Cost to Be the Boss' is as good an example of this school of song as any, though in the mid-sixties his repertoire was full of them: *His Best: The Electric B. B. King* also includes songs like 'Tired of Your Jive', 'Don't Answer the Door', 'Think It Over' and 'I Don't Want to Cut Your Hair', all textbook case-histories of male insecurity.) The bluesman's female counterpart fights back by insisting that it's not *her* fault if he's not making headway on the outside, and that she won't sit still while he takes his frustrations out on her. Aretha Franklin's confrontation with Matt 'Guitar' Murphy in John Landis's film *The Blues Brothers* is an intentionally trivialized, comic reduction of this conflict, but the conflict is still a very real and serious one, and the vehemence of Franklin's performance simply serves to underline it.

The problem, of course, is essentially one of class rather than race – working-class communities have, broadly speaking, tenaciously clung to traditional notions of gender roles – and therefore has more to do with crude economics than with any holdovers from either the callously divided families of slavery or from the residual patriarchal practices of West African polygamy (Bob Marley and Fela Kuti notwithstanding). The blues was, very specifically, the music of the poorest and least 'respectable' blacks, and, as many bluesmen from Muddy Waters to B. B. King have testified, was looked down on both by the hard-working, respectable church folks and by the educated, upwardly mobile, black professional classes, whose music of choice would be, respectively, gospel and jazz. However, when the urban poor are overwhelmingly black, then those who end up doing the kind of things that only the poorest and most desperate sections of any community are willing to do in order to 'get over' – mugging, dope-dealing, prostitution – will include a preponderance of blacks. It is therefore a simple matter for the terminally obtuse, or those with a racist axe to grind, to espouse the assumption that they're not doing it because they're poor, but because they're black.

Furthermore, idealism doesn't come easy to those who have been marginalized. Possibly the most cynical account of the alleged 'realities' of male-female relationships comes from Malcolm X in his autobiography, where he draws on his early experience as a pimp as well as his latter-day Islamic fundamentalism to state that 'the prostitutes said that most men needed to know what the pimps knew. A woman should be babied enough to show her the man had affection, but beyond that she should be treated firmly . . . all women by their nature are fragile and weak: they are attracted to the man in whom they see strength . . . I'd had too much experience that women were only tricky, deceitful, untrustworthy flesh.' Women, he originally believed, were essentially whores; men were, equally essentially, either pimps or johns. He would probably not have objected too strongly to Led Zeppelin's assertion (in 'Dazed and Confused') that 'many people talkin' but few of them know/the soul of a woman was created below', or (in 'Black Dog') 'I don't know but I've been told/a big-leg woman ain't got no soul.' The young Malcolm X had, however, led a bruising and victimized existence, which accounts for his sexism even though it doesn't remotely excuse it; the likes of Led Zeppelin were simply and complacently regurgitating half-understood clichés memorized from a stack of blues records.

For *his* part, Bo Diddley – the originator of 'I'm a Man' – recalled his early experience as a boxer in these terms, when interviewed for Michael Lydon's book *Boogie Lightning*: 'It wasn't that I wanted to be tough, but I figured you should like something rough, to be a *man*. I figure "man" means more than being male. Like the word "woman". What does a woman do? She bears children. This is something great, so she has a title: woman . . . "Man" means to me a cat is supposed to protect himself as well as his family, put his life on the line for them. Having the opportunity to be a husband, father and provider is a good title, if you live up to it.'

The 'sexism' of the blues retains the heat and passion of a full-blooded domestic spat between two people who, despite the occasional outbreak of yelling and a few thrown plates, have a deep and abiding commitment to each other. When its language was decontextualized and adopted by callow post-adolescents in search of an identity, it is probably not surprising that the result was a combination of lust and misogyny that comes dangerously close to the legitimization and glorification of rape. When Ted Nugent could call an album *Penetrator*, Whitesnake could name one of theirs *Slide It in*, and a band could actually adopt the numbskull title Great White, then the real agenda becomes obvious. And when the same Great White could use lyrics like 'Knockin' down the door, pull you to the floor/'cause you need it so bad . . . gonna drive my love inside you, nail your ass to the floor/down on your knees', we have indeed come a long way from the big-hearted brag of the blues.

One of the primary attractions of the blues to its youthful white early sixties constituency was its stark contrast to the more insipid aspects of the teen-angel school of pop songwriting. It would be nothing less than boorish to deny the intoxicating charm and swooning romanticism of the best of the girl-group songs – anybody who isn't moved by, say, The Shirelles' 'Will You Love Me Tomorrow' has no business listening to pop music in the first place – or to claim that the beautiful records that Burt Bacharach and Hal David constructed for Dionne Warwick have less right to an intelligent person's turntable time than the boys-town hard rock of The Who. However, songs of teddy bears, puppy love and living dolls were less than appealing to adolescent males whose hormones were in the process of going berserk. For them, the tough, knowing sexuality of the blues, and of the young white performers who had taken the blues on board, was far more attractive; it was the perfect antidote to the sugar-coated romantic stereotypes of conventional pop. (The intense loyalty which girls felt towards The Beatles was hardly accidental; they drew far more inspiration from Motown and Brill Building girl-group pop than they did from R&B and fifties macho rock, and the resulting tenderness which informed their music was not only received but understood. For this reason, they were far more a 'girls' group' than The Rolling Stones or any of *their* successors; and a far higher proportion of boys thus considered The Beatles, despite John Lennon's cynicism and aggression, to be a little 'soft'.)

Unfortunately, most of the youngbloods trapped themselves into identifying romantic stereotypes and the notion of monogamy with females and 'femininity' in general. In what was little more than an exaggeration of the traditional male need to define women according to masculine needs and ideas, the sixties songwriters yielded to the temptation of denying women any middle ground between the pedestal and the gutter. In songs like The Rolling Stones' 'Play with Fire' and Bob Dylan's 'Like a Rolling Stone', both of which are sneeringly and contemptuously sung to a spoiled rich girl whose ways are acutely offensive to Jagger's and Dylan's (fictitious) proletarian integrity, the reactionary stagnation of the social order was personified as female. Jimi Hendrix himself fell into this trap only once, in 'Are You Experienced', when he snarls at a young girl who is presumably unwilling to drop some acid and fall into bed:

> I know, I know you'll probably squeal and cry,
> That your little world won't let you go,
> But to who in your measly little world,
> Are you trying to prove,

> That you're made out of gold,
> And can't be sold?

That isn't a lover talking – that's a pimp.

Canadian bozo-rockers Guess Who even went so far as to identify American war-mongering and cultural imperialism as female, essentially blaming women for the Vietnam war. 'American woman,' they sang, 'Stay away from me.' It goes without saying that thousands of American women took Guess Who at their word. (More recently, the Anglo-Guyanese rocker Eddy Grant unconsciously echoed Guess Who by personifying apartheid as female in his 1987 hit 'Gimme Hope Jo'anna', which was otherwise *extremely* right-on.)

'Look at that stupid girl,' hooted The Rolling Stones, who deserve more than anyone the dubious honour of being the leading sexists of sixties rock. They juxtaposed mawkish tributes to helpless angels-with-broken-wings like 'Ruby Tuesday' with triumphalist anthems-to-domination like 'Under My Thumb', which suggested that the subjugation of woman was an essential rite of passage, the only road by which a boy could attain 'manhood'. Women, it seems from these songs, are ceaselessly seeking to trap men into settling down; they want domesticity (even though when they get it they don't enjoy it, and have to take refuge in tranquillizers – as per the Stones' 'Mother's Little Helper'). Men, on the other hand, want no-strings sex with no arguments and a little moral support thrown in, and ceaselessly seek to talk women into bed (and to talk them out of bed afterwards). Good women go along with this, bad women don't, and – irritatingly enough – persist in bringing their own needs and wants into what would otherwise be a simple uncomplicated business. At such moments, they need to be told 'Doncha Bother Me No More' or 'Baby, baby, baby, you're out of time'. (All these songs, incidentally, can be found on *Aftermath* (1966), which represents the peak of the Stones' post-adolescent sexism – as opposed to their grizzled, 'mature' sexism – and was, interestingly enough, their first album to consist entirely of songs composed by Mick Jagger and Keith Richards.) The nightmarish sexual violence of 'Midnight Rambler' ('Well, you heard about the Boston . . . Strangler/honey, it ain't one of those') and the lip-smacking sadism of 'Brown Sugar' ('Scarred old slaver knows he's doin' all right/he use'ta whip the women just around midnight') waited in the wings. Just a kiss away . . .

Though the primary influences on Jimi Hendrix's music come from the worlds of blues, soul, rock and jazz, his main man among contemporary lyricists was unquestionably Bob Dylan, whose conflation of Woody Guthrie's populist concerns and Arthur Rimbaud and William Blake's metaphorical and symbolist dreamscapes brought literary formalism (or, if you prefer, overweening pretentiousness) to the rock of the sixties. One of the most curious aspects of Dylan's *œuvre* is that his attitude to women – as expressed in the roles they have taken in the vast body of his work over the past thirty-five or more years – grew more rather than less reactionary as he aged, in sharp contrast to just about all of his peers. (Even Mick Jagger has been forced to reach some sort of accommodation with feminism, believe it or not; his first solo album was ruefully entitled *She's the Boss*. It didn't sell shit.)

The young Dylan of the acoustic years (1962–5) seemed to represent an egalitarian enlightenment on sexual politics as well as on issues of social justice. *Another Side of Bob Dylan* (1965) was book-ended by songs which explicitly rejected gender stereotyping on the grounds that it was in no one's real interests. 'All I Really Want to Do' was a distant descendant of Willie Dixon's 'I Just Wanna Make Love to You' (as recorded by Muddy Waters and The Rolling Stones), and listed, in a characteristic barrage of internal rhymings, all the manipulative things that Dylan did *not* wish to do to his subject, with the punch line 'All I really want to do/ is, baby, be friends with you.' At the other end of the album, 'It Ain't Me, Babe' rehearses the attributes of the idealized romantic lover and denies Dylan's own suitability for the fulfilment of that role. Implicit in the song is Dylan's acceptance of the woman's freedom to reject the application of masculine expectations to her own life; to say 'It Ain't Me, Babe' in her own right. However, the passing of time and the increasing influence of Judaeo-Christian fundamentalism later led Dylan to withdraw this privilege. By 1976's *Desire*, he was reduced to resorting to the lowest seducer's trick of all: claiming divine justification. 'Oh Sister' was Dylan's reply to feminism and a pretty shabby reply it was too: the song states that the Lord himself has decreed that the woman whom Dylan is addressing risks untold damage to her immortal soul if she does not subordinate her needs and preferences to his. It is a moot point whether this conceit is more repulsive or ludicrous; in the wake of his decaying marriage to Sara (the original 'Sad Eyed Lady of the Lowlands'), Dylan interrogates a prospective successor in terms which sound more like a job interview for the post of nursemaid-cum-companion than that of lover and muse to an artist who once redefined the concept of 'literacy' in post-rock songwriting. In the bleating 'Is Your Love in Vain', he enquires earnestly if the candidate in question can cook, sew, and 'make flowers grow'. It is almost impossible not to imagine legions of women chorusing: 'It ain't me, babe, no no no/it ain't me you're lookin' for, babe,' in response.

With his fog, his amphetamine and his pearls, Dylan cast an irresistible spell over virtually every rock songwriter of the sixties. Everybody was affected from John Lennon and Stevie Wonder to an entire school of singer-songwriters (led by Neil Young and James Taylor) who wore sensitivity on their sleeves to such an extent that they seemed to suggest that the only trustworthy man was an impotent one who moped around while a loyal and sympathetic 'old lady' sewed patches on his jeans, rolled an endless supply of joints and prepared exquisite little vegetable messes for all occasions. At the very least, this might have served as an interesting counterbalance to the King Dick posturing of Jagger, Plant and Morrison, if it hadn't been for a resentful undercurrent that suggested that impotence, too, was the women's fault.

So, what, you may ask, were female artists themselves doing to rebut this wholesale calumny of their gender? The answer is: not a lot. In the fifties, a tiny, corncrake-voiced rockabillette (rockabillene? rockawilhelmina?) named Wanda Jackson cranked out a series of fine singles, most of which covered well-known boys' songs and utterly transformed them. One of her best shots annexed Elvis Presley's 'Hard Headed Woman', a song from his *King Creole* movie which began 'A hard-headed woman and a soft-hearted man/been the cause of all the trouble ever since the world began', and went on to illustrate the point by encapsulating the stories of Adam and Eve, Samson and Delilah and other legendary male/female double-acts. Presley sang the song from the defensive, Jackson gleefully on the attack: the boys were on the run, and she was loving every last second of it. Another blistering counter-attack came from a fairly unlikely source: teen agonist Lesley Gore, whose previous contributions to the debate had been 'It's My Party (And I'll Cry If I Want to)' and its happy-ending sequel 'Judy's Turn to Cry'. 'You Don't Own Me' (1963) bucked the sixties consensus in terms which, by contemporary standards, were positively incendiary:

> You don't own me/I'm not one of your many toys,
> You don't own me/don't say I can't go with other boys,
> Don't tell me what to do/don't tell me what to say,
> And when I go out with you/don't put me on display . . .

Still, before we award Lesley Gore bonus points for being the most right-on woman of the decade, it's worth remembering that the song was actually written by two men. The two most prominent heroines of sixties hippie rock were Grace Slick and Janis Joplin. Slick was one of the lead singers of the ramshackle San Francisco electric post-folkie combo Jefferson Airplane and her stance was, at least, neither weepy nor vulnerable: in 'Somebody to Love', she mocked the lonely, a faction traditionally sacrosanct in pop dialectic. Slick was the only woman to take on the male hippie guru role of Trips Guide; she was the *real* Acid Queen, all frozen lysergic hauteur. By contrast, Joplin – often acclaimed as the greatest white blues singer of her time – was the archetypal female victim. She continually bemoaned the treatment she received at the hands of an endless succession of no-good men; a blowsy, drunken primal-screamer forever bawling what was at its best a genuinely scarifying inner pain and at worst an extended temper tantrum. One longed for her to sing, like Chicago blueswoman Koko Taylor, 'I'll Love You Like a Woman (But I'll Fight You Like a Man)'. When Taylor rears up and lets loose with *that* one, you can imagine even big bad swaggering Bo Diddley hastily stepping back to give her some space.

For young women all over the world, though, Joplin did indeed represent aspects of the new freedom. She may have screamed, but at least she didn't simper; she was no one's idea of either a dolly-bird (toothpick limbs, ironed hair, bush-baby eye make-up) or a suburban mousewife (perm, panty-girdle, hard-day-at-the-office-dear?), and her sexuality wasn't something turned on and off at the mains for any man's convenience. 'Women Is Losers', she announced angrily in one of her early songs, which is an important proto-feminist statement, to be sure, but nothing in her life or work suggests that she ever thought of any workable means of doing anything significant about it. She did what she wanted (theoretically, anyway), and stepped right outside the codes of acceptable feminine behaviour, but she was seen to suffer for doing so, drowning her myriad sorrows in booze and heroin, always deserted by the toy-boys she consumed like grapes. Inevitably, she was 'A Woman Left Lonely', receiving, for her temerity, the due punishment impartially determined by natural law. 'Blues are easy to write,' she said once. 'Just a lonely woman's song.'

It's safe to assume that if Joplin had been Bob Dylan's idea of the perfect woman, no one would ever have heard of her unless some man had deigned to write a song in her honour. In 'Love Minus Zero/No Limit',

Dylan paid tribute to the woman who would soon become his wife, and – twelve years later – divorce him. 'My love, she speaks like silence,' he begins, approvingly capping a verse with the ultimate accolade: 'She knows too much to argue or judge.' Dead convenient, that, especially for men who don't particularly like being argued with, let alone judged. Arguments and judgements are, after all, men's work.* Certainly the women (both real and symbolic) in Hendrix's songs would have plenty to say to the women in Dylan's: about how it was the master, rather than the pupil, who was the more likely to vent his spite, disgust and bile upon the female image.

'You know English people have a very big thing towards a spade. They really love that magic thing. They all fall for that kind of thing. Everybody and his brother in England still sort of think that spades have big dicks. And Jimi came over and exploited that to the limit . . . and everybody fell for it.'

Eric Clapton interviewed in *Rolling* Stone (1968)

'I think we all know that Clapton and the whole of that lovable Cockney scene have got problems. I'd've been interested to see if Clapton would've said that to Hendrix's face.'

Robert Wyatt, interview with the author (1987)

Pop mythology generally being a loose conflation of lies, rumours, old newspaper cuttings and snap judgements, it is less than surprising that unrestrained sexuality and all-purpose King Dick-ism remains one of the cornerstones of Jimi Hendrix's legend. The notorious 'nude' cover attached to Track Records' British edition of *Electric Ladyland* didn't help matters much, depicting as it did no fewer than twenty-one women, unclad except for a few strategically placed graphics of Hendrix. Not only was this not Hendrix's idea, but he actively loathed the cover and apologized profusely for it. The US version, released by Reprise, featured a cover design based on detailed instructions from Hendrix himself, but these instructions didn't reach Track in time for their production dead-

---

*Dylan is by no means the only artist to produce great work and yet be a disastrous influence on others; he has inspired as many dreadful songs as Hendrix, in his turn, inspired cataclysmically boring guitar solos. Nevertheless, Hendrix – like Lennon, like Wonder – rose magnificently to Dylan's implicit challenge. Dylan's impact on Hendrix was twofold: as well as inspiring him to explore his own inner world in his lyrics, Dylan convinced him that he could at least make an attempt to sing. Just as all new-born babies are said to resemble Sir Winston Churchill, so most would-be rock singers who 'can't sing' (Keith Richards in solo mode, for example) tend to sound like Dylan.

lines, so the company went ahead on their own. Apparently the lads at Track thought it was a hell of a good laugh. Hendrix didn't. Nevertheless, writers as disparate as fogey-moderne siren and Thatcher groupie Julie Burchill and poet/raconteur Hugo Williams have found this aspect of the man and his work sufficiently crucial for them to dismiss his music in its entirety as simply 'cock-happy guitar heroics'.

So were death and his cock all the world to Hendrix, as they were to his contemporary Jim Morrison? No more so than they were to Robert Johnson, who, for his sins, originated the 'Squeeze my lemon 'til the juice runs down my leg' line so ostentatiously co-opted by Led Zeppelin. Whether incarnated as 'love and death' or 'sex and violence', they are, after all, the Big Themes of most serious art (and for that matter, of most popular art as well). Hendrix's assumption of Johnson's legacy of existential dread and despair is dealt with in Chapter 5. His relationship with women, and with the feminine principle in general, was a deep, abiding and complex one.

For a start, it's worth reiterating that he was raised by a stern, disciplinarian father, and that he doted on his lively fun-loving mother until her premature death when he was sixteen years old. As a teenager and a young man, he was certainly nobody's idea of a macho Man's Man, and his earliest friends, champions and sponsors were almost invariably women, who would feed him, shelter him, clothe him, buy him guitars, and even hustle jobs for him. Men often disliked him intensely, and (before he became a big-time rock and roll star) were both puzzled by and jealous of his attraction for women, both on- and off-stage.

The British rock writer Nick Kent saw Hendrix play in Cardiff in early 1967. 'I was absolutely thunderstruck', he recalls, 'to see all these girls I knew from school, and who were always so demure, screaming and climbing over chairs to get at this man on the stage.' It wasn't just Welsh schoolgirls, either; Peter Townshend, leader of The Who, took his girlfriend Karen Astley (since 1968 Mrs T) on an extended club crawl when Hendrix made his début on the London circuit. He got slightly more than he bargained for; 'If I'd known then what I know now about how aroused my wife had been, I wouldn't quite so willingly have dragged her from club to club. *I* would have gone, but made sure that *she* went off to watch something more antiseptic . . . it was very sexual; not in an appealing way, in a kind of threatening way. And I talked to Karen about that, you know: "What was it like? Was it sexual?" She said, "What a fucking stupid question."'

Truman Capote once opined that Mick Jagger's 'erotic' stage act was 'about as sexy as a pissing toad'. Hendrix was certainly more knowing, more overt, more inflammatory. He would lean over to women in the audience, rapidly lapping his tongue in an explicit mime of cunnilingus (at a time when it was still considered an exotic sexual activity that only wicked, depraved men would perform and even wickeder and more depraved women would want); the guitar would become either a sexual partner or his own sexual organ. However, he would only use these moves when he was either exceptionally exuberant or exceptionally desperate to make an impact on his audience; at his early London club shows and in his breakthrough US performance at the Monterey Pop Festival, he was arguably both. Later in his career, though, he would prefer simply to sing his songs and play his guitar. Unfortunately, many of his audiences didn't consider that they had truly seen Hendrix unless they got sexual pantomimes as well as the music; like many another performer, he was ultimately hoist on his own petard.

'He used *everything*,' Robert Wyatt recalls. 'He was a total person, he was a total adult man. If there was anything he could do to make the show more exciting, he would do it . . . and in his act, because we're all sexual animals, that's in there too. It's all good fun, that.'

Incidentally, I cheated somewhat by using some highly selective editing on Eric Clapton's remark, quoted above, concerning Hendrix's exploitation of white myths about black sexuality. In the same 1968 interview, Clapton went on to point out, 'The stuff he does on stage, when he does that he's testing the audience. He'll do a lot of things, like fool around with his tongue and play his guitar behind his back and rub it up and down his crotch. And he'll look at the audience, and if they're digging it, he won't like the audience. He'll keep on doing it, putting them on. Play less music. If they don't dig it, then he'll play straight because he knows he has to . . . if you just scrape away all the bullshit he carries around you'll find a fantastically talented guy and a beautiful guitar player . . .'

Certainly Hendrix was aware of the effect he was creating. If Townshend escaped with nothing worse than a red face, he certainly got off more lightly than Mick Jagger. Townshend was a witness at the notorious occasion of Hendrix's public near-cuckolding of Mick Jagger with his ostentatious pass at Marianne Faithfull. 'And she was ready to get up and go out, he was that much of an electrifying sex machine. If you're in a nightclub and you watch someone who's obviously astounding and he comes and walks right past you and doesn't even take any notice of you, goes to your girlfriend, whispers something in your girlfriend's ear and she's obviously fucking *considering* it . . . whether or not she goes.'

Germaine Greer noted in her obituary for Hendrix in *OZ* (subsequently reprinted in her 1986 collection *The Madwoman's Underclothes*) that 'the groupies had always been further into prestige-fucking than honest sexuality'. This applied also to the musicians themselves, and Hendrix's grandstand play for Marianne Faithfull was, as much as anything else, a calculated slap at Jagger's own status as the king-pin (you should pardon the expression) of the London scene. Jagger had his revenge a couple of years later, when Devon Wilson – the New York super-groupie who was the model for Hendrix's song 'Dolly Dagger', and one of the most important women in Hendrix's life – walked out of Hendrix's twenty-seventh birthday party with Jagger on her arm.

The explosion of the 'groupie' phenomenon was one of the most enduring fables of the period: remember, we're dealing with an era that was post-Pill and post-miniskirt but pre-feminism and pre-AIDS. In the London club belt, groupiedom was comparatively quiet and contained. Townshend, again, recollects: 'You hear all these stories about London and all the groupies flocking around Jimi Hendrix, but it was a select group. There were only about ten, and they were the only women we knew apart from friends who were that kind of available at that kind of time. They were very seasoned music fanatics, but they were also hardened . . . they were nymphomaniacs! They wanted sex and they wanted excitement and they knew where to get it. It was *that clear* . . .'

America, however, was a different story. As groupiedom became a media event, what had originally been the province of a few dedicated fetishists became something of a craze. Young men wanted to become rock stars themselves, while many young women (then generally referred to as 'chicks', a term subsequently discarded by just about everyone except Keith Richards before its *faux*-ironic lad-mag revival in the 1990s) reacted to the shortage of positive role-models by settling for the next best thing, which was to become star-fuckers. In the absence of a feminist critique which would have recommended a boycott of phallo-centric chauvinist pigs, they demonstrated rejection of buttoned-down fifties moral values by devising exotic sexual entertainments which severely upset the equilibrium of the spotty English youths on whom they lavished their attentions. Eric Clapton: 'You were at school and you were pimply and no one wanted to know you. You get into a group and you've got thousands of chicks there. And there you are with thousands of little girls screaming their heads off at you. Man, it's power . . . *phew*!'

The most extreme were the Chicago Plastercasters, who – as their *nom de guerre* would suggest – dedicated their time to creating life-size models of rock stars' erections. One of them would specialize in the technical and sculptural aspects of the process, dealing with the plaster, clay and so forth, while the other would make sure that there was something worth casting. It speaks volumes – both about the elasticity of the term 'sexual liberation' and about the mood of the times – that for a year or two the Plastercasters were considered neither ludicrous nor pathetic, but avatars of sexual freedom and artists, to boot. When they held their first 'exhibition', the Hendrix 'exhibit' was deemed far and away the most 'impressive', and the resulting gossip made a contribution to Hendrix's legend which, in retrospect, he could well have done without.

Unlike the Rolling Stones and Led Zeppelins of this world, he was never known to indulge in the deliberate humiliation of these groupies. He certainly enjoyed sex – as part of a process of decompression from the intensity of a concert performance, as well as for its own sake – but in sexual matters, as in so many other aspects of his life, including (to his lasting frustration) his business affairs, Hendrix had a serious problem with saying 'no' to anybody. They wanted to make love to him (if 'make love' is indeed the appropriate term) and it was simply less bother to say yes than to say no. In a clip from Joe Boyd's biographical documentary, Hendrix described a typical on-tour encounter:

'And I get up at 7 o'clock in the morning and I'm really sleepy, and I open the door and see someone who really appeals to me, and first of all I ask myself "What in the world is she doing here? What does she even want?" or something like that. And then she says, "Uh, may I come in?" And I'm just standing there really digging her . . . she might be nineteen, twenty, past *that age* . . . so then I'll invite her in for a nap.'

The general consensus is that Hendrix was the very soul of boyish politeness to women, never presuming on his status as an excuse for boorishness. In *Days in the Life*, Jonathon Green's oral history of London in the sixties, Jo Cruikshank tells an illuminating little anecdote; she had vacated her seat in the Speakeasy Club to get up and dance, and when she returned, Hendrix – the most fashionable, sought-after person in London at the time – was sitting there. When challenged, he immediately leapt to his feet, apologizing profusely: 'Have I taken your seat? Here, have it back.' In itself, this is no big deal, but it would be disingenuous to assume that this response was typical of London rock stars of the time. A corroborating witness is Lemmy of Motorhead, whose first contact with the world of professional music-making was as one of Hendrix's roadies. 'He was the perfect gentleman,' Lemmy told the *Independent* in July 2000. 'With Jimi, if a woman came into the room he'd stand up as if he'd been goosed. And this even though he was a snake for women. You've never seen anything like it. He'd take four girls into a room and they'd all come out smiling.' However, when under heavy pressure, his gentle, stoned, mild-mannered façade could dissolve into frightening displays of violence directed at whoever was unfortunate enough to be in his way, be it Noel Redding, a female companion, Swedish cops or anybody else.

The two songs paired on his first single, 'Hey Joe' and 'Stone Free', are as intriguing a diptych of rock and roll's traditional male double standard as any since the famous twin-set of Dion & the Belmonts' hits 'The Wanderer' and 'Runaround Sue'. Just as Dion proclaims first his right to assert his masculine independence through promiscuity and then his horror of the woman who defies nature by daring to do the same, so Hendrix, in 'Hey Joe', declares his intention to shoot down the woman who he catches 'fooling around with another man'. 'Stone Free', by contrast finds him in the travelling musician's traditional hit-and-run mode:

> Women here, women there, try to put me in a plastic cage,
> But they don't realize it's so easy to break,
> Oh, but sometimes I feel my heart kinda running hot,
> That's when I got to move 'fore I get caught . . .

The usual bullshit, in other words. Sexual stereotypes being what they are, the world is full of whining or blustering men who presumably believe that sex is simply a bit of fun for them (and therefore putting it about a bit is perfectly all right), but a desperately serious matter for women (to be prevented at all costs if the man in question is not involved). Furthermore, men are the ones who take the initiative – who 'have' women – so a man who screws around is 'having' lots of women (lucky dog!), whereas a woman who screws around is 'being had' by lots of men (dirty cow!) As the man pleads with women not to tie him down in any kind of permanent relationship, he is simultaneously asking her to tie herself down; to give him the loyalty he is utterly unprepared to give to her. In his great slow blues 'Red House', Hendrix returns home after being away 'for about – uh – ninety-nine and one half days' to find that the lock has been changed and that his baby 'don't live here no mo''. He shrugs – after all, there's nothing he can do about it, and anyway, he's still got his git-tar – and trudges off to look for his departed girlfriend's sister.

Yet in the pair of songs which opened Hendrix's first album, *Are You Experienced* (1967), these clichés are tilted to reveal a rather more complex situation. 'Foxy Lady', set to a raucous, bulldozing funk-rock swagger, finds Hendrix almost literally licking his chops over some delightful young specimen who has just undulated into his line of vision. He can hardly believe his good fortune; she makes him want to get up and *scream.* He can't wait to get her home. But the turbulent, churning 'Manic Depression' which follows (incidentally, a curious musical hybrid with the rhythmic propulsion of a jazz waltz, the texture of hard rock and the formal structure of a blues), brings with it the morning after:

> Woman so willing, the sweet cause in vain,
> You make love, you break love, it's all the same,
> When it's over . . .

And 'over' it inevitably always was. Post-coital tristesse is simply another manifestation of the existential melancholy which subsumes all but the most overtly celebratory of Hendrix's songs, and 'Manic Depression' sketches out, in comparatively few lines, a profound world-weariness and despair. Sexuality represents an ever-proffered and perpetually-dashed avenue of escape from the manic-depression cycle ('I know what I want but I just don't know/how to go about gettin' it'), and his music is not only his life's sole justification, but his means of drawing a map of the world and understanding his own place within that world. 'Music sweet music/I wish I could caress and kiss/kiss . . .' Hendrix would occasionally introduce the song in performance with a throwaway line about wanting 'to make love to music instead of that same old everyday woman'; in Hendrix's art, as in that of so many of his predecessors, the Muse is always female. Which seems to place rather a heavy responsibility on 'that same old everyday woman'.

Gradually, a full gallery of female archetypes emerges from Hendrix's writings. There are strutting bimbos like 'Foxy Lady' or 'Little Miss Lover', who show out to Hendrix just as he does to them; these are the women cajoled in come-ons like 'Fire' and who, if they are not simply subjected to the three F's, can mutate either into the insipid clingers of 'Stone Free', '51st Anniversary', 'Ain't No Telling' or 'Crosstown Traffic', or the terrifying castrators of 'Dolly Dagger' or 'Stepping Stone'. Sometimes, they beat Hendrix to the punch and walk out on him before he walks out on them, leaving him lonely, confused and generally baying at the moon. In 'Stepping Stone', one of his most cynical songs, the woman is with him only to 'make it off in bed with my guitar'; to have the persona rather than the person, for status sex. On the fade of 'Dolly Dagger' (the pseudonym Hendrix chose for his fictional analogue of Devon Wilson is a specific reference to her concurrent relationship with Mick Jagger) he calls out, 'You better watch out baby, here comes your master,' but the line is delivered without conviction.

However, considering the extent of Hendrix's perceived mythic status as a swaggering macho *thing*, it should come as something of a surprise to anyone bothering to consider the actual content of his work that these bimbos and bitches – whose function within the songs is to mistreat him and be mistreated by him – by no means represent the female image obviously most central to him.

The feminine ideal that haunts Hendrix's most beautiful songs is no geisha, slave or groupie. She is stronger and wiser than he is, and she is his only hope of peace and salvation. With her he is no callous, arrogant stud; no strutting, well-hung alpha male. It is not so much that he is helpless before her; it is more that only in her presence can he bring himself to accept and acknowledge the helplessness that he already feels. He is lost, and only she can find him; he has fallen, and only she can raise him up; he is dying, and only she can bring him back to life. She owes him nothing; he can only give her everything because without her he has nothing. If she leaves him, he cannot bellow and stomp and storm off to console himself with the tender mercies of Dolly or Foxy; he can only wait helplessly for her to decide to return. His occasional fits of bluster cannot last for long.

She has many names and many guises. Sometimes she is a spirit, sometimes a fantasy, sometimes a woman as solidly, palpably physical as he is. Sometimes, lost in his purple acid hazes, his faith in his own senses is so poor that he can barely believe she's there at all; sometimes his inner turmoil paralyses him to the point where he is unable to reach out to her. He does not wish to drag her into his world; his world is the one which depresses him so (despite his superficial eminence within it), and he would rather be deemed worthy to enter hers.

She first appears in *Are You Experienced*'s 'May This Be Love', where her name is Waterfall. With her, 'nothing can harm me at all/my worries seem so very small'; her very presence constitutes sanctuary. She dominates *Axis: Bold as Love*, his most playful and carefree album (and why not; 1967 was probably the happiest year of his adult life). There, she is

Little Wing, an elfin playmate (*not* in the Hefner sense, I add hastily), a soulful, loving sprite; she is the heroine of the glowing, lustrous 'One Rainy Wish', waiting for him in an enchanted forest as irresistible and elusive as a dream; in her most earthly, non-hallucinogenic incarnation she chases his blues away in 'You Got Me Floating' and emerges, as beautiful and terrible as an army with banners, at the climax of 'Bold as Love', where Hendrix must conquer his own terrors and conflicts before he can be truly worthy of her. 'And all these emotions of mine keep holding me/from giving my life to a rainbow like you . . . but I'm, yeah, I'm bold as love.'

In 1968's *Electric Ladyland*, she is the Electric Woman who can cast out all doubt and fear. 'I'm so glad that my baby's comin' to rescue me,' he shouts in 'Long Hot Summer Night', where he has been suffering in her absence; a plight similar to that endured in the absence of his beloved 'Gypsy Eyes', who again arrives to save the day. 'My Gypsy Eyes has found me and I've been saved, yeah!/Lord, I've been saved/That's why I love you . . .' She is conspicuous by her absence in the desolate 'Burning of the Midnight Lamp': life without her is pointless, banal, empty.

> Now the smiling portrait of you,
> Is still hanging on my frowning wall,
> It really doesn't bother me too much at all,
> It's just the ever-falling dust that makes it so hard for me to see,
> That forgotten earring laying on the floor
> Facing coldly towards the door . . .

Maybe it is she with whom Hendrix, in the lengthy, shifting fantasia that is '1983/A Merman I Should Turn to Be', makes his final retreat from a war-torn, polluted world and takes up residence beneath the ocean waters (that's assuming that the seas haven't become hopelessly polluted in this particular scenario). Or maybe she *is* the ocean, or at least its microcosm, the briny waters of the womb.

Of course, it's easy to declare this kind of stuff simple sickly sentimentality, or masochistic self-abasement, or evidence of the mama's boy quavering behind a blow-hard façade, querulously waiting to have his spiritual bottom wiped clean of metaphysical shit. Hendrix, like that other ruff, tuff creem-puff John Lennon, lost his mother at an early age, but hopefully we can agree to take the pop Freudianism as read. There is no *direct* equivalent to Lennon's 'Mother' in Hendrix's work – unless we choose to interpret the entire cycle of songs which culminate in 'Angel' in that particular light – but if ever primal screams were emitted by an electric instrument, it was Hendrix's guitar.

> Angel came down from heaven yesterday,
> She stayed just long enough to rescue me . . .
>
> Jimi Hendrix, 'Angel'

'Jimi Hendrix was, like, I don't know, as if he really wasn't human . . . he was that way in private too. He would walk into a place and you could just feel him there. A lot of other big stars, when you meet them you realize they're just human, but it wasn't that way with him.'

Tommy Shannon, former Johnny Winter bassist now working with Stevie Ray
Vaughan, interviewed in Guitarist (1988)

'God? She's black'

Traditional anarchist joke

By the time She reappeared on record, Hendrix himself was dead, which lends songs like 'Angel' an eeriness not intended by their author. Two posthumous albums released in 1971, *Cry of Love* and *Rainbow Bridge* (the latter somewhat disingenuously billed as the 'Original Soundtrack' from what was undoubtedly the dumbest hippie movie ever made; thankfully, the album is nothing of the sort), were assembled from the most fully realized fragments of what was intended to have been the double album *First Rays of the New Rising Sun*. Both albums betray their makeshift origins – some of the tracks are obvious demos on which work was still in progress, hence the occasional fluffed lyric or out-of-tune guitar – but the phantom presence of the Muse is readily apparent.

In 'Drifting', he is pursuing her: 'Drifting/on a sea of forgotten teardrops/on a lifeboat/sailing for your love/sailing home'. In 'Night Bird Flying', she spends the night with him, but is only passing through, despite his pleas: 'Please take me through your dreams/inside your world I want to be'. And in 'In from the Storm', she comes, once again, to his rescue: 'I want to thank you, my sweet darling/for digging in the mud and picking me up,' he sings, 'it was you my love who brought me in.' However, it is in 'Angel' and the tantalizingly fragmentary 'Hey Baby (New Rising Sun)' where her role as Hendrix's saviour and redeemer is most clearly delineated.

'Angel' is one of Hendrix's most famous songs, thanks in part to a hugely successful 1972 Rod Stewart cover version, but mainly because of its theme and language ('came down from heaven', 'my angel, she said unto me', 'tomorrow I'll be by your side', and so forth), and its proximity to Hendrix's death. (The original, incidentally, was released as a single in 1971, to fairly unimpressive sales.) It is probably the most solidly constructed of Hendrix's later pop songs, with a stately, measured pace and a memorably gorgeous melody, and nowhere is the relationship between Hendrix and his Muse spelled out more clearly:

> . . . my angel, she said unto me,
> Today is the day for you to rise,
> Take my hand,
> You're gonna be my man,
> You're gonna rise . . .

It's a shame that 'Hey Baby (the Land of the New Rising Sun)' was never recorded properly, because the song was clearly of considerable importance to Hendrix. The *Rainbow Bridge* version is diffident and tentative, little more than a sketch: the guitar is treated with a wobbly, Leslie-cabinet effect which caused the pitch to fluctuate to the point where this listener, at least, begins to feel slightly seasick. Hendrix is heard asking an engineer, 'Is the microphone on?' before he launches into the song, neatly blowing the lyrics of the first line – unless, of course, he actually *meant* to sing, 'Hey, baby, where do you coming from,' which I doubt. (An even rougher demo version, with slightly different lyrics, showed up on *Midnight Lightning*, one of two albums where producer Alan Douglas overdubbed new backing tracks by studio musicians around Hendrix, but it is marred by a teeth-grindingly out-of-tune guitar which Hendrix would certainly have regarded as utterly unacceptable on anything intended for release.)

It's safe to say that we have never heard, and probably never will hear, a completed version of this song, as winsomely wistful as anything Hendrix ever wrote. She appears to him, as from a vision: clearly, She is Angel, Waterfall, Gypsy Eyes. She announces herself as being from the Land of the New Rising Sun, and he begs her to take him with her. 'Hey baby,' he pleads, 'can I step into your world awhile? "Yes, you can," she said . . . "we gotta help your people out right now/and that's what I'm doing here is all about."' She is revealed at last: not simply Hendrix's own personal saviour, but a redeemer for all of humanity.

Now, this isn't exactly the kind of notion which would occur to your average sperm-brained mannish boy, even though considering women to be simultaneously closer than men to the earth and to the spiritual realms has been a hardy perennial among sexist ploys designed to keep women out of serious business (you know – *man* talk). With Hendrix, there is no desire or need to co-opt this woman to be his side-kick; rather, his most devout wish is to be hers. Only a boy – of whatever age and experience – wants to rule or dominate women, to celebrate and re-enact an escape from the terrifying bogey of maternal power. To accept women and defer to them, even when not compelled to do so, requires someone else entirely.

Ain't that a man?

> I'm a man,
> At least I'm trying to be,
> And I'm looking for
> The other half of me . . .

Jimi Hendrix, 'Stepping Stone' (1969)

4

Room Full of Mirrors

The black artist and the white audience

'There's two kinds [of rock] – white and black, and those bourgeois spades are trying to sing white and whites are trying to sound coloured. It's embarrassing to me . . . all the white groups have got a lot of hair and funny clothes – they got to have on that shit to get it across . . . [but] Jimi Hendrix can take two white guys and make them play their asses off . . .'

> Miles Davis, interviewed in *Rolling Stone* (1969)

At lilac evening I walked with every muscle aching among the lights of 27th and Welton in the Denver coloured section, wishing I were a Negro, feeling that the best the white world had offered was not enough ecstasy for me, not enough life, joy, kicks, darkness, music, not enough night. I wished I were a Denver Mexican, or even a poor overworked Jap, anything but what I so drearily was, a 'white man' disillusioned.

> Jack Kerouac, *On the Road* (1949)

Knowing in all the cells of his existence that life is war, nothing but war, the Negro (all exceptions admitted) could rarely afford the sophisticated inhibitions of civilization, and so he kept for his survival the art of the primitive, he lived in the enormous present, he subsisted for his Saturday night kicks, relinquishing the pleasures of the mind for the more obligatory pleasures of the body, and in his music he gave voice to the character and quality of his existence . . . so there was a new breed of adventurers, urban adventurers who drifted out at night looking for action with a black man's code to fit their facts. The hipster had absorbed the existentialist synapses of the Negro, and could thus be considered a white Negro.

> Norman Mailer, 'The White Negro' (1957)

Even in the world of the hipster the Negro remains essentially what Ralph Ellison called him – an invisible man. The 'white Negro' accepts the real Negro not as a human being in his totality, but as the bringer of a highly specified and restricted 'cultural dowry', to use Mailer's phrase. In so doing, he creates an inverted form of keeping the nigger in his place.

> Ned Poisky, replying to 'The White Negro', quoted in Norman
> Mailer's *Advertisements for Myself* (1961)

'I'm through explaining this shit.'

> Ice-T

The 'cultural dowry' Jimi Hendrix brought with him into the pop marketplace included not only his immense talent and the years of experience acquired in a particularly hard school of show business, but the accumulated weight of the fantasies and mythologies constructed around black music and black people by whites, hipsters and reactionaries alike. Both shared one common article of faith: that black people represent the personification of the untrammelled id – intrinsically wild, sensual, dangerous, 'untamed' in every sense of the word. Within this fantasy, hipsters find everything to which they aspire, and their opposite numbers everything they fear, loathe and despise. The difference is that the hipster – in any of his succession of contemporary incarnations – is anxious to believe that his chosen favourite black entertainers are existential outlaws, while the conservative is willing only to accept reassuring images of blacks as non-threatening, mildly eccentric creatures, happy and willing to sing and dance for the amusement of their 'betters'. Ultimately, each stereotype is as fraudulent as the other: the black entertainer succeeds with the white audience either by embodying an aspect of blackness with which that audience feels comfortable, or else by appearing almost tangential to the black community: thus rendered unaffiliated, 'universal'.

Furthermore, neither 'the black artist' nor 'the white audience' are simple, monolithic entities answering to a single all-encompassing description: 'the black artist' can be anybody from Toni Morrison to Ornette Coleman, from Bill Cosby to Public Enemy, from Diana Ross to Spike Lee, while 'the white audience' could mean an urban teenager, a middle-aged rural conservative, or any of the myriad possible intermediate ranges of age, income, politics, taste or geographical location. So there are many white audiences and many black entertainers: the first and most fundamental error made by racists of both the liberal and conservative tendencies is the assumption that there is some sort of platonic ideal of the black person, and that any black who does not obviously conform to this ideal is either a hypocrite or a trickster. And this ideal has, of course, been defined by whites rather than by blacks themselves. It is the white pundit who, in the context of pop culture, decides who is black and who isn't: Mick Farren, writing in *New Musical Express* in 1975, managed to create a set of criteria which 'proved' that Bob Dylan was 'blacker' than Isaac Hayes; Nik Cohn, in the enormously influential *Awopbopaloobopalopbamboom*, denounced Otis Redding's gospel-derived freneticism as 'sweat-and-Tom', without ever showing any signs of having considered what a similar performance might have signified to a black audience.

Probably the most concise and explicit exposition of this attitude was provided in 1967 by the late Ralph J. Gleason, San Francisco's senior professor of pop-culch orthodoxy and *Rolling Stone*'s in-house guru:

The Negro performers, from James Brown to Aaron Neville to The Supremes and The Four Tops, are on an Ed Sullivan trip, striving as hard as they can to get on that stage and become part of the American success story, while the white rock performers are motivated to escape from the stereotype . . . The Supremes and The Tops are choreographed more and more like The Four Lads and The Ames Brothers and The McGuire Sisters. I suggest that this bears a strong relationship to the condition of the civil rights movement today in which the only truly black position is that of Stokely Carmichael, and in which the NAACP and most of the other formal groups are, like The Four Tops and The Supremes, on an Ed Sullivan/TV-trip to middle-class America. And the only true American Negro music is that which abandons the system of scales and keys and notes for a music whose roots are in the culture of the coloured peoples of the world . . .

In other words, equality of opportunity and participation in the cultural, social and economic mainstream of America was declared to be a worthless and contemptible goal, just when it seemed that black people had a chance of achieving it.* Furthermore, Gleason's definition of 'the only true American Negro music' seems designed to exclude all contemporary black pop, any harmonically sophisticated jazz and, indeed, virtually everything except free jazz and the rawest and most 'primitive' country blues: i.e. any music that black musicians might make which any appreciable quantity of white people might want to buy. The hippie, wrote Gleason,

is remarkably free of prejudice, but he is not attempting to join [black culture] or become part of it, like his musical predecessor the jazzman, or his social predecessor the beatnik . . . for the first time in decades, as far as I know, something important and new is happening artistically and musically in this society that is distinct from the Negro and to which the Negro will have to come, if he is interested at all, as in the past the white youth went uptown to Harlem . . .

Gleason is, to say the least, contradicting himself here: blacks *shouldn't* adhere to white standards or aspire to white goals, but *should* come around to hear the exciting things the white kids are doing. He wasn't the only one to indulge in barely veiled gloating; note the hostile glee with which Tom Wolfe describes, in *The Electric Kool-Aid Acid Test* (1968), the

---

*It's probably just as well that I didn't read Nelson George's *The Death of Rhythm & Blues* until this book was almost completed; otherwise, the temptation to quote him extensively – on this and many other related points – would have been irresistible.

discomfiture of 'Big Nig', who had provided the San Francisco venue for Ken Kesey's first Acid test: '. . . a big funky spade looking pathetic and square. For twenty years in the hip life, Negroes never even *looked* square. They were the archetypal soul figures. But what is Soul, or Funky, or Cool, or Baby . . . in the new world of the ecstasy, the All-One . . .'

Enter Jimi Hendrix.

'Man, I don't know what we're going to do now that Jimi Hendrix copped out on us . . . he was the only black cat who could play psychedelic.'

> Bo Diddley, quoted in *Boogie Lightning* by Michael Lydon (1974)

Hendrix arrived in a London hipoisie which worshipped Americana – and black Americana in particular – from across a seemingly unbridgeable cultural abyss. They had sedulously studied and reproduced blues and soul music in an attempt to attain some degree of empathy with these transcendent outpourings of joy and pain, trying to crack the façade of true-Brit reserve by appropriating the persona of the blues singer or soul man. They knew more about Motown, Mingus and Muddy Waters than all but a few white Americans, but the cultural context from which these musics had sprung was a mystery to them. They understood the vocal tricks and guitar licks, and the best of them could reproduce them virtually at will, but actual contact with black Americans had left them puzzled and confused. For the most part, the black bluesmen they had met were twice or three times their age and decidely cranky: the venerable reprobate Sonny Boy Williamson had used The Yardbirds, The Animals and others as backing groups, and had not been particularly impressed. 'Those cats in England want to play the blues *so bad*,' he told Robbie Robertson, later of The Band, 'and they play 'em *so bad*.' They, in turn, considered Williamson to be a fabulous monster, something along the lines of a centaur or a unicorn: a musician of awe-inspiring gifts, but chronically suspicious and secretive, almost perpetually drunk, either incapable of or unwilling to adhere to a set musical programme, and given to plucking chickens in his hosts' baths.

Sonny Boy Williamson, though, was a barely-literate sexagenarian from the Mississippi Delta, and it was scarcely surprising that he should find few points of contact with earnest young lower-middle- or working-class Englishmen; urban black Americans of the same age wouldn't necessarily have got much further with the old buzzard than The Yardbirds did. Nevertheless, British pop stars were just as likely to find themselves confused by encounters with their black American near-contemporaries.

On their first sojourn in New York, The Beatles – doubtless in search of some sexual dalliance and general excitement – invited The Supremes (the Motown female vocal trio who were the Fab Moptops' only serious competition in the best-seller lists at the time) to visit them in their hotel suite. When Diana Ross and her colleagues arrived, both parties were utterly dumbfounded. The Supremes found a room clouded with marijuana smoke and four guys in jeans sprawled around completely hammered; The Beatles saw three girls in neat suits, complete with gloves, fur wraps and a chaperone. The Supremes couldn't believe that The Beatles were such doped-out slobs; The Beatles were shocked at how 'prissy' and 'square' black girls from Detroit could be. Each side's notions of what the other should be like were based on a fundamental misunderstanding, and the encounter soon collapsed under the weight of the participants' mutual embarrassment. The Detroit contingent expected English 'class' and suavity à la David Niven from the Beatles, who in turn were convinced that The Supremes were raunchy, hell-raising party-timers – Bessie Smith songs come to life. The Fab Four failed completely to empathize with the aspirations of the upwardly mobile black proletariat; The Supremes utterly misread white rock and roll bohemia.

Jimi Hendrix, on the other hand, understood white bohemia quite instinctively, and white English rock and roll bohemia in particular; after all, he shared many of its tastes and obsessions, and for a while at least, he was perfectly happy to give them exactly what they wanted, to play the part of – to quote *Rolling Stone*'s John Morthland – 'the flower generation's electric nigger dandy, its king stud and golden calf, its maker of mighty dope music, its most outrageously visible force. Boil that down, and he's still being called a nigger. Hendrix must occasionally have felt that his new friends and admirers had grasped the wrong end of the stick and, in the guise of appreciation, were beating him with it. It was precisely this kind of role-playing which may have hindered acceptance by black audiences: he was enacting – in Summer of Love terms, admittedly – exactly the kind of stereotypes which many black Americans were so anxious to shake off. Even some of his new-found British buddies, like Eric Clapton, began to suspect the murderous irony with which he was pandering to those hoary old myths.

Hendrix was indeed flamboyant, exhibitionistic, obviously on drugs, fond of being photographed surrounded by blondes and almost totally lacking in the kind of dignity, discipline and restraint which black America had come to demand from its entertainers. It was the white critic

Robert Christgau who saw Hendrix at Monterey and called him 'a psychedelic Uncle Tom', but he undoubtedly echoed the feelings of a considerable number of black Americans who – initially, at least – considered Hendrix a stoned clown acting like a nigger for the amusement of white folks. Others, however, felt very differently. To a younger generation of black Americans, Hendrix's flamboyant self-assertion was a positive inspiration.

'You have to look at the society which makes us view ourselves a certain way,' says Vernon Reid. 'On one level, the idea of being flashy or outspoken is appealing because, from the time that you're small, if you're a black person, there is a social move to negate your existence. What is it like to be nothing? They don't come out and *say*, "You're nothing!" but Band-Aid is flesh-coloured, even if it's not the colour of *your* flesh . . . it's a lot better now, but at the time Hendrix was coming up, that was the status quo. So when you see people who are black being outrageous, they are asserting themselves. There is a psychological need to assert themselves because there's a feeling that if you're black, you're not anything.'

'I'm black. They never let me forget it. I'm black all right – and I'll never let *them* forget it.'

Brock Peters' closing speech on Miles Davis's *Jack Johnson* (1971)

To say that Hendrix had no black constituency at all, though, is to pander to myth, and racist myth at that. 'It had to be a new breed of blacks that would find him,' said Bobby Womack, ''cause the [record] companies didn't think [blacks] would relate to a nigger like him. I'd start seeing young black guys, fans, and they'd be dressin' just like him and I'd be thinkin' "*Damn*, I never saw black hippies before."' Hendrix biographer David Henderson points out in *'Scuse Me While I Kiss the Sky* (1983) that blacks *did* attend his shows, even though the scale of Hendrix's white support rendered their presence less conspicuous; and that they *did* buy his records, though the fact that he'd gone straight to the pop charts rather than registering first on the R&B lists meant that all his sales counted as pop. What was incontestable was that he received little or no airplay on black radio stations, which felt that his music simply wouldn't fit into existing formats. The easy acceptance of the notion that he had no black following not only bound him closer to his white audience, but reinforced Mike Jeffery's belief that he should cater exclusively to it.

As a result, white critics have simply deluded themselves and their readerships that Hendrix's lack of widespread acceptance by black audiences,

both before and after his London metamorphosis, was a result of the conservatism and lack of imagination of those audiences. Few critics of the
time were as honest about the underlying roots of their reactions to Hendrix as Richard Golstein. Reviewing *Electric Ladyland* on its release in
1968 for *Village Voice*, Goldstein described Hendrix as

flaying away at the business of being absurdly black with the kind of groovy contempt the English call Flash . . . when I think about my most gratuitous errors as
a critic, I can never escape my early outrage at Hendrix's vulgarity. Well, he does
pander to his audience, and it does feel humiliating. Coming from a white man
(Morrison or Jagger), I could still have accepted that jingle-jangle grace. But I
still demand dignity from a black performer . . . it's possible to excuse that criterion as a hold-over from folk-music, where blacks were allowed to be rebellious as
long as they were saintly as well. But it runs far deeper into the kind of adjust-
ment I had to make as a white man to the presence of aggressive (i.e. impolite)
blacks. It is still very hard for me to accept a black man who enjoys his own vulgarity. I can take the Panthers, with their cool aggression, or the preachers, with
their Christian charity. But Hendrix is a jiver, in the most threatening sense. Disguised as the corrupt Black Prince – Othello's Revenge – he is a mirror-image of
our own inner darkies, struggling to be clownish, sexual and free. Maybe that's
why Jimi Hendrix is so much less relevant to black culture. Ultimately, his is a
message blacks got long ago: everybody is his own spade.

Paradoxically, one of Hendrix's major assets in his campaign to capture
the hearts of the newly-emerged hippie rock audience was precisely that
failure to have made a mark for himself in black showbiz. He was black,
and he was about to become a star, but the one thing that he wasn't was –
in any traditional sense – a black star with a black audience, which meant
that his white fans never had the problem of being outnumbered by black
people at his shows. Eric Burdon had a telling anecdote which illustrates
that very point: during The Animals' first US tour in 1965, the band
wound up in Alabama and Burdon found himself in conversation with a
white girl who adored the same black stars that Burdon did. Noting that
Otis Redding had played the same hall the night before, he asked her if
she'd seen the show. 'Did I see him?', she replied incredulously. 'You got
to be joking, man, the place was full of niggers.' We have no way of knowing whether this particular customer, two or more years later, would have
wanted to go see Hendrix. If she had done so, she wouldn't have had to
deal with that particular problem. She might even have felt, as did Mick
Jagger, and Burdon himself in a different context, that 'he was *ours*'. It
was another two years before Otis Redding played the Monterey Interna-

tional Pop Festival and succeeded in 'crossing over', which was the one thing that Jimi Hendrix never had to do. His problem was crossing back.

In the jargon of music business marketing, *crossover* is a magic word. It refers to the process by which a black act, generally one already comfortably established with black audiences, begins to sell records to large numbers of whites. Sometimes this can only be accomplished at the price of sacrificing black popularity on the altar of mass acceptance by whites: to a certain extent, this fate befell Ray Charles in the wake of his success with country music in the early sixties. Other performers whose styles have been marooned by changing black tastes find that it is only their popularity with whites which keeps them in business. Bobby Womack remembers his mentor Sam Cooke being keenly aware of the pitfalls of crossover. 'When I record I got to sound white to cross over,' Cooke told Womack, 'but on the other side I sound black to keep my base. I'm gonna teach you this; never forget it.'

In the sense to which Cooke referred, Hendrix never had that base. In *The Death of Rhythm & Blues*, Nelson George describes Hendrix's music as 'the R&B sideman's revenge'; when he launched the Experience, he had five years' worth of frustration with the restrictions of the chitlin circuit to work off. By contrast, Sly Stone who had never gone through that particular mill – was far more willing to utilize R&B conventions even as he manipulated and expanded them, thus giving him simultaneous access to black and white crowds alike. Hendrix became more and more sensitive to his seeming inability to communicate to black audiences as time went on, especially after his relocation to the United States in 1968 and the dissolution of the original Experience in 1969. However, his management and record company were highly aware of the crucial importance of Hendrix's 'honorary white' status to his fans. 'The white guys and managers would say, "Don't play with these niggers, man; the fourteen-year-olds can't relate to all that space stuff. Get the cute English guys back,"' recalled Johnny Winter, the Texan albino blues guitarist who was one of Hendrix's regular New York jamming partners, 'and the black guys would tell him he was selling out to whitey. Jimi was a pretty sensitive person, plus he was pretty loaded all the time, and he didn't know what to do.'

'Jimi was the blackest guitarist I ever heard. His music was deeply rooted in pre-blues, the oldest musical forms, like field hollers and gospel melodies. From what I can garner, there was no form of black music that he hadn't listened to or studied, but he really loved the real old black music forms, and they poured out in his playing . . . Jimi's lyrics and clothes were stone white, but he's as black as they come.'

Michael Bloomfield, quoted in *Guitar Player* magazine (1975)

'To me Jimi wasn't a black man – he was a white man. He didn't think like a coloured guy and he certainly didn't appeal to a coloured audience at all. He wasn't playing coloured music.'

Gerry Stickells, Hendrix's road manager, quoted in *Hendrix: A Biography*
by Chris Welch (1972)

To say the least, we now seem to be dealing with a contradiction or three. Leaving aside Gerry Stickells' generalizations concerning how 'coloured guys' (or, for that matter, white guys) happen to think, we are once again faced with the question of exactly what 'coloured music' is. If it simply means any music played by black musicians, then Haydn's Trumpet Concerto became 'black music' as soon as Wynton Marsalis performed it, as did The Beatles' 'Yesterday' and 'Eleanor Rigby' when recorded by Ray Charles or Aretha Franklin; or Bob Dylan's 'Blowin' in the Wind' in the hands of Stevie Wonder, Bruce Springsteen's 'Pink Cadillac' à la Natalie Cole, or even the Doris Day standard 'Que Sera Sera' as interpreted by Sly & the Family Stone. How about the innumerable soul recastings of country hits and jazz transmogrifications of Broadway standards and show tunes? Do the songs of Rodgers and Hart become 'black music' once Charlie Parker, Miles Davis or John Coltrane have had their way with them?

Maybe what we're talking about is music consumed and enjoyed by black listeners and record-buyers; but that doesn't bring us out of the woods either. In the fifties, Bill Haley & the Comets' 'Rock Around the Clock' and Elvis Presley's 'Hound Dog' both topped *Billboard*'s R&B chart, and more recently we'd find ourselves stuck with – to name but a few – The (Young) Rascals, Kraftwerk, the Average White Band, Elton John, Hall & Oates, George Michael and Madonna, all of whom have scored heavily with black audiences at one time or another.

Let's try it another way: maybe the touchstone of True Blackness lies in the compositions and songs created by blacks. This particular theory leads us into still deeper and more treacherous waters: Pat Boone's notorious fifties 'whitebread' covers of songs like Fats Domino's 'Ain't That a Shame 'or Little Richard's 'Tutti Frutti' and 'Long Tall Sally' have now become 'black music', right alongside the entire 'white blues' and 'white soul' movements of the sixties, all the Claptons and Joplins and Bloomfields and Winters. If we extend *that* one a little further to include original music created by whites in what are technically black forms, idioms, styles and genres, then white seventies funksters like Kokomo, Wild Cherry and the Average White Band have now magically become black-by-extension, as has everyone from David Bowie and George Michael to The Beastie Boys and Eminem. This last argument not only serves to delegitimize black music which doesn't fit the arbitrary definition imposed by the late-sixties consensus – i.e. direct derivations from blues and gospel – but it magically gets rid of black music's major sticking point with many whites: black people.

In Alice Walker's short story *1955*, Traynor (a white 'king of rock') explains his central dilemma to Gracie Mae Still, the elderly blues shouter whose hit songs he has made his fortune by rerecording. 'They want what you got, but they don't want you,' he tells her. 'They want what I got, only it ain't mine. That's what makes 'em so hungry for me when I sing. They getting the flavour of something but they ain't getting the thing itself. They like a pack of hound dogs trying to gobble up a scent . . .'

Walker's 'Traynor' and 'Gracie Mae' are fictional analogues of Elvis Presley and the singer of the original 'Hound Dog', Willie Mae 'Big Mama' Thornton, who never met and conversed in real life – not that anybody knows about, anyway. Still, Traynor's confessionary monologue highlights the central thrust of twentieth-century American popular music; the need to separate black music (which, by and large, white Americans love) from black people (who, by and large, they don't). Thus in the thirties Paul Whiteman was the 'King of Jazz', in the forties Benny Goodman was the 'King of Swing', in the fifties Elvis Presley was the 'King of Rock', in the sixties Eric Clapton was the 'World's Greatest Blues Guitarist', in the seventies The Bee Gees – plus, of course, the unforgettable John Travolta – became the dominant international symbols of dance music, the eighties' best-selling rap album was by three middle-class Jewish ex-punks who'd reinvented themselves as The Beastie Boys and, as the nineties rolled over the millennial barrier, the rhyme roost was ruled by Eminem. Not for nothing did Sam Phillips, the boss of Sun Records in Memphis tell anyone who would listen that 'if I could find a white boy with a Negro sound I could make a million dollars'. Phillips had, ever since he opened his first studio, recorded some of the finest bluesmen in America, supplying record companies in Los Angeles and Chicago with seminal sides by Howlin' Wolf, B. B. King, Junior Parker and many others. He had, for example, given Chicago's Chess label the million-selling

'Rocket 88' by Jackie Brenston and his Delta Cats (actually, Ike Turner's Kings of Rhythm with saxophonist Brenston up front), an accelerated jump novelty nowadays considered to be the first true rock and roll record ever made. But Sam Phillips didn't get rich until he fulfilled oft-expressed (and even more frequently misquoted, thanks to the late Albert Goldman) wish by discovering Elvis Presley.

The entertainment industry has traditionally relied on white performers to provide black styles with their entry into the 'mainstream'; to render them acceptable to white audiences, and ultimately to disarm them. The white audience, superior both numerically and economically, is where the richest pickings are. A hit on the US R&B charts (compiled from black shops and black radio stations) is fine, but a pop hit is *serious*. 'R&B', asserts Bo Diddley in *Hail! Hail! Rock and Roll* – Taylor Hackford's biographical documentary film about Chuck Berry – 'don't stand for nothin' but rip-off and bullshit.' What he and Berry played, he continues, was called rock 'n' roll until Caucasians started playing it, and then suddenly '*they* was rock and roll and we were R&B'. And R&B meant the ghetto (unless you were on Atlantic): it meant cheap-jack record companies most if not all of which were white-owned, paying miserly or non-existent royalties; it meant ceaseless touring through the run-down theatres and bars of the 'chitlin circuit', where getting paid often meant pulling a gun before the promoter did. True enough, there was money to be made out of R&B, but it was a pittance compared to the rewards earned by pop stars. 'Pop meant selling whites,' summarized Marvin Gaye, 'and R&B or soul meant selling the brothers and sisters back in the neighbourhood. Everyone wanted to sell whites 'cause whites got more money. Our attitude was – give us some. It's that simple.' Of course, it wasn't.

The indignities often visited upon touring black performers, famous or not, could be nothing short of horrific. The South was undoubtedly the trickiest obstacle course, but the big Northern cities could be equally bad. Touring with the Count Basie Orchestra in the thirties, the light-skinned Billie Holiday was informed by the management of the Fox Theatre in Detroit that she was 'too yellow to sing with all the black men in [Basie's] band. Someone might think I was white if the light didn't hit me just right.' Against Holiday's furious objections, someone was sent out for a tub of grease paint. 'So I had to be darkened down so that the show could go on in dynamic-assed Detroit,' she wrote in her autobiography, *Lady Sings the Blues*. 'It's like they say, there's no damned business like show business. You have to laugh to keep from throwing up.' Things didn't improve when Holiday returned to the road a few years later with a white band, that of Artie Shaw.

It wasn't long before the roughest days with the Basie band began to look like a breeze. It got to the point where I hardly ever ate, slept or went to the bathroom without having a major NAACP [National Association for the Advancement of Coloured People]-type production . . . some places they wouldn't even let me eat in the kitchen . . . sometimes it was a choice between me eating and the whole band starving. I got tired of having a federal case over breakfast, lunch and dinner.

In *Hear Me Talkin' to Ya*, Nat Hentoff and Nat Shapiro's oral history of jazz, the great trumpeter Roy 'Little Jazz' Eldridge described how, during *his* stint with Shaw's band, he had difficulty gaining admittance to one of his own gigs:

'We were supposed to be playing a dance and they wouldn't even let me in the place. "This is a white dance," they said, and there was my name, right outside, and I told them who I was . . . [Artie Shaw] was real great: he made the guy apologize that wouldn't let me in and got him fired. Man, when you're on the stage you're great, but as soon as you come off, you're nothing.'

Ray Charles, in *his* autobiography, *Brother Ray*, testifies that little had changed by the early fifties:

We could be driving for hours and never find a gas station which would let us use the bathroom. If we stopped by the side of the road, we stood a chance of getting busted, so we'd open both doors of the car and piss between them. We could be hungry as bears and go half a day before we'd find a joint that would serve us. The race thing hit us where it hurt – in the stomach and in the balls.

Chuck Berry, off on tour in the wake of his breakthrough hit 'Maybellene', found that his countryish beat, clear diction and discreetly overexposed publicity photographs had gained him bookings from promoters who hadn't even realized that he was black. He was hurriedly and embarrassedly paid off at one such venue, and as he prepared to leave, he heard the white band who had been hired to back him playing his hit.

Black artists evolved new strategies to deal with such racist bigotry. 'We were breaking through the racial barrier. The white kids had to hide my records 'cos they daren't let their parents know that they had them in the house,' recalled Little Richard, easily the most influential of Hendrix's early employers. 'We decided that my image should be crazy and way-out so the adults would think I was harmless. I'd appear at one show dressed as the Queen of England and in the next as the Pope.' In other words, Richard became a clown, an escape-hatch used by many of his predecessors. Decades earlier, Louis Armstrong – the first great jazz soloist and one of the most important and influential artists America has ever produced – had virtually subordinated his superlative improvisatory talents to his desire to be loved by white people. The conflict between the need to establish jazz as a legitimate art form with Armstrong himself as its presiding genius, and the urge to become a successful and beloved popular entertainer was no contest at all, and indeed – considering Armstrong's background and the ethos of his times – it would have been quite remarkable if the outcome had been any different. Almost to the end of his life, Armstrong saw himself as a vaudevillian who played some trumpet as part of his act.

Armstrong's polar opposite was, of course, Miles Davis, who left the stage when his sidemen were soloing, frequently turned his back on the audience, never introduced either the tunes or the musicians and – despite maintaining many lengthy and cordial friendships with individual whites, and regularly employing white musicians (Lee Konitz, Bill Evans, John McLaughlin, Joe Zawinul, Mike Stern, John Scofield *et al.*) – cussed out whites in general every chance he got. Unlike Armstrong, Davis was – his assiduously cultivated bad-ass demeanor to the contrary – the scion of a wealthy and successful family. His father was a highly prosperous dentist, lived in a white neighbourhood, owned a considerable acreage of farmland and was, according to Eric Nisenson in *Round About Midnight*, 'as solidly bourgeois as a black family could possibly be in the early thirties'.

Duke Ellington came from a similar background, and it had required an educated urban visionary like Ellington to foresee that 'the music of my race is something which posterity will honour in a higher sense than merely the music of the ballroom,' but even in the thirties, the sophistication of Ellington's harmonic and textural innovations provoked the accusation (from James Agee and other – white – critics) that his music was 'effete' by comparison with the 'true' black music. It is hard to avoid the conclusion that the obsession of white pundits with the 'rootsy', 'funky' and 'authentic' – and, during the late sixties, with black separatist politics at their most extreme – seems designed to keep black people (and their arts) at the margins of white society (and its arts). Any attempt to penetrate the walls of the ghetto is frenziedly denounced as a sell-out by whites whose own access to bourgeois privilege had never been under threat, whether or not their whims led them, at any given moment, to choose to avail themselves of that access. Blacks, it seemed, had a

bounden duty to maintain themselves in a state of poverty and primitivism so as not to jeopardize their status as art objects; a duty to stay
poor, to stay oppressed, to stay funky, to stay ignorant, to remain as suf-
ferers in perpetuity. Blacks were told not to be ashamed of the blues, but
instead to be ashamed of The Supremes.

Ralph Gleason and his acolytes had thus arrived at a critical position
which enabled them to imply that all black musicians (other than a few
ageing blues players and militant avant-garde jazzmen) had become so
brainwashed by middle-class aspirations to wealth and social status that
their music was virtually worthless. Especially when compared to that of
The Grateful Dead or Jefferson Airplane or the holy Beatles, who – like
most of the white superstars – were regularly praised for the formal complexity, literary significance, political acuity and general Art Value of their
music. (Considering how advanced, aware, unprejudiced and generally
wonderful the rock audience and its critical wing have generally considered themselves to be, it is the 'pop' audience – who have never given a
shit about art, and who have only ever wanted a good noise to dance to
and a few doses of sentimental glop by which to hold hands and cuddle –
who have most enthusiastically welcomed black pop into their hearts,
homes and clubs. They may have been proportionately *less* willing to
extend an equivalent welcome to black people into their neighbourhoods
and workplaces, but that is another and a far longer battle. It is one of the
great liberal myths that people can live together in harmony once they
have learned to eat each other's food and dance to each other's music. Any
late-sixties-to-mid-seventies British skinhead with a taste for reggae
music and Indian food could have told you that.)

'I've found that the most unbeatable combination is black musicians recording
white people's music, but playing it black. Wes [Montgomery] and The Fifth
Dimension are perfect examples of that. A black man playing black music will not
sell as well.'

George Benson, quoted in *Guitar Player* (1974)

The great *bête noire* of the rock-as-art crowd was Motown, who – as Dave
Marsh put it in *Trapped: Michael Jackson & the Crossover Dream* – 'took
live performance and table manners, costuming and good grammar as
seriously as the bedrock of its hits, instructed kids from homes where
there were barely enough knives and forks to go round which spoon to
use first on white damask tablecloths, and did their best to saw the rough
edges off ghetto-bred vocabulary and speed up mid-South drawls.'

Motown released albums like *The Supremes Sing Rodgers and Hart*, and worried about whether allowing Stevie Wonder to record a song as 'controversial' as Bob Dylan's 'Blowin' in the Wind' was acceptable company policy. The corporation was decidedly over-cautious: by 1967, Detroit's ghettos were in flames. Motown may have been 'The Sound of Young America', but it literally didn't know what was happening on its own doorstep.

The 'irony' is, of course, that Motown was founded, owned and run by Berry Gordy Jr, a black man, and that all its producers, musicians and songwriters were also black. Atlantic Records, which distributed the impeccably down-home and ecstatically funky Memphis label Stax – the latter the home base of Otis Redding, Sam & Dave and Booker T & the MGs – was the hipster's choice of Cool Black-Music Label, but Atlantic's black singers – from Joe Turner to The Coasters to Aretha Franklin and beyond – generally fronted for the white producers, songwriters and musicians. As for Stax, it was a classic inter-racial team-up: the label's bosses and many of its backroom team were white – the most outstanding example being guitarist/composer/producer Steve Cropper, who undoubtedly contributed more to soul music than any other white person – and all of its singers were black. In terms of its music, solidly rooted in bluesy funk and post-gospel vocalizations, Stax was 'culturally blacker' than Motown, which is why it was a trendier taste for hippies not prepared to abandon *all* black music in exchange for the cultural treasures beginning to flow from San Francisco.

It was Stax, incidentally, that unwittingly provided Janis Joplin with her greatest humiliation. After the 1968 break-up of her shambolic band Big Brother and the Holding Company, she formed a new, horn-driven, heavily soul-influenced backing group and quixotically decided to début them at the Stax/Volt Christmas party in Memphis. Topping the bill and following Booker T & the MGs, The Staple Singers, Eddie Floyd, Albert King, Rufus & Carla Thomas, Isaac Hayes, Johnnie Taylor, The Bar-Kays and special guest Mr Jaaaaaaames Brown – all, with the exception of blues veteran King, delivering state-of-the-art soul showbiz – Joplin wandered on stage, sucking on her bottle of Southern Comfort, after her band had spent fifteen minutes setting up their instruments and chatting among themselves. This was the kind of carry-on that passed for exquisite naturalness and sincerity in San Francisco, but to black audiences – who respect professionalism above all – it was little less than an insult. After three numbers, most of the audience had left, and Joplin flounced off stage in a major snit. Joplin couldn't understand why they hadn't welcomed her with open arms, and the audience couldn't understand what the hell she thought she was doing there in the first place. Clearly, Richard Goldstein's 'everybody is their own spade' dictum worked better in theory than in practice.

'[Jimi Hendrix] was tryin' to fit in on his side of town, but it wasn't his side of town. He needed to be in another place . . . man, when he got to Europe he got with people that was like him, they was his family. I was glad that he found a place. And then a lotta blacks started sayin' how it's terrible that he had to go to the white side to make it, cause we treated him so bad. They was all runnin' round sayin' "Shit! He was in my band." All these people would come out of the woodwork: "He worked for me and I kicked him out . . ."'

Bobby Womack, interview with the author (1988)

'He'd been in the black milieu as the sideman for this musician and that musician and this was his chance to not only draw himself out of the mire of mediocrity but also to do something for the black cause . . . there was a tremendous sense of him choosing to play in the white arena, that he was coming along and saying, "You've taken this, Eric Clapton, and Mr Townshend, you think you're a showman. This is how *we* do it. This is how we can do it when we take back what what you've borrowed, if not stolen. I've put it back together and *this* is what it's all about, and you can't live without it, can you?" And the terrible truth is that we *couldn't* live without it. There was a real *vengeance* there . . .'

Pete Townshend, interview with the author (1986)

The day after Hendrix's triumph at Monterey, Pete Townshend wanted to make amends for the back-stage contretemps about who was going to follow whom. He walked up to Hendrix at the airport and said, 'Listen, no hard feelings. I'd love to get a bit of that guitar you smashed.' Hendrix speared the gangling Townshend with an arctic stare and sneered, 'Oh yeah? I'll autograph it for you, *honkie*.' Townshend was devastated. 'I just *crawled* away,' he remembers ruefully. Such eruptions of overt racial hostility were exceedingly rare for Hendrix, even under intense provocation, but there was something about Townshend which must have gotten quite a distance up Hendrix's nose. Townshend was acutely jealous of Eric Clapton's friendship with Hendrix; he was desperate for Hendrix's acknowledgement and affection. And he didn't get it.

'I thought, Eric's getting the big hugs, why aren't I? And I think the difference is that Eric feels perfectly natural with his adoption of blues music. He feels it inside; I don't. I don't even really feel comfortable with black musicians. It's always been a problem with me, and I think Jimi was so acutely sensitive in his blackness that he picked that up. [After Monterey] I felt a lot of hate, vengeance and frustration. Possibly because of my sensitivity, my uneasiness with black people, I felt I deserved it somehow.'

The differences between British and American racial politics were quite considerable in the mid-sixties. There is no living American who can remember a time when there were no blacks in the USA, but large-scale black immigration to the UK was a phenomenon of the fifties, and the vast majority of white Brits – to whom most blacks were still 'foreigners' – were even less familiar with them than their American counterparts. Sting, an adolescent when he first saw Hendrix playing a Newcastle club in late 1966, had literally never seen an actual in-the-flesh black person in his life before. As a result, there was plenty of scope for mutual misunderstandings: Hendrix once refused to be interviewed by Caroline Coon, founder of the Release drug advisory centre, because when her name was mentioned he thought it was a tasteless racial jibe; and his first roadie, the late Howard 'H' Parker, was fired in Sweden one morning when he told a hungover Hendrix that he resembled 'a gorilla who's just lost his bananas'. Hendrix was insecure enough to think that H meant to insult him; H was insensitive enough to think that Hendrix could possibly interpret his 'quip' in any other way.

Similarly in *'Scuse Me While I Kiss the Sky* – despite its flaws the most illuminating and insightful to date of all the formal Hendrix biographies – made much of alleged racial tensions within the Experience, claiming that Mitchell displayed a 'strange contempt' for Hendrix, and claiming that both Mitchell and Redding used terms like 'nigger' and 'coon' as part of their day-to-day banter. Both of them were deeply hurt by Henderson's implications, apparently derived from conversations with Buddy Miles. Many who knew the band well at this time have failed to recall any such incidents, expressed puzzlement at these charges, and confirmed that, even if they were true, the genuine warmth of the relationship between the trio meant that neither Mitchell nor Redding could conceivably have wanted to hurt Hendrix. 'Noel came from Folkestone, where there weren't any black people,' said Robert Wyatt. 'He doesn't have a malicious bone in his body, so it would have been unwitting.'

Back in the States, there was no ambiguity about such matters. Robert Wyatt was then the drummer/vocalist with Soft Machine, also managed by Chas Chandler and Mike Jeffery, and spent almost a year on tour as Hendrix's opening act. In the South, he remembers,

'. . . things really got tricky. We were playing in the South for a promoter called Bob Cope. He was a really nice Southern gentleman, big reception and meal for the artists and all that, and suddenly at the table one of the waitresses came in and did something wrong, put something in the wrong place, and he snapped at her. I don't remember if he actually called her a nigger, but the whole Texas white Southern *thing* suddenly came out at this waitress. Cope looked round and remembered that Hendrix was there, and I think it was the first time he'd ever realized that Hendrix was black . . . Hendrix was very upset by this, and he was very conscious of the explosive connotations of the very Scandinavian-looking groupies who used to come from the big Southern towns and stay with the band. You would see the local dignitaries from the radio station – or even the mayors – come to welcome the band to town going beetroot-red with embarrassment, being polite to him as an entertainer but not being able to handle what was going on in the dressing rooms. You don't have to go round making political statements on top of that. He was *living* a political life of great importance.'

Nevertheless, the longer Hendrix spent in the States, the more pressure was put on him to make an explicit statement about the open racial conflicts of the time, particularly after the turning point: the assassination of Dr Martin Luther King Jr in 1968. Hendrix was, after all, the only black rock star with a massive white audience, and he was correctly perceived by the Black Panther Party and others as having a vast influence on the young whites who followed him. He was thus courted by the Panthers – Noel Redding was once highly miffed to find himself virtually excluded from the Experience's dressing room by a Panther delegation with whom Hendrix was having a meeting – but he gave them little solace. His sympathies lay more with Martin Luther King than with Black Panther Party activists like Huey P. Newton; he was suspicious of all analyses which saw race as the eye of America's hurricane, and more suspicious still of black organizations which sought to recruit him.

However, not only was the movement not monolithic, but it didn't even represent a straightforward continuum between 'extreme' and 'moderate'. True, at one end were relative quietists, such as the National Association for the Advancement of Colored People (NAACP) (the name alone gives the game away), who saw nothing much wrong with American society except that blacks were denied full participation in it; but elsewhere were such radically different players as the Oakland-based Black Panther Party for Self-Defense, and the Detroit-based Nation of Islam. Apart from agreeing that, when it came to white supremacy, enuff was way more than enuff, their policies and programmes could not have been less congruent. The Panthers wore paramilitary uniforms – black leather jackets, turtleneck sweaters, berets and shades: *cooool!* – and freaked out cops and squares alike by carrying guns in public. The Panthers, formed and led by Huey Newton and Bobby Seale, were essentially socialists of the Maoist variety, happy to work with white radicals who were prepared to endorse and abide by their ten-point programme. Detroit rabble-rouser John Sinclair did just that, forming his own White Panther Party with the fabulous MC5 as their musical wing.

On the other hand, the Nation of Islam (informally known as the 'Black Muslims') were mystical racial nationalists. They demanded separatism, albeit on their terms, and considered white people to be racially inferior 'devils'; it was after joining the NoI that Muhammad Ali had renounced his 'slave name' of Cassius Clay. Their stellar spokesman, Malcolm X, had fallen out with the leader, Elijah Muhammad, and following a pilgrimage to Mecca during which he observed Muslims of all ethnic origins peacefully worshipping together, renounced the NoI's separatism in favour of the more inclusive spirit of orthodox Islam. He died in a hail of bullets at a 1965 press conference, shot down by black gunmen. Malcolm's death benefited both the NoI leadership, threatened by his challenge to one of their central tenets, and the US government, to whom Malcolm was infinitely more dangerous once armed with a message that could appeal to whites as well as blacks than he ever was as a radical separatist.

And looming over the entire movement was Dr King, whose towering 'I have a dream' speech, delivered in Washington DC in 1963, had extended his message from the South to the nation, and thence to the world. Dr King was growing steadily more radical, addressing not simply domestic racism but the war in Vietnam and the fundamental premises upon which American society was based, just as Malcolm was becoming more inclusive. Their paths were growing ever closer, and ultimately it took bullets to keep them apart.

Hendrix was not, to put it mildly, a particularly political animal. He was, first and foremost, a musician and his entire focus was on being a musician, improving his craft as a musician, expressing his inner life through his role as a musician and – most fundamentally – being able to make some kind of a living as a musician. His views on the Vietnam war were, initially at least, those of an ex-paratrooper rather than a putative hippie figurehead. In BBC2's *Reputations* show, Eric Burdon recalled a discussion of the war during which Hendrix rolled out the whiskery (and subsequently utterly discredited) 'domino theory' beloved of the US government and its apologists: that if the North Vietnamese were not defeated, then all the neighbouring Asian nations would successively fall to the Chinese.

That would change: and what changed it was, essentially, the experience of returning to the US as a celebrity whose views on life, the universe and everything were sought and listened to. Hendrix didn't so much 'get involved' in the black and anti-war struggles as come to terms with the extent to which, like it or not, he was already involved.

> Oh baby why d'you burn your brother's house down?
> Jimi Hendrix, 'House Burning Down' (1968)

'Black kids think the music is white now, which it isn't . . . The argument is not between black and white; that's just another game the establishment set up to turn us against one another . . . and the grooviest part about it is that it's not all this old-time thing that you can cop out with. The easy thing to cop out with is sayin' black and white. That's the easiest thing. You can see a black person. But now to get down to the nitty-gritty, it's gettin' to be old and young – not the age, but the ways of thinkin'. Old and new, actually. Not old and young . . . most [people] are sheep. Which isn't a bad idea. This is the truth, isn't it? That's why we have the form of Black Panthers and some sheep under the Ku Klux Klan. They are all sheep . . .'

Jimi Hendrix, quoted in David Henderson's *'Scuse Me While I Kiss the Sky* (1981)

Hendrix was being unfair to the Panthers: they weren't racial exclusionists like the Nation of Islam. The Black Panther street-vending the party newspaper outside the Electric Lady studio knew that brother Jimi was generally good for a sale, but Hendrix withheld the public endorsement the Panthers sought from him. He was nevertheless aware of their attendance at his shows. 'They come to the concerts, and I sort of feel them there – it's not a physical thing but a mental ray. It's a spiritual thing.' It was often suspected that Hendrix's decision to record Ed Chalpin's pay-off album with Band of Gypsys – Buddy Miles and Billy Cox, both black – was a conscious attempt to defuse black criticism of him, but it seems more likely that he simply wanted to recharge his batteries by playing with his oldest and most trusted friend and with his most entertaining new pal. There had also been a consensus within the Experience camp that it would be inappropriate for Chalpin to get his hands on any of Hendrix's current studio recordings or, indeed, any performances involving Experience material or Experience personnel. So Mitch Mitchell took a holiday (as opposed to a hike) and in came

Buddy Miles, who has subsequently claimed to have been the 'leader' of Band of Gypsys.

Still, Hendrix did take more and more interest in 'the community', and he was furious when Mike Jeffery booked him on to a TV talk show on a night when he had planned to play a benefit for The Young Lords, a Puerto Rican activist group. And when he appeared with blues singer Big Maybelle at a Harlem street party, David Henderson wrote, 'a black nationalist type came up to Jimi and said, "Hey, brother, you better come home." Jimi quickly replied, "You gotta do what you do and I gotta do what I got to do *now*."'

'We was in America. We was in America. The stuff was over and startin' again . . . and it's time for another anthem, and that's what I'm writin' on now.'

Jimi Hendrix (1969)

Hendrix never quite got to write his anthem, though this author, at least, would argue that he said a great deal of what needed saying by remodelling the old one. He also never survived to realize just how unreachably utopian his vision turned out to be. America was indeed divided in terms of old and new, but the old ways included much racism, and the old ways won. A few concessions were necessary, but they were made – albeit somewhat grudgingly – and America moved, sullenly and anxiously, into the seventies. A significant number of blacks had made genuine inroads into the professions in the wake of the upheavals of the sixties; they were better represented than ever before in local government and the police, less condescendingly ignored and stereotyped on TV and in the movies. Nevertheless, this 'progress' was resented by large numbers of whites, liberals as well as rednecks. The institution of 'affirmative action' (or 'positive discrimination') was regarded as discrimination against whites – as if 'affirmative action' in favour of whites had not been operating in America ever since the first heisted African set foot on American soil. The kind of racial *rapprochement* which had put James Brown's 'Say It Loud, I'm Black and I'm Proud' into the pop Top Five (it was, naturally, an R&B number one) was dead and gone.

The music business was certainly no exception. Record companies like Atlantic had come under increasing pressure from newly assertive black artists and producers who wanted to control their own destinies and reap the profits from their own music, and whites – whatever their credentials – were made increasingly unwelcome. Atlantic responded by chasing the rock market, sinking more and more of its resources into Led Zeppelin, Yes, Crosby, Stills, Nash & Young and its distribution of Capricorn Records, a label set up by Otis Redding's former manager Phil Walden as a showcase for The Allman Brothers Band and a whole slew of lesser Southern rock lights. The conversation between rock and soul gradually petered out, each community addressing its own concerns in its own manner. James Brown's run of Top Ten pop hits abruptly dried up.

> Don't call me nigger, whitey,
> Don't call me whitey, nigger.
>
> Sly & the Family Stone, 'Don't Call Me Nigger, Whitey', *Stand* (1969)

> Run Charlie run, the niggers is comin',
> The NIGGERS is comin'!
>
> Norman Whitfield for The Temptations, 'Run Charlie
> Run', *All Directions* (1972)

In retrospect, it is not surprising that there was so much overt racial hostility in the lyrics of the black pop of that era. What is surprising is that there was so little. Sly, of course, put his finger on it with the sneering playground taunt of 'Don't Call Me Nigger, Whitey', but if things had gone so far that a perfectly respectable mainstream black vocal group like The Temptations would bait honkies so openly (would they have done it in 1965 or 1985?), then it takes little imagination to imagine what was bubbling beneath the smooth surface of the seventies. Black pop continued to sell to whites through the disco era, but dance audiences – in a spontaneous and unselfconscious application of the 'death to the individual' theory – simply bought records they liked no matter who they were by, rather than followed and supported specific artists. Successful disco performers were thus considered 'faceless' by a rock audience hopelessly mired in personality-cult. The two black personality cults which the rock audience did accept were those of Stevie Wonder and Bob Marley, both of whom amply met the rigorous rockist criteria of the post-hippie consensus.

At a time when the domination of soul music by backroom writers, session players and label bosses was highly suspect to rock fans – who, broadly speaking, adhered to the post-Beatles/Dylan concept of individualist autonomy – Stevie Wonder was highly qualified. He had had a well-publicized war of independence with Berry Gordy's Motown plantation; he was a composer of vast resource and ability, and – thanks to his mastery of synthesizer technology – he damn near played everything himself as well as writing and producing it. He turned out the most exquisite love songs ('You Are the Sunshine of My Life') and some of the toughest funk ('Superstition') of his generation, and he wasn't in hock to anybody. Stevie was cool, that was sure. He'd been around long enough to qualify as a veteran, and he was still young enough to have absorbed the influences of Sly Stone, Bob Dylan and The Beatles. He'd jammed with Hendrix in London in 1967 and recorded much of the material for his first few 'adult' albums at Hendrix's Electric Lady studio. No seventies artist enjoyed such access to both black and white ears.

Bob Marley was a different kettle of fish. He'd grown up within earshot of the sixties consensus – Beatles, Dylan, Sly, Motown, Hendrix – but in the vastly different atmosphere of Jamaica. Born in 1945 to a Jamaican country girl and a broken-down English army captain, Marley developed into possibly the most extraordinary figure in the history of Western pop culture: not only the acknowledged leader of his chosen musical idiom, but the world's most prominent spokesman for a religion previously unknown to almost all but its practitioners, and finally the most politically influential recording artist of the twentieth century. He was the foremost performer in the export of reggae, Jamaica's home-grown pop – its funk, blues and gospel, all in one music – the living symbol of Ras Tafari (more commonly known as 'Rastafarianism'), and a prophet of Pan Africanism whose songs became the anthems of the triumphant ('successful' is another matter) Zimbabwean revolution. When he and his band, The Wailers, were invited to perform at Zimbabwe's independence ceremony in 1980, most previous claims concerning the 'importance', 'influence' or 'relevance' of popular music in the context of actual world affairs seemed, by comparison, little more than promotional blabber'n'smoke.

His mass breakthrough eventually came via Island Records – founded by the Anglo-Jamaican entrepreneur Chris Blackwell – a company with considerable experience in promoting and selling both 'progressive' rock and Jamaican music. The original Wailers (a vocal trio involving Marley, Peter Tosh and Neville 'Bunny Wailer' Livingston) enabled them to combine both areas of their expertise, especially when Blackwell convinced them to overdub rock guitarist Wayne Perkins on a few of the tracks. This wasn't as much of an imposition as a bald recitation might suggest; Peter Tosh already played a mean, drawling wah-wah guitar, and when he and Bunny Wailer quit in protest at the continued emphasis on Marley, the new-look Bob Marley & the Wailers hired a succession of mostly American post-Hendrix R&B-trained guitarists, including Junior Murvin (not to be confused with the reggae singer Junior Marvin), Al Anderson and Donald Kinsey (the latter a former Albert King sideman who subsequently formed a *very* snappy Chicago blues quartet called The Kinsey Report, which came close to becoming the missing link between Robert Cray and Living Colour). The peak of Marley's infatuation with rock guitar came on the 1979 world tour which eventually yielded the *Babylon by Bus* live double-album; in an ill-judged concession to rock sensibilities and his own Hendrix nostalgia, he allowed Murvin and Anderson to blitz out completely, thus radically upsetting the balance of his music.

British rock audiences took gladly to Marley; Caribbean music was not exactly unknown in England, Marley was as charismatic as any extant rock person, and he had evidently learned more songwriting craft from studying The Beatles and Smokey Robinson than had any of his compatriots. And, of course, he had been a favourite of Caribbean ex-pats for years. The situation was quite different in the USA. Only a tiny percentage of black Americans had Caribbean roots, and since, as a committed and militant Rastaman, Marley proclaimed the divinity of Haile Selassie, smoked ferocious amounts of ganja, declared that all people of African descent were Ethiopians and evidently hadn't cut or combed his hair since 1971, his black American constituency was not vast. White Americans loved him all the more for it, and reggae – like the blues, like Ornette Coleman, like Hendrix – became something that the white hipoisie considered the black American masses were simply too bourgeois to appreciate. Bunny Wailer didn't help with a solo album on which he implored 'black Yankees' not to be 'follow fashion monkeys' (that must've gone down a storm in Detroit). Tosh, for his part, was more openly hostile to white journalists than any performer to emerge before Public Enemy revived the old Black Muslim ploy of calling white folks 'blue-eyed devils', and – for the record – he was more hostile still to black writers whose racial integrity he considered inadequate. The indicator he chose was often hairstyle; far from leading naturally to Rasta dreadlocks and African styles, the Afro which had ruled the late sixties and the seventies had retreated in favour of the processed, wet-look 'do. To any ideological Rasta, this was Babylon's triumph incarnate.

What reggae eventually donated to pop was not its content but its technological creativity. Self-contained performing bands along Western lines were unknown in Jamaica before the advent of The Wailers; the bands worked the studios and the deejays ruled at massive dances, where they 'jammed' with the records, applying echo and equalization to resculpt the music as the record was played. They also 'toasted' – rhythmic chat over the music, the ancestor of rap – against instrumental remixes of current hits supplied on a custom basis by the producers. The 'sound system' style spread from Brooklyn's Jamaican community, the disco-mix 12″ single (complete with 'dub' side) became a commonplace, first in disco and then in rock, and the combination of rap and Eurobeat synthesizer imports metamorphosed into hip-hop.

> It's like a jungle
> Sometimes it makes me wonder
> How I keep from going under . . .
> Don't touch me
> 'Cause I'm
> Close to the . . . EDGE
>
> > Duke Bootee for Grandmaster Flash & the Furious Five,
> > 'The Message' (1982)

> We slay all suckers who perpetrate,
> And lay down the law from state to state
>
> > Run-DMC, 'My Adidas' (1986)

> Radio stations, I question their blackness
> They call themselves black but we'll see if they'll play this,
> Turn it up! Bring the noise!
>
> > Public Enemy, 'Bring the Noise' (1988)

Hip-hop turned out to be the next street culture to eat the world: its ultimate impact was as ubiquitous as that of rock music itself. Indeed, for film-makers and commercial directors, hip-hop displaced rock as instant aural shorthand for 'youth culture'. It upset any number of apple-carts. First of all, it was – like punk – almost deliberately 'unmusical', requiring – in its purest form – only a drum machine and a voice; in performance, the rappers were backed by deejays who 'cut up' and 'scratched in' excerpts from any number of records – spontaneous collage work which acknowledged no boundaries of style or period. It was also even more deliberately anti-social. At its lightest and poppiest, hip-hop threw up some of the most enjoyable novelty dance hits for years, and hundreds of rap records took a strong moral line on subjects like dope, guns and street crime. Others took graphic misogyny to depths undreamt-of by all but the scuzziest heavy metal bands, and resounded with images of Uzi-powered gang warfare, crack-houses and general urban collapse. It was what white punk rock had pretended to be about; it was the soundtrack to everything that makes Manhattanites want to move to the suburbs. As far as 'outlaw chic' was concerned, it beat the hell out of everything since Jimmy Cliff's performance as Ivan the gunman in the Jamaican gangster movie *The Harder They Come*. Radicals, style victims, political conservatives, tabloid journalists and concerned members of the public immediately assumed their traditional positions. *Is subway graffiti Art or Vandalism? Discuss. Should hip-hop concerts be banned? In a recent incident at a Run-DMC concert . . .*

Philly gangsta pioneer Schooly D ('I put my pistol up to his head/I said, "You sucka-ass nigga, I'm gon' shoot you dead"') may once have seemed like the last word in streetwise ultra-nihilism, but he was soon overtaken by meaner and more resourceful ghetto fabulists like NWA (featuring Dr Dre and Ice Cube) and Ice-T. Then the floodgates opened and rappers became Middle America's new bogeymen: the likes of 2 Live Crew, The Geto Boys and Sister Souljah were denounced in churches, courtrooms and even from presidential podia. Ironically, Ice-T found himself in Big Trouble not over any of his rap albums, but for a hard-rock song called 'Cop Killer', which he'd recorded with his thrash-metal band, Body Count. They'd been touring the length and breadth of the US with the 'Lollapalooza' mobile festival and playing to hordes of young white rock fans, which presumably made him more of a threat to the established order than when he'd confined himself to rapping for black youth. Body Count's album had been available all summer without generating any particular brouhaha – no mass outbreaks of anti-police violence that could possibly be attributed in any way to the song – until a Texas police department started making a fuss. Next thing anyone knew, a cop-driven 'boycott Warner Bros' campaign was in full effect, led by no less an American icon than NRA spokesman Charlton Heston. Ice's label, Sire Records, backed their artist, as did Warner Bros Records itself, Sire's distributor. But with untold millions in ad revenue at stake, the board of Time Warner overrode the record-company bosses, and Ice had to take his next album, the eagerly awaited *Home Invasion*, elsewhere.

However, no rap act to date has walked a more precarious tightrope than Public Enemy. Boasting state-of-the-art production by The Bomb Squad, their classic first three albums, *Yo! Bum Rush the Show*, *It Takes a Nation of Millions to Hold Us Back* and *Fear of a Black Planet*, were as uncompromising and inflammatory as anything pop music has ever produced, but their accompanying rhetoric took matters several stages further. The four principal members of Public Enemy – rappers Chuck D and Flavor Flav, deejay Terminator X and 'Minister of Information' Professor Griff – would appear surrounded by their bodyguards, the Security of the First World, sometimes toting plastic replicas of Uzi machine-guns. They were proud followers of Louis Farrakhan, leader of the Nation of Islam, and as such professed the old-time Black Muslim exegesis, as passed down from W. D. Fard to Elijah Muhammad, and as firmly repudiated by Malcolm X shortly before his assassination. White people are 'devils', created through genetic engineering by a mad scientist called Yakub – and therefore not true humans at all. In fact, Caucasians are descended from cave-dwellers who fucked dogs. This stuff went down a treat in interviews; white hacks were often reduced to pleading that they aren't devils and don't fuck dogs, which must have given Public Enemy a few good laughs now and again. Farrakhan himself was at one time fond of praising Adolf Hitler as 'a great man' and denouncing Judaism as 'an incorrect religion'. (Personally, I'd say that anyone who can even consider the terms 'correct' or 'incorrect' to be applicable to religious belief is probably dangerous.) Public Enemy made their début on Def Jam Records, co-owned by Jewish devil Rick Rubin.

'The great irony of [the] infamous is–Public-Enemy-anti-Semitic controversies', Nelson George pointed out in his characteristically exemplary *Hip Hop America*, 'was how many Jews were working for and with the band at the time . . . their tours were organized by the Jewish Lyor Cohen . . . much of their spin doctoring at the time was done by the Jewish Bill Adler at Rush Management. And Chuck D and [co-producer] Hank Shocklee were partners in Rhythm Method Productions with two Jews, Ed Chalpin and Ron Skuller. If PE hated Jews, then they must have been applying the gangster ethos: "Keep your friends close and your enemies closer."'

Ah yes, Ed Chalpin, that great philanthropist, that selfless sponsor and mentor of young black talent. It is doubtful whether Chalpin's association with PE gained him as spectacular a dividend as the million-to-one return on the single buck he advanced Jimi Hendrix, but them's the breaks.

Chuck D has a solid point, however; what whites may think of Public Enemy is less relevant to him than the knowledge that the band's expression of unvarnished hatred provides 'therapy for blacks'. In sharp contrast to the late sixties and early seventies, the mainstream black music of the eighties provides few clues that many blacks are seriously pissed off about the way things are. In their heyday, Public Enemy did that and more, and, by way of a bonus, provide a convenient index of the boundaries of white liberalism. A few days before this was originally written, I saw a blond five-year-old toddling down the street in a miniature black wind-breaker with a huge Public Enemy logo on the back. (The little devil . . .) And, of course, Edward Furlong, in his capacity as Archetypal Teenage Rebel of the Week, sported a PE logo T-shirt all the way through the mayhem and carnage of James Cameron's *Terminator 2*.

Real sparks flew when hip-hop collided with its mirror-image, Heavy Metal. Apart from the fact that black homeboys and white suburban poodle-heads hated each other cordially, their musics had more in common than either had with anything else: both are crushingly loud, unrelentingly macho and designer-perfect for reinforcing male adolescent power-fantasies. Scratchers had long been fond of 'borrowing' drum and guitar noises from Led Zeppelin or AC/DC records alongside the mandatory James Brown samples, and the process was codified by Run-DMC, who first hired studio guitarist Eddie Martinez to contribute a few crunches to records like 'Rock Box' and 'King of Rock', and then teamed up with seventies Stones-clones Aerosmith for a rap version of their oldie 'Walk This Way', complete with a smart, astute video which explicitly played on and then mocked the tensions the record pretended to resolve. Both parties benefited: Run-DMC sneaked on to rock radio and MTV, and Aerosmith were able to advertise the fact that despite all reasonable expectations, they were not only still alive, but sufficiently well to parlay what then seemed like a moribund career into an extravagantly thriving concern still going strong over a decade and a half, several million dollars and a good few platinum discs later.

The success of 'Walk This Way' followed on from an important battle previously fought over access to MTV, the 24-hour rock cable television channel. In the tradition that once led Vernon Reid and Greg Tate, co-founders of the Black Rock Coalition (respectively guitarist-leader of Living Colour and columnist for *Village Voice*), to define AOR as 'Apartheid Oriented Rock', MTV had refused to screen the ground-breaking 'Billie Jean' video from Michael Jackson's *Thriller* on the grounds that Michael Jackson was not suitable for their audience. Since Jackson was one of the most popular entertainers in the world, this was obvious bullshit. To their credit, CBS Records threatened to pull all their acts' videos off the air unless Jackson's was aired. The sky did not fall, and no crosses were burned outside MTV's headquarters. But, the point was made: 'rock' broadcasting was less integrated than its black equivalents, which have democratically opened their airtime to the likes of George Michael, resulting in his *Faith* album topping the R&B charts, and an R&B Grammy in 1989.

Phil Collins once complained, somewhat disingenuously, that he was the victim of 'reverse racism' because some black stations wouldn't play his records. Presumably he didn't worry about the fact that each black play for him meant one less play for a black artist who might not receive strict reciprocal courtesy from a white station. Even more gracelessly, Sammy Hagar, lead singer for Van Halen (who enjoyed R&B sales of their single, 'Jump', as a direct consequence of Eddie Van Halen's jaw-dropping guitar break on Michael Jackson's 'Beat It'), celebrated their *5150* album displacing Whitney Houston from Number One by sneering, 'See, it's no fair. We don't sell to black people and she sells to white people, too. She and Prince and Michael Jackson have something over on us. I got to start dancing.' Hagar doesn't have that much to complain about, though. White stations, according to Bobby Womack in 1988, 'play Prince, Michael Jackson and Whitney Houston, and they figure that takes care of all of us.'

Womack was exaggerating, but not by much. There was always Lionel Richie, who is such a downhome, Sunday-afternoon-car-washing type of guy that he is almost as acceptable as Phil Collins, only considerably better looking. No romantic 1980s interlude was complete without a soundtrack by Anita Baker. George Benson – who in another incarnation is by far the most impressive of the post-Wes Montgomery jazz stylists – sells truck-loads of the kind of pop records that make you want to use the word 'sophisticated' as an insult. Robert Cray's popularity was sustained by the pop, rather than R&B, market. But that still leaves Womack's Big Three.

Prior to the invention of Mariah Carey and the arrival in her life of clean-living Bobby Brown, Whitney Houston was the anointed successor, as if by divine right, to the Bob Mackie sequined throne of Diana Ross; graceful, elegant and empty enough to render her the patron saint of airline stewardesses everywhere. Michael Jackson's much-publicized eccentricities – not to mention his pancake make-up and absurd little designer nose – have rendered him almost as un-black as he is non-white, thus laying him open to the Wrath of Farrakhan. His views on poor Jacko are not that different from those of the Iranian Ayatollah Abbas Va'ez-Tabassi, who declared 'Satan appears in all forms and guises. One of his latest manifestations is in the shape of that sodomite black boy from America whose senseless wailings can have no place [in our land].' One shudders to think what Farrakhan – or any of the Ayatollahs – made of Prince Rogers Nelson.

The image and title [of *Purple Rain*] are only the latest manifestations of Prince's longstanding Jimi Hendrix obsession. His priapic posturing, moustache, gipsy-ruffle clothes and flowery packaging of the *Purple Rain* soundtrack have direct antecedents in Hendrix . . . Prince couldn't have chosen a better role model in the last black musical artist to make the race issue redundant . . . Hendrix signified rebellion, Prince reconciliation – between male and female, rock and funk, black and white . . . Hendrix also outraged audiences with his sexual flamboyance, but here again their approaches diverge. In the days before women's lib, Hendrix relied on macho swagger. [Prince's] sex appeal is more gentle and teasing than overbearing. Hendrix played up the reputation of having a large phallus; Prince would rather be known for having a shapely ass . . .

Scott Isler, *Musician* magazine (1984)

Hmmmmm. Well, Hendrix – to my knowledge – never performed in his underwear, hooked up a gadget that would enable the head of his guitar to squirt milky liquids into the front row of the audience as the 'climax' of a solo, brought a bed on stage to hump, or hired a go-go dancer whose clothes he would tear off – but there's no accounting for tastes. Nevertheless, the parallels are extraordinary, as are the differences. Both tell us much about the changes which took place between their respective eras.

Similarities first. Both men's home-towns (Hendrix's Seattle, Prince's Minneapolis) were 'whitebread' communities with small and isolated black populations, far away from the major centres of the music business. Both were oddball introverts whose only known interests were music and girls, both were from 'broken' homes (Hendrix growing up without a mother, Prince without a father), both decided as teenagers to make music their careers, both were black kids who refused to abide by the limitations of what black kids were 'supposed' to do or be, both were possessed by grandiose, ambitious, 'orchestral' visions which cut giant raw swathes across arbitrary genre-lines.

But Hendrix was born in 1942 – a contemporary of The Beatles – and, like theirs, his childhood and adolescence spanned the first generations of urban blues, bebop, R&B, rock and roll, and soul music. The possibilities of pop – as a manipulable symbolic language, as cultural guerilla warfare, as a long-term, large-scale cash-cow; hell, as *permanent employment* – had barely been recognized, much less explored, much less still codified and mechanized. The only people who had an idea of how any specialized aspects of the music business worked – from engineering a record to engineering a media campaign – were the professionals themselves, and most of *them* were making it up as they went along. Nothing had been around long enough for anybody to be *knowing* about it. Hendrix knew his music and his instrument; that was as far as it went. To say that he started out green is an understatement. He had no idea where he was going, except that he knew he wanted to play.

Prince, on the other hand, was born in 1958 (like Hendrix, a Sagittarian). To him, pop was a known quantity. It was something that had always been there; a fully-fledged part of the entertainment industry, a massive treasure-trove of stylistic devices and potent images; at once professionalized and demystified. Both the making and the marketing of music had been rationalized: Stevie Wonder had proved that a studio-wise musician can make records virtually unaided; David Bowie and The Sex Pistols that a thorough knowledge of rock's subtexts and devices could be exploited by the media-wise for riches, fame and controversy; Hendrix, Sly and The Beatles that there were no musical and social barriers that couldn't be trashed. Hendrix developed his voice and vision through concentrating on one instrument; Prince gained access to a multitrack studio and became not only a one-man band but a master arranger and producer.

Prince's uniqueness lies in his overall command of a variety of processes and skills. He plays bass, drums, keyboards and guitar; all of them more than competently, none of them particularly distinctively. Prince's music still sounds like Prince whether he is playing all the instruments – as he often does in the studio – or none. If he wants to do an entire show without touching a guitar or a keyboard, then any team of skilled and willing musicians seem to be able to produce his sound. His music and his stage show abound with references: to Hendrix, James Brown, The Beatles, Little Richard, David Bowie, The Rolling Stones, Elton John, Curtis Mayfield, Joni Mitchell, Chuck Berry, Elvis Costello, Carlos Santana, Charlie Parker, Sly Stone . . . The Moody Blues! He knows every trick in the book – from drop-dead James Brown dance-moves to bug-eyed, coquettish, Little Richard cutie-pie poses and empty, bravura guitar flourishes – and he practises a lot. He has ousted David Bowie from his former privileged position as the brilliant magpie at the cutting edge of pop weirdness; as the most astute collector and perverse manipulator of pop devices. Prince is both perversely unpredictable and – there's that word again – slyly *knowing*. He understands the rules and processes of self-mythologization in a way that *no one* in Hendrix's era possibly could. His approach is analytical, systematic; it is his ideas which are fresh and unorthodox, not his methods.

'Am I black or white?/Am I straight or gay?', he once asked in a lyric. As a light-skinned black man playing a music which deliberately transcended genre, he muddied the waters of his personal history in a way which Hendrix would never have dreamed of. In the mock-autobiographical movie *Purple Rain*, Prince depicted 'The Kid' (his screen self) as having a black father (moody, violent, self-destructive) and a white mother (noble, loyal, victimized). The implication is that when The Kid is being a shit (which is most of the time until his inevitable enlightenment shortly before the end of the movie), he is being his father's son; when he nices up, his mother's. He is, of course, at his most charismatic when he's being bad. Are we being told something here?

Hendrix bust his chops as a soul sideman and finally got picked up by the rock crowd; Prince was promoted from the first in both markets at once, simultaneously working New-Wavy rock clubs and opening slots for heavy funk acts like Cameo. Along the way, he reinvented a concept which had virtually atrophied; the black rocker.

> Who says a jazz band can't play dance music?
> Who says a rock band can't play funky?
> Who says a funk band can't play rock?
> Oh yeah!
>> George Clinton, W. 'Junie' Morrison and Mike Hampton for
>> Funkadelic, 'Who Says a Funk Band Can't Play Rock?' (1978)

> At fifteen I was raised as a funker,
> At seventeen I was made to discover
> That funk or rock and roll alone
> Is not enough
>> Robert Reed, Tony Fisher, James Avery and Harold Morton Jr
>> for Trouble Funk, 'Funk N Roll' (1983)

In many ways, the racial segregation of seventies pop has been transformed rather than eliminated. More and more mainstream pop has been affected by hip-hop and dance music – which have inevitably both rendered the overall complexion of said mainstream 'blacker' and earned black performers a bigger slice of the pie. Seeing black and white musicians working together behind both black and white leaders became commonplace; Sting's all-black band and Tina Turner's all-white bands barely excited comment. This was both utterly healthy and long overdue but, as the appalling Michael Bolton's success regrettably testifies, the white soul-boy came out of the deal far better than the black rocker. The likes of George Michael, Mick Hucknall and Jamiroquai were praised for the excellence of their taste and the bold sweep of their eclecticism, but even after Prince, the black rocker was anathema, considered ludicrous, demeaning, inconvenient or Lenny Kravitz. Black rock fell right through the cracks in the Anglo-American cultural continuum. Hard rock is not included in the spectrum of styles which constitute the black pop mainstream, as innovative bands like Bad Brains, 24/7 Spies and Fishbone subsequently discovered to their cost. The likes of Rage Against the Machine and Britain's Asian Dub Foundation notwithstanding, successful ethnic and multi-ethnic rock bands are few and far between.

The now-defunct Living Colour spent a very long time indeed as the hottest unsigned band in New York. As Reid explained, 'The white side of the industry claims that it can't put a black band on the album cover and sell them in suburban malls. The black side of the industry claims that black audiences don't want to hear rock and roll.' Reid was keenly aware of the razor-edged irony his band straddled – a 1988 London show began with singer Corey Glover announcing, 'Hi there – I's yo' new neighbour' from a darkened stage – but rock is symbolic turf which cries out to be desegregated. Or, to be more precise, 'decolonized'. Rock is directly derived from black music, and from the music of whites who were primarily inspired by black music. For that music then to turn its back on black musicians is not so much wicked as pathetic.

As a small indication of just *how* pathetic things can get, a favourite anecdote of Reid's:

'I went to [a musical instrument trade show] and check this out: I'm there with my guitar company ESP puttin' me up in a hotel, and they had the players doubling up. I was shuttled to this room and there was this guy from a heavy metal band. When I walk in, this guy is getting out of the shower, right, and he says, "It's not time to clean the room up yet." More than being rejected by record companies or told that my music can't be marketed, that incident told me more about what's happening racially than just about anything else. The guy was *terribly* embarrassed, and I couldn't even get angry with him because it was so ludicrous. He couldn't help it, it was just the way he was raised.

'Now, to bring it back to Hendrix, he was someone who wasn't gonna be invisible . . . he was a person who went against the idea that black people aren't anything. He just said, "I'm somebody," and he had the talent to back it up.'

> No I'm not gonna rob you
> No I'm not gonna beat you
> No I'm not gonna rape you
> So why you wanna give me that
> Funny Vibe?
>
> Vernon Reid for Living Colour, 'Funny Vibe' (1988)

Sadly, black America is still getting that 'funny vibe'. The massive popularity of black entertainers and athletes has not materially improved the relative position of the black underclass; indeed, many are worse off than they were before the Civil Rights era. The case of Bernhard Goetz – who shot four black teenagers on a New York subway in 1984 because one of them made a remark he interpreted as threatening – has revealed a horrific undercurrent in what are euphemistically referred to as 'race relations'. Goetz received considerable public support; the implication appeared to be that many white New Yorkers considered teenage black males to be part of a single entity – some sort of insect-like hive-organism. Because much street-crime is indeed committed by young black males, any of them can – by some alchemy – be considered responsible for the crimes of any others; for Goetz to shoot four kids he didn't know and who had never done anything to him was held by many to be a legitimate and acceptable response to the city's crime wave. Goetz was eventually acquitted of all charges except illegal possession of firearms, even though two of his victims had been shot in the back, and despite Goetz's own videotaped confession that he had deliberately gone out seeking a confrontation. No white politician pointed out the obvious: that if Goetz had shot four white teenagers – or, indeed, if a black man had, under identical circumstances, committed an identical act – he would have been put, to quote Bo Diddley's 'Cops and Robbers', 'so far back in jail they're gonna have to pump air in to him'.

In *Quiet Rage*, her 1986 account of the Goetz affair, Lillian B. Rubin draws some disturbing conclusions: that young blacks excluded from the nation's institutions have instead taken over the streets, and that even though the majority of victims of black street crime are themselves black, the issue has been used to legitimize ancient white paranoias about blacks in general. She describes a black Congressman visiting an ice-cream parlour in his own constituency: 'as [the Congressman and his aides] walked through the door, the white waitress eyed them suspiciously and moved behind the counter for protection. "Why are you in Howard Beach?" she demanded. "This is your Congressman," one of his aides explained. "I don't believe you," she replied.' Howard Beach itself was subsequently the scene of a horrific incident when a black driver whose car had stalled approached a local diner to phone for aid, and ended up – literally – running for his life.

Since then, Americans have watched the rollback of civil rights legislation under Reagan and Bush, including an actual decline in black voter registration in the South. They've witnessed the beating of Rodney King and the minimal official response to the very real issues which that beating raised. They've observed a so-called 'war on drugs' manifesting as a war on the poor; specifically the black poor. They've seen exactly what 'zero tolerance' means in Mayor Rudy Guiliani's New York, and exactly who gets zeroly tolerated, with some of the most horrific cases of racist police brutality in recent times. They've noted the disproportionately high representation of the black male population behind bars and on death row. They've registered the number of politicians happy to sign a death warrant on a black man come election time, and the high number of voters who are susceptible to that kind of persuasion. Some may even be aware that the Land of the Free actually has, by all consensual indices, one of the worst human rights records in the world. Business as usual, then.

It is no wonder that the term 'black' – championed so proudly in the sixties – is now being supplanted by the more conciliatory 'African-American'. The implication is that 'African-Americans' are simply one ethnic group among many – Italian-American, Irish-American, Greek-American and so forth – and that it is time for a retreat from the explicit polarization of 'black' and 'white'; the classic metaphor for mutually exclusive opposites. In the fourth decade after the assassinations of Malcolm X and Martin Luther King, crosstown traffic still faces formidable roadblocks.

> I turn on the TV, your America's doing well.
> I look out the window, my America's catching hell,
> I just want to know
> Which way do I go
> To get to your America
> Vernon Reid for Living Colour, 'Which Way to America?' (1988)

Once I asked Bobby Womack what was the most serious obstacle facing the black artist who wanted to get over to a white audience. He looked at me with some incredulity and replied, 'Bein' black'.

5

Never to Grow Old

Robert Johnson, Charlie Christian and the
meteorite syndrome

Jimi Hendrix had played music for his living ever since he was invalided out of the army in 1962, but the period of his mature work as a leader spanned a mere four years: from his arrival in England on 21 September 1966 to his death on 18 September 1970. Like Buddy Holly and Eddie Cochran, he crammed an astonishing amount of creative work into a comparatively short span of time – though neither man's influence extended over such a broad range of different musics as did that of Hendrix. It is indeed possible (though unlikely) that – like Chuck Berry, Elvis Presley and Little Richard – his time as an innovator was up, and that had he not died so prematurely, all that he would have produced for the remainder of his life and career would have been mere footnotes to a body of work that was, for all practical purposes, complete. Berry, Presley and Richard, after all, were virtually different men after the watershed experiences of – respectively – jail, the army and the church.

Hendrix, though, died on the threshold of an entirely new phase in his career. He had, after much typical dithering, decided to sort out the horrendous tangle of his business affairs, and was preparing to work with the legendary arranger Gil Evans on an album and concert which could well have launched him on a fresh career as a jazz musician. The truest parallels to Hendrix's fate – and to the perennial mystery of which path he would eventually have taken from this particular crossroads – are to be found in the lives, careers and work of two men, both comparatively young, both black, who met premature ends before Hendrix was born. One was the spiritual ancestor of nearly every guitarist who ever plugged into an amplifier, the jazzman who played guitar like a horn and virtually invented the instrument as an amplified solo voice. The other was the shadowy Delta bluesman who, according to myth and legend, sold his soul to the devil.

In Walter Hill's movie *Crossroads*, an eager teenage blues fan obsessed with the legend of Robert Johnson traces an almost-forgotten Mississippi Delta harmonica player to an old folks' home in New York City. The harp man, he believes, is Johnson's last living confidant, the 'poor Willie Brown' mentioned in the last verse of 'Crossroad Blues'. The reason our fresh-faced young hero is so anxious to find the old man is that he believes that Brown is the sole remaining conduit to an unrecorded Johnson song which can make him famous. Johnson, he babbles as he chases Willie Brown down a corridor, only recorded twenty-nine songs before his mysterious death in 1937, but there was one more which he never got around to recording. If he can persuade this old man to teach him the song, why then, he can make a record the equal of famous Johnson interpretations like The Rolling Stones' 'Love in Vain' or Cream's 'Crossroads', and this will become his ticket to legendhood.

Our downy protagonist is played by Ralph Macchio, and *Crossroads* follows a pattern established by *The Karate Kid*, a previous success of his. Hollywood wisdom had decided that audiences preferred Macchio in the role of a snotty but sensitive youth who discovers his own inner path and attains manhood through initiation into an exotic, esoteric discipline by a cantankerous but infinitely wise old coot – and John Landis's film *The Blues Brothers* had previously demonstrated that white R&B fans like to go to the movies just like everybody else does. It must have seemed – on paper – like an easy winner, but the combination of elements evidently cancelled each other out, because *Crossroads* was not remotely successful. Like *The Blues Brothers*, it was not so much a movie about the blues as an insight into the fantasy lives of white blues fans, but the relative grosses of the two movies proved that the ones who secretly see themselves as hard-living roughnecks, stomping and hollering in front of a hammering big band, definitely outnumber those who want to play Grasshopper to an elderly harp man from the Delta.

Crossroads is considerably more likeable than the average Boy-Becomes-a-Man movie – it is certainly preferable to *Ferris Bueller's Day Off* (but then so is an evening at the launderette) – and the simple fact of its existence is a potent tribute to the enduring mystique of the mysterious, haunted bluesman whose contemporaries firmly believed that he had sold his soul to the devil. Its opening sequences and occasional flashback episodes, depicting Johnson, clad in the uneasy finery of a new suit, fulfilling his supernatural assignation in a flat, bare Delta landscape before making his first recordings in a Texas hotel room, seem to have come from an entirely different movie, and a much better one. Unfortunately, that wasn't the one that Hill decided to make. *Crossroads* is content to exploit the most obviously sensational elements of the Robert Johnson legend – one can almost hear the drunken newspaper editor played by Edmund O'Brien in John Ford's *The Man Who Shot Liberty Valance* pontifically announcing, 'When a fact becomes a legend, print the legend' – while doing casual violence not only to the facts, but to their nuances and, ultimately, their significance.

For a start, 'Willie Brown' was a real person, but he was Johnson's senior by at least a dozen years. The brother-in-law of Chester (Howlin' Wolf) Burnett, Brown was a formidable musician in his own right (on guitar rather than harmonica), and the composer of at least one great song of his own, 'Future Blues'. Furthermore, he died in 1952, whereas the film is set in the late eighties. Robert Johnson's closest friends were undoubtedly his stepson, Robert Junior Lockwood – still, at the time of writing, alive, well, cantankerous and playing the blues – and Johnny Shines, who died in 1992. If Johnson's legacy had included some blues equivalent of the Holy Grail, the Lost Ark of the Covenant, or a splinter of the True Cross, Shines and Lockwood were the ones who would have had it; and neither of them were exactly sitting in wheelchairs waiting for a little white boy to come and catch up the torch from their sickly old fingers. They were both vigorous and creative men, and though more than capable of evoking the phantom presence of Robert Johnson, neither had stood still musically since the thirties. Furthermore, neither fitted the stereotyped image of the Delta bluesman so beloved by folklorists: that of a decrepit old drunk with ill-fitting false teeth, pathetically grateful to be hauled out of obscurity to bang out a few tales of hoboing and cotton-picking for hushed, respectful audiences of white college kids, all of whom would be deeply insulted if anybody suggested that there was even a hint of condescension involved.

The Johnson legend is certainly an intriguing one. It links a variety of compelling myths, each one a tried and trusted favourite: we have the alienated young man of titanic gifts, forced by a crushingly harsh environment to channel his talents into a lifestyle and art form which were then heartily despised; the intensely romantic myth of the tortured artist who dies young and – like Van Gogh – fails to live to enjoy the eventual recognition of his genius; and the enigma of a man who left virtually nothing behind except his recordings. For years there was no authenticated photograph of him, nothing but the occasionally contradictory anecdotal accounts left by his peers and contemporaries. Finally, there was the irresistible *frisson* of the supernatural: the all-pervading odour of the graveyard and the conjure.

I. Psychedelic or what? Spectacular lysergic graphic. (Bill Nitopi)

2. Hendrix (far left) and Billy Cox (second from left) prepare for a 1962 Nashville nightclub date with The Casuals.

3. James Brown models interesting psychedelic-print ensemble, 1970. (Rex)

4. The Chairman of The Board of Blues Singers: a svelte and stylish B.B. King hits another *those* notes, 1968. (Pictorial)

5. Miles runs the voodoo down, 1970: *out* go Italian suits and show tunes, *in* come funny sunglasses and wah-wah pedals. (David Redfern)

6. Ain't that a man? The magisterial Muddy Waters, late sixties. (David Redfern)

7. The quintessential rocker: Chuck Berry in one of his less alarming shirts, 1971. (David Redfern)

8. A love supreme: John Coltrane 1966. (David Redfern: photo by C. Stewart)

9. The début Jimi Hendrix Experience performance. Supporting Johnny Hallyday at the Paris Olympia, 1966. (Jean-Pierre Leloir)

10. What the well-dressed nocturnal mammal is wearing: London, 1966. (Gerard Mankowitz).

11. The Jimi Hendrix Experience: Mitch Mitchell (drums),
Noel Redding (bass), and some bloke in a hat, London, 1967.
(Dezo Hoffman).
Insets: 12. With band of Gypsys (Buddy Miles and Billy Cox),
1969. 13. Young, loud and spotty: Hendrix with Eric Clapton at
London's Speakeasy Club, 1967. (Rex) 14. Star and starmaker:
Hendrix and Chas Chandler confer at the Albert Hall, February
1969. (LFI)

15. Rollin' and tumblin' at Paris Olympia, 1967. (Jean-Pierre Leloir).

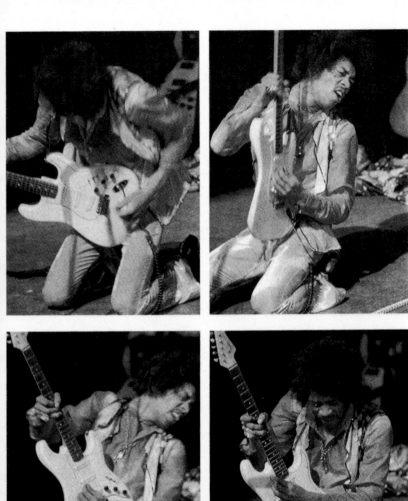

16. "UHHHH ... the name is Bootsy, baby ... " Ex-James Brown bassist Bootsy Collins in full effect. (Paul Cox/LFI)

17. Vernon Reid of Living Colour, 1988: who says a black band can't play hard rock *and* go platinum? (George Bodmar)

18. Prince's favourite guitarist is Carlos Santana; the resemblence is remarkable. (SIPA Press)

19. Sitting on top of the World: Jimi Hendrix, 1968. (Linda Eastman).

Robert Johnson, they said, entered into his Faustian pact so that he could play the blues the way he did, to describe and convey worlds of experience thankfully closed to mortal man. His songs dwell in realms of existential terror where he and the devil walk side by side, where stones are for ever in his pathway, where he is both consumed by lust and stricken with impotence, where the blues come walking like a man or falling down like hail, and tear mama-child all upside down, where God is if not dead then at least supremely indifferent to the fate of poor Bob, and the hellhounds are for ever on his trail. And he paid for it; he paid both in life and death. His voice sounds like bare trees clutching hopelessly at a grey sky: Robert Johnson was serving life without parole on Desolation Row before Bob Dylan was even born.

The blues that Johnson recorded in those pitifully few sessions during 1936 and 1937 resound with the torments of the damned. He died alone in a strange town. Some said that he was poisoned by a jealous woman, others that he was shot by a jealous man. And some hinted that he died from a conjure, cursed and hoodooed, died crawling on his hands and knees, barking like a dog.

No one knew for sure, it was said, where he died or when, or who claimed the body. After all, of what importance was the death of an itinerant black musician in the South of the thirties? Robert Johnson – the Johnson of myth and imagination, that is – drifted in and out of this life like a gust of chill wind, rattling the windows and fluttering the curtains before vanishing once more, leaving those twenty-nine songs recorded on wax discs in a Texas hotel room as the only proof that he had ever been here. And those twenty-nine songs were the finest, fullest flowering of the pre-war Mississippi Delta blues; at once a proudly, fiercely traditional example of the art of the Delta bluesman, deeply rooted in and drawing freely from the themes and techniques of his predecessors, and the work of a uniquely sensitive and creative individual artist, fully the equal of any American artist of the twentieth century. As myth, as legend, as symbol, as totem, as metaphor, this version of the story of Robert Johnson is well-nigh irresistible.

It is, of course, this Robert Johnson whose shadow hangs over *Crossroads*. In the movie, that is all that the Macchio character – or the audience – needs to know about Johnson, simply because it works better that way. Johnson remains a silhouette, a blank outline into which can be projected anything his listener wishes to imagine. Like all romantic stereotypes, it persists because it is far easier to deal with a legend or a stereotype than with a genuine human being. Both our heroes and our enemies are simpler propositions once they have been thus dehumanized; gods and devils are by their very nature incomprehensible to us, and we are thus relieved of any obligation to attempt to comprehend them.

Even during his lifetime, Johnson's impact on audiences was unearthly. Once, in broad daylight, he scared the young Muddy Waters half to death:

'He was in a little town called Frye's Point, and he was playing on the corner there. People were crowding round him, and I stopped and peeked over. I got back into the car and left, because he was a *dangerous* man . . . and he really was *using* that git-tar, man . . . I crawled away and pulled out, because it was too heavy for me . . .'

Interview with the author, *New Musical Express* (1977)

These days, we know far more about Robert Johnson than we did when his work – both released and unreleased – was finally collected on to album. We know that he was born Robert Leroy Dodds – his mother was married to someone other than his natural father – in Hazelhurst, Mississippi, on 8 May 1911. The couple separated, and young Robert was raised – and resented – by Charles Dodds, who, for reasons that need not concern us, had changed his name to 'Spencer'. Later, Robert Leroy Dodds Spencer rejoined his mother and her new husband Willie 'Dusty' Willis, thus acquiring yet another stepfather and yet another surname. When he was seventeen, he learned of his real father, Noah Johnson, and adopted *his* name, thereby finally becoming 'Robert Johnson'. As soon as he was able, he started hanging around the local jooks and dances, much to the displeasure of his mother and stepfather. He had a harmonica and by all accounts played it pretty well, but the big men around there were the guitar players – men like Willie Brown and Son House and the great Charlie Patton. Little Robert, as the older men half-derisively dubbed him, would grab their guitars during breaks in the dances and essay a number or two of his own, but he'd be making such a horrible noise that Son or Charlie or Willie would soon snatch their instruments back after complaints about Robert from the customers. In 1928, he made a serious attempt to settle down, marrying fifteen-year-old Virginia Travis, but the following year she died in childbirth whilst Robert was once again away on his musical wanderings. The baby did not survive, and the local community never forgave him. Possibly he never forgave himself.

Then one day, Robert Johnson just took off. Where he went and what he did no one knows, but about a year later he surfaced again. Son House and Willie Brown were playing a dance in 'a little place east of Robin-sonville called Banks, Mississippi'. Son House takes up the story:

'We were playing there one Saturday night and all of a sudden somebody comes in through the door. Who but him! He had a guitar swinging on his back. I said, "Bill!" He said, "Huh?" I said, "Look who's coming in the door." He said, "Yeah, Little Robert." I said, "And he's got a guitar." And Willie and I laughed about it. Robert finally wiggled through the crowd and got to where we were. He spoke and I said, "Well, boy, you still got a guitar, huh? What do you do with that thing? You can't do nothing with it." He said, "Well, I'll tell you what." I said, "What?" He said, "Let me have your seat for a minute." So I said, "All right, and you better do something with it, too," and I winked my eye at Willie. So he sat down there and finally got started. And man! He was so good! When he finished all our mouths were standing open. I said, "Ain't that fast! He's gone now . . ."'

Quoted in *The Bluesman* by Julio Finn (1986)

So within less than a year, Robert Johnson went from being a kid whose guitar-playing was so poor that people would actually tear guitars out of his hands to make him stop, to being a performer good enough to shake up Son House, one of the founding fathers of Delta blues. What happened? How did he do it? What transformed this green kid into the man whose music both consolidated the Delta tradition and extended it into new realms, the most consummate artist of his tradition, a bluesman with the jittery energy of a young man and the sand-blasted, experienced voice of one far older than his years? The most prosaic suggestion is that Little Robert holed up somewhere during his wanderings and spent the time engaged in feverish songwriting and guitar practice. Another possibility is that he ended up in jail, which is by no means unlikely – after all, a young itinerant black man with a guitar wouldn't exactly have had to commit any major breaches of the law to get himself put away in the Delta of the thirties. Even being in the wrong town after dark would constitute a sufficient offence, as Johnson implies in 'Crossroad Blues': 'Sun goin' down, boy, dark gonna catch me here.'

So why would the venerable likes of Son House ascribe Johnson's star-tling progress to the African-diaspora equivalent of a Faustian pact? Another prosaic suggestion: the old masters were simply jealous that this young whippersnapper had leapfrogged them and catapulted the hal-lowed tropes of Delta blues into funky new realms. Unwilling to acknowl-edge his talent and imagination as such, they ascribed his newly earned prowess to demonic intervention. Any other explanation might have forced them to accept that they'd been comprehensively outvibed by a mere stripling, and clearly they weren't up for that.

But if, for the purposes of argument, we take House's testimony at face value, the Johnson of flesh and blood now intersects with the Johnson of legend, for it is during this period of limbo that he made his rumoured 'pact with the devil'. We must now leave the realm of 'facts' and enter a metaphysical realm where 'facts' simply do not apply, because – if we choose to accept what Son House has to say – the transformation of Johnson and his music was simply too extraordinary to be attributed to a period of wood-shedding. According to Julio Finn in *The Bluesman*, his pioneering study of black American retentions of West African religious practices, Johnson spent that limbo period becoming an initiate of a Voodoo cult down in the bayous somewhere. 'The tradition of making a pact at the crossroads to obtain supernatural prowess', writes Finn, 'is neither a creation of the Afro-American nor an invention of blues lore, but originated in Africa and is a ritual of Voodoo worship. It is doubtful whether Johnson could have written the lyrics of his songs without having been initiated into the cult . . .' Not surprisingly, this interpretation has generally not found favour with white critics, most of whom feel more comfortable with historical or sociological explanations. Me, I'll take the Fifth Amendment on this one, except to say that unless the claims Johnson made in some of his key lyrics were intended to be no more than simple braggadocio, and if this is what he believed happened, then for all practical purposes it *is* the truth.

The precise form of the transaction has been described by bluesman Tommy Johnson (no known relation of Robert), as quoted by his brother Ledell:

'If you want to learn to play anything you want to play and learn how to make songs yourself, you take your guitar and you go to where the road crosses that way, where a crossroad is. Get there, be sure to get there a little 'fore 12:00 that night so you know you'll be there. You have your guitar and be playing a piece there by yourself . . . a big black man will walk up there and take your guitar and he'll tune it. And then he'll play a piece and hand it back to you. That's the way I learned to play anything I want . . .'

Quoted in *The Bluesman* by Julio Finn (1986)

The 'big black man' is Legba (Ellegua? Elijah?), mischief-maker, trickster and god of the crossroads. To the Christian, Legba – along with all the other African deities whose worship the whites tried so hard to expunge from their slaves and supplant with Christianity – represents the devil. To the Voodoo initiate, he is part of the power that drives the universe, and not necessarily a wholly benevolent power at that.

Far from being a 'primitive superstition', Voodoo is a highly complex and sophisticated belief system. Voodoo symbolism and reference resound through the country blues, and through the urbanized electric country blues of the Chicago school. Muddy Waters performed many such songs, most notably Willie Dixon's 'Hoochie Coochie Man' ('Got a black cat bone/got a mojo too/got a John the Conquer root/gonna mess with you') and his own 'Got My Mojo Working' ('Goin' down Louisiana/ get me a mojo band'), not to mention 'Rollin' Stone', and explicit reference to sacred stones of power which Africans carried over with them on the slave ships by the rather drastic expedient of swallowing them (a reference that casts an interesting sidelight on the British rock band who named themselves after Muddy's song). The 'mojo' is another voodoo charm; an object of power which, according to legend, can be used to manipulate probability, and control people and events.

It was these beliefs and references that contributed so much to the bluesman's pariah status among respectable folks, who were, after all, overwhelmingly Christian (though Finn provides chapter and verse to demonstrate the extent of West African retentions in the black Christian churches). And by rejecting all that downhome mumbo jumbo, city blacks were demonstrating their urban sophistication. But thirty years after Johnson's death, Jimi Hendrix proudly summoned up his 'old evil spirit' by proclaiming 'I'm a Voodoo Chile!' Like the Delta bluesmen, he claimed for himself (in the two versions of that song) both supernatural powers ('I stand up next to a mountain/chop it down with the edge of my hand') and a supernatural origin ('Well the night I was born/you know the moon turned a fire red').

In Hendrix's case, this has always been assumed to be pure metaphor: three decades and hundreds of miles separated him not only from Johnson but the entire milieu which Johnson inhabited, and there was no way that he could have been a Voodoo initiate in any formal sense. However, in his liner note for the original 1994 edition of the compilation *Blues*, Michael Fairchild quotes an intriguing assertion from former John Lee Hooker sidekick Eddie Kirkland: that in 1956 Kirkland had met a thirteen-year-old Jimmy Hendrix in Georgia. Presumably he had been brought there, without his father's knowledge, by his mother Lucille, who had kin down in Macon. It was there, Kirkland says, that young

Jimmy first became obsessed with the guitar and with the blues. Clearly, that suggests that he was initiated into *something* down there; if, that is, the trip took place at all. Al Hendrix denies it, but then he was the last person Jimmy or Lucille would have told. Nevertheless, both with 'Voodoo Chile' – and, most specifically, with the West African even-before-Bo-Diddley beat he percussively scratches from his guitar and wah-wah pedal at the beginning of 'Voodoo Chile (Slight Return)' – he is announcing as explicitly as possible that he is a man of the blues, and one who honours, respects and understands its deepest and most profound traditions.

When Robert Johnson was summoned to San Antonio to make his first recordings, the golden age of downhome Delta blues was almost over. In the urban centres of America, far away from the Southland, it was the age of swing, and nationwide radio hook-ups brought the music of Duke Ellington and Count Basie (not to mention Benny Goodman, the Dorsey brothers' bands, Artie Shaw and others) into the homes of anybody who could get their hands on a radio. In Chicago, the old-time Delta blues was already beginning its transformation into an urban music as Delta migrants like Big Bill Broonzy were recording with jazz musicians. The electrified-ensemble, citified country blues generically known today as 'Chicago blues' – typified by the Muddy Waters bands of the fifties – was still a decade and a half away, but in the Southwest Territories of Texas, Kansas and Oklahoma, as well as on the West Coast, a new kind of blues was emerging; one which set big-voiced blues shouters against funkier variations on the swing-band format. Charlie Patton and Blind Lemon Jefferson were dead. Son House and Skip James were virtually in retire-ment, Muddy Waters had only taken up the guitar a few years earlier, B. B. King was just eleven years old, and in Los Angeles, a transplanted Oklahoman named T-Bone Walker was already a featured soloist on elec-tric guitar with Les Hite's big band. In 1936, the notion of recording a downhome singer/guitarist without even the rudimentary support of bass and drums was already verging on anachronism.

Still, a talent scout named Ernie Oertles decided to take a chance on the young man, and arranged for him to record for Don Law of ARC Records. Unlike the bluesmen of even a few years earlier, Johnson was familiar with recorded blues. Indeed, he was one of the first bluesmen to have learnt significantly from the recordings of others rather than simply reworking and extending the ideas of local musicians through the 'folk' process, and his songs were virtually conceived to be recorded: tightly constructed both musically and lyrically, custom-built for the three-minute format of the 78 rpm record. Though he could entertain in a bar or a country dance just as well as any other bluesman – extending a song with improvised verses, and keeping the beat going for as long as the dancers could stay on their feet – his recorded blues are complete, final. Each one builds on its themes – lashed around the scaffolding of his taut, sinewy guitar – reaches its climax, and is over. It is as if the sheer fact of the existence of recording shaped Johnson's music, the notion that a song's ultimate destiny was to become a single, rather than a boogie for dancers which might go on for as long as half an hour. Recording had broken down and irrevocably transformed the folk process, and Johnson demonstrated this perfectly, both in the manner in which he assimilated musical materials from records, and explicitly designed his own music for the recording process. For Johnson, in short, it was not the song which was the final stage in the process, but the record.

Robert Palmer has, in *Deep Blues*, described Johnson as 'the Mississippi Delta's first modern bluesman' and the description can hardly be bettered. The music he recorded for Law on his first day in front of a microphone – Monday 23 November 1936 – included: 'I Believe I'll Dust My Broom' (derived from a throw-away line in an old Kokomo Arnold record and most frequently associated with Elmore James, though the first electric post-war recording of the song was by Johnson's step-son Robert Junior Lockwood); 'Ramblin' on My Mind' (borrowed by Eric Clapton for his début as a lead vocalist on John Mayall's *Blues Breakers* album); 'Come on in My Kitchen' (performed by Mick Jagger in Nicholas Roeg's *Performance*, and the basis for Bob Dylan's 'Pledging My Time'); 'Sweet Home Chicago' (another derivation from the work of Kokomo Arnold and a staple of Chicago blues bands right up to the – ahem – Blues Brothers; a quick flip through my own collection finds versions by Junior Parker, Magic Sam, Earl Hooker, Freddie King and others less distinguished); and 'Terraplane Blues' (the most successful of his songs to be released in his lifetime, the one by which he was best-known during the last year of his travels, and the source of Johnny Shines' 'Dynaflow Blues', as well as most white folkies' first slide-guitar exercise). Along with the plaintive 'Kind Hearted Woman' (later to become a staple of the young Muddy Waters' repertoire), the brilliant sustained metaphor of 'Phonograph Blues' and 'When You Got a Good Friend', these were more than enough to convince Law that he and Oertles had made the right decision, even though the second session three days later produced only the Skip James-derived '32–20 Blues'.

On the third day of recording, Friday 27 November, Johnson recorded 'Crossroad Blues' – virtually his anthem, thanks to the Eric Clapton/ Cream reading best-known simply as 'Crossroads' – as well as half a dozen more songs, ranging from the southern medicine-show 'hokum' of 'She's Red Hot' (allegedly composed by one of Johnson's brothers) to the terrifying 'If I Had Possession over Judgement Day'. A highly personalized version of the Delta staple variously known as 'Minglewood Blues' and 'Rollin' and Tumblin'' (the latter most familiar through later recordings by Muddy Waters and Cream), it is an utterly driven performance, the beat revved up to the point where it almost shakes itself apart, the voice cracking with fear and rage. 'If I had possession over judgement day,' Johnson sings furiously, 'Lord, then the little woman that I'm lovin' wouldn't have no right to pray.' A line which transfixes the listener with its pitiless unforgiving rancour, it insists on a life without hope, a life where all possible recourse to a benevolent higher authority has been blocked – the life which Johnson himself led. As he insists in another song recorded the same day, the 'Last Fair Deal Gone Down'. In other words, from here on in the dice are loaded against you, and you're betting against the house.

Also recorded that day were the Son House derivative 'Preachin' Blues' and the most explicit of Johnson's series of songs about impotence. Because 'Dead Shrimp Blues' is more graphic than 'Terraplane Blues' or 'Stones in My Passway', it is less celebrated – after all, it is hardly possible to get *more* graphic than 'I got dead shrimps, baby, someone is fishing in my pond/I tried my best bait, baby, and I can't do that no more.' No greater contrast is imaginable with the standard phallic brag of the country blues: we are a long way away from Blind Lemon Jefferson (and John Lee Hooker after him) boasting of the 'black snake crawlin'' in his room. It would seem that, even in order to become the greatest living singer and composer of down-home blues, dealing with the devil had its drawbacks.

Seven months later, Johnson was back before Law's microphone, this time in a disused warehouse in Dallas. The first day's recording produced three songs: the lilting, ragtimey, Carolinas-styled 'Four Till Late' (borrowed by Cream for the same album on which they had included 'Rollin' and Tumblin''); 'Steady Rolling Man' (a relatively relaxed piece of sexual braggadocio recorded by Eric Clapton on his first post-heroin album); and one of Johnson's towering masterpieces, 'Stones in My Passway'.

Once again, the singer is trapped; this time, 'I got stones in my passway and my road seems dark as night/I have pains in my heart, they have taken my appetite'. He can desire his woman only when she rejects him, his potency deserts him when he is with her, and he has been betrayed by his enemies (an interesting turn of phrase; one's enemies can torment and frustrate, but surely it takes a friend to betray). The music is wound up tight as an over-tuned guitar string; just like the singer himself, you expect the strings to snap under the strain to which he subjects them, but in the universe inhabited and depicted by Johnson, relief cannot come that easily.

The next day was Johnson's last as a recording artist. It resulted in ten songs going down, amongst them his most exquisitely painful and hope-less love song, 'Love in Vain' (a derivation from Leroy Carr's '[In the Evening] When the Sun Goes Down', recorded twice by The Rolling Stones, once rather stiffly in the studio and later, far more successfully, in concert) and his two most explicitly haunted pieces, 'Hellhound on My Trail' and 'Me and the Devil'. Here, all ambiguity vanishes; all mists are dispelled by an icy blast, leaving Johnson's view of his relationships with the powers that rule the universe utterly and horrifyingly specific. 'Hell-hound on My Trail' was the first song he cut that day, and the bottleneck he wore on the little finger of his left hand makes the treble strings of his guitar moan like wind through dead trees; the discomfort is increased by the eerie dissonance between the vocal line and the guitar. 'Got to keep moving, I got to keep moving/blues falling down like hail/got to keep moving, got to keep moving, hellhound on my trail,' he sings. Then the vision of endless pursuit by implacable damnation is interrupted by a heart-breaking vision of domestic bliss: Johnson and his lover on Christ-mas Eve, just 'passing the time away' before the horror returns. This time, the woman is his nemesis: she 'sprinkled hot foot powder all around my door' to prevent him from ever settling down. He is back out on the road somewhere ('I can hear the wind rising, the leaves are trembling on the trees'), the hellhound is still on his trail, and he is hoping against hope for that domesticity which had for ever been forbidden him.

'Me and the Devil Blues', cut less than an hour later, affords little more comfort. This time, there is a knock on Johnson's door early one morn-ing; he greets his visitor with the simple chilling line, 'Good morning Satan, I believe it's time to go'. Terror has given way to acceptance; the horror has become mere commonplace, and Johnson and the devil now go 'walking side by side'. In the earlier 'Kind Hearted Woman', he had reflected on his inability to share his life with another ('I mistreated my babe, and I can't see no reason why/every time I think about it I just wring my hands and cry'), but now things are more stark and unjust even than before: 'I got to beat my woman before I can get satisfied'. Far from fearing death, he now longs for it: 'Bury my body down by the highway side/so my old evil spirit can grab a Greyhound bus and ride.' This is not the song of a man on the edge; it is the work of someone who has long ago crossed that shadowy border and is trying to send word back. Even in the comparatively light-hearted Lonnie Johnson derivation 'Malted Milk' (one of the lesser songs in his repertoire), he remarks, 'My doorknob keeps on turning, must be spooks around my bed/I have a warm old feeling and the hair rising on my head.' It is little wonder, then, that the optimism of 'Honeymoon Blues' is so transparently unattainable; in 'Love in Vain', we find him accompanying his lover to the station, carrying her suitcase. She leaves, he stays, and all his love is in vain; another instalment of the price he has paid. 'Love in Vain' is undoubtedly Johnson's most beautiful song, one that aches with a sense of perpetual loss.

That last session included a few other songs: 'Travelin' Riverside Blues' uses the same 'Rollin' and Tumblin'' pattern as 'If I Had Possession over Judgement Day', and it has suffered the unusual fate of double cannibalization. Eric Clapton borrowed one of the verses and inserted it into Cream's 'Crossroads' after the guitar solo, and Led Zeppelin lifted the now-notorious line, 'You can squeeze my lemon 'til the juice run down my leg' for their 'Lemon Song'. 'Stop Breakin' Down' surfaced on The Rolling Stones' *Exile on Main Street* album; they doubtless relished the contrast between the brag of the chorus ('stuff I got'll bust your brains out, baby, it'll make you lose your mind') and the travails of the verses. 'Drunken Hearted Man' is a warning against sin and booze combined with a plaint about 'no good womens', and was probably borrowed, like 'Malted Milk', from one of Lonnie Johnson's late twenties recordings.

And that was it. Twenty-nine songs and *gone*. They packed away the microphone and the disc-cutter, and that was the last that the world at large heard of the lean, twitchy drifter with the guitar. Johnson resumed his wanderings, but before Law could set up more sessions, word came down from New York that producer, entrepreneur and jazz-fan John Hammond wanted to present Johnson at Carnegie Hall. As Hammond wrote in his autobiography, *John Hammond on Record*:

For several years I had wanted to present a concert in New York which would bring together for the first time, before a musically sophisticated audience, Negro music from its earliest beginnings to the latest jazz. The concert should include, I thought, both primitive and sophisticated music, as well as all of the music of the blacks, in which jazz is rooted. I wanted to include gospel music . . . as well as country blues singers and shouters, and ultimately the kind of jazz played by the Basie band.

After a not inconsiderable search for sponsors (Hammond was turned down by the NAACP on the grounds that jazz and blues were not the sort of things with which they wanted to be associated), he eventually found sufficient financial backing to go ahead, and Carnegie Hall was booked for 23 December 1938. Hammond immediately got to work booking his acts:

Above all, I wanted Robert Johnson as our male blues singer. Although he was virtually unknown to the general public, I considered him the best there was. We discovered, however, that earlier in the year he had been killed by his girlfriend. Years later, when his records were reissued, he influenced artists as widely divergent as The Beatles, Bob Dylan and The Rolling Stones. Ironically, his death occurred just as the blues he sang were becoming popular with jazz fans. Instead, we signed Big Bill Broonzy, another primitive blues singer whose records I loved.

When Don Law heard from John Hammond, he sent Ernie Oertles out on the road to track Johnson down, but their quarry had seemingly vanished into the Delta. Eventually, Oertles pieced together information from other travelling musicians and discovered that Johnson had died somewhere out there under fairly mysterious circumstances. Subsequent research has clarified events to the point where we now know that Robert Johnson died in Greenwood, Mississippi on 16 August 1938. He had been playing a local house-party, and had thrown caution to the winds by flirting with the host's wife. Someone slipped him a bottle of poisoned whisky, and when he collapsed he was taken home to spend several days in agony before dying. He was buried in Mississippi, right next to Highway 7. As Robert Palmer drily pointed out, 'From there, it would have been easy enough for Johnson's spirit to catch a Greyhound bus and ride.'

The genial, urbane and highly adaptable Bill Broonzy played Carnegie Hall (alongside the Count Basie Band, harp man Sonny Terry, gospel singer Sister Rosetta Tharpe and a Kansas City boogie summit involving pianists Albert Ammons, Meade Lux Lewis and Pete Johnson plus vocalist Big Joe Turner) and made a reputation which kept him comfortably ensconced as the Godfather of Chicago Blues until he was eventually dethroned by Muddy Waters at the end of the forties, as well as sustaining him through years of touring the world as a much-loved and versatile entertainer. To speculate on the impact of Robert Johnson on such an audience – not to mention his fellow musicians – had he appeared in 'From Spirituals to Swing' as Hammond had originally intended, is to create a virtual alternative history of American popular music; one in which the blues of the Mississippi Delta, and specifically Johnson's wintry, hellish vision, became part of the cosmopolitan mixture that was New York's black music scene. The blues has – to this day – never been important in New York and the appearance of Robert Johnson on the stage of Carnegie Hall that day in 1938 could well have changed that. Furthermore, the influence would have worked both ways; the musical and technological sophistication of New York City in general and Harlem in particular could not have failed to affect the shy, wild Delta wanderer. Who can imagine what kind of blues Johnson would have produced if Hammond's patronage had established him in the Big Apple? Johnson was, if nothing else, considerably more ambitious than Bill Broonzy, in terms of both his career and the scale and importance of the music he was so determined to create.

So what distinguished Robert Johnson from so many other Delta bluesmen? Why did men like Oertles and Law go to such pains to record him, even though he was working in a style which was considered dated even in parts of the South, let alone among the black diaspora of the rest of the USA? On the basis of that first session, his work displayed an almost unprecedented degree of discipline. Where a Blind Lemon Jefferson would loosen the beat to the point where it virtually disintegrated – a sung line would be answered by a guitar flourish, the beat relaxing and contracting, bar lines disappearing – Johnson's work was driven by a funky beat which, whether explicitly stated by voice or guitar or simply implied by their interaction, would have been more than enough to tell a bass player, drummer or second guitarist what they ought to be doing. His guitar would snap out a bass line and answer it with a high, lonesome slide riposte – all within the framework of a tough, danceable rhythm. The man sounded almost like a band, and indeed there is anecdotal evidence of Johnson working juke joints way down in the country with pianists and drummers, sometimes even playing an electric guitar. (One reason, incidentally, why electric guitars took considerably longer to take hold in the country blues than they did in jazz and urban music generally is that comparatively fewer homes in the Delta were wired up for electricity. Itinerant bluesmen would play anywhere they could – street corners, so-and-so's shack – and even if a man was prepared to travel with an amplifier, there was no guarantee that he'd find a place to use it outside of the bigger towns. Muddy Waters, for example, didn't get his first electric guitar until he'd been in Chicago for a while and found that his old acoustic simply didn't cut it in the noisy taverns. He didn't like it much at first, either, until he realized that the amplifier didn't just make the guitar *louder*, it made it sound *different*. After that, Muddy threw himself whole-heartedly into the wonderful world of electricity, and during the early fifties, led what was probably the toughest band in America.)

Robert Johnson was probably the first of the Delta bluesmen whose work mounts an explicit challenge to the folklorist theory that individual singers are simply agents of their tradition, and that it is the tradition itself which is truly the artist. Certainly, Johnson borrowed musical and lyrical themes from Son House, Kokomo Arnold, Lonnie Johnson and others – just as *they* undoubtedly borrowed from their predecessors. But as recording first documented and then supplanted the purely oral tradition, the singer-as-agent theory becomes more and more difficult to sustain. (This doesn't mean that people have stopped trying to apply it: Harry Oster, for one, has bemoaned the corrupting influence of radio and records on 'pure' folk music to such an extent that it would not be hard to imagine him attempting to preserve a community of Georgia sharecroppers under glass so that they could continue to produce untainted country blues for his delectation and that of a few of his fellow collectors.) There is no doubt that Shakespeare and Beethoven also worked in traditions established by their predecessors, but I have not heard it suggested that *their* personal contributions were negligible, and that the tradition did all the work for them. It is because their work has survived – in the form of written words and written music – that we know what it was that they achieved; and Johnson's work has also survived, thanks to Don Law and his unwieldy wax discs, as more than simply a series of echoes in the work of others.

His music ushers us in to a distinct and personal world; recognizably the Mississippi Delta as it existed during the thirties, a world depicted also by many of his fellow bluesmen, but seen from a perspective utterly peculiar to him. Johnson's world – or, to be precise, the inner world he superimposed on the actual, physical Delta, which he and his music inhabited – was uniquely and personally his. This is the key to his greatness, and it is true of him in a way it is not, for all their achievements, true of Son House or Charley Patton or Kokomo Arnold or Blind Lemon Jefferson. This is the quality perceived by Law, Oertles and Hammond.

In their introduction to the anthology *The Existential Imagination*, Frederick R. Karl and Leo Hamalian define existentialism in terms of

. . . its emphasis upon the alienation of man from an absurd world and his estrangement from normal society, his reception of the world as meaningless or negative, his consequent burden of soul-scarring anxieties, bringing with it his need to distinguish between his authentic and inauthentic self, his obsessive desire to confront his imminent death on one hand and his consuming passion to live on the other . . .

This description could perform such excellent service as a guided tour of the themes and preoccupations of Johnson's work, that it is highly tempting to proclaim the bluesman as some sort of proto-existentialist. Unfortunately, Johnson and the existentialists – despite their extensive common ground – part company before their journey even commences. Existentialism proceeds from the assumption that God is dead, and for Robert Johnson to embrace this philosophy would have meant abandoning not one, but two systems of belief. Johnson was split by his warring allegiances – not, as the simplistic explanation goes, to the neat Christian duality of God and the Devil – but to Christianity itself and the West African retentions we call Voodoo. No matter how heartily Johnson might have wished to be free of both, he lived and died in the belief that the entities and deities of the spiritual world held dominion over him – and none of them would hear his pleas. Poor Bob was laid low by the classic nemeses – the wrong woman and the wrong bottle of whisky – but such is the power of his music a full half-century after his death that it takes no great effort of the imagination to visualize the contract that he signed at those ghostly crossroads stamped, in letters of fire, PAID IN FULL.

One of his two surviving photographs depicts him neatly clad in white shirt and black braces. A cigarette droops from his lips. He is clutching an acoustic guitar capoed at the second fret; the fingers of his left hand seem as impossibly long and spidery as those of Chuck Berry and Jimi Hendrix. His hair is cropped close to his skull and bisected by an immaculately razored centre parting. His left eye is partially masked by a drooping eyelid; his right meets the camera's lens with a hard, challenging gaze. The face of Robert Johnson is the face of a man who had made his commitment – and who knew that he couldn't back down whether he wanted to or not. The last fair deal's gone down.

Or maybe it was the next-to-last. In 1990, Sony released *Robert Johnson: The Complete Recordings*, a two-CD boxed set containing not only the twenty-nine original Robert Johnson masters but also eleven previously unheard alternate takes, most of which demonstrated Johnson's highly disciplined approach to recording by being almost identical, in both lyrics and musical arrangements, to their well-known counterparts. The collection went on to sell almost half a million copies, a result which both gladdened the heart of blues believers everywhere and provoked the likes of ZZ Top's Billy Gibbons to utter quietly wry remarks concerning the incongruity of the Phantom of the Blues ending up as in-car entertainment for BMW-driving yuppies.

In the summer of 2000, one Claud Johnson, a sixty-three-year-old Mississippi farmer, was revealed to be, and legally acknowledged as, the sole authenticated surviving heir of Robert Johnson. Armed with this validation, he came calling on the rock community to start paying its dues – it was estimated that there were at least a million bucks' worth of song-publishing royalties floating around the various bank accounts of rockers who'd cut Johnson songs before copyright law was retroactively altered. The first court case centred around The Rolling Stones' versions of 'Love in Vain' and 'Stop Breakin' Down', and the verdict went in Johnson's favour. An appeal is pending at the time of writing, but it's probably safe to assume that Eric Clapton and Led Zeppelin – to name but two – may well be hearing from Mr Johnson's representatives in the immediately foreseeable future.

And if that ain't a fair deal goin' down, then nothing is.

As Robert Johnson's career was gasping to a close, that of Charlie Christian was just about to begin. Superficially, the two men could hardly have been more different. Christian was an 'impossible rube', a good-humoured country boy who loved to play music and party, and if there were any hellhounds on his trail, he dealt with them in private. As a member of the Benny Goodman Sextet, he found a national audience in 1939; ill-health forced him into retirement in 1941, and by 1942 he was dead, still only twenty-two years old.

Yet in those two years, he had two major achievements under his belt: he had not only dragged the guitar out of the rhythm section and into the spotlight as a convincing jazz solo voice, but – thanks to his after-hours jamming with the likes of Thelonious Monk, Charlie Parker, Dizzy Gillespie and Kenny Clarke – he had played a decisive role in the creation of be-bop, and thus helped to lay the foundations for most post-war jazz. He had been a friend and colleague of T-Bone Walker, the pioneering electric blues guitarist whose style provided the basis for those of B. B. King and the unnumbered hordes who came after him, and the unwary modern listener will no doubt be astounded to find what every rock guitarist knows as 'Chuck Berry licks' popping out at them from Christian solos cut with various Goodman bands. Wes Montgomery got through his first jobs by the simple expedient of reeling off Charlie Christian solos that he'd learned by heart, and then keeping quiet when the chords got too thick for him. In short, not only every single jazz guitarist, but quite a few rock and blues guitarists as well, are still standing on Charlie Christian's shoulders to this very day – and that doesn't even include the numerous performers on other instruments who were affected by his work. On top of this, through his friendship and informal musical contacts with the highly influential steel guitarist Noel Boggs, Christian helped to shape – via Boggs' eventual membership of the Bob Wills band – that intriguing county-jazz fusion form known as Western Swing.

Charlie Christian was born in 1919 in Dallas, Texas, and brought up in Oklahoma City. He came from a highly musical family; his father was a trumpeter and his mother played piano, and as a duo they would accompany the silent films in local movie houses. According to Pete Welding in *The Guitar*, Christian Sr went blind shortly after the family moved to Oklahoma, 'and, to support his family, sang and played guitar on the streets. Eventually, his three sons joined him in his sidewalk minstrelsy, Clarence playing violin and mandolin, Edward string bass and Charlie guitar.' By all accounts, Charlie Christian was a natural-born musician. He studied music formally at school and took as his model Lester Young, the great alto saxophonist whom Billie Holiday dubbed 'Prez' in recognition of his pre-eminence. (Young was a key member of the great Count Basie band of the time; like Basie himself, he was a graduate of the Bennie Moten band. He later became the finest studio foil Billie Holiday ever had, and a crucial influence on Charlie Parker and the first generation of bop saxophonists.)

Christian experimented with his parents' instruments, trumpet and piano, but the former proved unsuitable for one of his limited lung-power, a subtle warning of the tuberculosis which was eventually to destroy him. However, his piano-playing was more than adequate to gain him local work, and he would still entertain on the streets. When Christian was fourteen, he and the twenty-three-year-old Aaron 'T-Bone'

Walker would alternate on guitar and bass, and in Walker's words 'we'd go dance and pass the hat and make money. We had a little routine of dancing that we did.' As if this wasn't enough, he would play what was by all accounts highly proficient string bass in an ornately funky and musically adventurous style which prefigured that of the Duke Ellington band's young virtuoso Jimmy Blanton (yet another youthful prodigy who died before he could do more than scratch the surface of his vast potential) and Charles Mingus. At fifteen, he was playing bass with Alphonso Trent's band – a typically swinging, stomping Territories outfit – and both appeared and toured under several other leaders, including his brother Edward. By 1937, he was leading his own band – as a pianist – when he met Eddie Durham, then playing with the Territories' top band, that of Count Basie.

Christian's achievement has been so immense that critics and historians have often attempted to gild the lily by claiming that he was the first electric guitarist ever recorded. He was undoubtedly the most inventive and the most influential of the early electric guitarists, but the honour of being first belonged to Eddie Durham. Primarily a trombonist – he had held down the trombone chairs with the Bennie Moten band, the forerunner of Basie's definitive Territories big band, and with Jimmie Lunceford's band – Durham doubled on guitar, and ended up fulfilling the same right-hand-man co-arranging and co-composing role with Basie that Billy Strayhorn did with Duke Ellington. (Durham eventually quit Basie in the early forties, and took up a lucrative behind-the-scenes role as an arranger for Glenn Miller. White bands who did not wish to feature black musicians on the stand were generally eager to get their hands on black arrangements. When Fletcher Henderson's pioneering twenties band broke up, Benny Goodman bought 'the book': Henderson's arrangements.)

Meeting Durham and receiving informal instruction from him convinced Christian to lay his other instruments aside and become a born-again guitarist. He discovered the home-made cigar-box guitars which he and his brother had constructed as children, as well as what Durham described as his 'old beat-up $5 acoustic guitar'. He bought himself a Gibson ES-150 and an amplifier, and got to work.

Less than a year later, he was back on the bandstand once more. He rejoined Alphonso Trent, this time as a guitarist, and settled in for a residency at The Dome, a small club in Bismarck, North Dakota. He speedily became such a sensation that a local music store displayed their selection of Gibson electric guitars with a sign proudly proclaiming 'as featured by Charlie Christian!' A seventeen-year-old named Mary Osborne – no mean jazz guitarist herself, as it turned out – was passing the club and heard what sounded like an alto sax distorted by a PA system. Once inside, she discovered that it was Charlie Christian. Back in Oklahoma City, Christian took a band of his own into a club which – rather optimistically – called itself the Ritz Café. He was working there three nights a week for the princely sum of $2.50 per man per night, when pianist Mary Lou Williams heard him. She ended up singing his praises to her friend John Hammond.

Hammond may have been too late to catch the end of Robert Johnson's career, but he was in at the start of Charlie Christian's. No lover of the electric guitar, he was still sufficiently intrigued by Williams's enthusiasm to stop off in Oklahoma City – which at the time involved changing planes in Chicago and numerous local stops – as part of a scheduled trip to Los Angeles to supervise a few recording sessions by his brother-in-law Benny Goodman. He was met by 'one of those old pregnant Buicks with six Negroes inside'. They took him to get checked in at the hotel where Charlie's mother worked as a maid, and from there to the club, where Hammond and Christian were introduced. The guitarist was wearing a purple shirt and very narrow, pointed yellow shoes, but as soon as he plugged in and blasted off, Hammond knew he was in the presence of something – some*one* – extraordinary. He got straight on to the phone to Goodman and persuaded him to have Christian flown out to California – which took some doing – but once Goodman was reassured that it would be the sponsors of his radio show who would ultimately pick up the tab, he somewhat grumpily agreed.

The clarinettist's first meeting with his future star was less than auspicious. In the midst of a hectic recording session which had to be completed before that evening's show, Goodman was confronted with a skinny apparition in a huge ten-gallon hat and the aforementioned purple shirt and pointy yellow shoes – not to mention a luminous green suit and a string tie – lugging a guitar case and an amplifier. It was less an audition than a flat-out brush-off: Goodman requested Christian to play him the chords of 'Tea for Two' without even allowing him to plug in. Hammond wasn't going to give up that easily. After the first set of the evening performance, he and bassist Artie Bernstein lugged Christian's amp on to the bandstand and plugged it in. When Goodman came on stage, he found the guitarist there and waiting for him. He was *not amused*. Goodman was allegedly quite an intimidating fellow when Not Amused: he had a bespectacled glare which only became truly obsolete once the laser had been invented. Raking the bandstand with said glare, he called a tune called 'Rose Room', which – since it was not based on blues changes – he felt would be beyond the grasp of the 'impossible rube'. Christian sat there for a couple of choruses listening as the changes whizzed past, and then he cranked up his volume and started to blow. Goodman virtually dropped his clarinet as Christian force-fed him dazzling solo after dazzling solo, finishing up with an unmissable cue for the leader's own re-entry. Goodman and Christian swapped 'can-you-top-this?' solos – as legend hath it, anyway – for almost three-quarters of an hour, after which the Benny Goodman Quintet became the Benny Goodman Sextet.

'He wasn't the most imposing figure in the world,' Goodman remembered in an interview forty years later. 'He was retiring and reserved, thin, rather shy. He enjoyed a good laugh. But, by gosh, when he sat down to play the guitar, he was something.' In other words, he behaved like any sensible young black man from the Territories would at that time when spending a lot of time around white folks. He was neither stroppy nor servile – neither a bad motherfucker nor a Tom – and he resolutely kept his own counsel, but he was certainly not reserved or retiring once he had his guitar in his hands. Barney Kessel – one of the most distinguished of the first generation of post-Christian jazz guitarists – has recalled his surprise at the sheer volume and aggression of Christian's playing when the two men jammed, back when Kessel was an awe-struck sixteen-year-old. 'I like to hear myself,' was Christian's gnomic explanation.

Within days of that first meeting, Christian was playing with Goodman on nationwide radio. By now Goodman was paying him $150 a week, though he performed but rarely with Goodman's big band. The clarinettist was a trail-blazer when it came to featuring black musicians with the smaller sub-groups like his quartet, quintet and sextet – pianists Count Basie and Fletcher Henderson and the great vibraphonist Lionel Hampton all featured as guest stars with the small groups, as did Duke Ellington's star trumpeter Cootie Williams, the master of the wah-wah plunger mute – but the big band was a very different matter. This did not, however, prevent Christian from becoming, in his time, the most influential guitarist in America.

It is difficult to assess Christian's work on record as the expression of a fully formed personal vision, simply because the bulk of his recordings over those vital two years were made as a sideman. Despite the fact that – as Mary Osborne has testified – many of the key phrases and melodies of Goodman tunes like 'Gone with What Wind' (credited to Goodman and Lionel Hampton) were simply licks that Christian had been playing with his various bands in Oklahoma City and Bismarck, when he or anybody else played with Benny Goodman, what they were playing was essentially Benny Goodman's music. Goodman was one of the titans of the age of swing, but his inspiration was essentially New Orleans, from Sidney Bechet and other Old Masters of the liquorice stick; the clarinet itself was an instrument on the way out, soon to be superseded by the soprano saxophone. Goodman was a formidable musician and a highly gifted improviser, but the fact remains that he is almost invariably the most dated-sounding player on his own small-group recordings – and that Christian is the most 'modern'.

Like most jazz guitarists of the time, who had had most of their hands-on experience with acoustic guitars (or even, Lord save us, the banjo), Christian had cultivated considerable speed of execution. This was necessary because of the short duration and fast decay of notes struck on the unamplified instrument, and the facility to play easily and fluently in sixteenth-notes (i.e. four notes to each beat; sixteen notes to the bar) was a basic requirement. Christian's electric guitar enabled him to hold a note for far longer than an acoustic guitarist (even though the extreme sustain which was later to become a fetish of blues and rock guitarists was still unavailable to him), and this gave him an unparalleled degree of choice and flexibility in his phrasing. His tone was rich and warm, but not as utterly devoid of edge as the plummy sound which many jazz guitarists subsequently used (probably in emulation of saxophonists like Ben Webster).

Critics have disagreed over Christian's rhythmic flexibility – James Lincoln Collier in *The Making of Jazz* accuses him of stiffness, while Pete Welding and others admire his ability to phrase around the beat – but all in all, his effect was smooth yet jaunty, witty and urbane; harmonically more advanced than most of his colleagues and yet firmly rooted in the blues. Nineteen-thirty-nine was the breakthrough year of the electric guitar: Les Paul, already a popular radio personality, was recording his electric guitar; T-Bone Walker, Christian's old spar from Oklahoma City, had just recorded 'T-Bone Blues' with Les Hite in Los Angeles; Eddie Durham cut ground-breaking solos with the Kansas City Five and Six. And Charlie Christian was the acknowledged champion.

Yet his ambitions, both artistic and personal, far outstripped his role with Goodman's small groups. Amateur recordings made with an anonymous band in a Minneapolis nightclub depict a very different Christian from that heard on the Goodman records. Blowing uninhibitedly over the changes of the standard popular songs generally used by musicians of the time as vehicles for improvisation – 'Stardust', 'I Got Rhythm', 'Tea for Two', and so on – Christian takes extended solos which vault off into harmonic realms generally ignored by the Goodman bands. The 'voice' of his guitar and amplifier is thicker and rougher; as distorted and rough-edged as that of T-Bone Walker or fifties guitarists like B. B. King or Chuck Berry. The difference between those recordings and the Goodman sides is the same as the difference between a man in his best clothes and on his best behaviour at a party where he is unsure of his relationship with his host, and meeting the same man a few hours later in his own neighbourhood bar with a few drinks inside him, his jacket unbuttoned and his tie loosened, speaking freely among friends. It is a shame that so many of his successors and imitators based their sounds on those produced by Christian in the studio (where his amp was barely on), and ended up with tones of an almost painful gentility – rather than developing the raw, vital, intensely eloquent sound he made when playing for himself.

Yet for all Christian's success and influence as a member of the Goodman organization, it was his extra-curricular activities which ended up having the most far-reaching musical consequences. Whenever he was in New York, he made his second home on the bandstand at Minton's, a Harlem nightclub on 118th Street. Run by ex-bandleader and saxophonist Teddy Hill, who had employed trumpeters Roy Eldridge and Dizzy Gillespie and led his band through Europe as well as touring with Bessie Smith in the twenties, Minton's speedily became known as a place where musicians could get together and blow after hours. Since it was only seven blocks away from the legendary Apollo Theatre, Minton's attracted top-class musicians, and it wasn't long before Christian became a regular at the late-night jams. He would arrive after Goodman's shows, still soaked with sweat, haul his guitar and amp out of a cab and hold court on the stand. Eventually, he obtained a spare amplifier which was permanently installed on the stage: whether Teddy Hill bought it for him as a gesture of friendship and appreciation or whether he purchased it himself is still a matter of dispute, but what is universally acknowledged is that Minton's was the breeding ground of what later became known as 'be-bop', and that Charlie Christian was the king at Minton's.

The house rhythm section there included drummer Kenny 'Klook' Clarke and a twenty-year-old pianist named Thelonious Monk. Since 1937, Clarke had been experimenting with a radical new approach to drumming which involved moving the time-keeping function from the bass and the snare drums to the ride cymbal and using the rest of the kit for 'dropping bombs'; emphasizing other beats with the clattering rim-shots which gave him his nickname. Indeed, Clarke's drumming probably gave be-bop its name: he would hit a piercing, metallic rim-shot – *klook!* – and follow it with a resounding *mop!* on his bass or snare. From *klook-mop* to *be-bop* was a short linguistic step. Monk, at the same time, was a gifted young stride pianist in the Kansas City tradition of Basie and the Pete Johnson boogie school, but *his* burgeoning radicalism was ignited by the advanced chords and harmonies which Christian would generate from the blues and from the well-worn changes of the pop standards. (B. B. King credits Christian with introducing the diminished chord into the blues, for example.) Combined with the adventurous rhythms of Kenny Clarke, the result was an intensely challenging music which could force the unprepared or unimaginative musician right off the stand. Clarke, Christian and Monk could turn the chonking, rigid 4/4 beat and four chords of 'I Got Rhythm' into something both intimidating and exhila-rating. The resident trumpet player was Joe Guy, an amiable soul whose position in the history of jazz owes more to his subsequent musical and marital relationships with Billie Holiday than his instrumental talents. His solos served principally to allow Christian time to recharge his batter-ies before unleashing *his* next extended improvisation.

Ambitious young musicians like Dizzy Gillespie and Charlie Parker would line up to jam, and in doing so, play crucial roles in forging a new jazz which was to combine with the economic trends that took the big bands of the thirties off the road, and consign all but the greatest of the swing bands to the history books. The only surviving recordings allow us a precious window on to those epoch-making sessions. They were made by an enthusiastic young amateur named Jerry Newman, who lugged a wire-recorder up to Harlem to catch Christian in action. Unfortunately, while Newman admired Christian and Dizzy Gillespie with a fiery inten-sity, his zeal did not stretch to Charlie 'Yardbird' Parker, the unorthodox young alto saxophonist who was Gillespie's running buddy. When 'Bird' stepped forward, Newman would switch his machine off. Still, it is thanks to Newman that we have any aural evidence at all of how Christian sounded when he was playing for himself and his peers rather than for

Goodman and his public: combining the harmonic daring and sophistication which was bop's hallmark with the assertive funk of the Oklahoma bluesman.

It is impossible to overestimate the importance of bop to the development of jazz: it was where everything that used to be referred to so loosely as 'modern jazz' started. The musical revolution launched at Minton's may have commenced as a research and development lab, or as a means of sorting out who could blow and who couldn't, but it ended up as a musical meta-language: a 'music about music'. It took the basic materials of swing and the blues and deconstructed them, and just as Kenny Clarke took the 4/4 beat apart and reassembled it, Christian, Monk, Parker and others rearranged the harmonies. Parker's famous description to Nat Hentoff of the creative processes he used to arrive at what Cab Calloway and the old guard scornfully described as 'Chinese music' will serve as well as any other to illustrate the radicalism of the bop approach:

'I was jamming in a chili house on 7th Avenue between 139th and 140th. It was December 1939. Now I'd been getting bored with all the stereotyped changes that were being used all the time at the time, and I kept thinking there's bound to be something else. I could hear it sometimes, but I couldn't play it. Well, that night, I was working over "Cherokee" [one of the standard changes of the era] and as I did, I found that by using the higher intervals of a chord as a melody line and backing them with appropriately related changes, I could play the thing I'd been hearing. I came alive . . .'

As did many other young musicians. To perform the kind of musical conjuring of which Bird was speaking, you require more than a good ear, fast fingers and a rudimentary ability to read; all of which could see a player all right in the swing bands. Bop raised the stakes: a musician needed a fearsome degree of knowledge and theory just to understand what was happening on the stand at Minton's, let alone to participate. The demands of the new music created the new élite which was to dominate jazz for the next fifteen years. Charlie Christian was all set to be at the forefront of that élite: he was very young, and developing his skills almost daily; he was thoroughly conversant with the vast body of musical theory which bop required of its practitioners, and in addition to considerable popularity with Goodman's pop audience, he had a nationwide reputation as America's foremost guitarist. There was no reason why – as the influence of bop spread – he would not have remained as much its boss as he was whenever he climbed 'Teddy's Hill' – the stage at Minton's. The only problem was his health. Against medical advice, he was still not only fulfilling all his commitments to Goodman, but continuing to show up and jam up-town. Something had to give.

As early as the summer of 1940 – less than a year after joining Goodman – he had collapsed coughing during a date in Chicago. An X-ray had detected a spot on one lung. He had never told either Goodman or Hammond of his tubercular susceptibility, but the road-life was telling on him, and his refusal to slow down had aggravated matters considerably. By the spring of 1941, Christian was seriously ill and became a patient at a sanatorium on Staten Island. Loyal friends like John Hammond, Teddy Hill and Harlem physician and jazz buff Dr Sam McKinney were regular visitors, bringing him chicken and chocolate cake and new records, but – much to Charlie's sorrow – he never heard from Benny Goodman. Unfortunately, some of his *other* friends had slightly different notions concerning his welfare. They would bring him marijuana and booze, and help sneak him out to jams and parties so that he could continue to get high and have sex. That winter, the TB became pneumonia, and in February of 1942 Charlie Christian died. He was twenty-two years old, had been a professional musician for seven years, and had been 'on the scene' a mere twenty months.

Gifted people who die young invariably become the focus of romantic necrophilia. They are adopted like Christ-substitutes, dying for 'our' collective sins, depicted as somehow too beautiful or too sensitive to live. In real terms, they are either stupid or unlucky. Robert Johnson may have died because he attempted to welsh on a deal with the devil, or – more prosaically – because he was too reckless and cocksure to care about which woman he was fooling with or whose bottle he was drinking from. Charlie Christian died because the lifestyle of a jazz musician in the late thirties and early forties was simply too demanding for a youth with a susceptibility towards tuberculosis. Even then, he might have survived if he had pushed himself less hard, wrapped up warm and gone to bed after a show instead of heading up-town in sweat-soaked clothes in order to climb up on to the stand of a smoky club and play for yet more hours; if he'd heeded medical advice earlier and risked losing his job with Goodman by undergoing treatment which could have taken him off the road for years; or if he'd obeyed the rules of the sanatorium once installed there, and patiently waited out his cure. But he was young and eager and possessed of awesome musical powers: he was established both with one of the leading bands of the old guard and the hot Young Turks of what was to be the next major wave of jazz. He could have been sensible, conserved his energies, protected his health and stayed around long enough to become an elder statesman.

Ultimately, all we have left are memories and might-have-beens and a few records and rumours: legends and lies. All these young shooting stars and comets ended up ripping themselves off as well as us: James Dean was a spoiled brat and a lousy driver; Jimi, Brian Jones and Janis Joplin just took too damn many drugs (or, in Chuck Berry's words, 'were proven wrong in taking too strong and rolling too long'); Buddy Holly, Eddie Cochran, Richie Valens and Otis Redding were unlucky, plain and simple. But what they all have in common is that we will always remember them as young, frozen in their youth, cut off abruptly in the middle of furious activity, left amidst the clutter of unfinished business both artistic and personal; incomplete people arbitrarily halted in the process of incomplete lives.

Robert Johnson played the most eloquent and evocative blues of his time or any other. Charlie Christian created a new and expressive voice for an infant instrument, the electric guitar. Jimi Hendrix embodied and extended the achievements of both of them . . . in a few short years.

> Misty blue and lilac too, never to grow old . . .
> Jimi Hendrix, 'One Rainy Wish' (1967)

6

Blue Are the Life-giving Waters Taken for Granted

Jimi Hendrix as bluesman

'Blues is easy to play, but hard to feel.'

Jimi Hendrix

'The blues is real, it's not perverted or thought about, it's not a concept. It is a chair, not a design for a chair, or a better chair or a bigger chair or a chair with leather on . . . it is the first chair. It is a chair for sitting on, not for looking at or being appreciated. You *sit* on that music.'

John Lennon, interviewed in *Rolling Stone* (1970)

'The blues are not wrote; the blues are lived.'

Johnny Shines, quoted in *Blues* by Robert Neff and Anthony Connor (1975)

On the face of it, what could be simpler than the blues? Twelve bars; divided into three lines of four bars each, the second of which is generally a repetition of the first. Three chords: the first (tonic), fourth (sub-dominant) and fifth (dominant) of the scale, which means that in the key of E, the blues is played on E, A and B, or in the key of C, on C, F and G. A couple of pentatonic scales, one major and one minor: each containing five notes out of the standard eight in the octave, one of which is smeared between the major and minor third and another between the major and minor seventh, thus becoming bent or 'blue' notes. Anybody who can play a musical instrument (guitar, piano, harmonica, saxophone or whatever) can learn, in a comparatively short time, to play something which sounds like the blues.

It'll only be something which *sounds* like the blues, though. To play or sing something which *feels* like the blues can take a lifetime.

In pop terms, the blues has been around for ever, but most published accounts place its emergence in recognizable form somewhere around the turn of the century, ten or fifteen years after the guitar's arrival in America, and fifteen or twenty before the advent of recording. Broadly speaking, it subdivided itself almost instantaneously into two strains: one urban, performed mainly by female vocalists accompanied principally by piano and optional brass and reeds; the other rural, performed by male singers either solo or in duos, generally self-accompanied on guitar or harmonica, which gradually replaced the fiddle. The men were often itinerants, and as a result were considered less 'respectable' and 'sophisticated' than the women, and it was the country blues which transformed itself into the rocking electric combo music of the immediate post-war years.

The music of the women soon declared a greater affinity with the jazz world (a woman with a good voice could make a far better living from jazz or pop), but in the late thirties – following the lead of the great T-Bone Walker – the more 'progressive' of the male singers joined forces with the swing bands, and featured both as instrumental soloists (on piano or electric guitar) and as part of big, brassy ensembles. From T-Bone Walker came B. B. King, Lowell Fulson, Clarence 'Gatemouth' Brown and the other 'lead guitarists' of the blues, and by the fifties the likes of Otis Rush and Buddy Guy had merged post-King, post-Walker guitar stylings (which drew heavily on more advanced harmonic variations on the traditional structures) into the Muddy Waters-derived Chicago idiom.

Just as gospel (or 'spirituals', as they used to be called) is present-day black America's religious music, jazz its classical music, and soul and R&B its pop, blues is its folk music. Naturally, that is something of an oversimplification: attempting to place living music into neat, watertight compartments is a mug's game (except as a map reference for browsers in record shops). None of those classifications – 'gospel', 'jazz', 'soul' and 'blues' – represents one homogeneous form of music, and all of them persist in talking to each other while rock eavesdrops.

Just as there are multifarious strands within the broad terrain of the blues, there are also innumerable definitions of the blues, and even more aphorisms which explain that the blues is *this* or ain't nuthin' but *that*. Some definitions are musical, describing the form in terms of its rhythms, scales and harmonies. Others are ethnomusicological or historical, tracing its musical elements back to their various roots in Africa or Europe. Some are inherently political, seeing the blues as the collective diary of the black underclass struggling for survival as captives in a racist, capitalist 'Babylon'. Others still are primarily emotional, adhering to the concept of the blues as a state of mind: 'if it ain't a sad song, it ain't the blues,' Robert Cray, the doyen of the young contemporary bluesmen, defiantly insists. Then there's the psychological interpretation, which centres on the cathartic and expressive functions of the music. The sociologists wheel out their tables and flow charts tracing the patterns of migration from the rural South to the big cities. And the linguistics department, not to be outdone, produce their tortuous textual analyses of country blues lyrics. It's enough to make you long for a stack of Little Walter albums and a bottle of Jack Daniel's.

'I don't really separate [Eric] Dolphy from Sly [Stone] from [Thelonious] Monk from [John] Coltrane because the common thing that links all those people together is the blues. The blues is what links [Ornette] Coleman to The Temptations or Hendrix to 'Trane .'

Vernon Reid of Living Colour, interviewed in *Village Voice* (1986)

Amplifying these remarks to *Guitar Player*'s Joe Gore in 1988, Reid added, 'The blues is really more than a structure, it's a real feeling.' He's right, of course – just as the proponents of all the previously cited theories are also perfectly correct within the terms of their chosen turf – but the blues is even more than simply 'a feeling'. The emotional range of the blues is as broad and rich as that of any body of art or literature I know about, and the quality of expression is considerably greater than most. If the blues is more than a sociological phenomenon, or a bunch of chords, licks and scales, or a group-therapy session with guitars and booze, it is an index of the *quality* of expression that can be brought to bear with instrument or voice. There is a saying that no jazz player who cannot play the blues, no matter what their musical prowess and knowledge, could truly be considered great, and while many blues players are indeed formidable technicians, what distinguishes masters from journeymen is not so much quality of execution as quality of expression.

In others words, blues is at least as much a *how* as it is a *what*. Its 'how' is the distinguishing factor which separates real deep soul from straightforward black pop (no matter how groovy), and serious jazz from both cocktail-lounge drivel and 'can-you-top-this?' musicians' twiddling. Its 'what' was swallowed almost whole by sixties rock, though no black bluesman (up to and including B. B. King and Robert Cray) has derived as much economic benefit from the music's successive waves of popularity as have its white popularizers (up to and including Eric Clapton and ZZ Top).

'If a young B. B. King with talent to burn walked in here today I'd have to show him the door because there's no future in it.'

Calvin Carter, A&R man for Chicago blues label Vee Jay,
quoted in *Urban Blues* by Charles Keil (1966)

'The kind of blues I play . . . there's no money in it. You makes a good livin' when you gets established like I am, but you don't reach that kind of overnight million-dollar thing, man . . . no way. If you play nuthin' but blues, it's hard to get big off of it. It takes years and years and years, and still kids come in and go "Who he?"'

Muddy Waters, interview with the author, *New Musical Express* (1977)

As Howlin' Wolf once said of Elvis Presley, Jimi Hendrix 'started from the blues. He made his pull from the blues.' His most fundamental musical instincts were those of a bluesman, and had he been born even five or ten years earlier, he would most likely have become one of the 'younger bluesmen'. Until the emergence of Robert Cray in the 1980s, this was the description generally applied by blues critics to the likes of Buddy Guy and Junior Wells. They were born, respectively, in 1936 and 1934; members of the last generation of gifted young black musicians to see the blues as a viable outlet for their talents and ambitions. Which tells us, fairly accurately, just when the blues ceased to express what black America wanted to hear itself expressing.

Guy and Wells were Southerners by birth, and they migrated to Chicago in the fifties, following in the footsteps of thousands of blacks who had quit Mississippi, Alabama, Louisiana or Georgia to head for one of the big cities, all of which were thriving and distinctive musical centres. Chicago, St Louis, Detroit, Los Angeles and Houston were the strongholds of the blues outside the Southland at that time, and ghetto taverns and theatres played host to the great travelling blues revues, from the cranked-up Mississippi Delta blues of Muddy Waters or Howlin' Wolf to the brassy jump and swing of the more polished B. B. King or Bobby 'Blue' Bland. The blues was dear to the hearts of the first-generation Southern migrants who formed the 'working class' within the black communities of the big cities, but by the end of the fifties, the vast majority of younger, urban-bred blacks regarded the music as an anachronism. Muddy Waters describes what happened to the older, more rural-rooted bluesmen thus: 'I'm dead outa Mississippi, the country,' he told me in 1977. 'I play cotton-patch music, cornfield, fishfry. B. B. and Albert [King] are a different style, a higher class of people'd see them, more middle-class people – in those days, anyway. Now you talkin' direct to black, because white people, if they like you, they don't give a damn.' That's a polite way of putting it. Whites, traditionally, have little awareness of or sensitivity to cultural or class distinctions within black communities. 'I have [white] doctors and everything who come around,' he continues. 'Doctors, lawyers, maybe even a judge slip in there sometime.

'But in those days some clubs would rather have B. B. in there than me, because a more white-collar guy comes in to see him. They'd want to be *sophisticated*, they'd say they don't dig the *deep* blues like me and Wolf were playing, John Lee Hooker, maybe Lightnin' Hopkins. What the hell, you can't please everybody. What do I care? Back when I was playin' for only black I always had my house full, you couldn't even get *in*. I didn't need no guy in the necktie, y'know wh'mean?'

'I hate down-home – it's so embarrassing.'

> An unspecified member of The Four Tops, cited by
> Jonathon Green in *The Book of Rock Quotes*

To Hendrix, it was nothing of the sort. Like his inheritor Prince, who grew up in whitebread Minneapolis, he came from an area without a significant black population; as previously noted, Seattle lacked an indigenous black music scene and thus Hendrix's primary musical influences came from his father's record collection and from the radio. Nevertheless, even amidst the *mélange* of musics available over the airwaves, the blues made an immediate impact on him as he told *Rolling Stone* in 1968:

'When I was upstairs while the grown-ups had parties listening to Muddy Waters, Elmore James, Howlin' Wolf and Ray Charles, I'd sneak down after and eat potato chips and smoke butts. That sound was really – not evil – just a thick sound. The first guitarist I was aware of was Muddy Waters. I heard one of his old records when I was a little boy and it scared me to death, because I heard all of those sounds. Wow, what is *that* all about? It was great.

Muddy Waters, the Godfather of Chicago Blues, migrated to Chicago from Mississippi in 1943. He got himself a job in a paper factory, but pretty soon was earning more money with his guitar; roaring the down-home Delta blues to homesick transplanted Southerners in the noisy, bustling taverns of Chicago's Southside. The step to amplification was a short but necessary one, and in the wake of his first hit record – 'I Can't Be Satisfied', cut in 1948 for the Aristocrat label, which was soon to become Chess – he formed what was almost certainly the first all-electric blues combo. At a time when the 'electricity' of the rockabilly sides which Sam Phillips was cutting down in Memphis was limited to the use of electric lead guitar and the odd touch of slap-back echo, Muddy Waters was leading the world's first real rock and roll band. His rich, chesty baritone and piercing, keening slide guitar replaced the spooky, ectoplasmic solitude of the country blues with a solid physicality and a palpable sense of community; traditionally the music of loners and transients, the Delta blues was transformed by Waters into a collective, rooted experience.

He was born McKinley Morganfield in Rolling Fork, Mississippi, on 4 April 1915; was taught by Son House and inspired by Johnson. In turn, he became a teacher and an inspiration. His bands launched a second wave of Chicago blues stars, including guitarist Jimmy Rogers, harmonica players James Cotton, Junior Wells, Walter Horton and – the greatest of them all – virtuoso and innovator 'Little Walter' Jacobs. Little Walter, who died in a street brawl in 1967, gave the harmonica both the tonal and harmonic resource of a tenor sax, and as visionary a notion of the possibilities of amplification as Hendrix himself. His strengths were his soaring imagination and his hypersensitive ear; his weaknesses were for alcohol and the demands of a massively-developed ego. Even a full decade after Little Walter's death, Waters spoke of him with the intensity of the freshly bereaved, comparing him to Charlie Parker, John Coltrane, Billie Holiday . . . and Jimi Hendrix. 'Awwwww man, he was another Robert Johnson. It's hard to find them kinds of peoples. Yeah man, those guys . . . you don't run into 'em too often. They *born* with that.'

Waters steered Chuck Berry to his first recording contract, allowed Rogers and Little Walter to cut sides of their own at his sessions and on his recording time. Like Miles Davis, he taught others to lead. 'I had a lot of mens in the band. That's why I feels that I did a lot more for blues players than anybody else I know ever lived. I took 'em into my band and made good blues stars out of 'em.' And when the young white boys started coming around, he adopted them too. Paul Butterfield, Nick Gravenites and Michael Bloomfield in Chicago, Johnny Winter in Texas, Eric Clapton in London: all of them became his 'sons'.

Jimi Hendrix, too, made a pilgrimage to sit at Muddy Waters' feet; back when he was still a struggling itinerant, he walked into the Chess studios in Chicago and found the great man in session with his band. Hendrix demonstrated a few of his new-age blues techniques and received, for his pains, a good-natured oblique lecture on the pitfalls of straying too far from the tradition. In Michael Fairchild's *Blues* liner-note, Howlin' Wolf's master guitarist Hubert Sumlin recalled a young, pre-London Hendrix sitting in with Muddy's near-contemporary and perennial rival and cutting such a dash that Wolf ended up offering him Sumlin's job. Years later, however, Hendrix sat in with Wolf again, this time as a reigning superstar, and received a savage, public put-down from the old man, who regarded the wah-wah pedal with approximately the same degree of warmth and fondness reserved by James Bond for Ernst Stavro Blofeld. Eccentricities that Waters or Wolf would tolerate from

Bloomfield or Clapton they would not accept from Hendrix. They were, after all, white boys and couldn't be expected to know any better. Hendrix was a brother and was supposed to know the rules.

Wolf's disdain for the new psychedelic blues was understandable, though. In 1968, Chess executives, who had successively marketed their downhome bluesmen as rock and rollers and folk singers (depending on what the dominant pop trend was at any given moment), had sent Wolf and Waters into the studios to record what they fondly imagined to be 'psychedelic' versions of their greatest hits. Waters' *Electric Mud* turned out to be an abomination, and *Howlin' Wolf's New Album* was worse. The cover proclaimed, in huge red lettering, 'This Is Howlin' Wolf's New Album. He Doesn't Like It. He Didn't Like His Electric Guitar at First Either.' Wolf – born Chester Burnett in 1910 in West Point, Mississippi – was a cranky old man, and he took violent exception to the blurb as well as the music: he had taken to electric instruments with great enthusiasm, and had in fact led the first all-electric blues combo in West Memphis in the early fifties. The album featured Wolf and a team of Chicago session players, including Wolf's own lead guitarist Hubert Sumlin, engaged in the curious task of imitating young players who'd started out imitating *them* – and doing an extremely poor job of it. The fuzz-boxes which Sumlin and the others (among them Pete Cosey, who later recorded some astonishing noise guitar on Miles Davis's 1975 album *Agharta*) used to mimic the overdriven guitar sounds produced by Clapton, Hendrix and their imitators as a response to Freddie King, Sumlin and *their* contemporaries, ended up sounding like a gnat in a matchbox. With the kind of publicity sense that tempts press officers to slash their wrists, Wolf told anyone who would listen that the album was 'dog shit'. He probably blamed the whole ghastly business on Hendrix.

As the black market for downhome blues declined and the old masters began to seek the support of a newly-emerging white public, they were more than occasionally exasperated by the contradictory demands which their new audiences made on them. When the blues was swept into campus clubs and concert halls in the wake of the folk boom, sophisticated entertainers like Big Bill Broonzy, who'd played electric instruments and worn good suits for years, were expected to show up wearing sharecroppers' overalls and playing old acoustic guitars. John Lee Hooker, a Delta migrant who'd settled in Detroit and recorded a series of reverb-laden blues hits which literally crackled with electricity, solved the problem by developing different acts for different settings. For a black club, he would put his suit on, arrive with a band who'd open with a medley of current soul hits, and play his electric guitar; for the white folkies, he'd dress down, bring an acoustic and perform solo. Simultaneously, he would release punchy, rocking city-blues singles for Chicago's Vee Jay label, and acoustic 'folk blues' albums for the New York-based jazz label Riverside.

In 1958, Muddy himself had received a harsh reception on his first British tour, when his fierce electric guitar and Otis Spann's amplified piano had actually driven electrophobic jazz critics from concert halls. Why, they complained, this was little better than that nasty rock and roll stuff. Six years later, he returned – acoustic guitar in hand – with a specially rehearsed repertoire of old-time Delta tunes, only to find the country crawling with groups named after his songs (The Rolling Stones, David Bowie's Manish Boys, The Mojos) and audiences packed with mods and art students screaming for songs they'd first heard at shows by The Yardbirds, Manfred Mann or the holy Stones. Still, Muddy Waters' magisterial presence and hood-eyed authority enabled him to transcend, with effortless disdain, any damn-fool white-kid notion about what his music ought to sound like, or – for that matter – what constituted an acceptable width of lapel. Other R&B veterans were less fortunate. 'The irony was', Pete Townshend says, 'that they all looked so pathetic, John Lee Hooker in his checkered jacket doing his cabaret, which he still does to this day. Somehow, they weren't able to attend to the quantum jump that we'd made. Hendrix did . . . and he went way ahead.'

Hooker, Waters, Jimmy Reed, Sonny Boy Williamson and the others surfed the vogue for what was referred to as 'rhythm and blues', but the term 'rhythm and blues' was subject to drastically different interpretations in Britain and the USA. As originally coined by Atlantic Records producer/executive Jerry Wexler, it simply meant black pop music: any music primarily produced by and for the black community, a meaning subsequently reactivated in the nineties. But its early sixties British definition came to mean anything performed by The Rolling Stones and the bands who came to varying degrees of prominence in their wake. 'British R&B' was a loose conflation of Chicago blues, fifties rockabilly and early sixties soul. The early Stones repertoire borrowed from first-generation electrified country bluesmen like Muddy Waters ('I Just Wanna Make Love to You', 'I Wanna Be Loved', 'I Can't Be Satisfied'); Jimmy Reed ('Honest I Do') and Slim Harpo ('I'm a King Bee'); the pioneering rock and roll of Chuck Berry ('Come on', 'Bye Bye Johnny', 'Carol', 'Down the Road Apiece', 'Around and Around', 'Confessin' the Blues', 'You

Can't Catch Me'), Buddy Holly ('Not Fade Away'), The Coasters ('Poison Ivy') and Bo Diddley ('Mona'); early Motown ('Money', 'Can I Get a Witness', 'Hitch Hike'); and the extravagant post-gospel testifying of Wilson Pickett ('If You Need Me'), Otis Redding ('That's How Strong My Love Is'), Irma Thomas ('Pain in My Heart') and Solomon Burke ('Everybody Needs Somebody to Love').

What all these sources had in common was an emphasis on ensemble playing; the Stones showed little interest in the strain of blues derived from T-Bone Walker and exemplified by stellar soloists like B. B. King, Albert King and Freddie King or the Chicago 'West Side' school of Buddy Guy, Otis Rush or Magic Sam. The only British guitarist capable of drawing creatively on those influences (or even mimicking them convincingly) was Eric Clapton, who rapidly turned The Yardbirds from a second-string Rolling Stones along the lines of The Pretty Things (who in turn resembled nothing so much as *Spitting Image* puppets of the early Stones) into a platform for his startlingly fluent and aggressive soloing. The dual result was a fetishization of lead guitar playing as an athletic event (who could be faster, louder and more audacious?), and a rapid split between the progressives (who used R&B as a foundation for increasingly eclectic and eccentric pop) and the purists (who craved 'authenticity' at all costs and regarded any departures from the gospel according to their favourite bluesmen as near-blasphemy). As good a demonstration of shifting allegiances as could be desired came when Clapton first quit the increasingly 'progressive' Yardbirds (he was replaced by the dazzlingly flamboyant and dizzyingly eclectic Jeff Beck) to join the earnestly 'purist' John Mayall's Bluesbreakers in 1965, and then the following year abandoned Mayall to form the 'progressive' Cream.

To put it mildly, the purists had some remarkably narrow and dogmatic notions of what constituted true 'authenticity'; by comparison, the Albanian Communist Party was an open-minded and liberal organization. Among the things they disliked: any concession to 'entertainment' or 'performing', or such 'commercial' devices as horn sections. 'Commercial' was the deadliest insult in the purist lexicon, even though the Chicago blues records produced by the Chess and Vee Jay labels were as 'commercial' as the artists and producers could possibly make them. The British blues purists were desperately serious; 'fun' was counter-revolutionary. Their music had been derived exclusively from records, and from encounters with touring American bluesmen who were most likely to be older musicians like Muddy Waters, Sonny Boy Williamson and

Jimmy Reed. What they would have made of T-Bone Walker's repertoire of hot moves (sinking into a full splits while playing the guitar behind his back or head), B. B. King's extended, preacherly monologues concerning domestic relations, Buddy Guy's fondness for playing the guitar with a handkerchief, a microphone stand or anything else that might have happened to come to hand, or the time-honoured stunt of leaping into the audience furiously soloing at the end of a 100-foot cable (a favourite trick of Buddy Guy and Guitar Slim) hardly bears thinking about. Come to that, they would probably have had a collective heart attack if confronted with the twenties performances of the legendary Charley Patton, Howlin' Wolf's original model and a guitarist given to slinging his acoustic guitar around in a manner remarkably similar to Guitar Slim, Johnny Guitar Watson and Hendrix himself. Patton was renowned for playing his guitar behind his back or neck, throwing it in the air and catching it, or pretending to ride it like a mule, stunts which his audiences adored. He was lucky that he didn't live to try pulling any of this stuff at the Newport Folk Festival.

B. B. King, for his part, invariably worked with horn sections: even in his leanest years when he was reduced to a five-piece backing group, two of them were brass players – but as late as 1966, the stern Mayall was stating in his liner notes for *A Hard Road* that 'I find [horns] an advantage on some numbers but I would reassure all our followers that I have no intention of augmenting the Bluesbreakers in the future, except for recording purposes.' (By 1967, he had hired a three-piece brass section, but life is full of small betrayals.) Needless to say, the blues purists considered Motown to be soppy girls' music and the brassy funk of Stax and Atlantic intolerably vulgar, which is pretty ironic considering that 'real soul' is currently fetishized by some of the same people who considered it 'commercial' and revisionist at the time; 'authenticity' was a matter of adherence to the letter of the blues rather than its spirit, and a fairly distorted view of said 'letter' at that.

'Can you imagine a British-composed R&B song? It just wouldn't make it.'
>> Mick Jagger (1963, shortly before The Rolling Stones realized how
>> much money The Beatles were making and started writing their own material)

'We were blues purists who liked ever so commercial things but never did them on stage because we were so horrible and so aware of being blues purists, you know what I mean?'
>> Mick Jagger, interviewed in *Rolling Stone* (1968)

'Authenticity', therefore, meant sedulous mimicry of vocal and instrumental mannerisms, rather than the emotional authenticity without which blues is simply an intriguing variant of *rock ordinaire*. For some obscure reason probably related to regional variations in vowel-sound pronunciation, Britain's most 'authentic' imitators of black American singers came from the North and the Midlands (The Animals' Eric Burdon from Newcastle, the Spencer Davis Group's Stev(i)e Winwood from Birmingham and – a little later – Joe Cocker from Sheffield), while the hotbed of British neo-blues guitar was London and the Home Counties (Eric Clapton, Jeff Beck and Jimmy Page all came from Surrey, probably the most solidly *haute-bourgeois* county in the entire nation).

Clapton, apart from anything else, was the figure who linked the two separate waves of UK R&B. As the guitarist with The Yardbirds, he was part of the post-Stones 'R&B boom', which concentrated primarily on Chuck Berry, Bo Diddley, Muddy Waters, John Lee Hooker, Howlin' Wolf and Jimmy Reed, but his subsequent period with John Mayall spearheaded the 1967-and-onwards 'blues boom' (Fleetwood Mac, Chicken Shack, Savoy Brown *et al.*), which was far more guitar-solo-intensive and drew therefore on the Three Kings (B. B., Freddie, Albert), Otis Rush and Buddy Guy. As the lynchpin and primary drawing card of Cream, he also enjoyed five or six months as the unchallenged king of psychedelic neo-blues: in other words, he maintained that status until Hendrix came to town.

'Hendrix plays Delta blues for sure – only the Delta may have been on Mars.'
Tony Glover, *Rolling Stone* (1971)

During the seventies and eighties, there were quite a few excellent reasons why most people avoided listening to the records Jimi Hendrix made before he came to London. The first, and most telling, is that most of them sounded dreadful; the recording quality was at best indifferent and at worst disgraceful, and it would verge on outright flattery to describe the vast majority of the musicians with whom Hendrix performs as being better than mediocre. The second was that the packaging of the bulk of these prehistoric sides reached truly spectacular heights of disingenuousness and deceit: one set of New York demo sessions arrives in an ornate four-volume box entitled *The Genius of Jimi Hendrix*, while the liner note for *Guitar Giants Volume I* (a random clutch of 1965/1967 Ed Chalpin/ PPX tracks issued in Germany on the appropriately named Babylon

Records label) claims – with truly breathtaking chutzpah – that 'the Jimi Hendrix sound was originally created by Ed Chalpin . . . it is rumoured that Jimi was unhappy with the way things were going after this session and . . . this album was, and is, the last of Jimi's recordings produced in the way he wanted.' It was not surprising that anyone impulse-buying one of these albums was unlikely to come back for more, especially if they were more familiar with Hendrix's reputation than his work. It wasn't until the summer of 2000 that a reasonably listener-friendly indication of what Hendrix sounded like with Curtis Knight was finally issued under the title of *Drivin' South*. Recorded at a club gig in Hackensack, New Jersey, on Boxing Day of 1965 – a mere seven months before his transatlantic jaunt – it finds Hendrix beating a bunch of blues standards to within an inch of their lives.

Nevertheless, wading through the morass of Hendrix's New York recordings can be an intensely instructive process, even if an only intermittently enjoyable one, simply because it provides a fairly reliable indication of what kind of musician he was before his discovery by Linda Keith and Chas Chandler. Among other things, it demonstrates, fairly unanswerably, that Jimi Hendrix had learned everything that he needed to know about the vocabulary of modern blues guitar by the time he was twenty-three. Scattered among the mung are a handful of performances which display a fully-formed and individual 'voice', both utterly steeped in the richest juices of the post-T-Bone tradition and restlessly eager to create within it. From B. B. King, Hendrix had learned to form long, smooth, elegantly-flowing lines; from Buddy Guy he derived jagged, angry, spitting clusters of notes; from Albert Collins and Albert King he inherited a ferocious, snapping attack at the leading edge of a note; and from Bo Diddley an eagerness to incorporate both electronic effects and the 'bad' noises that most guitarists strive to eliminate, like the screech and grind of a pick rasping against the wire windings of the lower strings. Finally, he was more than capable of travelling back to the earliest electrifications of the ominous drones and rumbles of Mississippi Delta blues, incorporating the rolling bass-string riffing of Waters and John Lee Hooker into the more modern styles.

Most important of all, he had developed a personal tone and sound all his own; one which didn't depend on any of the gadgets he used so inventively in later years. No fuzz-box, no wah-wah pedal, no stacks of huge, high-powered Marshall amplifiers, not even the Fender Stratocaster tremolo arm with which he duplicated the soaring, sliding effects of the great bottle-neck guitarists like Muddy Waters and Elmore James. Using an old Fender amplifier and a Fender Duo-Sonic guitar (a cheap, student model with a short scale-length, no tremolo and two single-coil pick-ups), he proved the validity of the old guitarists' adage that whatever instruments, amps and gadgets are used, ultimately a player's sound comes from the fingers. As a blues singer, he made up for his relative lack of vocal power with a light, insinuating drawl which was as shy and self-deprecating as his guitar was confident and assertive. Plus, of course, Hendrix had no problem sounding exactly like a black American man; no need to resort to Mick Jagger's updated Al Jolson routines.

With Curtis Knight & the Squires, he can be heard recreating and expanding B. B. King's trademark counterpoints and obbligatos on 'Sweet Little Angel' behind Knight's vocals, and synthesizing elements of all his heroes into his own personal voice on a custom-tailored varia-tion of Albert King's 'Travellin' to California', a dead ringer, in both structure and mood, for his 1967 perennial 'Red House'. His personality as a bluesman was already clearly established: his voice expressed a shoul-der-shrugging mock-indifference to disappointment, while his guitar scarcely masked the sorrow and rage behind the defiant, insolent ease with which he tossed off his licks and runs. By comparison, Eric Clapton and Michael Bloomfield were gifted, precocious boys; Hendrix was already a man.

'Hendrix put black culture on the map . . . but it was almost an archaic black style he was working in . . . it was extraordinary that he would have used the most primitive kind of electric rock as a basis for his stuff. Night after night, after he had thrown everything at everybody, the high-spot of the night where everybody would hold their breath would be 'Red House'. Everything would go quiet, he would go quiet, he would sing and play and he wouldn't even need a band. The core of it all was John Lee Hooker and stuff like that, in the end . . . just the coun-try blues, where people would have very quiet voices, almost whispery, like Jimmy Reed. In the early days of blues, there were a lot of really *intimate* singers. It wasn't all Little Richard and Otis Redding and big declarations on one knee, there was a whole other side that he used, like Robert Johnson. In the middle of all that maelstrom, he was as intimate as a country blues singer.'

Robert Wyatt, interview with the author (1987)

It is fascinating to scan the contents of Hendrix's London record collec-tion, as preserved by Kathy Etchingham and now on display at the Expe-rience Music Project in Seattle. The blues people represented therein include (in alphabetical order) Blind Blake, Canned Heat, Guitar Slim,

John Lee Hooker, Lightnin' Hopkins, Howlin' Wolf, Elmore James, Albert King (though, interestingly, not B. B.), Leadbelly, John Mayall, Charley Musselwhite, Jimmy Reed, Washboard Sam, Muddy Waters, Junior Wells and Sonny Boy Williamson: a selection ranging from the most traditional acoustic sounds through to the contemporary white bands, with the heaviest stylistic bias concentrating on the grand archetypes of the city blues of the fifties.

In later years, Hendrix would occasionally confide that he felt bored by the blues. Certainly he felt confined by its overt subject-matter ('The content of the old blues was singing about sex – problems with their old ladies – and booze. Now people are saying so much more with music'), but he could no more separate himself from the blues than he could cut off his right hand. He was keenly aware that the blues had stopped growing when black musicians and listeners had shifted their interests elsewhere, and that – despite their undeniable gifts – the young white blues-rockers had only two options available to them. One was to move the furniture of the blues into their rock and roll crash-pads; the other was to produce finely detailed but ultimately sterile reproductions of the epochal performances of the greats. On the other hand, the venerable titans, and even their younger successors, were unwilling or unable to adapt their music to the changing tastes of the sixties, and were therefore doomed to become oldies acts performing their classics to a new-age equivalent of the folkie crowds who had hauled the country bluesmen of the pre-war years out of sharecropper obscurity.

The two great exceptions shared an instrument (guitar), a surname (King) and a birthplace (Indianola, Mississippi). Albert King (born Albert Nelson, 1923–92) and Riley 'B. B.' King (born 1925) were not related – though B. B.'s father's name was Albert, and Albert King's publicists claimed for a while that the two were half-brothers – but both men were, in their different ways, capable of finding new musical direction without compromising their idiom.

B. B. was a knowing, eclectic musician, a master showman and a warm, winning personality: he had eagerly absorbed the lessons of Django Reinhardt and Charlie Christian, embellishing the blues scales with the ninths, elevenths and thirteenths with which most earlier bluesmen hadn't bothered; his bands featured first-class horn men who flavoured his music with the jump of Louis Jordan and the swing of Count Basie, and he was a fluent, rich-voiced, gospel-trained singer. Most important of all, people liked him. Like Otis Redding, his gifts were supplemented by the sheer personal warmth he projected; even when he sang outrageously male-chauvinist lyrics like 'Don't Answer the Door', 'Paying the Cost to Be the Boss' or 'I Don't Want You Cutting Off Your Hair', his unmistakable niceness communicated itself to the women who came out in force for his shows. B. B. was, after all, only bluffing; if he was *their* man they'd soon cuddle all that nonsense out of him and he'd realize that he didn't have to talk big to get respect. He was a big soulful man, a teddy bear with a guitar; when he sang about being hurt by love everybody felt sorry for him, and when he got happy everybody felt happy for him. For what it's worth, that's not simply an onstage pose; B. B. King has been in show-business for forty years and no one has a bad word to say about him.

In his definitive work, *Urban Blues*, Charles Keil was able to say,

B. B. King has never been to Europe, never done a college concert or appeared at a folk club; he has never been on a jazz festival stage or . . . directed his efforts towards a pop or teenage market. In other words, he is still singing to the same audience he has always had . . . B. B. King is the only straight blues singer in America with a large, nationwide and almost entirely Negro audience . . . though he rejects the possibility [he] may find that his blues style will in time win for him a substantial white as well as Negro audience.

Keil was utterly correct: in 1968, B. B. King played Bill Graham's Fillmore West in San Francisco. He was introduced by Michael Bloomfield and the audience gave him a two-minute standing ovation before he'd played his first note; two years later, 'The Thrill Is Gone' became a massive hit with pop and soul audiences. Since then, he's done all the things enumerated above by Keil (except appear in folk clubs with overalls and an acoustic guitar), and – though Robert Cray may yet surpass him – he is currently the most-travelled, best-known and best-loved bluesman alive. And going pop with a bang by sharing U2's 'When Love Comes to Town' in 1988 certainly didn't hurt.

B. B. and Hendrix first met in the early sixties when Little Richard and B. B. were double-billed on a string of dates in the South; one night in Kentucky, all the guitarists on the bill got together to talk after the show. Hendrix was earnest and respectful, quizzing the older man for blues lore and guitar hints, and B. B. looked forward to meeting the young guitarist again next time his path crossed Little Richard's. But by the time the two co-starred again, Hendrix was no longer in Little Richard's band; the acquaintance was not renewed for another five years, by which time Hendrix was already a major star. B. B. was opening for Janis Joplin's Big

Brother and the Holding Company in New York, and Hendrix – who had been playing a concert of his own – dropped by to say hello.

'I think he kind of saw me as a father figure,' B. B. reminisced in a 1989 television interview. 'There was no threat there because he was Jimi Hendrix and nobody could be like him, but he respected me like you would a father or somebody who's been around a long time. That's the way he seemed to look up to me . . . he would sit down and play little things to me and ask me "What d'you think of *this*?" He was still shy to me, but I could still feel the friendliness, that bit of buddy feeling. And I thought of him a bit like I do one of my sons.' B. B. was in no doubt about Hendrix's mastery of the blues. 'Jimi played blues, and he did it well. He played good blues; he just did it Jimi Hendrix's way.'

Albert King was the grizzly to B. B.'s teddy bear, and he took a different route to his breakthrough. In 1965 he signed to Stax Records in Memphis, and with Booker T & the MGs' drummer Al Jackson Jr as his producer and the rest of the Stax crew writing his songs and backing him up, he effortlessly slotted his big, fat, crooning voice and lean, mean, slicing guitar into the same punchy country-funk backdrops which worked so well for soul stars like Otis Redding, Wilson Pickett and Sam & Dave. He had hits, too – 'his influence was as inescapable among blues players as [John] Coltrane's was in jazz,' wrote Robert Palmer – and tunes like 'Crosscut Saw', 'Oh Pretty Woman' and, most of all, 'Born Under a Bad Sign' rapidly became blues standards. His guitar-style was massively unorthodox: as a left-hander, he tuned his guitar to an open chord (instead of the conventional 'Spanish' tuning of E, A, D, G, B and E, from low strings to high) as did many country bluesmen, but instead of restringing the guitar like Hendrix, Paul McCartney and most other left-handed players, he simply turned the instrument over so that the treble strings were at the top and the bass strings at the bottom. King and Hendrix had met briefly in Nashville in the early sixties and King had demonstrated a few of his tricks for the younger man: Hendrix knew King's solos so well that he and Buddy Miles were able to sing them in unison, with or without the records. 'I like Albert King,' he enthused to *Rolling Stone* in 1968; 'he plays completely and strictly in one way, just straight funk blues. New blues guitar, very young, funky sound which is great. One of the funkiest I've heard. He plays it strictly that way so that's his scene . . .'

The paradox of Albert King's playing was the knife-edge tension he created between aggression and repose. He concentrated utterly on sound and his timing, as slow, methodical and irresistible as the bulldozer he used to operate before he got into music full-time. He may have played off the same fistful of two- and three-note runs all night, but he sand-bagged you with them every time. Despite the rhythmic flexibility which enabled him to work so successfully with the dance rhythms of soul and funk, Albert's taciturn, menacing understatement was utterly country: his reticence was eloquent in itself.

His polar opposite is the frenetic, hyper-thyroid Buddy Guy, a player whose manic, skittering note-clusters Hendrix adored so much that in New York he would follow Guy from club to club with a portable tape recorder to capture each performance for private study. Playing the Ann Arbor Blues & Jazz Festival in 1967, Guy recalled in Robert Neff and Anthony Connor's *Blues*,

'. . . after playing maybe 45 minutes, I started doing some tricks with my guitar, playing it with drumsticks and stuff like that. Someone from the audience hollered out, "You been watching Jimi Hendrix!" I didn't even know who he *was* back in '67 so I called back, "Who is that?" And they thought it was a big joke . . . I went to Canada and people said "Wow! You're copying Jimi Hendrix." Well, I just kept on trying to find out about Hendrix 'til I finally made it back to New York.

'In New York, in steps Hendrix with a tape recorder. He say, "I've been follow-ing you for years. I want to tape what you're doing." I say, "Well, from what I been hearing, I've been following *you*." He said, "Well, you and I know better. Don't pay no mind to those people." . . . When I was mostly playing for black audiences in Texas and Tennessee, they would sit there and wait for [the theatrics]. But if I go out there tomorrow and clown on stage, somebody gonna call out, "You're doing Hendrix!"'

Ironically, Guy spent almost two decades under the shadow of his illustri-ous disciple before the resurrection of John Lee Hooker's career in the 1990s sparked a reawakening of interest in vintage blues stars to comple-ment the blue-wave hotshots like Robert Cray and Stevie Ray Vaughan. Guy was even the subject of a devastating put-down from the late Albert Collins, a Texas bluesman and near-contemporary whose savage, tooth-and-claw guitar attack is somewhere between the styles of Albert King and Guy himself, and who not only influenced Hendrix with his late-fifties instrumental hits, but temporarily succeeded Hendrix in Little Richard's band. 'Well, see, Buddy's been introduced to Jimi Hendrix,' Collins told *Guitar Player*'s Dan Forte in 1988. 'Buddy don't really play blues no more. He's into the Jimi Hendrix thing. I'm not sure, but I hope he knows what he's doing because, like, if I wanted to play like Jimi Hendrix – I'm noted as a blues player – people say, "Hey man, what you doin'?" *Ain't* no more Jimi Hendrix.'

Sadly, there ain't no more Albert Collins, either. The Master of the Telecaster died of lung cancer in 1993, though he was still delivering astonishingly intense performances until a few months before the end: one such late show, captured on video, featured him in a head-to-head cutting contest with Buddy Guy in which Collins actually sliced Buddy into tiny little pieces: no negligible feat by any means. Guy, however, seized the time with a series of incandescent, and highly successful, nineties albums, commencing with *Damn Right I've Got the Blues* and *Feels Like Rain*. By the arrival of the millennium, only those venerable maestri John Lee Hooker and B. B. King, respectively nineteen and eleven years his seniors, outranked him in the contemporary hierarchy of Planet Blues.

'Speaking of the modern young blues players that I've heard "live" I would certainly cram Jimi Hendrix, Buddy Guy, Otis Rush, Eric Clapton and Peter Green on the same pedestal. In my opinion they all sound completely individual but they all share the same emotional greatness.'

John Mayall, liner notes to *A Hard Road* (1967)

Earlier on I remarked, somewhat facetiously, that one problem which Hendrix did not share with Jagger or Eric Clapton was that of figuring out how to sound like a black American man. This is not so much because he *was* a black American (after all, very few black Americans are blues singers) as because he had absorbed the culture of the specific strata of black American life in which the blues had held its strongest sway. He had lived as an itinerant with a guitar, like the country bluesmen of the thirties, and, like them, he had played whatever music someone was prepared to pay to hear. His predecessors had played hillbilly music, vaudeville songs and pop ballads as well as blues; any music that they could learn off the radio or someone's Victrola. But even though the music Hendrix had played for a living was generally the R&B Top 40 and whatever hits his employers might have had, he had lived the blues in a way that none of his white contemporaries had done, whatever their talent and sensitivity, and despite the diligence of their studies.

America's erstwhile king of white blues, the late Michael Bloomfield, takes literally dozens of slow-blues choruses on 'Albert's Shuffle' and 'Really' from 1968's *Super Session*: they are awesome in their fluency, masterful in their phrasing, and idiomatically utterly faithful to the text of the law as laid down by B. B. King, Albert King and T-Bone Walker. Unfortunately, they are emotionally as flat as so many pancakes. Hendrix was 'authentic' not simply because he *was* a black American, but because he had lived as one rather than simply fantasized about doing so, as the Brits did. 'I would try to picture what [an ideal bluesman] would live like,' Eric Clapton once explained. 'I would picture what kind of car he drove; what it would smell like inside. Me and Jeff [Beck] had this ideal of one day owning a black Cadillac or Stingray that smelled of sex inside and had tinted windows and a great sound system . . . if I wanted to emulate somebody I would try to picture what they would live like and try to live that way.' Hendrix had no alternative but to 'live that way'. He spoke blues as his native tongue.

Eric Clapton, on the other hand, played the blues something like Vladimir Nabokov wrote English: with the masterful formal grasp of one who has studied so intensely that he learns the rules of his chosen language or discipline to a far greater extent than many who have always simply assumed them and instinctively operated within them. Like Nabokov – and, for that matter, like Joseph Conrad and Jack Kerouac, both of whom came to English from, respectively, Polish and French – what Clapton was able to create and express through his acquired outlet was both a revelation to and an influence on many native 'speakers'. Yet the cultural distance which provides perspective also imposes isolation; and in an art form where nuance is all, sterility is the almost inevitable result. One is reminded of the Jewish joke about the mother who sees her whiz-kid son on his yacht, proudly sporting a captain's peaked cap. 'To *you* you're a captain,' she points out sceptically. 'To *me* you're a captain. But to a *captain* are you a captain?' Sad to say, of very few of the white bluesmen could it be said that to captains they were captains.

Instead, they were rock and roll bands. They were 'R&B' or 'Blues' bands by comparison to the average run of rock and pop groups, and they were absolutely right to distinguish themselves as such, but compared to even those practitioners whom they disdained as pop musicians (like James Brown or post-crossover Ray Charles), they were rock musicians, and the smarter ones – including Clapton, Jeff Beck, The Who and The Rolling Stones – realized the fact pretty rapidly. To captains, they were deck-hands, except that they were far more highly paid. British blues bands ran the emotional gamut from A (I'm feeling sorry for myself) through B (I'm well 'ard, me) to C (I'm not tough really but I'm going to pretend that I am) to D (I'm pissed off), which is pretty much par for the post-adolescent males who staffed them and whom Robert Wyatt describes as 'a kind of slobbish aristocracy where everyone becomes like a young Eton boy on acid'. By contrast, Hendrix seemed very different. 'He was *experienced*, to use his own catchphrase, and he really knew what he was doing. He was an adult.'

The Jimi Hendrix Experience was never a blues band *per se*; apart from anything else, neither Noel Redding nor Mitch Mitchell were blues players. The former was a rock guitarist whose ambition, according to Robert Wyatt, was to be in a band like The Move or The Small Faces, and who'd never played bass prior to his job with Hendrix; while the latter was a one-time child prodigy whose previous experience had been principally in jazz, and who brought to the band a style halfway between John Coltrane's master-drummer Elvin Jones (who was Mitchell's hero) and The Who's Keith Moon. (In fact, about the only thing that can be said in favour of the musicians with whom Hendrix had played in Curtis Knight's band was that they were far more at home with the blues than the Experience, as otherwise seriously flawed early performances of songs like 'Sweet Little Angel' and the various versions of 'California Night' demonstrate fairly convincingly.) The name of the game, though, was 'progressive blues', and the use to which Hendrix put the blues was as a continuing source of inspiration for his own explorations of the common ground between what had hitherto been considered different and discrete musics.

One method he used frequently was to take a blues standard, rearrange it, and then replace the original melody and lyrics with compositions of his own. As an example, his performance at the Monterey Pop Festival included a drastic revamp of B. B. King's 'Rock Me Baby', which he transformed from an easy, swinging medium shuffle into a romping, stomping, up-tempo dance piece which would have recalled the mid-sixties heyday of the Stax-Volt sound if the guitar hadn't been playing *all* the band parts and Mitchell had stayed 'on the one' instead of circling the beat with his trademarked Jones/Moon flourishes. Eventually, Hendrix wrote, a new set of lyrics, the 'Rock Me Baby' vocal parts disappeared, and – hey presto! – there was a new song entitled 'Lover Man'. This was considerably more creative, as well as more honest, than what the Jeff Beck Group (then featuring Rod Stewart as lead vocalist and Ron Wood on bass) did with the same B. B. King song on their 1968 album *Truth*, which was to play the song almost exactly like B. B. used to while appending their own title ('Rock My Plimsoul') and composer credit. On the same album, they also hijacked B. B.'s 'Gambler's Blues' (retitled 'Blues De Luxe') and Buddy Guy's 'Let Me Love You Baby' (retitled 'Let Me Love You'). This kind of thing was standard practice among less scrupulous blues-rockers. Led Zeppelin were the most notorious – *Led Zeppelin II* lifted two Willie Dixon songs, one without even changing the title – mainly because their sales were so much higher than either their immediate competitors or, for that matter, those of the original artists. Led Zeppelin were also the most disingenuous, claiming that their lifts were simply part of the same folk process by which Delta bluesmen had reworked and further adapted each other's variations on traditional materials. Eric Clapton and The Rolling Stones were notable exceptions, being highly and laudably conscientious about giving credit (and royalties) wherever due. The Stones' collective copybook did not, however, remain entirely blotless: their first 'self-composed' hit, 'The Last Time', owed a considerable debt to The Staple Singers' fifties gospel hit 'This Could Be the Last Time'. And, as noted in an earlier chapter, Claud Johnson has come calling to demand his father Robert's dues, paid in full.

However, the most remarkable example of the alchemical processes whereby Hendrix extended the power and mystery of the country blues into his own personal dreamscape is 'Voodoo Chile', where he draws one unbroken line from the spooky, tranced-out Delta moans of the twenties and thirties to the baddest polyrhythmic street-funk of the seventies. It begins with an October 1967 session for BBC Radio One's *Top Gear* show, where the Experience recorded 'Catfish Blues', a Muddy Waters staple also known as 'Two Trains Running' and, as Muddy originally titled it, 'Still a Fool'. Muddy's version was recorded in 1951, though it is derived from a 'Deep Sea Blues' recorded at least ten years earlier by Mississippi bluesman Tommy McLennan as well as 'Catfish Blues' by McLennan's close friend Robert Petway. The song was, incidentally, a primary source for Muddy's own anthem 'Rollin' Stone'. Like 'I'm a Man'/'Manish Boy', Hendrix's favourite from his Curtis Knight/John Hammond Jr days, 'Catfish Blues' is solidly rooted in the tonality of E, without any chord changes, but its verses are of set lengths and its structure is correspondingly tight. It is, none the less, loose enough to allow Hendrix to throw in specific allusions to Bo Diddley's 'Oh Yeah' and Muddy Waters' 'Rollin' and Tumblin'', another Delta standard which shares lyrics and guitar motifs with Muddy's 'Louisiana Blues' and Robert Johnson's 'If I Had Possession over Judgement Day'.

In Hendrix's 'Catfish Blues', he improvises in (rather than on) the tradition, demonstrating his unrivalled ability to create unison guitar and vocal lines.* Here Hendrix enacts the time-honoured Delta rituals with a combination of passion and formal grasp which annihilates the barriers between emotional and structural authenticity. John Hammond Jr has claimed that Hendrix knew little about the blues until he relocated to the USA; this performance alone (even without the evidence of the Curtis Knight tapes) demolishes *that* one. Despite the inclusion of one of Mitchell's Elvin Jones-derived mini-drum solos and a few of Hendrix's state-of-the-art distortion effects, this is a *blues* performance – in every sense of the term – from start to finish.

The story does not, of course, end here. The following year, Hendrix recorded 'Voodoo Chile', a rambling fifteen-minute jam co-featuring Stevie Winwood on Hammond organ and Jefferson Airplane's Jack Casady deputizing for Noel Redding on bass, which takes up most of the first side of *Electric Ladyland*. Its opening vocal and guitar statements, performed out of rhythm before the entrance of the band, refer back explicitly to the earlier performance and, by extension, to the entire wealth of Delta-gone-to-big-town blues lore from which his 'Catfish' was in turn derived. The relationship between the blues and Voodoo as a hold-over from West African religious and mystical practice and philosophy has been the subject of at least one first-class book-length study (Julio Finn's *The Bluesman*, to which the inquisitive reader is hereby directed), but in the context of the life and work of Jimi Hendrix, it is worth reiterating that his self-identification as the Voodoo Chile functions as his statement of black identity: a staking of claim to turf that no white bluesmen (with the exception of the great Southern pianist/vocalists Mose Allison and Mack 'Dr John' Rebennack, the latter's forked tongue virtually sticking through his painted cheek) could even hope to explore, let alone annex. Whether Hendrix intended 'Voodoo Chile' as an explicit challenge to the hegemony of Western rationalism and black American Christian culture is ultimately not the point. That Hendrix was announcing, explicitly and unambiguously, who he thought he was, is.

---

*It is no accident that virtually all the pre-eminent blues masters combine the functions of singer, composer and instrumentalist (among the few exceptions are Bobby Bland, who neither plays nor composes, and Howlin' Wolf's remarkable and highly influential guitarist Hubert Sumlin, who rarely sings), whereas their most prominent British equivalents tended to specialize in either vocals (Jagger, Burdon) or guitar (Beck, Page, pre-Derek & the Dominos Eric Clapton).

> Somebody done hoodoo'ed the hoodoo man
>> Junior Wells, 'Hoodoo Man Blues' (1966), after John Lee
>> (Sonny Boy I) Williamson

> I'm a voodoo chile . . . Lord knows I'm a voodoo chile . . .
>> Jimi Hendrix, 'Voodoo Chile' (1968)

'Voodoo Chile' is virtually a chronological guided tour of blues styles, starting with the earliest recorded Delta blues and travelling through the electric experiments of Muddy Waters in Chicago and John Lee Hooker in Detroit to the sophisticated swing of B. B. King and the cosmic blurt of John Coltrane, eventually arriving at a glorious free-form noise which onomatopoeically evokes the blurring and collapse of history and category. Its lyrics, which were considered *highly* psychedelic at the time, express alienation and an inescapable sense of *otherness* by means of metaphors absorbed from Hendrix's porings through Chas Chandler's collection of science fiction paperbacks; favourites included Ray Bradbury, Arthur C. Clarke, Fred Hoyle and Isaac Asimov.

The lyrics begin with a claim to supernatural origins, epic in the scope of its myth-making and its sense of the blues as legendary:

> Well, the night I was born
> Lord I swear the moon turned a fire red . . .
> Well, my poor mother cried out 'Lord, the gypsy was right!'
> And I see her fall right down dead. Have mercy!

> Well, mountain lions found me here
> And set me on an eagle's wing
> He took me past the outposts of infinity
> And when he brought me back he gave me Venus witch's ring . . .

Again, 'the gypsy was right' refers back to Willie Dixon's 1954 composition 'Hoochie Coochie Man',* as definitively interpreted by Muddy Waters. 'Hoochie Coochie Man' has one of the most famous opening stanzas in the post-war blues:

---

*Hendrix recorded 'Hoochie Coochie Man' twice, though neither version was intended for public consumption. In October 1967 he performed the song for BBC radio's *Alexis Korner's Rhythm & Blues Show*, with his host sitting in on slide guitar; Hendrix blew the words of the last verse, but it was kept and broadcast anyway. Two years later, he, Buddy Miles and Billy Cox goofed around with it at a New York studio jam session, where he contrived to send up both Muddy Waters and the Harlem drag queens he remembered from his first Big Apple sojourn.

> Gypsy woman told my mother
> While 'fore I was born,
> Said 'You got a boy child comin'
> Gon' be a son of a gun . . .'

Finally, he paraphrases William Blake as he launches the blues into space ('Well, my arrows are made of desire/from far away as Jupiter's silver mines'), before ending with an *après moi le déluge* shrug in the face of the apocalypse as powerful as that in 'If 6 Was 9' ('Fall, mountains – just don't fall on me'):

> Well, I float in liquid gardens and Arizona's new red sands,
> I taste the honey from a flower named blue down in California . . .
> And New York drowns as we hold hands. Yeah!

'Voodoo Chile' is part of a long, long line of supernatural brag songs – in which the singer lays claim to magical and mystical as well as temporal and worldly powers – which stretches from all those early 'devil music' songs, through the hoodoo hokum of Muddy's tunes banging on about mojo hands, John-the-Conqueror-roots and so forth, right up to the 1969 psychedelic-soul masterpiece 'I Can't Get Next to You', written by Norman Whitfield and Barrett Strong for The Temptations:

> I can turn back the hands of time, you best believe I can,
> I can make the seasons change just by waving my hand,
> I can turn a river into a raging fire,
> I can live for ever if I so desire . . .

It was, after all, only poetic justice when Al Green covered the song for his first album and turned it 'back' into the blues it always really was. Yet 'Voodoo Chile' had one further metamorphosis left: a spontaneous jam with Mitchell and Redding at the behest of a film crew who wanted footage of the group recording. Hendrix combined a chant-like guitar riff he'd been working on with a percussive, muted strum accented on his wah-wah pedal, and extemporized a new set of lyrics. The ominous, chattering wah-wah sound he created for what was eventually included on *Electric Ladyland* under the title of 'Voodoo Chile (Slight Return)' became one of the dominant motifs of seventies soul and funk. It was speedily adopted by guitarists Melvin 'Wah Wah Watson' Ragin and Dennis Coffey on a whole slew of ground-breaking Temptations hits written and produced by Norman Whitfield for Motown, and taken to its apogee on Isaac Hayes' title music for *Shaft* and subsequent black-oriented shoot-'em-up movie scores like Curtis Mayfield's *Superfly* and Bobby Womack's *Across 110th Street*. The lyric, however, raised Hendrix's fusion of his personal mythology and the lore of the blues to its greatest heights:

> Well, I stand up next to a mountain
> Chop it down with the edge of my hand . . .
> I pick up all the pieces, make an island
> Might even raise a little sand.
>
> I didn't mean to take up all your sweet time,
> I'll give it right back one of these days . . .
> If I don't meet you no more in this world,
> I'll meet you in the next one, and don't be late . . .

A pre-occupation with death is not common to all bluesmen: in *Blues and the Poetic Spirit*, Paul Garon analyses a number of blues lyrics under various theme-groupings including Eros, aggression, humour, travel, alcohol and drugs, male supremacy, liberation of women, night, animals, work, the police and the church, crime and magic, but surprisingly he did not consider it worthwhile to scan for expression of attitudes to mortality. Now, if we first do Garon the courtesy of assuming that this is not simply sloppy scholarship and then discount songs which refer to death by violence, we're left with the conclusion that Hendrix's intense feelings of rootlessness and frequent suggestions in his songs that death will provide his only escape from what he regards as an intolerable existence are the expression of an existential angst that has only one genuine precedent.

And that brings us, inevitably, back to Robert Johnson. The old evil spirit of the man with the hellhound on his trail is evoked almost by rote in biographies of the sixties blue-rockers – Ray Coleman's *Survivor* (about Eric Clapton), Stephen Davis's *Hammer of the Gods* (Led Zeppelin) and Ed Ward's *Michael Bloomfield: The Rise and Fall of an American Guitar Hero* are three examples which come readily to mind – and if the subject happens to have died young, then so much the better. But the hellhound takes many forms. If Hendrix never walked side-by-side with the devil – he generally left cheap diabolism to the Stones, Led Zeppelin and the post-Black Sabbath cartoon merchants who followed in their wake – his songs are nevertheless haunted by the distinctively clammy presence of the beast's most deadly incarnation: despondency.

The deadliest traps are the ones we set for ourselves.
Raymond Chandler, *The Long Goodbye*

There must be some kind of way out of here . . .
Bob Dylan, 'All Along the Watchtower' (1968)

Entire songs of Hendrix's seem as if they are spun off from that one line of Dylan's; it is the greatest line Hendrix ever sang that he didn't write, and when Dylan returned to live performance with The Band in 1974, their performance of the song paid explicit homage to Hendrix's. (It was as if Hendrix had taken such complete possession of 'All Along the Watchtower' that there was no other way for Dylan to reclaim it.) True enough, not all of Hendrix's songs are despairing, and in many of those that are, he still retains hope that the Angel will descend to his rescue. But where Hendrix and Johnson fuse most perfectly is in those moments when they both seem to accept that, no, there *ain't* no kind of way out of here this side of the grave. And maybe not even then.

In 'Manic Depression', the churning 9/8 blues from *Are You Experienced*, there is something terribly matter-of-fact about Hendrix's world-weariness. It isn't even melodramatic; he just sounds disgusted (in the bluesman's sense, as when Albert Collins explained why he quit music for several years by saying, 'I just got *disgusted* with it'). 'I think I'll go turn myself off and go on down,' he sings, 'really ain't no use for me hangin' around.' The same album's 'I Don't Live Today' – frequently dedicated in concert to the American Indian – asks 'Will I live tomorrow? Well, I just can't say/well, I know for sure I don't live today.' It is set to a traditional Cherokee drumbeat which Hendrix learned in his childhood, and continues, 'No sun coming through my windows, feel like I'm living at the bottom of a grave/ won't you come on and rescue me, so I can be on my miserable way . . .' The steady beat has disintegrated by now as Hendrix enquires caustically, 'Ain't it a shame to waste your life away like this?' and the guitar screams like a wounded pony before Hendrix's voice, panned across the stereo picture, exclaims, 'Awwwwww . . . there ain't no life *no where!*' In concert, he performed parts of this particular section unaccompanied, as in the 1969 San Diego version included on *The Jimi Hendrix Concerts.* 'Existing! Nothing but existing!' he cursed . . . and wrenched the sound of a burning village from his guitar, sardonically interspersed with strains of 'The Star Spangled Banner'. It is chaos and carnage, an explicit link between the charnel-house of Vietnam, the riots at home, and his own deepest despair.

The Cry of Love, the first album released after Hendrix's death, ended

– poignantly enough – with 'Belly Button Window', a simple little blues performed virtually solo: just Hendrix picking and singing under a single over-dubbed wah-wah guitar playing what are essentially harmonica parts. Whether the tune would have assumed any great significance had Hendrix not died – or, indeed, whether it would have been released at all if Hendrix had been around to prepare the final running-order of what was to have been the double album, *First Rays of the New Rising Sun* – is moot; but its central conceit is as complex as its structure is elementary. In 'Belly Button Window', Hendrix imagines himself in the place of a baby waiting to be born; he wonders whether his parents really want him or, for that matter, whether he himself is ready for the stresses and pain of another life. 'If you don't want me, make up your mind,' he sings, ''cause I ain't comin' down this way too much more again.'

Ultimately, Baby Jimi opts for life, not without some trepidation:

> So I'm coming down into this world, daddy,
> Regardless of love or hate,
> I'm gonna sit up in your bed, mama,
> And just a-grin right in your face,
> And then I'm gonna eat up all your chocolates,
> And say I hope I'm not too late . . .
> I'm here in this womb,
> Looking all around,
> And I'm lookin' out my belly button window,
> And I swear I see nothing but a lot of frowns,
> And I'm wondering if they want me around . . .

Sadly, he isn't comin' down this way again.

'Blues today is mostly white people'

Otis Rush, *Guitar Player* (1987)

> Woke up this morning, both my cars were gone,
> I felt so suicidal, I threw my drink across the lawn.

Martin Mull, 'Ukelele Blues' (1973)

> Can blue men sing the whites,
> Or are they hypocrites,
> To sing the blues?

The Bonzo Dog Band, 'Can Blue Men Sing the Whites?' (1968)

By and large, the blues field has failed to respond to the challenges Hendrix laid down. He was the first and last of the space-age bluesmen; the only one to create an entirely new set of possibilities for the future of the cornerstone of twentieth century popular music, the only one to propose new ways of creating *within* the blues field rather than to heist its treasures and stash them elsewhere. Where his precursors used their instruments to mimic the rural sounds of trains and animals, or the urban clamour of police sirens and traffic jams, Hendrix reproduced bombs and riots, air raids and helicopters, exploding buildings and the screech of tyres. In the truest sense of the term, it was *modern* blues, and the gauntlet is still lying where he left it.

The blues is currently healthier than it's been for a long, long time. Paul Oliver, in his liner note for *The Story of the Blues, Vol. II*, suggests that it was the arrival of Otis Rush in the late fifties that 'presaged the final flowering of the blues as an essentially Negro music before it became the popular music of the world,' but I would argue that the blues remained black until considerably later, maybe until the end of the seventies. To suggest otherwise simply gives the white bluesmen credit which, at that time, they had not earned. The generation of bluesmen which consisted of Robert Cray and his contemporaries was the first in which black and white musicians have started out more or less equal, simply because the blues life – as it lived for so long – no longer exists in its traditional form. Everybody is learning from records, and from the reminiscences and tutelage of those bluesmen who still recall the way it was. (The everswelling suburban hordes seeking the ghetto *frisson* of eavesdropping on the voice of the black underclass these days grab themselves a handful of rap records: if there is a new music which fulfils that aspect of the blues' function, it's being made by Mos Def, Wu-Tang Clan and Busta Rhymes. But be warned – there is nothing rueful, plaintive or accepting about *this* music.)

Since the late 1970s, successive waves of fine younger blues players, black and white, have emerged and charted the peaks and troughs of the blues economy. The breakthrough which led to the major upsurge of interest in the mid-eighties, however, was the advent of two young Stratwielders, both with a decade or so of fully paid-up blues-circuit dues behind them, who between them not only made blues sexy again, but determined the course of the next few years' worth of its history. Stevie Ray Vaughan (1955–90) and Robert Cray (1953–) not only became the frontrunners of a revitalized blues scene, but achieved sufficient lift-off from Planet Blues to attain major mainstream visibility.

Cray had been a protégé of Albert Collins and his composition 'Phone Booth' was covered by Albert King, but his real forte was updated Southern soul: his synthesis of O. V. Wright's funky balladeering and his own Collins-meets-Guy raw-nerve guitar created a far more potent blend than its deceptive smoothness might suggest, paying off with the massive pop success of *Strong Persuader* and *Don't Be Afraid of the Dark*. His success helped float the boats of already established names like Collins, Johnny Copeland and Joe Louis Walker.

Vaughan, by contrast, was a scrawny street-rat from Dallas, Texas, and a major Hendrix buff whose repertoire included an insanely protracted workout on 'Voodoo Chile' and a bravura instrumental version of 'Little Wing'. He was the younger brother of The Fabulous Thunderbirds' guitarist Jimmie Vaughan, but where Vaughan Major was a virtuoso practitioner of less-is-more stylings in the tradition of Steve Cropper or Pop Staples, Vaughan Minor was a monumentalist: a hi-octane old-school showman who wrapped Hendrix's sonic mantle around gleanings from Albert King, Hubert Sumlin, Buddy Guy, Albert Collins and Lonnie Mack, serving up the resulting mix jam-hot at delivery point.

However, it wasn't until he'd emerged from rehab following a full-on substance-abuse crash-and-burn that he developed a songwriting voice to match his guitar pyrotechnics. Finally, he had found a story of his own to tell – as opposed to recounting, albeit with phenomenal fire and flair, bits and pieces of someone else's – and the resulting album, *Crossfire*, finally brought his extraordinary gifts into full focus. Sadly, it was his last as a leader: he died in a 1990 helicopter accident, only minutes after sharing the stage with Eric Clapton, Buddy Guy, Robert Cray and his elder brother Jimmie at a Chicago-area open-air show's triumphant jam finale. His death sparked a massive outpouring of collective grief from the blues community, and John Lee Hooker and Buddy Guy both dedicated their next albums to him. 'Stevie Ray Vaughan helped revitalize the blues scene,' said John Mayall. 'He was a monumental figure, as important in his own way in the eighties as Jimi Hendrix was in the sixties.'

The all-important difference was that Hendrix was an innovator and Vaughan, for all his brilliance, was a popularizer. Maybe that tells us something about the crucial differences between the sixties and the eighties.

Even before his death he had been massively influential, spawning a whole heap of post-Vaughanists, many of whom were most definitely guitarists first, singers second and songwriters a very poor third. The most idiosyncratic is undoubtedly Bobby Radcliff; the youngest include Kenny

Wayne Shepherd and Jonny Lang (both of whom were doing extraordinary things with the six-string razor before they were old enough to
require regular application of the non-metaphorical variety); and the odd
one out is Sue Foley, if only because she's female, Canadian and plays a
pink paisley Telecaster.

So what does the blues look and sound like nowadays? The last few
years of the twentieth century saw a seemingly paradoxical reawakening
of interest in pre-war blues on the part of younger black musicians like
Keb' Mo', Eric Bibb and Alvin Youngblood Hart, not to mention at least
one Grand Eclectic in the dreadlocked shape of Ben Harper, a lap-steel
innovator whose Hendrix debt is readily apparent as soon as he applies
boot to stomp box. The pre-war blues was also one of many ingredients in
the post-modern stew brewed by Beck, new-age polymath and slacker
Prince.

As was hip-hop. The genre which ate virtually all of popular music
during the nineties has left blues virtually untouched. From the hip-hop
side of the fence, overtures came from Arrested Development (who sampled Buddy Guy and Junior Wells' 'Snatch It Back and Hold It' for
'Mama's Always on Stage' from their début album *3 Years, 5 Months and
2 Days in the Life of.* From across the divide, Taj Mahal enlisted DJ Jazzy
Jay to spin a sample from Slim Harpo's 'Shake Your Hips' into the
groove, thereby turning the sublimely titled 'Squat That Rabbit' (from
Like Never Before) into one of the most hypnotic boogies on record. And
a post-Living Colour Vernon Reid made spectacular use of a John Lee
Hooker sample on his underrated *Mistaken Identity.*

Second-generation bluesman Chris Thomas's *21st Century Blues . . .
from Da 'Hood* (Private Music, 1994) was a timely and audacious, if not
altogether successful, attempt to blend blues and hip-hop. Taking as his
watchword Taj Mahal's dictum that the music is indigenous not to a place
and time but to a community, Thomas launched a determined assault on
the generational and musical barriers separating two key forms of
African-American ghetto-realist storytelling. Unfortunately, he wasn't
helped by the overly rock-friendly production, which buried his raps
under an avalanche of guitars, failing to give him the vocal space and clarity necessary for effective rap communication. And the raps weren't that
groundbreaking to begin with. Nevertheless, it represented a formal
accomplishment of some magnitude, creating something which didn't
exist before and demonstrating that it's impossible to get from Robert
Johnson and Peetie Wheatstraw to Ice-T and Public Enemy without

travelling via Jimi Hendrix. Maybe Thomas should have called himself Ice Blue. Well, somebody should.

Rather more successful, both artistically and commercially, was Little Axe's *The Wolf That House Built* and its successor, *Slow Fuse*. Little Axe, a project from Brit dubmeister Adrian Sherwood's On-U Sound System, is helmed by guitarist Skip McDonald and features his long-time colleagues Doug Wimbish (bass) and Keith LeBlanc (drums): the trio played together in the Sugarhill Records house band, providing the backing tracks for classics like 'The Message' before morphing into the dubrock terrorist cell known as Tackhead. Doug Wimbish also participated in the final stages of Vernon Reid's Living Colour project and was briefly in the running to replace Bill Wyman on The Rolling Stones' bass throne, before the final selection of ex-Miles Davis and Sting man Daryl Jones. McDonald and producer Sherwood – plus stellar guest percussionist Talvin Singh, still a few years away from winning his Mercury Prize – create an inner-space Delta soundscape both lush and ghostly, something like Hendrix's 'Pali Gap' played for ominousness rather than tranquillity, and furnish it with lyrical, ambient and sampled (Howlin' Wolf's speaking voice, Robert Johnson's guitar, and more) allusions to the worlds of dub, funk, rap and South African choral music.

Little Axe don't so much bring the blues into the modern world, as bring the modern world to the blues. The contemporary instrumentation of McDonald, Wimbish, LeBlanc and Singh is recorded and mixed to sound deep and full and rich; the samples are almost purposefully flat and tinny, as if to demonstrate the extent to which they come from, and still belong, somewhere long ago and far away. Ultimately, Little Axe's work, deliriously entrancing though it is, only emphasizes the music's distance from our own time and space, rather than its nearness. This is the exact opposite of what Vaughan and Cray, or the revitalized John Lee Hooker and Buddy Guy, or even the seemingly eternal B. B. King, showed us in the eighties: a living music comfortable in our world, rather than lovingly preserved artefacts from another.

Most successful of all, and most recent, is guitar-spanking dance wizard Moby, who sampled thrilling extracts from Alan Lomax's field recordings of the fifties into hits like 'Natural Blues' from his best-selling album *Play*. But even the title 'Natural Blues' drops the listener down a lift-shaft: the 'naturalness' of the samples itself belongs to the past.

ZZ Top combined a deep, scholarly love of the music and its attendant lore and culture with a strain of absurdist, self-mocking humour and an eager technological inquisitiveness which not only simultaneously meets both traditional and contemporary demands, but represents the most honest and creative response to the overflowing ironies of the white blue-man's role in the eighties and nineties.

However, if the blues is going to survive as more than a series of eerily scratchy voices and riffs sampled into dance hits, or as a cosy nostalgia trip for roots-music purists, it's going to require some genuinely inspiring new standard-bearers capable of creating an impact on the post-millennial soundscape equivalent to that generated by Vaughan and Cray in the mid-eighties.

Because there's still no getting away from it: *ain't* no more Jimi Hendrix.

7

With the Power of Soul . . . Anything Is Possible

Jimi Hendrix and soul music

Can you feel the spirit? . . . In the dark
Aretha Franklin, 'Spirit in the Dark' (1970)

Hallelujah I love her so!
Ray Charles, 'Hallelujah I Love Her So!' (1955)

When Ray Charles converted the spiritual 'My Jesus Is All the World to Me' into the 1954 R&B hit 'I Got a Woman', the veteran bluesman Big Bill Broonzy was shocked. 'He's got the blues, but he's cryin' sanctified,' Broonzy complained. 'He's mixin' the blues with the spirituals. I know that's wrong . . . he's got a good voice, but it's a church voice. He should be singin' in a church.' Brother Ray was indeed dealing with a potentially explosive mixture: the sound of gospel and the subject-matter of the blues, the divine and the profane, the Lord's music and the devil's. In bringing together the church and the tavern, he invented modern soul music, and nothing was really the same after that.

Nineteen-fifty-four was Year Zero in many other ways: it was the year that the US Supreme Court – in what became known, appropriately enough, as 'the Brown Decision' after a Kansan named Oliver Brown took the Topeka Board of Education to court over the barring of his daughter Linda from a local school – decreed that racially segregated education was unconstitutional. It was also the year in which a long-haired introvert-exhibitionist Memphis high-school drop-out named Elvis Presley combined Arthur Crudup's blues 'That's All Right Mama' and Bill Monroe's hillbilly standard 'Blue Moon of Kentucky' for his first single release on a local label hitherto best-known for its R&B product. And it was the year in which the popularity of blues records with black consumers began its inexorable decline. In Seattle, Jimi Hendrix celebrated his twelfth birthday; in London, the author celebrated his third.

To say that Charles's move – any more than Presley's – was not calculated is certainly not an attempt to drag out all the old racist arguments about 'primitivism': Ray Charles had – and has – a piercing musical intelligence, and when Frank Sinatra (of all people) described him as 'the only true genius we have', he was giving Charles nothing less than his rightful due. Musically, he knew exactly what he was doing, as the rapturous reception accorded to 'I Got a Woman' and its numerous successors demonstrates so eloquently, and he was also fully aware of the furore he was about to create by bridging the most profound cultural abyss that existed within the black American community of the time. Ray Charles was an intensely, restlessly creative twenty-four-year-old who knew what sounded good to him, and if he didn't realize that what he was about to do was to create a new genre which was eventually to subsume most of the black music of the time (and a good proportion of the white), then it's only fair to point out that neither did anybody else.

The profound gap between sacred and secular music wasn't simply a matter of style (8- and 16-bar patterns instead of the traditional 12 bars of the blues, juxtaposition of major and minor chords in the same song, emphasis on repeated call-and-response exchanges to raise the emotional temperature, and so on), but a matter of world-view. It was certainly not uncommon for people to patronize both the bar-room on a Saturday night and the church on a Sunday morning; T-Bone Walker's 'Stormy Monday', a blues standard which virtually every blues singer has performed at some time or another, sums the whole thing up in the lines: 'The eagle flies on Friday, on Saturday I go out to play/Sunday I go to church, I kneel down and I pray.' However, singing the blues and preaching the gospel were considered mutually exclusive practices, as the careers of many performers serve to illustrate. Blues singer Georgia Tom, responsible for some of the filthiest blues of the twenties, later got religion and metamorphosed into the Rev. Thomas A. Dorsey, author of 'Peace in the Valley' and 'Take My Hand Precious Lord', as well as Chicago's leading publisher of religious songs. (Incidentally, Rev. Dorsey made far more money from this devout activity than he ever did from singing the blues. B. B. King's experience was directly the opposite: as a teenage street-singer, he noted that those who enjoyed the gospel songs he sang never tipped him, whereas the ones who liked the blues did. B. B. therefore decided to become a blues singer.) Little Richard, one of Jimi Hendrix's more regular employers in the early sixties, has oscillated between pulpit and stage for most of his career, Solomon Burke is a full-fledged bishop, and Big Bill Broonzy himself put in time as a preacher. They all agreed that no man could serve two masters, and that the secular and divine musics must be kept rigidly separated.

Ray Charles was primarily considered, by the comparatively small number of people who'd heard of him at the time, to be a blues singer, and – shocking as his co-opting of gospel devices was then considered – it wasn't half as bad as it would have been if he'd been a gospel singer moving the other way. Three years later, Sam Cook – lead singer with The Soul Stirrers, a leading gospel quintet – had to cut his first secular record under the pseudonym of Dale Cook (the 'e' suffix was a later addition). Even so, his vocal style was so readily identifiable by gospel *aficionados* that he was speedily ostracized by God-fearing church folks who would not allow what they literally considered to be the Devil's Music in the house, and when, at the height of his fame, he showed up as a guest at a Soul Stirrers concert, the devout booed him off the stage.

The same beliefs also affected later singers like Bobby Womack and Terence Trent D'Arby, even though they were born nearly twenty years apart: Womack's father would only consent to his sons forming a group if they swore to stick strictly to gospel, and D'Arby's, who was a preacher, enforced such strict discipline that young Terence could only listen to his beloved Jackson 5 records at the homes of friends with less strait-laced parents. Many years later, after he had followed the Hendrix route and become a star in Europe, D'Arby visited the church where Al Green, one of the most influential soul stars of the seventies, was preaching. Green, informed that the young sensation of the moment was in the house, called D'Arby to the pulpit to sing. Ashen-faced and mute, Trent D'Arby stayed in his seat and left shortly afterwards, visibly distressed. Even Tina Turner, who has made a career, if not several, out of acting the *wild thang*, is still faintly disapproving of all that stuff. 'If I see a good-lookin' guy,' she snorts, 'I don't wanna sing him no *spiritual*. I just wanna let out a wolf howl!' As far as she was concerned, what Brother Ray did with gospel music was *naughty*, a little bit *dirty*. Wrinkling her nose, she likens it to Ray 'leaving a little sump'n *nasty* under the table'. And Tina isn't even a Baptist any more; she's been a Buddhist for the last twenty-odd years. Go figure.

> Some people say a preacher won't steal,
> I found two in my cornfield
> > Traditional country blues couplet, last heard in Muddy
> > Waters' 'Can't Get No Grindin'' (1973)

It wasn't just black communities that felt so strongly about it, either. At around the same time as Ray Charles was performing the musical equivalent of splitting the atom by fusing gospel and blues, a bunch of white crazies in Memphis were crossing another barrier by shoving hillbilly music and rhythm and blues into an electric blender at Sam Phillips' Sun studios. Piano-molesting Jerry Lee Lewis, the wildest and craziest of all the white-trash rockers, underwent agonies of religious doubt when confronted with 'Great Balls of Fire', a song that incorporated apocalyptic Pentecostal imagery into an account of how hot and bothered he got about his girlfriend. He was convinced that singing the song would condemn him to eternal damnation, but after prodding from Sam Phillips, he went ahead and sang it anyway.*

Thumbnail sketches of the geneses of rock and soul – the dominant genres of post-war pop – generally state that the former was the fusion of blues and country music and the latter of blues and gospel. In reality, both musics are more complex than that, and call for explanations of corresponding complexity. Sun rockabilly, as perpetrated by Presley, Lewis, Carl Perkins and assorted others, was essentially what happened when hyperactive young red-necks copped a bunch of blues tunes and sped them up to a near-bluegrass tempo. By the same token, the soul music of Ray Charles and James Brown, whose first record 'Please Please Please' was issued two years later, was indeed the application of the galvanic techniques and principles of Baptist church music to the everyday subject-matter of the blues. However, neither of these twin cornerstones of conventional pop-lore takes into account either the full extent of gospel's importance as an essential ingredient in the mix of musics generally referred to as 'country-and-western', or – even more crucial – the vital role played by the church in the saga of twentieth-century black America. It is next to impossible to understand either black American politics or black American showbusiness without considering the role of the church. Virtually every soul star, and not a few bluesmen, learned to sing in church – Marvin Gaye, Otis Redding and Aretha Franklin, to name but three examples that come rapidly to mind, were the children of preachers – and God generally gets a credit on their album sleeves (albeit somewhere between the hairdresser and the second assistant engineer). Church provided on the one hand, the organization and leadership necessary for any kind of social stability in intensely embattled communities, and on the other, catharsis, release and the will to persevere.

Its political role lay in providing the sustaining metaphor for survival, progress and ultimate deliverance: the tale of the Israelites in their

*Greil Marcus quotes the argument between Lewis and Phillips in an appendix to his *Mystery Train*.

Egyptian captivity. The words of the great spirituals and gospel songs are about one thing; the received meaning about something else entirely. Gospel's most enduring legacy to black music is the ability to communicate an infinity of layers of meaning through the nuances between the lines and between the notes, through emphasis and pronunciation and vocal (or instrumental) texture. Even the most banal pop song can be animated by a soul singer who has something urgent to communicate: you have only to compare Engelbert Humperdinck's 'Release Me' (the most hated and despised British Number One single of 1967, as far as everybody I knew was concerned) with Esther Phillips's take on what was virtually the same arrangement of the same song.

To cite the most extreme and unfair example I can think of, let's compare Paul McCartney's Beatle classics 'Yesterday' and 'Eleanor Rigby' with Ray Charles's interpretation of the same songs. McCartney sings as a young man who sounds even younger; his boyish tenor seems unblemished by experience. Brother Ray, by contrast, is a dozen or so years McCartney's senior, and his seamed, grainy voice bears the audible scars of a lifetime's joy and pain. When McCartney sings, 'Suddenly/I'm not half the man I used to be', the line is almost too big for him: *what* kind of man did he used to be? Charles's reading of the same line carries a sense of loss that is almost painful in its immediacy; an entire lifetime is evoked, the entire tragic history of black people in America adds its shading and weight. Similarly, Charles translates 'Eleanor Rigby' from the dank Liverpool Irish Catholic church conjured up by McCartney to a store-front Baptist church in a big-city ghetto or a small southern burg somewhere. Where McCartney sings like a compassionate angel looking down on Father McKenzie and poor Eleanor, Brother Ray is right there in the congregation.

It isn't even a simple matter of Ray Charles being a 'better' singer than Paul McCartney, or a 'better' anything else; both men have strung the tightrope of their brilliance over the abyss of their capacity for banality, and have both triumphs and pratfalls aplenty in their dossiers. It's not even that Ray has 'soul' and Macca hasn't. It's simply that some people allow their soul closer to the surface than others. (Even this interpretative genius can be taken too far, though: by the late seventies, it seemed as if Aretha Franklin had been told so often that she could sing the phone book and render it transcendental, that that had indeed become her aim. Eventually, her sales slackened to the point where she had to stop singing the damn phone book and get back to *songs*.)

Gospel's message of hope also transferred itself seamlessly to the black political struggle. An aspiring black politician doesn't actually have to be a preacher (Rev. Jesse Jackson notwithstanding), but he does have to know how to move a gathering like one. Likewise, in showbusiness terms, the preacher provides the soul singer's most essential role model. Curtis Mayfield's sixties recordings with The Impressions ('We're a Winner', 'Keep on Pushing' and, most explicit of all, 'People Get Ready') are merely the most overt examples of the linkage between the ideas of divine and temporal salvation, and the *œuvres* of Aretha Franklin (the daughter of Rev. C. L. Franklin, the most popular and admired preacher this side of Martin Luther King himself) and Al Green (whose ministry began after a St-Paul-at-Damascus type encounter with a very angry woman and a tub of hot grits) present easily the most convincing equation of religious and sexual passions.

> Good God Almighty, the man sho' makes me feel . . . so . . .
> Gooo-oooo-oooo-ooooodd!
>
> Aretha Franklin, 'Dr Feelgood' (1967)

Black church is a *show*, and – except in the Deep South – white church is *boring*. Black Christianity, after all, still draws heavily on West African notions of the relationship between the physical and spiritual realms; whereas white folks go to church passively, to receive instructions from God, black church is about active participation, and a transcendental experience of being possessed by God. (Can you *feel* it? Can I get a witness?) Ultimately – for a few blinding, rapturous moments – it is about *being* God. As one celebrant said in a recent film about Brazilian variations on West African ecstatic religion, 'They threw a party for the gods – and the gods came.'

Himself a former preacher and the son of a preacher, the late James Baldwin wrote in *The Fire Next Time* (1966): 'There is no music like that music, no drama like the drama of the saints rejoicing, the sinners moaning, the tambourines racing, and all those voices coming together and crying holy unto the Lord . . . I have never seen anything to equal the fire and excitement that sometimes, without warning, fill a church, causing that church, as Leadbelly and so many others have testified, to "rock".'

That is the central experience of soul music encapsulated right there. For believers and non-believers alike, the soul singer is the catalyst for the audience's experience of the divine paradox: of simultaneously getting outside yourself and into yourself, of using transcendence both to fly away and to inhabit the moment you're in more fully than ever before.

Whatever the technical definitions of soul music in terms of structure or instrumentation, a 'soulful' performance is one which fulfils these theoretically contradictory imperatives, and the greatest soul singers aren't necessarily the ones with the most extensive bag of vocal tricks (otherwise Whitney Houston would be the greatest soul singer alive), but the ones who make you *feel* most intensely. If you believe it, it's soul music. If you don't, it's simply a display of the kind of empty virtuosity best left to heavy metal guitarists. Can y'all dig it? A-*men*!

> Ain't no heaven . . . ain't no burnin' hell
> John Lee Hooker, 'Burnin' Hell' (1949)

> I been down so long that down don't bother me
> Albert King, 'Down Don't Bother Me' (1966)

There are many dimensions to that age-old dichotomy between gospel and the blues. One common aspect of both the churches and the taverns was that they were, for a long time, just about the only autonomous institutions which black Americans had, and – as might be expected – they not only hosted very different activities but represented equally distinct philosophies. The blues people existed in a continuous present where every day was a struggle, pleasure was transitory, and the only possible reactions were to bemoan foul circumstance or to boast of the snappy style or 'stoical irony' (Baldwin again) with which they managed to survive. The church folk lived right, praised the Lord, and looked forward to a better day. In many ways, the most vital distinction was that the church folk saw themselves as a community whereas the bluesman was an outsider, always ultimately alone. Naturally, this was part of the blues' romantic appeal to sensitive white oddballs. As Eric Clapton explained in 1987 to Melvyn Bragg on the British television arts programme *The South Bank Show*:

'I felt, through most of my youth, that my back was against the wall and that the only way to survive was with dignity and pride and courage. I heard that in certain forms of music, and I heard it most of all in the blues, because it was always an individual. *It was one man and his guitar against the world.* It wasn't a company, or a band, or a group; when it came down to it, it was one guy who was completely alone and had no options, no alternatives other than to sing and play to ease his pain.'

Clapton is a sensitive and perceptive man – at least, when he's not talking about immigration and race relations in Britain – and here he puts his finger not only on the mystique which the blues had for him (and, for that matter, for Jimi Hendrix), but on the reason why it ceased to be an adequate musical outlet for black Americans. Black people had had quite enough of feeling 'completely alone' and without options and alternatives, quite enough of the notion of one man or woman (with or without a guitar) against the world. By secularizing gospel and thereby implicitly transferring the concept of transcendent salvation into the real world, Ray Charles articulated a potent political metaphor: one of an attainable heaven on earth. And by replacing the romantic individualism of the blues with the community spirit of gospel, his music spoke volumes about the leverage that black America could exert through collective action. Soul music was about an end to 'divide and rule'; it was – and *is* – about black America getting itself *together*.

Despite the presence of magnificent *auteurs* like Ray Charles and James Brown – and Aretha Franklin, and Otis Redding, and Stevie Wonder, and Marvin Gaye, and Sly Stone, and George Clinton, and Al Green, and many more – soul is a team-player's music, and the qualities which it both depends on and respects most absolutely are discipline and appropriateness. The notion of community and collective effort isn't simply an abstraction, but a reality which permeates the soul aesthetic down to its deepest cells and fibres. A traditional soul revue is just about the most disciplined spectacle you're ever likely to see in popular music, and its greatest triumphs occur either when something that's been rehearsed a hundred times and performed a thousand times more comes off looking and sounding like a spontaneous improvisation, or vice versa. Young white renegades from the bourgeoisie, seeking to escape from a culture which regards spontaneity as something akin to the black plague (no *overt* pun intended) regard this aspect of soul music with some suspicion, and are therefore more drawn to blues, folk or free jazz; working-class whites generally understand *exactly* what is implied, which is why – in England, at least – they were the ones who responded most enthusiastically to soul, while their middle-class counterparts preferred to twitter on about the music's lack of alleged 'authenticity'.

The great soul bands are the ones that play most unselfishly, who place their resources most wholeheartedly at the disposal of the needs of the singer and the song, like the great James Brown ensembles or the Stax and Motown studio groups. There are indeed some great lead instrumentalists – mainly saxophonists like King Curtis, Junior Walker and Maceo Parker – but they, too, only serve to stand and wait before they blow.

Maceo Parker plays when James Brown – excuse me, *Jaaaaaaaames Braaaaoowwn* – grunts 'Maceo!', but then he shuts up when James gets ready to take it to the bridge. Soul is not, to put it mildly, a soloist's music.

> Baby Child as a man
> as a living grain of sand
> Sitting on the ever changing shore
> Greeting the sunrise . . .
> Picked up upon the Gypsy Woman
> Hair flaming night as ravens even sleep . . . rainbow cloth
> Tambourine complementing her chant and choice of graces
> And Love Her God . . .
>
> I actually looked upon her on my right . . . coming forth
> And Baby Child then secondly looked her left to eye
> And 11 or 12 women, men and little ones approached;
> They clad in their master's wish
> White robes swaying to be baptised
> These two worlds crossed each other in front of me, when
> Afterwards, Baby Child sipped a heartful of ocean . . .
> Spat out the waste and walked upon the New Day.

Jimi Hendrix, liner note to Band of Gypsys (1970)

They took an express straight to the Electric Church. Many times we come across this scene: a brother and cousin emptying their burdens a little ways on down the railroad tracks; the bro' . . . kicking a can . . . trying to kick out his blues and jealous blues and in his back pocket he carries a bootful of raw violent silk but sometimes frustration spills from his house of pain and feeds the weeds around his yard . . . fat to the bone they grow as they attempt to crawl towards his all . . . But he doesn't have to even cry . . . because his natural soul shall be washed soon . . . and he knows . . . and taps his cousin on the shoulder who was aware of the rumbling tracks . . . shaking his head, heart and feet . . . and the brother and cousin say without speaking a word . . . 'I can really see those tracks swaying.' THE EXPRESS has made the bend, He is coming down the tracks. Shaking steady . . . shaking funk . . . shaking FEELING – shaking LIFE – 'Buddy Miles EXPRESS is here' cries them both . . . the cousins say . . . 'Yes bro' . . . I am with you . . . but where are we going?' The conductor says as they climbed aboard 'small we are going to the Electric Church . . .' the Buddy Miles EXPRESS took them away . . . and they lived and heard happily and funkily ever after. And uh . . . excuse me . . . but I think I hear my train coming.

Jimi Hendrix, liner note to *Expressway to Your Skull* by Buddy Miles Express (1968)

Do you know Hendrix's face? Then you know Roger Mayer's Classic Fuzz, the very same fuzz distortion circuit that Roger Mayer designed for Jimi Hendrix during his tenure as the master's sound technician . . . the combination of circuit design ingenuity and an innate knowledge of the amplified tone – the much sought-after 'human tone' that made Hendrix's sound so haunting and 'religious' – are the ingredients that Roger 'Mr Wah-Wah' Mayer has packaged . . .

Ad copy for Roger Mayer's effects pedals, *Guitar World* (1987)

They threw Jimi Hendrix out of church when he was eight years old because he was always dressed funny. It broke his heart, because Childe Jimmy adored the music and excitement of church so much that Sunday morning was virtually the high spot of his week. Eventually he considered starting his own; in interviews where he felt more than usually comfortable – or when he was more than usually stoned – he would talk about something he called the Electric Church, or Sky Church, or Electric Sky Church, or any such combination. With all due respect to the efficacy of Roger Mayer's gadgets, if there was a 'haunting and "religious"' quality to Hendrix's sound, there may have been more to it than his choice of stomp boxes.

To put it mildly, the Electric Church was a somewhat (you should pardon the expression) fuzzy concept; Hendrix referred to the group with which he played Woodstock (Mitchell on drums, a scared-stiff Billy Cox making his début on bass, rhythm guitarist Larry Lee – who took lead vocals for a decidedly extemporized version of Curtis Mayfield's Impressions ditty 'Gypsy Woman' – and percussionists Jerry Velez and Juma Sutan) as Sky Church, and the loose jamming circle he assembled in upstate New York in late 1969 was also either the Electric or Sky Church. As Hendrix used the term when it wasn't applied as a band name, Electric Church was a context for participatory worship, learning and communion without regard for denomination or demeanour. It was the kind of place which would never have thrown him out when he was a kid. 'The background of our music,' he said in 1968,

'is a spiritual-blues thing . . . we're making our music into electric church music – a new kind of Bible you carry in your hearts, one that will give you a physical feeling. We try to make our music so loose and hard-hitting so it hits your soul hard enough to make it open. [Rock] is more than music, it's like church, like a foundation for the lost or potentially lost . . . we're trying to save the kids, to create a buffer between young and old. Our music is shock therapy to help them realize a little more of what their goals should be. We want them to realize that our music is just as spiritual as going to church. The soul must rule, not money or drugs. You should rule yourself and give God a chance . . .'

You can kick the boy out of church, but you can't kick the church out of the boy. By the same token, you can starve the boy out of soul music – as they did a dozen or so years later, and for much the same reason – but you can't starve soul out of the boy. The five years Hendrix spent on the 'chitlin circuit' were absolutely miserable for him. At the same time, that period provided him with the kind of musical education which *nothing* can buy: a first-hand exposure to the legends of soul and R&B. In 1962, working on what he later referred to as 'the Top 40 Soul R&B Hit Parade package with the patent leather shoes and hairstyle combined', he was thrown into contact with the young Bobby Womack. At the time, Womack was singing and playing guitar alongside his brothers in The Valentinos, protégés of Sam Cooke, who was co-headlining the tour with Jackie Wilson. It's worth repeating that whatever Hendrix may have claimed subsequently in order to boost his credibility in England, he didn't actually accompany Cooke or Wilson, but played behind 'Gorgeous' George Odell, who would open the show with a few songs and then, as MC, introduce the more celebrated acts. While we're on the subject, Hendrix's claims to have backed Ike & Tina Turner are dismissed by no less an authority than Tina Turner herself, which is good enough for me. 'If Jimi Hendrix had ever been on our stage, believe me I'd remember him,' La Turner assured me in 1988. 'I'd've given him a *big kiss*!' If Hendrix did indeed audition for Ike one afternoon in a St Louis bar and didn't get the job, it must have been because Ike didn't want someone like Hendrix anywhere near his audience, his Ikettes and his Tina. However, according to the chronology provided in Harry Shapiro and Caesar Glebeek's *Electric Gypsy*, Hendrix did indeed play a few dates with the Turners, so – Tina's testimony notwithstanding – the jury is still out.

Womack (who bought Hendrix's old guitar from Gorgeous George Odell's grandmother sometime in the eighties), remembers Hendrix this way:

'Jimi Hendrix was like an outcast. He was so weird, you know, he would dress so weird. People would say, "Look at that motherfucker, he ain't gonna get no work, he ain't gonna do *nuthin*'." 'Cause they didn't *understand*. They'd say, "Look where he's at, he's got an earring in his ear . . ." George would go onstage, he'd pull off his shirt, he'd be doin' all that clown stuff and he wouldn't even realize that all the girls be screamin' for Jimi. Jimi'd upstage him all the time, but he wasn't even tryin' to, he'd just say, "I'm tryin' to make your show better." Jimi would take the git-tar and be playin' it with his teeth [while] George be singin' a ballad. Then George would turn round and say, "I'm gonna tell you one more time, Jimi, I'm gonna make you *eat* that git-tar the next time I see it in your mouth; this is my show and you're embarrassin' me, turn around and see this motherfucker eatin' his git-tar." Jimi say, "I'm only tryin' to help you." George say, "Don't do *nuthin'* to help me" . . .'

With variations, this incident was repeated throughout Hendrix's time on the soul circuit. 'He could never have played with Sam or Jackie,' says Womack,

'. . . because he played them long *screamin'* lines . . . in those days, if you didn't have a process, a trim haircut and a suit and tie, you wasn't in it. He dressed so raggedy, all his clothes looked like they came from a rummage sale. He always wore strange-lookin' jewellery, he had real long hair stuck all out. When I see guys look like that now, I say no *wonder* people didn't like Jimi Hendrix! This was twenty-seven years ago! Later on, of course, they was all runnin' round sayin' "Shit, he was in my band!" King Curtis say, "I used to put him out 'cause I would make him wear a tie and he didn't want to wear no tie. He would leave the sleeves of his shirt all loose. I would say, 'Man, put these cufflinks in and wear it neat.' He'd say, 'I like it like this.'" Curtis used to say, "He can play, but he didn't fit with the guys, nobody wanted him around." All these people would come out the woodwork: "He worked for me and I kicked him out. Guy came in lookin' like he'd been sleepin' in the street for twenty years." He'd turn his git-tar down but he would still over-shadow a person like King Curtis. Everybody he would play with, people wouldn't be payin' no attention to the artist, they'd be sayin' hey, look at *him*. When he would play with his teeth, they'd give him an ovation because they thought he was crazy, but the artist at the front would think he was tryin' to take the show.'

Traditionally, white critics have interpreted Hendrix's travails as a putative soul sideman as an example of how all those ignorant, narrow-minded blacks simply weren't smart enough to understand his brilliance, and generally speaking, Hendrix himself never saw fit to contradict them. What neither they nor he acknowledged was that those singers and musicians regarded the knife-edge discipline of their stage-shows and the sharkskin-and-mohair opulence of their costumes as evidence of exactly how far they had travelled from their beginnings. Most of them were originally from the rural South; even the superflash, superbad Wicked Wilson Pickett was raised up in a shack miles from the nearest town, which was the teeming metropolis of Prattville, Alabama. They were proud men, and they hadn't fought their way every inch of the journey from Dogpatch, Mississippi in the face of every obstacle that the Land of the Free could throw at them just so's some drugged-out space-case from

Seattle could show up for a gig looking like a street bum and then put on his *own* show at stage left while they were trying to go to work. That wasn't just an irritation, that was an *insult*. If Hendrix got fired from every single job he had in those years, it shouldn't've come as that much of a surprise.

Nevertheless, he learned his trade, and in the first half of the sixties, there was an awful lot to learn. Three great soul empires – Atlantic, Motown and one-man empire James Brown – dominated that era, and each one of them contributed a vital piece to the jigsaw. Atlantic Records, founded by Ahmet and Nesuhi Ertegun in New York in 1947, had provided the platform for Ray Charles' ground-breaking 'I Got a Woman' and the multiplicity of hits which had followed it, and even though Brother Ray had split to cut his country albums for the ABC conglomerate by the time the sixties rolled round, Atlantic were still in there with their unique juxtaposition of Big Apple smarts and grits-and-groceries Southern soul. Ben E. King, who'd racked up an impressive gallery of hits both as one of The Drifters' succession of lead singers and as a solo artist, characterized his hardy-perennial smash 'Stand by Me' (revived in the eighties as the theme for both a Levi's commercial and a movie adaptation of a Stephen King novella) as 'straight out of church and a few parts Harlem, sweetened up with some plush Broadway strings', but any number of Atlantic's New York productions would fit that description. Their inspired mix of sophistication and roots would allow them to take a stone preacher like Solomon Burke (or, a little later, Aretha Franklin) and team them up with their New York session A-team, led by saxophonist 'King Curtis' Ousley, and including at various times guitarist Cornell Dupree, drummer Bernard 'Pretty' Purdie and bassists Chuck Rainey and Jerry Jemmott. Hendrix played briefly with Curtis – discographers are still arguing about whether he played on Curtis's 'Soul Serenade' or not – and if he'd behaved himself he might well have ended up as a leading New York studio player, knocking down a decent living but limiting himself to delivering whatever Curtis or the producer ordered. Cornell Dupree told *Guitar World* that Curtis had hired Hendrix away from The Isley Brothers because he wanted to update his band's sound, and that at the time 'Jimi wasn't playing the acid thing . . . it was more R&B. I mean *greased*. I mean *funky*. I mean he could do some Albert King, but in a different definition.' Chuck Rainey remembers 'constantly going to my bass and trying to play lines the way Hendrix played them'.

From their Manhattan offices, the Ertegun brothers and their head honcho Jerry Wexler had a hotline to the Southland. Not only did they distribute the masters they received from the Memphis-based independent label Stax Records, but they would assign head-office signings like Wilson Pickett and Sam & Dave (both of whom employed Hendrix in their road bands, but not for long) to record in the converted movie theatre on McLemore Avenue with Booker T & the MGs, Isaac Hayes, the Memphis Horns and the rest of the Stax in-house operation. The jewel in Atlantic's Memphis crown was a bluff, stocky farm-boy from Macon, Georgia, named Otis Redding.

'This is the love crowd, right? We all love each other, don't we? Am I right? Let me hear you say YEAH!'

Otis Redding at the Monterey Pop Festival (17 June 1967)

Recently, it's become fashionable to claim that Otis Redding was over-rated, or that Solomon Burke or James Carr were *really* the greatest of the sixties Southern soul men. It's true that he was more than occasionally guilty of what Jerry Wexler called 'oversouling' (hollering, screaming and y'alling as a substitute for rather than a means of expression), that he could occasionally become entangled in his favourite clichés (in his Monterey Pop Festival performance of 'Try a Little Tenderness', he suffixes virtually every line with either 'Oh yeh yeh' or 'Oh no no', wherever applicable), and that his vocal range was fairly minimal; but when the Big O got to cooking, somehow none of that mattered. Otis had the rare ability to make his listeners care about him – B. B. King was his only real peer in this particular respect – and willingly share both his rejoicing and his sorrows. Of the four performers who achieved the real ears-and-tail-maestro triumphs at the 1967 Monterey Pop Festival – Hendrix, The Who and Janis Joplin (with Big Brother and the Holding Company) were the others – it was Otis who had the least opportunity to capitalize on that breakthrough. Monterey was his coronation as the Love Crowd's favourite soul man, but just before Christmas of 1967, three days after recording 'Dock of the Bay' and exactly three years after the killing of Sam Cooke, Otis and most of his road band, The Bar-Kays, died in a plane crash.

Steve Cropper, a bony farm boy from the Ozarks, played guitar on virtually every record cut at Stax between 1962 and 1968 (including the Albert King records, produced by MGs' drummer Al Jackson Jr, which Hendrix loved so much), as well as collaborating on songs as memorable as 'Knock on Wood' (written with Eddie Floyd, who sang it), '634–5789' (written with Floyd and sung by Wilson Pickett), and Pickett's biggest hit, 'In the Midnight Hour'. Cropper's funky, understated but piercing approach made him one of the most copied guitarists in R&B as soon as Booker T & the MGs' 'Green Onions' was released in 1962. Hendrix was understandably delighted when, that same year, he ran into Cropper in a soul food restaurant in Nashville, and the pair immediately commandeered a nearby studio for a brief jam. An acetate recording was cut (it has long since disappeared from mortal ken), but nothing came from the encounter; except that Hendrix can be heard performing a letter-perfect Cropper-style introduction to Little Richard's epic 1965 soul ballad, 'I Don't Know What You've Got (But It's Got Me)'.

Stax and Atlantic were both companies owned by whites, staffed by whites and blacks, and dedicated to selling records to adult black audiences. Their opposite number was Berry Gordy Jr's Detroit-based Tamla-Motown combine, owned and staffed by blacks and concentrating on selling to teenagers of all races. Speedily establishing a stable of superstars – The Supremes were far and away the most successful, racking up more pop hits than any early sixties stars apart from The Beatles – their triumph was rooted in the achievements of their house band, whose most celebrated members were bassist James Jamerson and drummer Benny 'Pops' Benjamin, and a gallery of Midas-fingered writer-producers including the team of Eddie and Brian Holland and Lamont Dozier, and the ubiquitous Smokey Robinson. The purity of Robinson's falsetto was second only to that of The Impressions' singer-composer-guitarist Curtis Mayfield, and his songwriting was sufficiently sophisticated for Bob Dylan to declare him 'America's greatest living poet', and for Britain's most erudite music critics to declare The Beatles geniuses when they borrowed a few of Smokey's patented chord changes for some of the songs on their second album. The Motown production style centred around a less syncopated beat than most of their black independent competitors, smoothed-out pop-gospel vocals, and a multi-layered sound incorporating orchestrations almost as elaborate as those of Atlantic's New York productions, generally using at least three guitarists (Joe Messina, Robert White and Eddie Willis) all playing interlocking, complementary parts. (This particular Motown device made life hell for the guitarists in their acts' road bands, let alone for rock groups trying to replicate an entire Motown arrangement with one or two guitars standing in for an entire batallion of horn, string and keyboard players. A few years of covering complex studio arrangements like Motown's had a lot to do with the development of Hendrix's extraordinary one-man-band approach to the guitar.)

The Motown sound was as sweetly intoxicating and utterly irresistible to dancers, pop fans and young lovers as it was simperingly corrupt and vaguely blasphemous to black-music purists and blues-oriented folkies, but then the company's records weren't made for purists and folkies. Sprinkled with Motown's unique glitter-dust, Detroit became a sonic Hollywood, an index of the aspirations of the urban black proletariat. Still rooted in church music and the blues, Motown's music was utterly urban; stripped of the defiantly downhome Southern intonations of Stax, and shorn of any associations with the bad old days. Nevertheless, even though the company shied away from anything which smacked of radical politics or militant confrontation, they caught the *Zeitgeist* of the Civil Rights movement with the celebratory urgency of Martha & the Vandellas' 'Dancing in the Street', an ostensibly straightforward juke-box anthem which managed to sound like some funky victory parade the morning after the revolution. Some commentators, including Peter Guralnick in his *Sweet Soul Music*, define soul purely in terms of Southern music, effectively banishing Motown to the 'pop' shelf, but to British kids at least, Motown certainly seemed soulful enough. After all, what did the UK have to compare it with? Freddie and the Dreamers?

> If you got funk, you got style
> George Clinton (Funkadelic), *Hard Core Jollies* (1976)

The third great pillar of sixties black American pop fulfils Eric Clapton's formulation: 'one man against the world . . . [not] a company, a band or a group.' James Brown wasn't a company (though he ended up running several) or a band (likewise); instead, he was a one-man genre. Unlike conventional performers, who built their show around the demands of their music, Brown constructed his music around the requirements of his show. On the one hand (or perhaps 'foot' would be more appropriate), this meant extraordinary post-gospel theatrics where Brown would enact mini-melodramas of loss and redemption while he performed 'Please Please Please', 'Try Me' or 'Prisoner of Love'; on the other, it resulted in orgiastic extravaganzas of polyrhythmic virtuosity which enabled Brown to develop, refine and flaunt the vocabulary of gymnastic dance moves passed on to subsequent hoofers like Prince, Michael Jackson and Terence Trent D'Arby. From 1965's triumphal 'Papa's Got a Brand New Bag' onwards, Brown's music discarded more and more of the conventional devices of Western song structures and concentrated ever more strongly on the holy science of THE FUNK and THE GROOVE: propulsion created by the meshing of seemingly independent instrumental scraps which were juxtaposed to form a tensile, interactive pulse over which Brown would deliver his trademarked grunts, screams and exhortatory proto-raps. The results were resonant with subtexts, and easily more eloquent and relevant than most people's fully-fledged 'lyrics', but the success of those shows and those records was only possible because of what is arguably *Jaaaaaaaaames*'s central attribute: his skills as a bandleader.

James Brown is, of course, the most influential dancer to emerge between Fred Astaire and Michael Jackson; he is also a formidable post-gospel soul screamer, a competent (if unremarkable) pianist and drummer, a dubious political philosopher and a walking disaster area as a businessman. But as a bandleader, he is one of a particularly select group; his only true peers are Duke Ellington, Count Basie, Miles Davis, Muddy Waters, Sun Ra, Art Blakey, Gil Evans, Fela Kuti, Sly Stone, George Clinton, John Mayall, Frank Zappa and Prince. The bandleader's art is a specialized one: many gifted singers, instrumentalists, composers, arrangers and performers have never mastered it. It is the ability to weld musicians together to realize the leader's vision, while simultaneously allowing that vision to be enriched and inspired by what the individual players are personally able to bring to the party; to exist in a veritable symbiosis while never ceasing to maintain overall control. It requires an instinctual, Zen-like mastery of the ebb and flow of human relations: an overly loose grip creates shapelessness and an overly tight one, sterility and frustration. The records Brown made with his greatest bands are proof of these skills: when his great mid-sixties band walked out in protest against his disciplinarianism, his stinginess and his unwillingness to credit them on his album sleeves, they formed their own group and, under the name of Maceo & the Macks, created a series of staggeringly dull records which merely provided an explicit negative example of exactly what J. B. had been doing on records which seemed as if he simply went HEH! and YAAAOOOOWWW! while the band went their own sweet way.

Brown, incidentally, replaced Maceo *et al.* with a gaggle of Cincinnati teenagers including brothers Phelps (a.k.a. 'Catfish') and William ('Bootsy') Collins on, respectively, guitar and bass. They too quit in their turn to join George Clinton in his Parliament/Funkadelic thang alongside

Maceo Parker and the horn section; the original band eventually came traipsing back. They included guitarist Jimmy Nolen, whose ability to slice-and-dice a 4/4 beat a different way every time made him one of the most copied guitarists of the sixties. Unfortunately, since JB wasn't big on handing out personnel credits, only cognoscenti and the late Nolen's fellow-musicians even knew who he was, which is why people alluding to his distinctive rhythmic expertise talk about 'James Brown-style guitar', as if Brown himself was the guitarist. Playing with James Brown was a great way to learn the business and to participate in the greatest rhythm machine of the sixties. It was a very poor way to get rich, to get famous, or to try out one's own ideas. Brown would fine his musicians for missing a note or a step, for lateness, talking back or for breaching his stringent dress code. In James Brown's band, Hendrix would have lasted five minutes. *Maximum*.

'Hendrix was by far the greatest expert I've ever heard at playing rhythm and blues, the style of playing developed by Bobby Womack, Curtis Mayfield, Eric Gale and others.'

Michael Bloomfield, interviewed in *Guitar Player* (1975)

Discussing the same style on another occasion (recounting to author Ed Ward his failure to understand what New York studio guitarist Gale was really doing), Bloomfield cited Steve Cropper rather than Bobby Womack, but the principle remains the same. 'All I knew about black guitar playing was blues guitar,' Bloomfield told Ward, 'and I didn't know anything about a huge school of black guitar playing that . . . all those cats had synthesized out of gospel guitar.' If Bloomfield didn't know about it, then certainly Clapton and Beck and all the London boys didn't either. It is a style custom-made for accompanying vocalists, and it comes squarely out of the shared turf between gospel and country music. Its basis lies in an intimate knowledge of the scales and arpeggios on which chords and lead-lines are based, and it draws on two-string melodic obbligatos and three-string broken chords, incorporating allusions to the bass-line: a little bit of everything. Only rarely will it include any of the bent, sustained, horn-like notes on which blues-derived rock guitar is based; rather, it favours trills and hammer-ons, and it is both delicate and punchy. Franke Marino, the Canadian one-time boy wonder who formed Mahogany Rush after allegedly coming down from an acid trip in hospital and discovering that he was the reincarnation of Jimi Hendrix (I type this with a straight face and trust that you will read it likewise) told *Guitar World* in 1985, 'He played very much like a lot of black guitar players I know who don't play heavy music . . . if I turned their amps up and made them distort a bit, my God, they'd sound more like Hendrix than I do.'

It doesn't take an exceptionally acute ear to verify Marino's point, or Bloomfield's. Curtis Mayfield's introduction and halfway-mark break in The Impressions' 'People Get Ready' or Bobby Womack's rhapsodic fills on Wilson Pickett's 'I'm in Love' (or, for that matter, on any number of mid-sixties Atlantic sides by Pickett and Aretha Franklin) bear an instantly recognizable family resemblance to Hendrix's work on 'Wait until Tomorrow', 'Castles Made of Sand', 'The Wind Cries Mary' or any number of his prettier and more reflective tunes. The brief unaccompanied instrumental version of 'Electric Ladyland' which closed the posthumous Alan Douglas cut-and-paste album *Loose Ends* and which has, praise Jah, been resurrected on the four-CD *Jimi Hendrix Experience* boxed set, is probably the most eloquent example of his mastery of this most exquisitely subtle and graceful of rhythm and blues guitar styles, blending Mayfield's ruminative trills with Wes Montgomery's gliding octaves as if it was only due to some bizarre accident that they were ever separated at all.

Surviving live recordings of Hendrix playing various sleazy New York-area club gigs with Curtis Knight & the Squires provide a fairly clear picture both of the group's contemporary repertoire and of Hendrix's approach to the R&B hits of the period. The assortment assembled on *In the Beginning* . . . includes a couple of Joe Tex tunes ('You Got What It Takes' and 'Hold on to What You Got'), a pair of British Invasion classics that seem to have arrived via Otis Redding (The Beatles' 'Day Tripper' and the Stones' 'Satisfaction'), and Otis's own 'Mr Pitiful' alongside his illustrious Stax colleague Rufus Thomas's 'Walkin' the Dog' (as covered by The Rolling Stones). Tributes are paid to Ray Charles ('What'd I Say') and Motown (The Four Tops' 'I Can't Help Myself'), as well as to Hendrix's former employers The Isley Brothers ('Twist and Shout' as covered by The Beatles) and Wilson Pickett ('Land of 1,000 Dances'), and the set is spiced with blues tunes (Hendrix's perennial 'I'm a Man' plus Jimmy Reed's 'Bright Lights, Big City') and novelties like 'Wooly Bully' and 'Hang on Sloopy'. Throughout, Hendrix furiously rolls all the various interlocking guitar parts (and, for good measure, the horn and keyboard lines as well) into one churning ball of propulsive rhythm, occasionally breaking out into solos so dense with ideas that they seem to be on the verge of flying apart at the seams. He obviously knows all the rules of R&B and soul guitar, and just as obviously cannot wait to break them.

No matter how far he might later have strayed from the strictures of commercial soul, or however disdainfully he might have referred to 'penguin suits' and 'Flash Gordon shows', the rigorous lessons of the soul revue stayed with him. Noel Redding has recalled that at his audition for The Jimi Hendrix Experience, they jammed on such venerable R&B staples as Don Covay's 'Have Mercy Baby', Booker T & the MGs' 'Green Onions' and Solomon Burke's 'Everybody Needs Somebody to Love', before Hendrix attempted to teach him 'Hey Joe', already planned as the new band's first single. The band's first public performances at the Paris Olympia included Otis Redding's 'Respect' and Wilson Pickett's 'Land of 1,000 Dances', as well as 'Everybody Needs Somebody to Love' and 'Have Mercy Baby'; the latter was still on the set-list for the Experience's early London club-shows, as documented on a surviving bootleg tape from the now-defunct Flamingo club. It was on the soul tunes that the band cut its collective teeth; it was undoubtedly convenient, since Redding and Mitchell were familiar with the songs from their own delvings into contemporary R&B, but it was also the discipline with which Hendrix chose to weld three very disparate musicians (one jazz drummer, one rock guitarist turned bassist and one Hendrix) into a single coherent unit.

Hendrix once told Michael Bloomfield that 'he wanted to burn Clapton to death because he couldn't play rhythm'; so intense was the blues snobbery and lead-guitar fetishization of the British rock scene that very few of the local guitar hotshots (honourable exceptions being John Lennon, Keith Richards and Pete Townshend) could. Hendrix's ability to sound like all of the James Brown band playing at once was a vital part of what set him apart from his peers: Clapton did indeed play rhythm, but his approach was firmly rooted in the first-position folkie chords, and most of the other guitarists' idea of rhythm was based on the Chuck Berry or Jimmy Reed manner of bouncing between a straight major chord and its sixth or seventh. Hendrix's soloing concept was indeed derived from the blues, but his rhythms came from soul.

The fingerprints of the chitlin circuit were all over many of his early songs, though this was effectively disguised both by the fact that the guitar was doing most of the work normally handled by a full band, and by Redding and Mitchell's utter lack of resemblance to a soul bass-and-drum team. 'Foxy Lady', speeded up slightly and shorn of its end-of-the-world guitar noises, could have slipped straight into the Wilson Pickett bag, brag and all, right alongside the 'Land of 1,000 Dances' knock-off, 'Fire'. The self-deprecating shrug and chug of 'Remember' would have been just fine and dandy as a B-side for Otis Redding, from whose 'Mr Pitiful' it was clearly derived. Even 'Purple Haze', a stoned, surreal stomp in its studio incarnation, would frequently be revved up to a James Brown dance tempo in performance.

Sales of the first Jimi Hendrix Experience single, 'Hey Joe'/'Stone Free', were even tabulated in Britain's specialist soul chart as well as the regular pop listings, simply because of the assumption that since Hendrix was an American black man under forty years of age, what he was playing was soul rather than a new brew in which soul was simply one of the ingredients. Both sides were also compiled into a Polydor collection entitled *Soul Explosion* (packaged, like many soul anthologies of the time, with a cover photo of a black model sprawled on the floor wearing not a lot) alongside tracks by James Brown, Edwin Starr and others. This was considered highly inappropriate by both soul and rock buffs, but it wasn't to be long before Hendrix's innovations percolated back into the mainstream of black American pop. Apart from anything else, his records soon came to the attention of an alert, ambitious San Francisco deejay/bandleader named Sylvester Stewart. Stewart was better known by his professional name: Sly Stone.

> TIME!
> Has come today . . .
> Joe & Willie Chambers for the Chambers Brothers, 'Time Has Come Today' (1967)

> R-E-S-P-E-C-T,
> Find out what it means to me . . .
> Aretha Franklin after Otis Redding, 'Respect' (1967)

> YEAH! Giddon UP! And DANCE to the MUSIC!
> Sly & the Family Stone, 'Dance to the Music' (1968)

> Say it loud, I'm black and I'm proud!
> James Brown, 'I'm Black and I'm Proud' (1968)

Soul music was certainly neither static nor passive in 1967. While the white bohos of London and San Francisco were enjoying the Summer of Love, black America had its own solstice: what was referred to at the time as 'the summer of Rap [black-power activist H. Rap Brown], 'Retha and Revolt'. Otis Redding was at the peak of his popularity, James Brown was tearing up both pop and R&B charts with militant dance smashes which paid progressively less and less attention to traditional pop values and, in the process, forged an entirely new funk aesthetic.

Probably the most significant of all at the time, though, was the former teenage gospel queen Aretha Franklin, who emerged from five years of stultifying miscasting at Columbia Records and signed to Atlantic, where Jerry Wexler and the Erteguns sent her to church (metaphorically speaking) and turned her loose to transform Otis Redding's 'Respect' into a controlled explosion of triumphant autonomy. Addressed both by a woman to men and by a black to whites, 'Respect' served notice that the rules had changed. Over in Detroit, Berry Gordy was still having anxiety attacks about the possible consequences of young Stevie Wonder's insistence on cutting Bob Dylan's 'Blown' in the Wind'; by the following year, Motown too had joined the revolution.

One mammoth, apocalyptic slice of the new black music came from The Chambers Brothers, formerly a family gospel quartet who'd moved up from Mississippi to Los Angeles and started working the folk circuit. Like many of their white counterparts, they'd bought a bunch of Fender equipment, hired a drummer and become a rock band. The Chambers Brothers developed an act which blended their own compositions with cover versions of Otis Redding and Wilson Pickett tunes, but they performed them with a guitar-and-harmonica front line which put them closer to The Rolling Stones than to a mainstream soul revue. They recorded 'Uptown' (written by Betty Mabry, who would later marry Miles Davis and introduce him to Jimi Hendrix under circumstances which would contribute materially to the collapse of the marriage), but their greatest achievement was 'Time Has Come Today', an orchestrated pandemonium of fuzzed guitars, reverb, screams, laughter and the tick-tock of drummer Brian Keenan's cowbells and rim-shots. The Chambers Brothers were a rock band in everything but their unmistakable post-gospel harmonizing, but 'Time Has Come Today', rough and anarchic as it was, was essentially the first outbreak of psychedelic soul. It certainly wasn't the last.

> I wanna take you HIGH-YAH!
> Sly & the Family Stone, 'I Wanna Take You Higher!' (1969)

> Mommy, what's a Funkadelic?
> George Clinton on behalf of Funkadelic, 'Mommy, What's a Funkadelic?' (1970)

Being strongly drug-oriented, rock singers have distorted the sound of soul music with psychedelic effects. Unfortunately, some black artists have fallen into this bag, for The Temptations have lost their souls on 'Cloud Nine' (escapism through drugs), and have landed back on earth to have their 'fortune told' while they learn the 'meaning of soul' in some 'Psychedelic Shack' where black folk *ain't at*. Then, too, there is Sly & the Family Stone who sing such dope-infested lyrics as 'Stand/don't you know that you are free/well, at least in your mind if you want to be'. These songs . . . are 'counter-revolutionary' and should be boycotted by the black community.

A. X. Nicholas in the introduction to his anthology, *The Poetry of Soul* (1971)

If Nicholas didn't mention Hendrix by name in his verbal assault on black musicians whom he considered to be glorifying drug-use, it could only signify that as far as Nicholas's perception of the tastes of black audiences went, Hendrix didn't mean diddley (and I'm not talking about Bo). Despite the plethora of conspiracy theories suggesting that Chas Chandler, Mike Jeffery and Reprise Records were a gaggle of Macchiavellian racists scheming to isolate Hendrix from his people, or that Hendrix himself was an Uncle Tom who wanted to be white, the more plausible reasons behind this dubious assumption are comparatively prosaic. In the summer of 1967, when Warner/Reprise bought the US rights to the Experience's records, they were still a primarily middle-of-the-road company with no significant presence in the contemporary music scene. They had even less presence in black music, unless we include old Sinatra cronies like Sammy Davis Jr and Count Basie (though, to be fair, it should be pointed out that at the height of the apartheid era, Reprise also recorded Miriam Makeba and Hugh Masekela, two determinedly oppositional South African expats), and then throw in comedian Bill Cosby for good measure. (Cosby adapted 'Purple Haze' into an allegedly humorous psychedelic soul single entitled 'Hooray for the Salvation Army Band', which has quite rightly been utterly forgotten today.) This is undoubtedly why Seven Arts, who had recently purchased Warner/Reprise, decided to merge the company with Atlantic. Even if Reprise had desperately wanted to sell Hendrix to a black audience, it is doubtful that they would even have known how to do so. Chas Chandler wouldn't have been much use in this respect; his contacts and expertise lay elsewhere. Furthermore, Hendrix himself couldn't have cared less at that point: he was playing to bigger and more appreciative audiences (the Monkees tour débâcle notwithstanding) than he ever had before, and he entertained few warm feelings towards the soul establishment which had 'buked and scorned him for so long.

And even if Hendrix's records *had* been promoted to black radio stations and those stations had played them, his music would have sounded as bizarrely incongruous as it did on white Top 40 stations. 'It would have been hard to imagine any of Hendrix's records with that splashing drum sound and unfunky bass and all that looseness sitting neatly in the tracks of a Motown record,' as Robert Wyatt puts it. The majority of main-stream R&B fans may have initially reacted unfavourably to Hendrix – they must have undoubtedly shared Robert Christgau's initial perception of him as 'a psychedelic Uncle Tom' – but for black musicians it was quite another matter. By far the most influential was Sly Stone.

Anyone seeking to write a history of disc-jockeys-turned-performers will undoubtedly note that the phenomenon didn't start with Jamaican toasting, or with hip-hop. In the late forties, B. B. King was a deejay in Memphis, and his exposure to a wide variety of records contributed materially to the breadth and eclecticism of his music. Rufus Thomas, who cut the first Stax record, had his own radio show for years, and Sly Stone was himself a power in Bay Area radio. He programmed Bob Dylan and The Beatles alongside the R&B hits, wrote and produced records (including Bobby Freeman's million-selling dance-trash epic 'C'mon and Swim' and The Great Society's 'Somebody to Love', which became far better-known when the band's lead singer, Grace Slick, quit to join Jefferson Airplane and took the song with her), and had his own band on the side. Sly & the Family Stone were signed to Epic Records, and their first album, the modestly-titled *A Whole New Thing*, was standard-issue R&B tarted up with a few psychedelic trimmings like fuzz guitar and trick echoes. A transplanted Texan with an impressive pedigree as a musical child prodigy and reformed gang member, Sly had his own bag of tricks, and in 1968 he unleashed them with a vengeance. 'Dance to the Music', the title track of an otherwise undistinguished album, changed the course of popular music. It was succeeded by a clutch of pop-soul crossover hits which somehow contrived to meld James Brown's funk with The Beatles' tuneful optimism, records as universally accessible as anything since early Motown. The titles alone of those songs – 'Everybody Is a Star', 'Stand!', 'Everyday People', 'You Can Make It if You Try', 'Fun', 'I Wanna Take You Higher', 'Hot Fun in the Summertime', 'Thank You Faletin Me Be Mice Elf Agin' – form an evocative litany of the euphoric optimism of the brief liaison between black and white youth which Sly, even more so than Hendrix, epitomized. It is only fitting that he should precede Hendrix at the close of the *Woodstock* movie: before Hendrix's triumphal decon-struction of the American Dream (Mks I & II) with 'The Star Spangled Banner', there's Sly's happy family in their baddest threads doing that old-time boogaloo while their chief mocks and exorcizes generations of racial terror, shoving his huge grinning black mug into young America's face, going 'BOOM-lakka-lakka-lakka, BOOM-lakka-lakka-lakka . . .'

Sly and Hendrix couldn't have been more different as personalities. 'Jimi would come into a room', Bobby Womack recalls, 'and, as big as he was, he'd just *ease* over into a corner and sit down and just say, "Hey man, whisper whisper" like he was afraid to talk. Sly would *roar* in; they knew each other, but there was no closeness there. Sly was too macho; he thought it was about bein' *arrogant*, actin' crazy, but Jimi was different. I'd say, "Hey man, how ya doin'?" and he wouldn't say nuthin', he'd just smile.' Nevertheless, Hendrix was keenly aware of what Sly was up to. According to Robert Wyatt, Sly's music – along with James Brown's – was Hendrix's favourite listening when he was holed up in his hotel rooms on tour, and on one studio occasion where Hendrix offered to overdub a bass-line on one of Wyatt's compositions, the result bore a startling resemblance to Larry Graham's playing with Sly. (This tape vanished into limbo, incidentally, and only recently resurfaced.) Hendrix even alludes, tongue in cheek, to the principal riff of Sly's then-current 1969 hit 'Sing a Simple Song' during the Band of Gypsys' concert version of Buddy Miles' 'We Got to Live Together'.

Sly and Hendrix had started from a similar base. Sly was a bright young guy who'd learned the ropes of R&B orthodoxy and found them unbearably constrictive. He admired The Beatles' melodic invention and science-fiction production techniques, he was intrigued by Bob Dylan's linguistic ingenuity, and he was comfortable around whites. However, the differences were equally crucial. Sly had very little interest in the blues or in extended soloing, and though he was a gifted multi-instrumentalist who could handle himself on guitar, drums, keyboards, bass and harmonica with equal facility, his primary function was as a composer, producer and arranger whose main instrument – like Duke Ellington's – was his band.

Though self-contained bands that composed, played and sang their own music (or at least pretended to) had become the norm in rock music in the wake of The Beatles and The Beach Boys, they were virtually unprecedented in the soul world. The great bands either functioned as regular sidemen for *auteur*-stars like James Brown or Ray Charles, or else they backed all comers as house sessioneers for the likes of Stax or Motown. The 'groups' were generally vocal groups, requiring independent instrumental back-up and – unless they included major composers like The Miracles' Smokey Robinson, The Impressions' Curtis Mayfield or the '5' Royales Loman Pauling, or had some other regular source of quality material – they were at the mercy of the song-finding capabilities of their labels' A&R teams. Sly not only ran a band that was a 'group' in the sense that rock fans would use the term, but one which seemed like a virtual working model of a new society – joyous, diverse and inherently anti-hierarchical.

Sly & the Family Stone was a seven-piece band in which black and white and male and female musicians swapped roles continually. Sly nominally sang lead, but his guitarist brother Freddie, his keyboard-playing sister Rose, trumpeter Cynthia Robinson and Larry Graham all chimed in, Graham with a startling, oily basso which anchored the vocal ensemble as firmly and imaginatively as his extraordinary bass-playing did the rhythm section. Graham would turn out to be the most influential bass guitarist of the seventies: his technique of slapping the low strings with his thumb and plucking the top strings to produce a sharp, percussive snap (developed when playing duos with his organist mother and attempting to compensate for the absence of a drummer by 'slapping and popping' to mimic bass and snare drums) had virtually become standard practice by the early eighties. He made extensive use of a fuzz-box on many of his bass-lines (including 'Dance to the Music'), thereby anticipating many of the synthesizer-bass effects of post-electro dance music. He also carved out a fairly lucrative career as a vocalist: his greasy, cavernous croon stood him in good stead both as leader of his breakaway band Graham Central Station (where he pioneered the use of drum machines at a time when they were commonly disdained as mere toys) and as a solo lurve-man cutting a string of horrible records in the Isaac Hayes/Barry White/Teddy Pendergrass mode.

'Dance to the Music''s pass-the-parcel succession of lead voices, Outbreaks of bom–bom–bom scatting, party-time atmosphere and jubilant, whomping beat utterly transformed soul music. Most dramatically, Motown drafted writer-producer Norman ('I Heard It through the Grapevine') Whitfield to overhaul their current top male vocal group, The Temptations, with a view to bringing them into line with the New Thang. Whitfield deconstructed the standard approach of lead-vocalist-plus-harmonies-and-oowahs along Sly lines, thus precipitating the departure of lead singer David Ruffin, who was speedily replaced by the more malleable Dennis Edwards. Larry Graham's high vocal profile served to bring the Tempts' veteran basso Melvin Franklin up into the foreground, and Whitfield also augmented the house band with guitarists

Dennis Coffey and Melvin 'Wah Wah Watson' Ragin (the latter, like Jimi Hendrix and the Jackson 5, a former protégé of Bobby Taylor), both of whom were adept at handling exotic sound-processing devices. The most frequently used guitar toy was the wah-wah pedal, which – despite memorable and imaginative performances by Frank Zappa and Eric Clapton, to name but two – had rapidly become identified as Jimi Hendrix's signature sound.

The plaintive cries, angry jabberings and urgent, percussive chatter which Hendrix conjured from something which is, after all, nothing more than a foot-operated tone control, became an indispensable ingredient in the vocabulary of a new kind of soul music: one which brought all the subtexts to the surface, acknowledged ambiguities only when probing them till they bled, and discussed both the public and the inner lives of black Americans more explicitly than ever before. The rhythms of James Brown, the expansive orchestrations of Motown and the fifties Atlantic Drifters' sides, the volatile bubbling cauldron of Sly's vocal arrangements and acid-rock special effects, the Memphis Horns' stabs and blares, and Hendrix's anguished, sardonic 'talking guitar': each in their different ways said 'I'm black and I'm proud', and each ended up in Whitfield's psychedelic soul stew.

Whitfield applied both his high drama and Motown's traditional high gloss to a string of epic ghetto-realist singles, commencing with 'Cloud Nine' and climaxing with 1972's epochal 'Papa Was a Rolling Stone' before declining into knee-jerk self-parody. 'The Temptations,' says Bobby Womack, 'they come up with that polished act with everybody dressed alike and movin' at the same time. Yeah, they got psychedelic with their *music*, but not with their *life*. That was just the act part of it.'

Eventually, Motown co-opted Sly's sound even more perfectly by signing a young family vocal group named The Jackson 5, fronted by a spooky nine-year-old prodigy who could sing like a naughty little angel and do all James Brown's dance steps down to the last spin and slide. The fact of their extreme youth meant that their records could legitimately be shorn of the adult concerns which loaded Whitfield's Temptations' records, and 'I Want You Back' and its successors exploded with the carefree fizziness of a can of ice-cold Pepsi. And to emphasize their freshness and novelty, their new-age distinction from an older generation of soul stars, Motown's legendary grooming department kitted them out exactly like five miniature Jimi Hendrixes: flared pants, loose bright shirts . . . and great big puffball Afros.

'Buddy [Miles] is Superspade. If you melted down James Brown and Arthur Con-
ley and Otis Redding into one enormous spade, you'd have Buddy . . . he is the
quintessence of all R&B amassed in one super talented human being. His singing
is just superb, his drumming is just the best. He's the superman.'

Michael Bloomfield (possibly on drugs at the time), interviewed
in *Rolling Stone* (1967)

When Bloomfield quit the Paul Butterfield Blues Band in 1966, Butterfield took the opportunity to revamp the band's approach by hiring a horn
section (including future fusion-blah supremo David Sanborn) and
adding Motown and Stax covers to his Chicago-blues repertoire. Bloomfield, in his turn, was bent on forming a great big fat soul band to showcase a big fat drum prodigy he'd virtually kidnapped from Wilson
Pickett's road group. Buddy Miles was, apparently, quite something.
'Christ! He was like Baby Huey. Buttons popping off his overcoat,
weighed about 300 pounds', was how he was remembered by Nick
Gravenites, the lead singer in what was eventually known as The Electric
Flag. The group didn't last very long; partly because a significant proportion of its membership were messed up on either LSD or heroin, and
partly because – despite an intense academic appreciation of soul-revue
showtiming – Michael Bloomfield was acutely embarrassed by his obese
protégé's fondness for ordering audiences to say YEAH if they were having a good time and generally clap-yo'-hands-y'all-ing them to death.
The Electric Flag performed at Monterey, and though their performance
is missing from the movie, director D. A. Pennebaker thankfully did
include Bloomfield's attempt to beat the all-time land-speed record for
the number of times a person can say 'groovy' in one sentence. However,
the Festival gave Buddy Miles an opportunity for a reunion with Jimi
Hendrix, whom he'd last seen receiving his marching orders from a Pickett gig, 'for feeding back in "Midnight Hour" and so forth', as Hendrix
later described it.

They stayed in touch: Miles recorded one more album with The Electric Flag after the peripatetic Bloomfield abandoned his creation, collected a few Flag alumni into the first edition of his on-again–off-again
Buddy Miles Express, and wound up in New York playing drums on a
John McLaughlin album Alan Douglas was producing for his own Douglas label. Hendrix had recently installed Billy Cox as his regular bass-
player, and the three of them had taken to jamming informally as Band of
Gypsys. Ed Chalpin still had his teeth in Hendrix, Jeffery, Reprise and
Polydor's collective ankle over his one-dollar Hendrix contract, and it was

agreed that he would be given an all-new Hendrix album to sell to Capitol Records as an inducement to go away. As no one wanted Chalpin to have an Experience album – or, indeed, *any* of Hendrix's unreleased studio music – Band of Gypsys played two New Year concerts at Fillmore East, and Chalpin was given the resulting tapes.

Band of Gypsys is an inconsistent album: it contains only (only?) one of Hendrix's absolute masterpieces ('Machine Gun'), there's far too much of Buddy Miles singing (a little of which goes an extremely long way), and Hendrix himself has a few noticeable tuning problems. It's generally received a fairly unenthusiastic press, but the Cox/Miles rhythm section has a heavy, rolling fluidity which brings out a very different dimension in Hendrix's playing from the more familiar Redding/Mitchell team, which hinged on Redding's stiffness and Mitchell's flamboyant extroversion. For the record, the Gypsys remained Miles Davis's favourite Hendrix rhythm section. Despite Cox and Miles's R&B pedigrees, the result treads an intriguing path along the common border between hard funk and heavy metal; less psychedelic soul than black rock. 'Buddy Miles could be pleasantly messy', opines Robert Wyatt. 'He wasn't as tight as a Stax drummer. He was no drum machine; his rolls would clatter about a bit.' Wyatt is absolutely correct: Miles is less an Al Jackson Jr than a John Bonham, but the way Hendrix locks into the thick, lazy twitch of Cox and Miles's groove on the opening 'Who Knows' creates a brand new funk which he never attained with any other combination, and one which found its truest echoes in the seventies music of one of Hendrix's sixties influences. It wasn't surprising that Digital Underground used a sample of that groove as the basis for 'The Way We Swing' on their *Sex Packets* album.

In 1970, Curtis Mayfield left The Impressions to try his hand as a soloist. Just as the open racial conflicts of the late sixties tempered his euphoric optimism with a sharper, warier compositional edge, the hard confrontationalism and apocalyptic urgency of psychedelic soul, black rock and the new funk forged a fresh context for the sweetness and fragility of his falsetto musings. On *Curtis Live* (1971), he appears against the sparsest of backdrops: two guitars (one of which, of course, was his own), bass, drums and congas. His voice sounds almost touchingly naked when shorn of the churchy support of The Impressions, and his reworkings of the group's standards are disappointing; but on the sparse, eerie 'Stare and Stare', guitarist Craig McMullen's laconic wah-wah interjections provide the perfect counterpoint for Mayfield's pitiless analysis of the mutual distrust and animosity that lay behind the bright façade of Sly Stone and Jimi Hendrix's rainbow coalition.

Mayfield's triumph as a standard-bearer for post-psychedelic soul came when he composed and recorded the score for *Superfly* (1972), one of the blaxploitation thrillers which flooded the movie theatres when some exceptionally intelligent Hollywood people caught on that black people like to go to the cinema. There were quite a few such movies, all with scores by noted soul men: the most famous of these is undoubtedly Isaac Hayes's music from *Shaft*, which started the fad; and Marvin Gaye and Bobby Womack both produced interesting, if flawed, soundtracks for (respectively) *Trouble Man* and *Across 110th Street*. The blaxploitation craze petered out when some exceptionally intelligent Hollywood people realized that even though black people liked to go to the cinema, they weren't going to keep coming back to have their intelligence insulted by cynical, patronizing movies that typecast them as pimps, hookers and dope-dealers. Mayfield's *Superfly* music – as twitchy, clamorous and quintessentially urban as a subway night-ride from 4th Street to the Bronx – was like all Whitfield's Temptations' records played at once on competing ghetto-blasters with a samba school practising percussion, a music store playing host to all the neighbourhood guitarists, and a store-front church holding a service in the adjoining buildings. The soundtrack's big hit single, 'Freddie's Dead', hangs on a single snarling riff that sounds like Band of Gypsys' 'Who Knows' at the end of its tether – which, of course, is exactly what it was.

Yet the most extraordinary transformation wrought by Jimi Hendrix was that of the group that had employed him as their guitarist in 1964. The Isley Brothers – Ronald, Rudolf and O'Kelly – were a post-gospel family vocal trio whose late fifties hits, 'Shout', 'Twist and Shout' and 'Respectable', had become R&B standards in the hands of British acts. 'Shout' had launched Glaswegian teen prodigy Lulu, and despite her later descent into the hideous morass of British 'family entertainment', it was one of the most authentically galvanic British R&B performances of the sixties. (When Hendrix made his notorious 1968 appearance on her BBC TV show, one wonders if she appreciated the irony.) 'Twist and Shout' was a staple of The Beatles' live performances and one of their earliest hits, and 'Respectable' was a favourite of, among others, the Clapton-era Yardbirds. Kelly Isley, searching for a guitarist, had hunted Hendrix down in Harlem, inducted him into the brothers' backing band, and put him up in the family home in New Jersey.

Hendrix toured and recorded with the Isleys, and – unlike many of his other employers – they gave him scope to show his unique stuff during their performances (Hendrix, rather ungraciously, suggested later that they did this 'because they thought it might make 'em more bucks or something'). After he moved on, they signed to Motown, and under the supervision of Holland, Dozier and Holland, cut 'This Old Heart of Mine' and 'Behind a Painted Smile', two of the company's finest sixties singles. They embraced psychedelic soul with a vengeance, and by the onset of the seventies, had mutated into one of the best of the black rock bands. This was achieved by the simple expedient of drafting their younger brothers Ernie and Marvin and cousin Chris Jasper. Ernie was ten years old when Hendrix had been with the brothers, and his initial musical ambitions had then centred around drums, but under Hendrix's influence he had also mastered the guitar. Marvin played bass, and Jasper keyboards; in the studio, Ernie played both drums and guitar. They specialized in an odd combination of funk workouts and soulish adaptations of folk-rock hits by the likes of James Taylor and the Doobie Brothers, and one of Ernie's first tasks with them was to cut a medley of Neil Young's 'Ohio' and Hendrix's 'Machine Gun'. However, their apogee came with 'That Lady', a revamp of one of their early hits which led off their album *3+3*. Ernie, duly kitted out with the Stratocaster and head-band which became standard kit for soul guitarists in the seventies, was alternatively miffed and flattered by persistent rumours that his soaring, rhapsodic, fuzzed-out solos and fills on 'That Lady' had in fact been recorded by Hendrix himself.[*]

The sixties soul empires duly lost their ways, as empires will: Motown went to Hollywood, but their flagship act was now the grown-up Stevie Wonder, who had celebrated his adulthood by block-booking himself into Hendrix's Electric Lady studios and recording the material that made up most of *Music of My Mind*, *Talking Book* and *Innervisions*. Star went to the bankruptcy court; despite Isaac Hayes's enormous success as the definitive symphonic-soul lurve-man, the company faltered after terminating their distribution agreement with Atlantic in 1968. Atlantic in its turn went rock and roll jet-set, lavishing most of its energies on Led Zeppelin, Yes, Crosby, Stills, Nash & Young and The Rolling Stones. James

[*]In the early eighties, the generation gap finally hit the band; the younger half continued as Isley, Jasper & Isley, while the original brothers soldiered on even after Kelly's death reduced them to a duo.

Brown kept up the pressure until the mid-seventies, when disco did him in. And Sly simply went to pieces.

As the disintegration of the original Family Stone mirrored the collapse of the Woodstock dream it so exultantly symbolized, Sly externalized that disintegration with the eloquently chilling *There's a Riot Goin' on*. Most of its music was constructed via overdub by Sly himself, aided by Billy Preston's keyboards and Bobby Womack's guitar and bass. Its slowed-down, inward-looking songs dealt with hard drugs and hard knocks, though it produced the autumnal hit 'Family Affair'. Everything that followed, including the partial reclamation of Sly's original turf with the reasonably successful *Small Talk*, was little more than an exercise in damage limitation. His albums bore titles like *Back on the Right Track* and *Heard You Missed Me, Well I'm Back*, but these claims were near-fraudulent. Like Ike Turner before him, Sly fell victim to the Bad Motherfucker syndrome, so desperate for autonomy that he would rather destroy himself than allow anybody else – even acolytes like George Clinton, Michael Jackson or Prince – to save him.

Soul itself splintered into the lush, mink-lined world of the Lurve Men, led by Isaac Hayes, Barry White and Teddy Pendergrass (the latter the star of the Philadelphia International label, which self-consciously inherited the Motown mantle), and the hard-assed street-funk bands who picked up on James Brown, Sly and Hendrix. Some, like The Commodores and Kool & the Gang, ensured their longevity by either developing or hiring in-house lurve-men – step forward Lionel Richie and James 'J. T.' Taylor – while others, like the Ohio Players, eventually simply pimped themselves out. Easily the best of them was George Clinton's Parliafunkadelicment Thang.

'You know, I think I'm gonna start an R&B band . . . I think I'm gonna work with some horns and put together something like Otis [Redding] 'cause that's really where it's at.'

Jimi Hendrix, talking to Michael Nesmith of The Monkees in London
(September 1970)

Clinton had started out in the fifties singing doowop, drifted through various indie labels with a vocal group called The Parliaments, and eventually got heavily psychedelicized in the late sixties. He singularized the group's name to Parliament, named the back-up musicians Funkadelic, and in the seventies, pulled off the masterstroke of signing Parliament to one label and Funkadelic to another while making both acts' records with the same team. (Incidentally, the answer to the question 'Mommy, what's a Funkadelic?' is 'Someone from Carolina who encountered eternity on LSD and vowed to contain it in a groove.') A formidable polymath – part cosmic jokester, part piercing social critic, part master-organizer, part shaman – Clinton's organization ended up as something like a cross between Earth, Wind and Fire with a sense of humour and Frank Zappa's Mothers of Invention with a tolerance for groove. He employed a verit-able squadron of guitarists, including Eddie Hazell, Mike Hampton and the late Glen Goins, using them to conduct virtual invocations of Hen-drix's spirit; indeed, if Hendrix had lived to carry out the plan he con-fided to Michael Nesmith, it might well have sounded something like Funkadelic.*

In the eighties, it became fashionable for soul purists (virtually all of them white) to regard any soul record which included anything even faintly resembling a guitar solo as some sort of sell-out to nasty old rock-ists (i.e. to white rivals for the right to set black music's cultural agenda). To maintain this kind of critical position is a denial not only of the impor-tance of Jimi Hendrix as an individual, but of the vast tracts of African-American cultural history embodied in his music. Jimi Hendrix's music could not have existed without soul music – and modern soul music would have been inconceivable without his.

---

*As noted above, Clinton had had the great good fortune to inherit a sizeable contingent of James Brown's disaffected musicians, including the young monster bassist Bootsy Collins. To while away the time on the band bus, Collins would entertain his colleagues with impro-vised impressions of Hendrix's spacy mumble; Clinton was sufficiently intrigued to encour-age Collins to develop this comedy-turn into a full-fledged spin-off act. As Bootsy's Rubber Band, Collins would announce himself, with amiable wooziness, as 'Caspar the Friendly Ghost', and three of his albums (*Stretchin' Out*, *Ahhh . . . . The Name Is Bootsy, Baby* and *Bootsy? Player of the Year*) actually outsold those of the parent organization. In the liner notes of his 1988 comeback album *What's Bootsy Doin'?*, Collins credits Hendrix – ahead of Sly Stone, James Brown and The Temptations – as the chief innovator of the sixties.

8

Hear My 'Trane A-comin'

Jimi Hendrix and the jazz legacy

I can't stand to sing the same song the same way two nights in succession. If you can, then it ain't music, it's close order drill or exercise or yodelling or something, not music.

Billie Holiday, Lady Sings the Blues (1956)

PLAYBOY: In recent years, according to some critics, jazz has lost much of its appeal to the younger generation. Do you agree?

BOB DYLAN: I don't think jazz has *ever* appealed to the younger generation. Anyway, I don't think they could get into a jazz club anyway. But jazz is hard to follow; I mean, you actually have to *like* jazz to follow it; and my motto is, never follow *anything*. I don't know what the motto of the younger generation is, but I would think they'd have to follow their parents. I mean what would some parent say if the kid came home with a glass eye, a Charlie Mingus record and a pocketful of feathers? He'd say: 'Who are you following?' And the poor kid would have to stand there with water in his shoes, a bow tie in his ear and soot pouring out of his belly button and say: 'Jazz, father, I've been following jazz.' And his father would probably say, 'Get a broom and clear up all that soot before you go to sleep.' Then the kid's mother would tell all her friends: 'Oh yes, our little Donald, he's part of the younger generation, you know.'

Nat Hentoff interviews Bob Dylan, Playboy (March 1966)

Much of the stimulus to [post-bop, rock-derived, contemporary jazz guitar] developments came from the brilliant, self-tutored electric genius of the guitar, Jimi Hendrix, whose near-demonic forays into pure texture – in which distortion, feedback, sustain, and the like were turned into vital, integral components of the music he created with such abandon in the mid-60s – opened up an exciting, hitherto unperceived world of musical possibilities. Like many untutored visionaries, Hendrix had an imperfect understanding of the conventional disciplines of music, with the result that his playing, for all its brilliance and originality, frequently was chaotic, sprawling and, in the final analysis, inconclusive. Still, warts and all, he showed us what electric guitar might be, and in a very real sense, he is the true father of contemporary electric guitar, his experimental work leading to and influencing in many of its important aspects what is currently known as 'fusion' music.

Pete Welding in the 'Jazz' section of The Guitar: the History, the Music,
the Players ed. Gene Santoro (1984)

In one sense, Peter Welding's hard assessment of Jimi Hendrix's role in the development of contemporary jazz is almost fair, even if his use of the terms 'untutored' and 'self-tutored' as near-synonyms is more than a little condescending (you could, after all, say the same about Ornette Coleman, or even Gil Evans). In another important sense, though, Welding is disingenuously loading his critical dice; much of the improvised music of the sixties – the free jazz of Ornette Coleman, Archie Shepp, Cecil Taylor and the late John Coltrane as well as the psychedelic rock of Hendrix, Cream, Pink Floyd and The Grateful Dead – was indeed 'chaotic, sprawling and . . . inconclusive'. That was almost the point; most of the art, culture and politics of the sixties represented differing aspects of a wholehearted assault on the very notion of structure, which – in musical terms – served as a useful metaphor for the unacceptable face of authority.

Just how much 'structure' jazz had accumulated by, say, the mid-fifties was the root of much heated debate, most of which served to indicate the gaping abyss between what the music represented to the people who played it and what it meant to many of those who set the critical agenda. To the former it was, as Robert Wyatt – indirectly quoting Max Roach and Charles Mingus – puts it, 'this incredible repertoire of classical music . . . the body of technical knowledge invented and acquired and redisseminated from Ellington to be-bop is one of the most awe-inspiring that this century has produced.' By contrast, Eurocentrics like the late novelist Anthony Burgess appreciated it only as a kind of light comic relief from 'proper' (i.e. European classical) music. Jazz, as Burgess wrote in 1967, was 'illiterate, instinctual, impulsive, aleatoric, unscorable, unpredictable – therein lay its charm.' In other words, you didn't need brains either to listen to or to play jazz, which is presumably why blacks were so good at it. Burgess would presumably find the suggestion that you have to be smart to play this music either absurd or threatening, and the notion of a 'great jazz composer' – like Duke Ellington, Thelonious Monk or Charles Mingus – to be a contradiction in terms.

Even Igor Stravinsky – John Coltrane's 'ultimate musician', Charlie Parker's idol and the man under whom Bird yearned to study – originally considered it impossible for jazz to incorporate both improvisation and composition. 'Jazz', claimed the great man, 'has nothing to do with composed music and when it seeks to be influenced by contemporary music it isn't jazz and it isn't good.' Stravinsky's remark was made in the twenties, prior to his composition of *The Ebony Concerto* (composed in 1945 for Woody Herman) or the emergence of Ellington, and he subsequently modified his view. Others, however, with the benefit of considerably more evidence than Stravinsky had at the time, have continued to hold that the terms 'contemporary music' and 'composed music' *by definition* exclude jazz. At the very least, statements like these not only place an arbitrary critical ceiling on what jazz musicians and composers are or are not 'allowed' to do with their music – it is difficult to believe that anyone who has actually *listened* to Ellington could imagine that it is even remotely possible to do what he did and not be a composer – but they also represent a fundamental misunderstanding of what jazz improvisation is all about.

'Spontaneity in jazz is the elimination of the unwanted accident by a mind-numbingly thorough knowledge of the instrument you're playing and of the harmonic and rhythmic circumstances that you're going to have to negotiate.'

Robert Wyatt, interview with the author (1987)

True enough, many jazz musicians – particularly older ones – have often seemed to disdain theory. 'If you don't live it,' Charlie Parker once said, 'it won't come out of your horn,' but the last thing he meant was that 'living' – without discipline, study and practice – is all that is required. The super-compressed, high-pressure improvisation of Parker's forties be-bop revolution required the on-the-spot, random-access application of a fearsome amount of raw musical theory; as noted in Chapter Five, Parker could rearrange the harmonic furniture of a given tune in a seeming infinity of ways, and any bop musician worth the going pawn-shop rate on his instrument was expected to be able to do likewise. More than a decade later, John Coltrane took the process several stages further: he would produce 'sheets of sound' from his tenor saxophone by drawing on his knowledge of every chord which would fit at any given moment of a piece, 'spelling' the constituent notes of each chord as an arpeggio and creating a new, spontaneous melody line from the twenty-four-or-so notes thus made available to him. Sometimes they would spill out in groups of five or seven notes, instead of the customary neat fours, occasionally clocking in at a mind-boggling rate of a thousand notes a minute. This may be an 'instinctual' process – and even that is debatable – but it certainly isn't 'illiterate'. To put it another way, not only have monkeys with typewriters not yet produced Shakespeare, but they haven't even managed to produce a Jeffrey Archer novel or an average issue of the *Sun*.

Needless to say, a jazz musician performing creative feats on this scale is not *thinking* about scales, modes or the precise spelling of an E♭ aug9♭5 chord, which may go some way towards explaining why jazz is such an offence to the most sacred precepts of Western rationalism (according to which anything you do without thinking about it is by definition highly suspect). That musician is, however, performing an act of spontaneous creation by calling on knowledge in order to express feeling, which is both an entirely different process and a considerably more complex one.

It was against this very complexity that many jazz musicians revolted in the mid-fifties. 'Funk' and 'soul' – both of which became pop buzzwords in the sixties and seventies – were hallmarks of a new music which evolved both to assert black cultural identity at a time when the white-dominated West-Coast 'cool school' had become the most prominent public face of jazz, and to clear some blowing space in a music virtually choked by thickets of increasingly complex chords. The 'cool school' had been inaugurated by Miles Davis's collaboration with Gil Evans on a series of ground-breaking late forties sessions later collected on the album, *Birth of the Cool*, and typically it was Miles himself who signalled the new direction with his 1955 Newport Jazz Festival performance of 'Walkin'', a straight, soulful blues.

Soul-jazz arose out of hard, or post-bop (it's not *that* much of an exaggeration to suggest that all jazz produced after Charlie Parker's death in 1955 was post-bop), and it harked back to the most fundamental roots of twentieth-century black American music, to gospel and country blues. Ray Charles cut jazz albums for Atlantic (including the notable *Soul Brothers* with vibraphonist Milt Jackson, who – as a member of pianist John Lewis's Modern Jazz Quartet – was also a leading light of the cool school) alongside his pop singles, and was, needless to say, one of the movement's central inspirations. Soul-jazz also threw up a new breed of stomping, churchy organists, including Brother Jack McDuff, Jimmy McGriff and the best-known of all, 'The Incredible' Jimmy Smith. The latter, in particular, 'invented' the Hammond organ as a jazz instrument to the same extent that Charlie Christian 'invented' the electric guitar; indeed, the listenability of a jazz organist is in direct proportion to his (or her – let's not forget Trudy Pitts and Shirley Scott) resemblance to Smith. The titles of many of the crucial new standards tell the story: Smith's 'Prayer Meeting' and 'The Sermon', Horace Silver's 'The Preacher', Charles Mingus's 'Wednesday Night Prayer Meeting' and 'Better Git It in Your Soul', Bobby Timmons's 'Dis Here', 'Dat Dere' and 'Moanin''. (Mingus, incidentally, defies common patterns of stylistic chronology; he cut *Pithecanthropus Erectus*, his epic precursor of free jazz,

in 1956, and 'Wednesday Night Prayer Meeting' in 1958, when soul-jazz
was beginning its decline.)

One singularly tempting over-simplification which should nevertheless
be strenuously resisted, is the notion that the cool school represented
nothing more than a sell-out to Eurocentric notions of musical legitimacy. When John Lewis's Modern Jazz Quartet walked out on stage in
their formal evening dress to play their occasionally bloodless chamber
jazz, they were manifesting black pride just as emphatically as the funk
merchants with their studied down-hominess; their way was a statement
that they, as Robert Wyatt puts it, 'could do everything that a white academic conservatory musician could do, plus everything that they couldn't
do as well.' The fastidious Lewis and his colleagues – like other black
musicians before them, going as far back as Scott Joplin and the appro-
priately-named ragtime-opera composer James Europe – were attempting to take on the Western academic tradition at its own game. This
neo-classical 'third stream' music, though, turned out to be fairly unsatisfactory to all parties, just as much of the jazz-rock that came along later in
the wake of Miles Davis (and Jimi Hendrix!) proved to be bad jazz and
worse rock.

Where my own dreams sufficed, I disregarded the Western musical tradition
altogether.

Archie Shepp

By the end of the fifties, soul-jazz had virtually become absorbed into the
general canon of rhythm and blues as the staple sound of black bar-room
music; trios of organ, drums and either electric guitar or tenor sax working over soul, blues and pop-song changes. The players who'd sparked the
music, though, had moved one stage beyond; having junked the convo-
luted harmonic structures that the be-boppers had inherited both from
European music and big-band jazz, they then dumped the blues and
gospel chord progressions which had been used in their place. The result
was something infinitely more daring and dangerous; a jazz which abandoned key centres, bar lines and regular beats; field hollers for the big
city, Afro-American music in its purest sense. In other words, free jazz.

If jazz is, in Whitney Balliet's felicitous and oft-quoted phrase, 'the
sound of surprise', then nothing was ever more surprising than free jazz.
It split both critics and players more profoundly than any other innovation in the entire history of the music; it was considered infinitely more
dangerous than be-bop. Bop was, after all, a highly structured music

which demanded a fearsome and intimidating degree of musical sophistication – it was originally designed to keep time-wasters out of jam sessions by formulating a music which only an élite could even *begin* to play
– but the very density of its harmonic concept meant that it could easily
choke on its own formal devices. If bop was like walking a tight-rope
without a net, the New Thing was like walking a tight-rope without a
tight-rope: in other words, if you can't fly, don't bother. Just as daringly, it
went back to jazz's earliest New Orleans roots by emphasizing collective
improvisation and eliminating the distinction between the foreground
(i.e. the soloist) and the background (the accompaniment).

The dominance of the soloist in jazz began with Louis Armstrong, who
had emerged from the controlled *mêlée* of collective improvisation by the
sheer purity, volume, ingenuity and audacity of his playing. The new
music's disregard for structure referred back to the earliest country blues;
the solidification of the three-line blues into a rigid twelve-bar form
occurred when the emphasis shifted to band performance from the old
solo troubadors, who could improvise at will because they had no accompanists to confuse. As late as 1948, Muddy Waters' 'I Can't Be Satisfied'
uses an eleven-bar structure, and performers like John Lee Hooker and
Lightnin' Hopkins have often left putative back-up musicians gibbering.
Hopkins once responded to the lese-majesty of a very young ZZ Top
telling him that he had changed chord too late with an arctic stare and the
gnomic utterance, 'Lightnin' change when Lightnin' want to.' Free jazz
was deliberately and joyfully heading back to the dark ages. Furthermore,
it threw both musicians and listeners back to their most fundamental
resources. Players had learned to depend on their ability to play the
'right' harmonies with the 'right' sound, and listeners had learned to
depend on *their* ability to recognize when this had been achieved. Free
jazz said, 'Later for *that* shit; how does it *feel?*' This was not *comfortable*
music; it was the most uneasy listening imaginable.

Harmony is, after all, a metaphor as well as a musical device; not for
nothing do administrators speak of 'harmonious' racial or industrial relations; a soothing notion of a place for everything and everything in its
place. In Arthur Jacobs' *A Short History of Western Music* (in which, incidentally, Jimi Hendrix is the only cited rock musician apart from the
ubiquitous Beatles and Elvis Presley), the author quotes a fourteenth-
century papal decree that sets out which musical devices are and are not
permissible within the church. Harmony was suspect because any devia-
tion from strict homophony (unison) might distract the listener from the

verbal content of a work (prayers, in other words), though 'it is not our intention to forbid, occasionally, the use of some consonances, for example the octave, fifth and fourth, which heighten the beauty of the melody.' Short rhythmic values, like the semibreve (a 'whole note', or full bar of 4/4) and minim (half-note), were discouraged on the grounds that they were 'intoxicating the ear, not soothing it'. Thus the increasingly common use of thirds in the fifteenth century was initially considered sacrilegious; the seventh would have seemed outright blasphemy, and be-bop's most celebrated harmonic totem, the flattened fifth – known from medieval times as 'Diabolus in Musica' ('the Devil in music') – was explicitly banned in the sixteenth century by the Council of Trent. It's just as well that Pope John XII never lived to hear it emerging from a flurry of sixty-fourth notes, or, indeed, rather puckishly inserted into the introduction of Hendrix's 'Purple Haze': the song is in E, but instead of announcing the 'home' key the insistent bass Es of the opening are coupled with a repeating pair of non-harmonic B♭s an octave apart. The result is both jarring and exhilarating.

Improvisation, naturally enough, was *totally* out of order. 'Certain disciples of the new school', said the peevish pontiff, '. . . display their methods in notes which are new to us, preferring to devise ways of their own rather than to continue singing in the old manner. Moreover, they . . . deprave [the melodies] with discantus [improvisation] . . . we straitly command that no one henceforth should think himself at liberty to attempt these methods, or methods like them . . .' Furthermore, in 1562, Ignatius Loyola's Society of Jesus proscribed music 'in which anything impious or lascivious finds a part', though Jacobs claims that Loyola's proposal to ban polyphonic music altogether from the church was a 'nineteenth-century romantic forgery'. Nevertheless, the fear of being misunderstood by *Down Beat* pales into utter insignificance by comparison.

It is, however, worth remembering that jazz has never produced anything interesting that wasn't bitterly assailed at its outset. (Jazz itself has, of course, scared the shit out of everybody from *Isvestia* to the White Citizens' Council of Alabama; the former on the grounds that it represented the apogee of Western capitalist degeneracy, the latter on the usual grounds of 'find out what the niggers are doing and make them stop'.) The story of how the young Charlie Parker was derisively banished from a Kansas City jam session when the veteran drummer Jo Jones threw a cymbal at his feet has passed into legend (and into Clint Eastwood's *Bird* movie); Duke Ellington compared be-bop itself to 'playing Scrabble with the vowels removed', and Louis Armstrong called it 'Chinese music'; Miles Davis, finding himself on the same 1954 session as Thelonious Monk, demanded that Monk not play under his trumpet solo as the pianist's elasticated rhythmic sensibility and unusual chord voicings upset his concentration . . . and *everybody* hated Ornette Coleman.

The single most important figure in the genesis of free jazz (the style itself is named after a visionary Coleman album featuring a 'double quartet', all improvising collectively for the duration of an album's two sides), Coleman spent his first thirty years as an utter pariah. He was born in 1930 in Fort Worth, Texas (where he played in a school band which also included King Curtis), and exercised his self-tutored (thank you, Pete Welding) tenor sax chops in whatever bands would have him. Rarely hired and frequently fired, he was excoriated for his alleged lack of musicality wherever he went; he suffered in guitarist Pee Wee Crayton's R&B big band, and was once slung off the stand at a jam session by no less magisterial a figure than Dexter Gordon. (Coleman was by no means the only major jazzman to have cut – or lost – teeth in R&B ensembles: Charlie Parker was a graduate of Jay McShann's big band; John Coltrane played with Eddie 'Cleanhead' Vinson and Big Maybelle; Albert Ayler spent a couple of summers playing behind Chicago harmonica virtuoso Little Walter; Lester Bowie – best-known for his work with the Art Ensemble of Chicago – paid dues with Jackie Wilson, Little Milton, Joe Tex, Albert King and Jerry Butler; Bowie's Art Ensemble colleague Philip Wilson put in time with Paul Butterfield; Coleman's principal drummer Ed Blackwell worked with Ray Charles and Huey 'Piano' Smith; George Benson led his own R&B band for some years in Philadelphia, and so on *ad infinitum*.)

Coleman was considered highly weird for his odd clothing, long hair and bristling beard (in 1949!), and was once badly beaten in New Orleans by the buddies of a jealous guy who thought that Coleman was after his girlfriend. He switched to alto saxophone (favouring a white plastic instrument rather than the standard brass Selmers) and resettled in Los Angeles, where in tandem with trumpeter Don Cherry, he began painstakingly constructing his own revolution. His first real critical acclaim came not from his jazz peers (with the exception of John Lewis, who was deeply familiar with modern European concert music), but from white critics and academics like Gunther Schuller and Leonard Bernstein.

Does any of this sound familiar?

'[Roland Kirk, John Coltrane, Eric Dolphy and Miles Davis] took certain ideas and extended them beyond the known breathable atmosphere with startling effect, but as a complete and total music everything about jazz had been conceived of and worked out by about 1960, and all that happened after that was jazz musicians breaking away from it.'

Robert Wyatt, interview with the author (1987)

The key jazz events of 1960 were Atlantic's release of Ornette Coleman's *The Shape of Jazz to Come* and John Coltrane's departure from Miles Davis's group. Coltrane – born in Hamlet, North Carolina, in 1926 – had joined Miles in 1955 just as Miles was ditching the complexities of bop in favour of blues modalism, signalling the ousting of chord sequences by scales and melodies as the primary basis for improvisation. He was generally regarded as one of a group of rising tenor saxophone stars in the slipstream of Sonny Rollins, who would have been Miles's first choice if he hadn't been in the process of kicking a severe heroin habit at the time. 'Trane recorded a half-dozen enormously influential albums with Miles before his own drink and drug problems necessitated a forced sabbatical, during which time he replaced dope and booze with God and Thelonious Monk.

Despite his marriage to a Muslim woman and his association with numerous Muslim musicians, Coltrane's spirituality was non-specific and all-embracing. 'I believe in all religions,' he once said, and he enthusiastically investigated Muslim, Hindu, Buddhist, Jewish and Christian systems of belief, all of which spilled over into his music. The use of Indian scales and modes became a pop commonplace in the wake of George Harrison's sitar experiments, but Coltrane had drawn on the same (and many other) sources some years earlier, and indeed, The Byrds based their adventurous 'Eight Miles High' on a melodic fragment from Coltrane's 'India' even before George Harrison heard his first Ravi Shankar record. Just as the free jazzers never allowed the song to get in the way of the music (and pop, at its most thoroughly distilled, never allows the music to interfere with the song), 'Trane never allowed religion to come between him and God. Even the statement that the post-clean-up 'Trane rededicated his life to God and to music is misleading; it implies that he acknowledged a division between the two. Coltrane's all-embracing faith is at the vibrant, luminous core of *A Love Supreme* (1964), the most explicitly devotional work of his career.

Newly refreshed, Coltrane studied briefly with radical tenorist John Gilmore and his boss, Sun Ra. (An early proponent of electric keyboards and leader of his own Solar Arkestra, Sun Ra had recently arrived in New York from Chicago. He stunned the jazz community with his big-band improvisations complete with lengthy recitations, and his incorporation of ethnic Africana with science-fiction trimmings into both his music and his dress attracted a fanatical coterie while encouraging the vast majority to dismiss him as a mere oddball.) Finally, 'Trane joined Thelonious Monk – himself recently emerged from fifteen years in the wilderness and finally acknowledged as the pioneer he was – for a legendary engagement at a New York jazz bar. That six-month stand at the Five Spot saw Coltrane crowned as the new king of the tenor, and led to his rejoining Miles Davis for the epochal *Kind of Blue* and *Milestones* sessions, where the contrast between Miles's burnished, understated melancholy and Coltrane's fervid volubility created astonishing degrees of exquisite tension. He had recorded sporadically as a leader for Prestige throughout the fifties, but most of these sessions were simply jams; his first utterly distinctive music was made for Atlantic during his last months with Miles. His Atlantic year produced, among others, *Giant Steps* and *My Favourite Things*; he even teamed up with Don Cherry and other Ornette Coleman sidemen to record *The Avant-Garde*, a programme of Cherry and Coleman tunes which Atlantic unaccountably sat on until 1966.

In 1961, he took his quartet to ABC's newly-formed jazz subsidiary Impulse, and allied himself more and more closely with the post-Coleman New Thing. His drummer of choice was the phenomenally loud and frenetic Elvin Jones, with whom he carried on a non-stop musical conversation that lasted for almost five years, and as he performed and recorded with Young Turks like Eric Dolphy, Pharoah Sanders and Archie Shepp, his music became ever more radically non-Western. 'Trane, Dolphy, Sanders, Albert Ayler and their successors incorporated into their music all of the 'bad' sounds which saxophonists had traditionally attempted to lose as their command of their instruments grew; from the honks and squeals beloved of R&B hornmen to the rattle of the keys and the 'split' reed sounds which generated multiple notes instead of the traditional clean tone. This was anathema to the reedmen of the old school, to whom a pure, clean sound was a veritable grail; almost as much the universally-recognized badge of maturity and competence as it had traditionally been to the European classical musician.

Despite the extraordinary work of Cecil Taylor – you'll believe a piano can scream – the New Thing's abandonment of tonality and orthodox harmony placed progressively less and less emphasis and reliance on the chordal instruments, specifically the piano. As a result, guitars had virtually no place in the New Thing. When Amiri Baraka (LeRoi Jones as he was then) compiled his 1961 list of who mattered in the avant-garde, Taylor was the only cited pianist alongside five saxophonists, two trumpeters, four bassists, three drummers and no guitarists whatsoever. The premature death of Charlie Christian – who, with Charlie Parker, Dizzy Gillespie, Thelonious Monk and drummer Kenny Clarke, had after all been one of the founding fathers of be-bop – essentially exiled the guitar to the peripheries of the jazz world, and despite the excellence of many post-Christian players (Barney Kessel, Sal Salvador, Kenny Burrell, Grant Green and Herb Ellis, to name but five), there it had remained. As Robert Wyatt astutely points out, Kessel sounds as if he comes *before* Christian, rather than after; and indeed, if *all* jazz guitarists who emerged between Christian and Wes Montgomery were to be strangled at birth by some homicidal time-traveller, the course of the music's overall development would be virtually unaltered.

Guitarists are the big boys in rock and blues – try, if you will, to imagine either music without what Mott the Hoople's Ian Hunter dubbed the 'six-string razor' – but in jazz, the brassmen rule; guitarists are definitely the poor relations. 'Guitar like a horn' may have been the ideal, but in practice, most jazz guitarists had adopted a pianistic approach, rigidly orthodox in technological terms, using big-bodied acoustic-electric guitars and moderate amplification. When the sounds of the horns changed, the guitars stayed put. Most jazz guitarists sounded, in rock terms, as if they were playing with the covers still on their amps. (By contrast, the most sonically experimental rock guitarists, like Jeff Beck and Pete Townshend, probably thought at that time that a 'diminished scale' meant a pay cut.) The price the jazzbo guitarists paid for their conservatism was exclusion from the New Thing.

True enough, Miles Davis had occasionally augmented his sixties band with guitarists Joe Beck (whose life has been continually plagued by people who confuse him with Jeff Beck) and George Benson. The soul-jazz guitar master Wes Montgomery, whose thumb-stroked octave lines eventually enabled him to make his fortune and ruin his reputation with an endless series of M.O.R. albums, rehearsed with Coltrane's early sixties group for a couple of weeks before bailing out for less mysterious musical terrains. The first jazz guitarist to challenge the prevailing orthodoxy was Warren 'Sonny' Sharrock, a Sun Ra protégé who made his studio début as a sideman on Pharoah Sanders' *Tahid* (1967). 'Pharoah had this technique of overblowing the horn,' Sharrock explained in an interview. 'It sounded like very fast tonguing, like a buzz-saw, I tried to copy it by trilling on the guitar, and found that I could get a huge sound, but more human, like a voice. Then I tried to stretch it by pulling strings and bending notes, and that was the beginning.' In 1969, Sharrock was hired as a calculatedly disruptive element in flautist Herbie Mann's otherwise lightweight soul-jazz combo. Since most of Mann's audience consisted of the kind of people whose reaction to Ornette Coleman's music or Jackson Pollock's abstract expressionism would be 'My kid could do that and he's only four', the results were somewhat mixed.

'I don't like guitars. I like drums and I like Coltrane. People used to get mad at me when I'd get hired for gigs. I'd say, "I ain't gonna play chords. That's guitar. I'm a horn player."'

Sonny Sharrock, interviewed in Musician (1988)

HENDRIX: Who's this other guy [Sharrock]? I think I've heard some of his things.
BURKS: He's all over the guitar. Sometimes it sounds like it's not too orderly.
HENDRIX : Sounds like someone we know, huh? (laughs)

Jimi Hendrix interviewed by John Burks (1970)

'Play like you don't know how to play the guitar.'

Miles Davis's instructions to John McLaughlin during the
In a Silent Way sessions (1969)

Among the earliest musical sounds Jimi Hendrix heard were the big bands of the forties. His father, Al Hendrix, had been an accomplished jazz dancer in his youth, and Jimi grew up with the Duke Ellington band's horn section ringing in his ears. One of Ellington's favourite effects was that of an entire trumpet and trombone line using plunger mutes to create a derisive or mournful 'wah wah' effect. The masters of the plunger mute were trombonist Joe 'Tricky Sam' Nanton, trumpeter Bubber Miley and Miley's successor Cootie Williams, and any of Ellington's numerous recordings of 'East St Louis Toodle-Oo' give a fair indication of the uncanny degree of vocalization the effect could create. In the service and on the chitlin circuit, Hendrix would occasionally confide to his intimates that one day he would be able to make that sound with his guitar, and this was taken as yet more confirmation that the boy was nuts. Al Hendrix also loved the hooting, growling tenors of the R&B of the late forties and early fifties, and their sounds were an integral part of the musical furniture of the young Hendrix's formative years. They also played a seminal role in determining how he 'heard' the guitar.

By the time Hendrix hit Greenwich Village, the most common sounds in the bars and coffee-houses were folk music (of both the traditional and post-Dylan varieties) and jazz. The market being what it was, the only jazzbos able to command concert audiences were the most popular, which essentially meant that everybody with less economic clout than Miles Davis or Dave Brubeck played places like the Half Note or the Village Vanguard, and the sounds of Roland Kirk, Charles Mingus, Ornette Coleman, Cecil Taylor and even 'Trane himself spilled out on to the sidewalks. Hendrix certainly acquired his taste for Bob Dylan at this time, not to mention the wilder British bands like The Yardbirds and The Who; but whether or not he actually attended the jazz clubs and sat at the feet of Sun Ra, Coltrane, Mingus and Coleman, their presence was inescapable.

In fact, it really doesn't matter whether Hendrix can be *proved* to have checked these men out or not. It is a matter of record that he arrived in London with a battered copy of Roland Kirk's *Rip Rig and Panic* in his luggage, and Billy Cox – who started out as a classically trained jazz bassist enamoured of Charles Mingus and Ray Brown – has attested to Hendrix's knowledge of lounge-bar standards such as 'Misty', 'Moonlight in Vermont' and 'Harlem Nocturne', which feature chords and scales more sophisticated than those used in standard blues-rock. However, it was Mitch Mitchell – who himself drew on Elvin Jones, Miles Davis's teenage prodigy Tony Williams and Keith Moon as his gurus among drummers – who introduced Hendrix to the music of the remarkable blind multi-instrumentalist Roland Kirk, whose ability to play two or more horns simultaneously provided an astonishing parallel to what Hendrix managed to achieve with the running octaves he appropriated from Wes Montgomery. Mitchell had played with Georgie Fame's Blue Flames – whose idiosyncratic blend of jump blues, soul-jazz, hard funk and ska novelties had made them one of the few British bands to appeal to black audiences – and had recently been fired by Fame for noisiness and insubordination. Nevertheless, whether Hendrix studied and applied the methods and techniques of the New Thing or the earlier jazz mode or whether he was simply plugged into the *Zeitgeist* and developed them independently, the fact remains that they're there.

'All I gotta say is . . . "Third Stone from the Sun". And for anyone who doesn't know about that by now, they should've checked Jimi out a lot earlier.'

Jaco Pastorius, explaining what Jimi Hendrix has to do with jazz to
Bill Milkowski in *Down Beat* (1982)

We could take many worse examples than 'Third Stone from the Sun' from *Are You Experienced*, recorded in February 1967 and released in June of that year. It begins with a sliding major ninth chord over a skipping, swinging Mitchell beat which manfully attempts to combine the elastic, polyrhythmic flow of New Thing drumming with the solidly anchored beat of rock; his bass drum is tightly locked into the rigid, metronomic bass guitar line, and the accents are distributed over the top of his kit. Hendrix's arpeggiated chords and Coltranoid mock-orientalisms are overlaid with the eerie swooshing of Hendrix's own breathing, recorded through a throat-microphone and slowed down. On another track, Hendrix provides a drawled recitative in which he portrays himself as a space traveller about to land on earth (the 'Third Stone from the Sun' of the title); hazy cosmic jive straight out of the Sun Ra science-fiction textbook. The first transition settles the beat down into a funky blues-rock groove as Hendrix swaps the oriental mode for a straightforward blues scale filled with Chuck Berry double-stops, before a vicious dive-bomb performed with the tremolo arm brings the proceedings to a crunching halt.

Then the jazz beat returns and Hendrix begins – in jazz parlance – to play 'out': of rhythm, out of tonality, out of notes. He unleashes his full arsenal of pure sounds: screams, whinnies, sirens, revving motorcycle engines, burglar alarms, explosions, droning buzz-saws, subway trains, the rattling of disintegrating industrial machinery, the howl and whine of mortar shells. Eventually, the music literally shakes itself to pieces.

Mitchell's precocious expertise with rhythms beyond the ken of the average rock drummer is demonstrated again on the same album's 'Manic Depression', a churning, thunderous 9/8 which combines rock textures, blues chord structure and jazz-waltz time. 'I Don't Live Today', a caustic evocation of the plight of the native American, uses a traditional Cherokee drumbeat and, once again, blues structures, but the patterns are no sooner established than they are discarded: the tempo escalates, the structure is demolished, and for a few seconds we are immersed in the ever-shifting landscapes of Coltrane and Elvin Jones. This emphasis is stronger still on the 1969 concert version of the same tune included on *The Jimi Hendrix Concerts*: Mitchell juggles the accents of the beat against Hendrix's muted strum, and a new central section leaves Hendrix alone to play utterly 'out'. Just as the radical tenor players had used a variety of embouchures and overblowing techniques both to generate two or three different notes simultaneously and to play an octave or more above the instrument's 'legitimate' range, Hendrix would use the sustain and feedback obtained by running his massive new Marshall amplifiers at maximum volume to turn the descending bass growl of a 'dive-bomb' into higher and higher overtones, gradually overwhelming the fundamental pitch of the original note. Here, he produces a series of eerie shrieks . . . and then, with the bitterest and most savage irony, he begins to play 'The Star Spangled Banner'.

Hendrix's adaptation of Francis Scott Keyes' anthem was still a few months away from evolving into the towering statement it became later that year when performed at the Woodstock Festival. Here, the opening lines are submerged in a demolition-derby collision between a Vietnam fire-fight and a home-front urban riot. Then the song's opening guitar riff reappears, revved up to double-time like a Wilson Pickett soul revue playing the first date of an eternal season in hell, before that, too, collapses in a percussive welter of damned souls in torment.

Hendrix's 'out' playing was not necessarily always an expression of pain, rage or grief: the brief exercise in pure crash-and-burn pyrotechnica with which he opened up 'Wild Thing' at the climax of his Monterey Pop Festival US début was Hendrix *playing* in the most literal sense of the word. It was playful, mischievous, exuberant, euphoric, extrovert; an ex-underdog's high-spirited slapstick display of hey-look-what-I-can-do. But as the mood of the times darkened, so did Hendrix's music; when he moved into his trick-bag, it was increasingly to express that which simply could not be communicated in any other way. There is no precedent in rock and roll, soul music or the blues for what Hendrix did to his national anthem that muddy Monday morning after that last fling of the notion of a mass counter-culture. Defiant and courageous in its ambition, deadly serious in its intent and passionately inspired in its execution, the Woodstock performance of 'The Star Spangled Banner' is Hendrix's key to the kingdom.

'At that moment, he became one of the greats, like Coltrane or Parker or Dolphy. He plugged into something deep, something beyond good or bad playing. It was just "there it is".'

Vernon Reid, interview with the author (1988)

At Woodstock, Hendrix was performing with Sky Church, an expanded band featuring Mitchell and including, for the first time, Billy Cox on bass. One Larry Lee (of whom little has been heard before or since) filled in on second guitar, alongside two percussionists: Jerry Velez on bongos and Juma Sutan, a former Coltrane associate, playing congas. (Unfortunately, a combination of the onset of fatigue among the sound crew and a misunderstanding of the nature of the music meant that the performances of Sutan and Velez barely registered on the eventually released recordings.) 'The Star Spangled Banner' came almost at the end of what many who were present apparently considered a lacklustre performance, evolving out of a jam finale to 'Voodoo Chile (Slight Return)' with Hendrix and Lee's guitars locked in an insistent three-note call-and-response. Then the band lays out and Hendrix plays, unaccompanied and out of time (all right, *a cappella* and *rubato*) the unmistakable signature motif of 'Voodoo Chile (Slight Return)'. He plays it as slowly and pensively as Miles Davis would, wringing every last drop of significance from each note. Then, without Lee or Cox but with Mitchell, Sutan and Velez raging behind him, he begins to play the tune – one which every American has heard several thousand times.

Or rather, he *tries* to play it, but somehow it gets ambushed along the way. That clear, pure tone – somewhere between a trumpet and a high, pealing bell – is continually invaded by ghostly rogue overtones; the stately unreeling of the melody derailed by the sounds of riot and war, sirens and screams, chaos and alarm. A year or so earlier, a British 'progressive' band called The Nice (led by organist Keith Emerson) had attempted a similar assault on Leonard Bernstein's 'America' (from *West Side Story*) which climaxed onstage with a burning of the US flag. But that was jejune by comparison. Hendrix presented a compelling musical allegory of a nation bloodily tearing itself apart, in its own ghettos and campuses, and in a foreign land which had never done anything to harm its tormentors. Time and again, the rich, clean statement of the melody would resurface, a proudly waving flag standing above the *mêlée*, and time and again, the tide of violence and horror would swell to engulf and drown it. Nation and melody alike were haunted and swamped, hopelessly fragmented and lost, uneasy dreamers drifting rudderless into nightmare. The feedback and distortion ate into the melody like acid, corroding everything it did not consume. Kurt Weill could have imagined it, Albert Ayler could have played it, but only Hendrix could have hefted the symbolic weight.

And then, as if to say 'Fuck it!' even before the last feedback mists had blown away, Hendrix whomped straight into what was perhaps the most perfunctory 'Purple Haze' he ever played in his life. Meanwhile, as the hippies wallowed in the garbage they'd strewn around what was originally a very nice field, Miles Davis was at work on an ambitious double album called *Bitches' Brew*.

> I got no kick against modern jazz
> Unless they try to play it too darn fast
> They change the beauty of the melody
> Until it sounds just like a symphony . . .
>
> Chuck Berry, 'Rock and Roll Music' (1956)

'When fusion grows up it may achieve the artistic significance of the "cool" jazz of the fifties.'

Robert Christgau on John McLaughlin, in *Rock Albums of the '70s* (1982)

The short history of fusion goes like so: as Miles Davis's sixties quintet (Miles, drummer Tony Williams, pianist Herbie Hancock, bassist Ron Carter and saxophonist Wayne Shorter) nears the end of its creative life, the Zen *brujo* of the trumpet picks up on some Sly, Hendrix and James Brown records and – bingo! – a genre is born. Within seconds, music stores are stripped of electric pianos and synthesizers, and suddenly there's no escape short of hermithood from Mahavishnu Orchestra, Weather Report, Return to Forever and Herbie Hancock's Headhunters. Like all short histories, it's broadly accurate but intensely misleading.

Jazz and rock had sustained a healthy mutual animosity ever since the mid-fifties. To the denizens of the jazz world, rock was a delinquent, retarded nephew who had, by some fluke, managed to inherit the family fortune; as far as rockers were concerned jazz was either blanded-out cocktail music or unstructured din, all of it played and enjoyed by snotty élitists who wouldn't know a good time if it came up and bit them in the ass. Nevertheless, diplomatic relations had been cautiously established throughout the sixties, mainly through the honest brokerage of R&B. Just as Bob Dylan's dive into folk-rock had allowed sundry unsuccessful American folkies (like the members of The Byrds, Jefferson Airplane and The Grateful Dead) to reinvent themselves as rock and rollers (though, as Robert Wyatt reminds us, they remained 'very loud folk bands'), the post-Rolling Stones boom in white R&B provided an entrée for young British jazzers. Groups like Georgie Fame & the Blue Flames, Manfred Mann and the Graham Bond Organisation (the latter including bassist Jack Bruce, drummer Ginger Baker and, at various times, guitarist John McLaughlin and tenorist Dick Heckstall-Smith) laid the foundations for a new *rapprochement*. Manfred Mann's group, for example, overdubbed flute, tenor and vibes on top of its standard R&B instrumentation, and was quite capable of juxtaposing a Chicago blues standard like 'Hoochie Coochie Man' or 'Smokestack Lightnin'' with a soul-jazz hit like Cannonball Adderley's 'Sack o' Woe' or Mongo Santamaria's perennial 'Watermelon Man' (composed by Herbie Hancock), all the while alternating Brill Building pop-soul croons like 'Oh No, Not My Baby' and 'Come Tomorrow' with Bob Dylan covers along the lines of 'With God on Our Side' and 'If You Gotta Go, Go Now'. Paul Butterfield's Blues Band, to many the epitome of Chicago blues revivalist orthodoxy, featured a hardswinging, sparklingly intense version of Cannonball Adderley's 'Work Song' on their second album, *East-West* (1966), but it was overshadowed by the title tune, a 13-minute 'raga-rock' improvisation which owed considerably more to John Coltrane's Shankarisms than to George Harrison's. In Britain, Polydor Records signed Chas Chandler and Mike Jeffery's protégés Soft Machine (featuring Robert Wyatt on drums and vocals), but couldn't make up their corporate mind whether the Softs were the label's best-selling jazz band or worst-selling rock group.

Probably the most courageous jazz-rock work – even though it wasn't recognized as such at the time – was by Captain Beefheart & His Magic Band, who combined fevered dadaist lyrics with music that made an explicit connection between early, irregular Delta Blues and ferocious post-Coleman New Thing improvisation. 'Beefheart' himself was Don Van Vliet, an occasional friend and colleague of Frank Zappa; he has now retired from music and makes a far better living as a painter. Zappa himself drew heavily on free jazz in his work with the Mothers of Invention; partly because he recognized its unique expressive potential, and partly because he knew it annoyed people.

More prosaically, the next step was an outbreak of rock groups with horn sections, the most notorious of which – Blood, Sweat & Tears and Chicago – blended brass riffs à la Stan Kenton with acid-rock guitar à la Jefferson Airplane, weighed them down with clumping rock rhythm sections, and welded the whole unwieldy mess to embarrassingly overwrought and hectoring 'white soul' hollering unworthy even of Tom Jones. Naturally enough, both groups were howlingly successful, and became the idols of Holiday Inn lounge bands everywhere. (Honesty compels me to acknowledge that Chicago – or 'Chicago Transit Authority', as they were known at the time – were one of Hendrix's favourite groups, though he recommended their concerts rather than their records. Historicity simultaneously demands the mention of 'Free Form Guitar', a six-minute New Thing thing performed on their first album by their late guitarist Terry Kath, touchingly ambitious, though no rival to either Sharrock or Hendrix.) Blood, Sweat & Tears had originally begun, like Michael Bloomfield's Electric Flag, as a 'progressive' soul band; its ousted founder, polymath Al Kooper, took refuge as a CBS A&R man, in which capacity he auditioned and rejected Lifetime, featuring Tony Williams and John McLaughlin. He also collaborated with Bloomfield to create 'His Holy Modal Highness' (*Super Session*, 1968), rock's most elegant and authentic tribute to Coltrane.

There were inquisitive sniffs from the jazz side of the fence, too. West Coast tenorist Charles Lloyd took his group into San Francisco's Fillmore Auditorium to rapturous responses and massive sales of albums like *Love in* and *Journey Within*, but despite the presence of illustrious then-newcomers Keith Jarrett (piano) and Jack De Johnette (drums), Lloyd's records survive only as curios of the era. The Gary Burton Quartet, a New York-based group led by vibist Burton and specializing in lightweight, Latin-inflected soul-jazz, wooed the hippies by sprouting moustaches and sideburns and allowing their guitarist, Larry Coryell, to dip a toe into Sonny Sharrock territory on tunes like 'General Mojo Cuts Up' from *Lofty Fake Anagram*, challenged only by Lloyd's *Journey Within* as the definitive 1968 hippie–jazz artefact.

If Chicago, Blood, Sweat & Tears and the other rock big bands depict most graphically the pitfalls facing rockers confronting jazz, it is Larry Coryell (and, for radically different reasons, Tony Williams) who provides the most eloquent example of the reverse dilemma. An abnormally fluent and resourceful player, Coryell careens through his be-bop runs with offhand deftness, but as soon as he kicks on a fuzztone and bends a string, he is magically transformed into a garage-band kiddy who's just smoked his first joint and wants to practise a riff he's copped from Barry Melton of Country Joe & the Fish. His downfall is his distance from the urban blues which was a primary influence on Jimi Hendrix, Eric Clapton and the other rock guitarists he admired; the use of bent and sustained notes, the pseudo-vocal colorations which were their second nature. There is an ancient adage about jazzmen who cannot play the blues: Coryell validates it. Like many jazz players, he assumed that rock was such a simple form that there was nothing he needed to learn in order to play it.

Robert Wyatt, whose Soft Machine toured the US as opening act with Hendrix for over a year, recalls, 'I saw Coryell once – he was one of the few people who ever got up and tried to cut Hendrix. It was at the old Scene Club in New York, and he was leaping backwards and forwards, his fingers flying, and Hendrix – when it came to his solo – just went 'ba-WO-O-O-OWWWW' and it just *erased* the last ten minutes [laughs] with one note. It was silly for Coryell even to try. It was like walking into a blowtorch . . . the fool!' Coryell, sensibly enough, later concluded, 'I better go back and practise be-bop and listen to my Joe Pass records, because it's going to be years before my version of rock is as together as his.'

More to the point, a magnetic storm was slowly building, pulling the more curious jazz and rock musicians together, and the calm eye at the centre of that storm was Miles Davis. While the 'leadership' of sixties jazz had been passed to Ornette Coleman and John Coltrane, Miles had led an elegant quintet whose music had been *sui generis*; above and to one side of the thrash and honk of the New Thing, yet freer and more fluid than the post-bop hordes. Intrigued by the sounds that Cannonball Adderley's pianist, Austrian expatriate Josef Zawinul, had been getting from the Fender-Rhodes electric piano, he had been demanding that Herbie Hancock feature the Rhodes and that Ron Carter switch permanently to electric bass. When Carter demurred and Hancock proved mildly dubious, Miles hired another pianist, Chick Corea, and flew in the British bassist Dave Holland, who was experienced with both acoustic and Fender basses. Holland brought with him tapes of a guitarist friend who had played with and (musically) grown up with jazz-rock veterans like Jack Bruce and Ginger Baker, and also moved easily between pop sessions and blues, rock or jazz gigs. Miles's young drummer, Tony Williams, had been getting increasingly restive, and when he heard those tapes, he took a chance and posted the guitarist a ticket to New York. Not too long afterwards, John McLaughlin arrived in town.

Miles and Hendrix had been sniffing around each other for some months; Hendrix somewhat intimidated by the older man's towering reputation, and Miles more than a little hostile, at least in part because of the powerful mutual attraction which existed between his new wife, the former Betty Mabry, and the young hotshot. (After her separation from Miles, Betty Davis launched a brief solo career as a singer; one of her songs, 'He Was a Big Freak', concerned a man who enjoyed being whipped with a lavender belt. The song was widely assumed to be about Miles; the trumpeter's counter-claim was that it was about Hendrix. I'd like to take this opportunity to wish the very best of luck to any future Hendrix biographer who sets out to authenticate *that* one.) When Betty decided to throw a party for Hendrix in the Davis Home, Miles himself contrived to be absent at a recording session, but he sketched out a tune on manuscript paper and left it in the music room for Hendrix to inspect. When Miles phoned up later to inquire about the guitarist's reaction, Hendrix had to confess that he didn't read music and couldn't make head or tail of it. Hendrix was keenly aware of his lack of the formal, technical knowledge so highly prized by jazz musicians, and in the last year of his life spoke increasingly often of taking a year off to study music, to fill in the gaps about which he felt so self-conscious. 'Tell me honestly, what do those guys think of me?' he would anxiously ask friends. 'Do they think I'm jiving?' The answer was that they didn't, but Hendrix was too unconfident to accept that.

Nevertheless, a loose jamming society began to emerge around the twin axes of Miles and Hendrix, involving Larry Coryell, Buddy Miles, John McLaughlin, Tony Williams, Dave Holland, Stevie Winwood, Jack De Johnette, Mitch Mitchell, Jack Bruce and organist Larry (Khalid Yasin) Young. Miles invited McLaughlin to the sessions for what was to become *In a Silent Way*, the prelude to *Bitches' Brew*, and his guitar became an alternative centre to Miles's own trumpet, though the album was dominated by the glistening, rippling pools of sound produced by no fewer than three electric pianos (played by Hancock, Corea and Josef Zawinul, the latter contributing the title tune. *Bitches' Brew*, recorded later in 1969, was similarly heavy on electric ivory, though Larry Young took the Hancock chair alongside Zawinul and Corea.) Williams, McLaughlin and Young formed Lifetime, whose rejection by Al Kooper, despite their undeniable musical excellence, may have had something to do with Williams's insistence on singing his own 'lyrics' and reciting his own 'poetry'. Jack Bruce toured in an unrecorded band alongside Coryell and Mitchell while Hendrix was off playing with Band of Gypsys, and in 1970 he briefly augmented Lifetime.

Yet Hendrix and Miles remained apart. Producer Alan Douglas, who had teamed McLaughlin and Buddy Miles for *Devotion*, the guitarist's first US recording as a leader, had been plotting with Gil Evans, the virtuoso arranger behind such Milestones as *Birth of the Cool*, *Miles Ahead*, *Porgy and Bess* and *Sketches of Spain*, to bring together Miles, Hendrix, Tony Williams and Evans's own orchestra, but Hendrix's management were dead against it, and both Miles and Tony Williams were asking very large sums of money. Eventually, Hendrix, Douglas and Evans simplified the project considerably; work was due to commence in late 1970 on rehearsals for a live album which Douglas would record at Carnegie Hall. Hendrix was to be the soloist in a programme of his own compositions, using Evans's orchestra and arrangements. As it was, Hendrix died the week before the first rehearsal. The concert took place in 1974, with guitarists Ryo Kawasaki and John Abercrombie attempting to fill the master's shoes; an album, *The Gil Evans Orchestra Plays the Music of Jimi Hendrix*, was issued later that same year.

> Trumpets and violins
> I hear in the distance . . .
>> Jimi Hendrix, 'Are You Experienced' (1967)

'[Hendrix] was the most incredible natural musician . . . he didn't know the names for the truly advanced musical forms that he created, but he didn't need to know them – that's for the academicians . . . he hadn't had classical or any other training, yet he had the talent of someone like Stravinsky or Berg.'

> Larry Coryell interviewed in *Guitar Player* (1975)

'Hendrix had no knowledge of modal music; he was just a natural musician, you know, he wasn't studied, he wasn't into no market, and neither am I.'

> Miles Davis (1974)

As a hint of what might have been, Gil Evans's album is fascinating; the closest indication of what would have resulted if Hendrix had realized this particular dream. 'I want a big band,' he said in one of his last interviews. 'I don't mean three harps and fourteen violins. I mean a big band full of competent musicians that I can conduct and write for . . . I think I'm a better guitarist than I was. I've learned a lot. But I've got a lot more to learn about music because there's a lot in this hair of mine that I've got to get out. With the bigger band I don't want to be playing as much guitar. I want other musicians to play my stuff. I want to be a good writer.' If Hendrix wanted to learn about orchestration, it would have been impossible for him to find a better teacher than Gil Evans.

In the entire history of jazz, only Duke Ellington himself has excelled Evans's ability to use the orchestral palette to produce tone colours both delicate and jarring, and the arrangements here are the ultimate vindication of the 'orchestral' nature of Hendrix's imagination. On records like *Miles Ahead* and *Miles Davis at Carnegie Hall*, Evans's orchestrations seem to emerge organically from the music of Davis's quintets, and on the Hendrix programme, everything the band plays is simply an expansion of what Hendrix himself played on a single guitar and the occasional overdub. It is not without flaws and errors of judgement, though: stompers like 'Foxy Lady' and 'Voodoo Chile' are next to pointless without the presence of Hendrix himself, an absence made even more blatant by the inadequacies of the guitarists. Neither Kawasaki nor Abercrombie are bad guitarists *per se* (quite the reverse, in fact), but it remains true that while rock guitarists are deficient in the kind of discipline necessary to work within the confines of arrangements as sophisticated as Evans's, their jazz equivalents – like Abercrombie and Kawasaki – lack the boldness to let go of the notes and enter the realms of pure *sound*. Even today, the only guitarists I can think of who could have done the job are Sonny Sharrock, Vernon Reid and Defunkt's Ronnie Drayton. Maybe Evans should have abandoned the notion of using guitarists at all, and hired Archie Shepp as the soloist.

Evans remained a devoted admirer of Hendrix's music all his life, including tunes like 'Up from the Skies', 'Little Wing' and 'Castles Made of Sand' in his band's repertoire right up until the end. In what was almost his last creative act, he recorded two of his Hendrix arrangements with jazz bassist turned all-purpose post-punk celeb Sting: 'Little Wing' appeared on Sting's *Nothing Like the Sun* album (1988), and a version of 'Up from the Skies', recorded at the same session, remains unissued. (Sting's live performances of 'Little Wing' often ended with guitarist Jeff Campbell blaring out 'The Star Spangled Banner' while standing on top of an amplifier.) At the time of Evans's death, I was trying to track him down for a detailed interview on this and related topics, but his comments to Bill Milkowski in *Guitar World* will have to suffice: 'I will play [Hendrix's] songs because I like them . . . I'm always going back to Jimi's music and finding new possibilities, and every time I listen to his tunes, I hear something new. That's the mark of a great composer.'

It is undeniable that, as Robert Wyatt put it, 'there was a whole lot of stuff that Hendrix didn't know that was actually out of his grasp'. He desperately needed a teacher, and the jazzers with whom Hendrix jammed during his period of retreat in Woodstock (1969–70) lacked the authority to fulfil that role. Albums have surfaced derived from his New Thing jams with Juma Sutan and pianist Mike Ephron; the latter sold the tapes to various budget-album houses under titles like *Jimi Hendrix '64*, which enabled him to maintain the fiction that the tapes predated Hendrix's contractual obligations to either Ed Chalpin or Chandler and Jeffery. Neither Sutan nor Ephron is powerful enough to lead Hendrix; he is insufficiently sure of himself to lead them. Result: nobody goes nowhere. (The Ephron sessions have also been marketed as *Jimi Hendrix at His Best Volumes 1–3*. I trust your admiration for the free-market economy remains as thoroughly undiminished as does that of the author.) The teacher Hendrix needed could well have been Gil Evans; it might also have been Roland Kirk, with whom Hendrix had jammed, and of whom he was in awe. But it *should* have been Miles.

'The jazz attempt to incorporate Hendrix – and I would include Miles Davis, my favourite musician of the century, in this – was and is a mistake, a fairly embarrassing mess . . . what I seem to remember is a lot of Coryells and McLaughlins thinking, "With my fluid jazz knowledge, if I turn up and use lots of feedback, I could leave Hendrix standing." In the end, the final impact [Hendrix] had on jazz was fairly disastrous. Miles gets all these psychedelic heavy metal guitarists in, and I don't, on the whole, think it works.'

Robert Wyatt, interview with the author (1987)

In the chapter on Ornette Coleman in his *All American Music* (1983), John Rockwell welds Hendrix and Miles together as the 'pioneering jazz-rock fusionists'. Indeed, Hendrix's shadow – as well as those of James Brown and Sly Stone – has hung over Miles Davis's music for the greater part of the last two decades, though it is nowhere more apparent in his seventies *œuvre* than on *Jack Johnson* (1971) and *Agharta* (1976). The former was soundtrack music for a docudrama about the great black heavyweight boxer, whose reluctance to conform to white standards of how a black person should behave no doubt struck a highly reverberant chord with Miles, and also probably had not a little to do with the Hendrix allusions which dominate the album's two side-long selections, 'Right Off' and 'Yesternow', from start to finish. For the *Jack Johnson* sessions, Miles used his latest bass player, Michael Henderson, an eighteen-year-old R&B prodigy he'd hired away from Motown and Aretha Franklin's road band, and Billy Cobham, a muscular young clouter who sounded like Buddy Miles with technique. Herbie Hancock came in to add some organ, and soprano saxophonist Steve Grossman contributed a few aimless Coltranisms, but the record's true star is John McLaughlin, who plays fierce, snappy wah-wah riffs throughout. For the closing sections of 'Yesternow', Sonny Sharrock augments the ensemble, his thunder-clouds of feedback drifting ominously through the music.

Still more explicit is the double-album *Agharta*, which comes as close as anything you'll ever hear to suggesting what might have happened if Miles and Hendrix had gone into the studio together and managed to collar Sly Stone, Larry Graham, Buddy Miles and a couple of Fela Kuti's percussionists en route to the sessions. Hendrix haunts *Agharta* from start to finish; Miles invokes him ceaselessly, both through guitarists Pete Cosey and Reggie Lucas and with his own wah-wah-processed trumpet and organ. Cosey launches into a series of head-on confrontations with the New Thing implications of Hendrix's onomatopoeic guitar improvisations; by contrast, Lucas represents Hendrix's soul-man side, the funky lyricism of his approach to the basic materials of R&B. Miles himself alternately grapples with the phantom and mourns him. Over the four sides, he plays a series of solos which are simultaneously laconic and eloquent, sobbing unashamedly, yet without the faintest hint of sentimentality. Interviewers had no need to ask Miles how he felt about Jimi Hendrix; everything they needed to know is on *Agharta*.

Beset by persistent ill-health, Miles went into retirement until 1980, but in a sense his thunder had already been stolen. An entire genre had sprung up in the wake of *Bitches' Brew*, most of it performed by his former sidemen, most of *that* on CBS Records, and most of it outselling Miles himself. Label boss Clive Davis had backed jazz-rock ever since the old Blood, Sweat & Tears/Electric Flag days; Chicago were on his label, and with the exception of Tony Williams's Lifetime and Chick Corea's Return to Forever, he picked up most of Miles's men as they departed the fold. Josef Zawinul and Wayne Shorter formed Weather Report, which started out dinky and then became severely funky when they acquired an extrovert young bassist named Jaco Pastorius. Herbie Hancock bought every electric keyboard in the shops and created a hi-tech update on soul-jazz called *Headhunters*, which not only outsold any jazz album ever issued (including *Bitches' Brew*) but ate the pop and R&B album charts alive. John McLaughlin and Billy Cobham formed The Mahavishnu Orchestra alongside Czech pianist Jan Hammer, hippie violinist Jerry Goodman and bassist Rick Laird, whom McLaughlin had known in London; their brief was to combine the massive weight and muscularity of hard rock with the high-octane spirituality of John Coltrane and the fleet articulacy of be-bop. Their admirers firmly believe that they succeeded; I state for the record that they were the most admired and imitated fusion band of the seventies.

Chick Corea's Return to Forever – spotlighting fusion's other premier bassist, Stanley Clarke – started out as an airy, all-acoustic Latin-jazz combo making albums like the appropriately-titled *Light as a Feather*, but soon acquired monstrous amplifiers and titles like *Hymn to the Seventeenth Galaxy*. Eventually, Corea's sidemen – Clarke, drummer Lenny White, and successive guitarists Al DiMeola and Bill Connors – all made their own records and formed their own fusion bands. Larry Coryell put together The Eleventh House; hell, *everybody* formed their own fusion bands. Even Jeff Beck, the king switchblade of British rock guitar, dived into the fusion pool on *Blow by Blow* and *Wired*, aided and abetted by Jan Hammer, among others, and developed a penchant for guesting on Stanley Clarke's albums. Amidst a flurry of the usual multi-noted fusoid tomfoolery, Beck revealed a thitherto-unsuspected and thoroughly bewitching way with a ballad; not only Stevie Wonder's 'Now We've Ended as Lovers' but Mingus's 'Goodbye Pork Pie Hat' yielded new, unexplored territory to his ironic, inquisitive guitar.

Basically, Robert Christgau, Robert Wyatt and all those who agree with them are absolutely correct; artistically speaking, fusion was a disaster. At its funkiest (Jaco Pastorius-era Weather Report and the better moments of Hancock and Stanley Clarke), it updated soul-jazz for the street-funk seventies, reopening atrophied lines of communication between jazz and contemporary black popular music. At its most 'artistic' (pre-Jaco Weather Report, the less deafening moments from Mahavishnu and Corea), it was modern Cool for proto-yuppies. At its noisiest, it was simple totalitarian bludgeoning; Heavy Metal with a Juillard diploma. In general, fusion combined rock's elasticity with jazz's concision; jazz's populist urge with rock's élitist ambitions; be-bop's catchiness and danceability with rock's appropriateness as a showcase for marathon solo improvisations. God, it was awful. And many people are still blaming Miles Davis and Jimi Hendrix for Stanley Clarke's 'Vulcan Princess' or Return to Forever's *Romantic Warrior*.

In short, fusion was undone by its humourlessness and by its weakness for corn-ball monumentalism. Both Hendrix's and Miles's 'voices' are human, quirky, vocal; mostly, they resist the temptation of grandiosity to which successive practitioners of fusion have so easily succumbed.

Hendrix's soloing was definitely in the jazz tradition, and a lot of members of the jazz community picked up on it. Not everyone, of course – there's a lot of players from the old school who couldn't stand to listen to Hendrix. But of my generation, most everyone will admit he was a leader.

Al DiMeola, *Down Beat* (1982)

The most eloquent tributes to Hendrix from the post-*Bitches' Brew* fusion school have come from the bass players rather than the guitarists, who favour McLaughlin as their model. Stanley Clarke, who at his most hyperactive sometimes appeared to be taking on Jimi Hendrix and Larry Graham at the same time, used both a piccolo bass (a short-scale instrument tuned up an octave to bring it into guitar register) and session guests (Jeff Beck, McLaughlin and Ray Gomez) for some uncanny moments on his mid-seventies albums; though his eeriest, prettiest and most explicit Hendrix reference came as late as 1985 with the musing prelude, seemingly extrapolated from the introduction to *Axis: Bold as Love's* 'One Rainy Wish', to his startling rap version of Bruce Springsteen's 'Born in the USA'. The late Jaco Pastorius, who was – for all practical purposes – the 'inventor' of the fretless electric bass, demonstrated his view of Hendrix's importance to contemporary jazz by merging quotations from Charlie Parker's 'Donna Lee', John Coltrane's 'Giant Steps' and Hendrix's 'Third Stone from the Sun' into his solo medley (a version of which, entitled 'Slang', appears on Weather Report's 1979 live album *8:30*). However, Hendrix's influence on jazz did not reach its fullest flowering until the eighties, and it took two old masters' return to the public arena to realize it.

'Hendrix was one of my idols. To me, he was one of the gods, and that's the only name that'll go because he played like nobody's business. Hendrix was beyond all the categories, and that's the kinda stuff I like, stuff that transcends those earthly categories. To hell with the rest of it, the most interesting thing in music is the magic. That's what we're after – pure magic!'

Steve Lacy, the man who turned John Coltrane on to the soprano sax, and the only white saxophonist who understood Thelonious Monk

'There was a fairly general consensus y'know, among the leading jazz musicians who had taken the opportunity to get into Hendrix, that had he taken a strict jazz direction with his music, which he was certainly capable of doing, that Jimi would have been one of the jazz greats.'

Miles Davis, who should know

Miles came back in 1980; wizened, gnomic and more idiosyncratic than ever. Fronting a stripped-down band built on the hard, springy foundation of Marcus Miller's steel-thumbed funk bass, and using the guitars of Mike Stern and/or John Scofield as his principal instrumental foils, his new music (most impressively showcased on 1981's live double *We Want Miles*) seemed to pick up where *Jack Johnson* left off. While he let Scofield go his own post-boppy way most of the time, he leaned on Stern (and, in the final years before his death in 1991, upon piccolo-bassist Foley) to be his Hendrix surrogates. But as Vernon Reid points out, 'What's missing in Mike Stern's playing is that sense of abandon. Hendrix had that uncontrolled *fury*: the uncontrollable spirit of the thing that makes him extraordinary.'

Of central importance was a musical flurry building up around Ornette Coleman, who, in the late seventies, had gone electric with a vengeance. A startling album cut with his new Prime Time band, *Dancing in Your Head*, used a melodic motif from Coleman's 1972 symphony *Skies of America* as the starting point for bumpy, exuberant improvisations which compacted funk and rock in much the same way as be-bop had compacted swing. It introduced Bern Nix and Charles Ellerbee, the two guitarists who have been Prime Time's mainstays, and launched a whole new musical continuum that stretched from Coleman's Texas home-base to New York's SoHo art scene. Under the disingenuous blanket heading of 'no wave', a school of musicians sprang up to explore avant-funk and Coleman's 'harmolodic' theory. (I've had this explained to me several times by some very smart people and I *still* don't understand it, but the consensus is that harmolodics frees melody from the constraints of harmony and allows full chromatic improvisation.) The most prominent harmolodicians include drummer Ronald Shannon Jackson, a Prime Time graduate who speedily formed his own Decoding Society, which featured Vernon Reid on guitar and bassist Melvin Gibbs; and guitarist James Blood Ulmer, who made a startling début, *Tales of Captain Black*, on Coleman's Artists House label alongside bassist Jamaladeen Tacuma, Coleman's son Denardo on drums and the great man himself on alto. Ulmer's career has been erratic, to say the least; he cut *Black Rock* and *Free Lancing* for Columbia at the height of his fame, but his music has stayed pretty much where it was. Generally working against the thunderous funk bass of Amin Ali – the eldest son of drummer Rashied Ali, who displaced Elvin Jones for Coltrane's last years – Ulmer is, in his own way, as much a missing link between John Lee Hooker and Sonny Sharrock as Hendrix was himself. 'Ornette Coleman opened the way for a particular kind of jazz,' explains Robert Wyatt, 'and out of that Ulmer was able to use the Hendrix in himself. *That's* really where Hendrix enters jazz. The door was opened by Ornette's funny theories and by Blood being the kind of guitarist who could use the information that Hendrix left behind.'

The eighties also saw the renaissance of Sonny Sharrock, who recorded and performed solo, with his own band and in one screaming tornado of an improvising funk-rock band with saxophonist Peter Brotzmann, drummer Ronald Shannon Jackson and bassist/producer Bill Laswell, who was responsible for mixing the proto-rap Lightin' Rod single 'Doriella DuFontaine', a spontaneous collaboration between Hendrix, Buddy Miles and Jalal of The Last Poets. Jackson also played with Melvin

Gibbs in Power Tools, a trio featuring guitarist Bill Frisell, and Coleman himself returned to the public eye with *Song X*, in which he rescued the immensely popular guitarist and guitar synthesist Pat Metheny from sinking into the New Age blahs. Add Defunkt – a blistering avant-funk-metal band led by trombonist Joe Bowie, younger brother of the Art Ensemble of Chicago's Lester Bowie – to the stew, and you have a new, strange brew in which not only the guitarists, but the hornmen and rhythm sections, have at last been able to 'use the information Hendrix left behind' and create an explicit working definition of his role in the perpetually-evolving tradition of 'black classical music'. The only surprise is that it took so long.

Coda:
The English and American Combined
Anthem (Slight Return)

'Hey! Whew! Rock and roll!'

Jeff Bridges introducing the *Legends of Rock* TV special (1978)

'Power is the ability to define phenomena and have them react accordingly.'

Huey P. Newton, co-founder of the Black Panther Party

Categorization is a wonderful thing. Back in the dying days of the First Vinyl Era, I was combing through the racks of a major British record chain searching for replacements for a hideously scratched-up copy of *A 25th Anniversary in Show Business Salute to Ray Charles*. However, I couldn't find Brother Ray anywhere. I checked out the soul rack; I looked under blues; I flipped through jazz. Finally I admitted defeat and asked an assistant: he directed me to 'easy listening', where I found what I wanted nestling amongst the Barry Manilow and Julio Iglesias records. That was laughably inappropriate, to say the least; even more traumatic was to find that another leading chain had their Jimi Hendrix records binned under 'heavy metal'; right up there with greats like Iron Maiden and Guns 'N' Roses.

This kind of brutal reductionism reflects, quite accurately, the way popular culture actually works. Ultimately, you see what you want to see, and what you see is what you get. What a writer thinks a book may be about – or a director a movie, or a composer a song – is ultimately not the point; what the reader, viewer or listener thinks it's about *is*. It is utterly pointless for artists or critics to ascend their respective high horses and either mope about being misunderstood or deliver querulous pronouncements about the hegemony of philistinism. Their customers are only interested in the sufferings of artists if they make for good gossip, and they are only interested in art if it *delivers* – a good story, a good dance beat, laughs, tears, loud noises, whatever. (A critic thereby becomes Culture Hut's *de facto* head waiter; the trustworthy kind who'll *really* tell you what's good and what's 'off' tonight.) In order for said customers to find what they want with the minimum of fuss, it's just as well that retailing layouts emphasize the uses to which the stores' patrons put certain musics rather than the intentions, ambitions and actual achievements of the performers concerned. (The notion of a store which classified its records under headings like 'Albums Done to Get out of Contractual Obligations, A–Z', 'Albums Designed to Annoy the Artist's Ex, A–Z', 'Records Men Like to have Sex by, A–Z' and 'Records Women Like to have Sex by, A–Z' is admittedly rather attractive, but it would take a hell of a long time to find all the Marvin Gaye records.)

Nevertheless, the very notion of 'easy listening' seems a massively incongruous description for the extremes of uninsulated pain and joy in the music of Ray Charles. And Hendrix as Heavy Metal? Phallic strut, death-obsession, science-fantasy imagery, Fender-Marshall meltdowns . . . what else could it be?

Finally, who cares? Hendrix was fond of saying that 'there are only two kinds of music: good music and bad music', and while he didn't originate the line – it's been around at least as long as Louis Armstrong – it is certainly one which he fervently believed. (Now *that's* how to run a record store: 'Good Music, A–Z' and 'Bad Music, A–Z'.) His own music drew freely on anything he had heard which appealed to him and he had a lifetime's worth of experience to tell him how demeaning and deadening it is for anybody – any music, any culture, any artist, any people, any *person* – to be defined from outside and then made to conform to the limitations of that definition, especially when that definition is explicitly hostile. Perhaps this is why, finally, Hendrix's vision, and the legacy of that vision, means so much more than a burnt Stratocaster and a sweaty headband.

> Hey Joe
> Where're you gonna run to now?
> I'm goin' way down south
> Way down where I can be free
> There ain't NO ONE gonna find me!
>
> Jimi Hendrix (after William M. Roberts), 'Hey Joe' (1966)

Appendix:
Music, Sweet Music, Drips from
My Fender's Fingers

Hendrix and hardware

That's all right, I still got my git-tar.
Look out, baby!

Jimi Hendrix, 'Red House' (1967)

'Every guitar player has to go to the father.'

Bobby Womack, interview with the author (1988)

If the musicians of the sixties were, as Robert Wyatt says, 'dragged along in the wake of their audiences' expectations', then the instrument manufacturers and recording engineers were, in turn, dragged along in the wake of the musicians' imaginations. Just as wars have traditionally been fought with strategies that proved successful in previous conflicts, so equally, each new stage in the evolution of the music was created with an older generation of technology. The earliest sound recordings served a purely documentary function as snapshots of 'real' events; the electric guitar was initially considered as simply a louder version of its acoustic ancestor. A recording engineer's job was to get everything sounding as 'realistic' as possible; a producer's – inasmuch as the term 'producer' existed at the time – was to coax or bully the best performance he could from the musicians. Records were cut fast to reduce costs; Jerry Lee Lewis once boasted that 'Whole Lotta Shakin' Goin' on' took 'about as long to record as it does to listen to'. The ten songs from The Beatles' first album which hadn't been previously released as singles were recorded in a single fourteen-hour session. When they played their legendary Shea Stadium show to an open-air audience of 55,000, The Beatles used less amplification than today's bands would bring into a good-sized club.

In the sixties, Phil Spector became recording's equivalent of a D. W. Griffith or a Cecil B. de Mille: he worked on a grand, Wagnerian scale, staging awesome spectacles – five guitarists, three drummers, platoons of strings – for his microphones, just as Griffith and de Mille did for their cameras. George Martin, spurred on by the drug-addled aural visions of

The Beatles, put to work everything he had learned as the producer of The Goons' surreal comedy records, creating the extraordinary *trompe l'oreille* conjuring tricks of the fab moptops' later fantasias. Martin's production of The Beatles' records caught Jimi Hendrix's imagination as powerfully as Bob Dylan's lyrical virtuosity had done: like Martin, he saw the recording studio as an extension of his instrument, as a brush rather than a canvas.

Both as a guitarist and as a recording artist, Hendrix was following in the footsteps of Les Paul, a pivotal figure in the development of twentieth century music technology. Paul – born Lester Polfuss in 1916 – was first and foremost a musician, and a very successful one, but his greatest impact was as an inventor. At nine, he 'amplified' his acoustic guitar by stabbing the needle of his parents' gramophone into the instrument's vibrating wooden top; he pioneered multitrack recording and was building himself solid-body electric guitars in the early forties. The best-selling records he made with his wife Mary Ford were masterpieces of sound-on-sound collage, pasting together as many as twenty overdubs of guitar and voice, some speeded up or slowed down. His instrument designs were eventually adopted by Gibson – one of America's leading manufacturers – and their first mass-produced solid-body guitar still bears his name. (Initially, Gibson's executives were so dubious about the 'plank' guitar that their first instinct was to market the Les Paul without the company's logo.) If anybody is the missing link between Charlie Christian and Jimi Hendrix, it is Les Paul; he was the first person who really understood the extent to which the electric guitar was a new instrument, as different from the acoustic as a Hammond organ is from a Steinway piano – or a car from a horse.

Literally hundreds of companies have marketed electric guitars over the years; the best of them have produced instruments with distinct sounds and applications. The Beatles' early records primarily showcased the rockabilly plunk of George Harrison's favoured Gretsch instruments and the bright jangle of John Lennon's Rickenbackers, but from the early fifties onwards, electric guitar manufacturing in the USA was essentially dominated by Gibson and Fender, two companies utterly distinct in both their individual histories and their design philosophies. Gibson was established in the late nineteenth century by the brilliant, autocratic luthier Orville Gibson, and the expansion of the company and the evolution of its products was a stately but inexorable march of progress; technological innovation and traditional, conservative styling combined at every turn. The body of the Gibson Les Paul may have been a thick, carved chunk of prime solid mahogany, but it was also a miniature version of the company's pre-eminent line of premium jazz guitars. As with its big, hollow ancestors, its mahogany neck was firmly glued in place, and the crucial 24¾″ 'scale' length (the quantity of string between the bridge and the nut) remained.

Fender guitars were an entirely different sort of animal. Leo Fender certainly didn't invent the solid-body guitar – Les Paul had been there before him, as had Californian inventor Paul Bigsby and not a few others – but he was the instrument's Henry Ford; he was the one who figured out how to mass-produce and mass-market affordable solids. His first guitar, the Broadcaster – introduced in 1950 and renamed Telecaster two years later – was manufactured in modular form and then bolted and wired together; its neck was a single piece of rock maple with frets applied directly into the blond wood, its headstock was angled with all the tuners in one row to keep the strings straight for their entire length, and Fender's 25½″ scale gave the Tele a higher string tension which complemented the high-frequency bias of his pick-ups. Leo Fender didn't even play the guitar himself: he was a former radio-repairman whose company had been founded on his amplifier line. The Telecaster was as untraditional as a guitar could get; no greater contrast with the plush opulence of the Gibson range could have been imagined.

Jimi Hendrix was a Fender man through and through. He experimented with various Gibsons, including the massively ostentatious Flying V model, of which he owned two: a mid-fifties 'Black Beauty' Les Paul Custom and a white three-pickup SG Custom complete with Gibson's somewhat eccentric 'Vibrola' system, which he must have found seriously inadequate by comparison with the far more usable unit fitted to the Fender Stratocaster, unveiled in 1954. He owned more than a hundred 'Strats' over the years, very few of which are known to have survived. (Buddy Miles, Monika Danneman, Al Kooper, Frank Zappa and Mitch Mitchell owned authenticated Hendrix Strats; Billy Gibbons of ZZ Top has one of slightly less impeccable pedigree.) To this day, UK instrument dealers refer to Stratocasters made between 1966 and 1971 (or reissues thereof) as 'Hendrix Strats'.

Leo Fender and his crew designed the Stratocaster as a more elegant and elaborate development of the plain, workman-like Telecaster. The Telecaster's body was a flat plank; the Stratocaster's was contoured at the back to fit around the player's ribcage and tapered at the front to accommodate the right forearm. Where the Telecaster mimicked the single cut-away of previous electric guitars, the Stratocaster's body was cut away above and below the neck, like horns. The Telecaster had two pickups – one at the butt of the neck and the other just above the bridge – to the Stratocaster's three. Fender had originally intended the Strat's pick-ups to be heard separately, since he didn't like the sound they made when combined; however, guitarists disagreed, and soon discovered that by carefully lodging the pick-ups' selector switch between the designated positions, two further sounds were available. (In the early seventies, spare-parts companies began to manufacture five-way switches for instal-lation in Stratocasters; a few years later, Fender conceded and began sup-plying Strats with five-ways as a standard feature.)

Unlike Gibson's guitars – and, for that matter, the Telecaster – the Strat's volume and tone controls were placed close to the bridge, so that the player could manipulate them without having to interrupt the music by reaching down. Gibson, still thinking of the electric as a different sort of acoustic guitar, presumably worked on the principle that a player would carefully adjust the sound to suit his or her requirements, and then concentrate on playing. The Stratocaster's design assumed that the gui-tarist might conceivably want to modify tone, volume and pick-up selec-tion *while playing*.

Finally, the Strat came equipped with the most elegant and reliable hand-vibrato system then available; a thin metal bar which protruded from the bridge and raised or lowered the tension (and therefore the pitch) of the strings. Most of the musicians Fender knew played country music, and the Strat's accessible volume control and hand vibrato (gener-ally, and inaccurately, referred to as a 'tremolo') enabled a guitarist to mimic the swells and bends of the pedal steel guitar. What Fender had in mind when he designed the Strat tremolo, though, was something far more genteel than the pedal-to-the-metal savagery Hendrix inflicted upon it; it is therefore not so surprising that on many of his live record-ings Hendrix was so frequently out of tune. The tremolo system simply wasn't up to it (neither, for that matter, were the guitar strings available at the time), and guitarists unwilling to undertake drastic retuning between – or even during – tunes generally fought shy of serious trem action until more stable, lockable (and, unfortunately, more unsightly and cumber-some) versions were introduced in the early eighties by the Floyd Rose and Kahler companies.

The Stratocaster had been a favourite of some of the radical blues guitarists of the fifties – Buddy Guy, Ike Turner, Otis Rush, Pee Wee Crayton and others had found it eminently suitable for their needs – but until the arrival of Jimi Hendrix, it was most commonly associated (in the USA) with Buddy Holly and (in the UK) with Hank B. Marvin of The Shadows. Both of them were gifted, inventive guitarists who loved the Stratocaster for its clean-cut tones, versatility and general ease of handling, but as far as the new blues-rock hotshots were concerned, it was a guitar for skinny, bespectacled nerds. The most prized snob guitar to own in 1966 was the Gibson Les Paul, both because its thick, rich sound (jointly attributable to its body construction and to the feedback-reducing double-coil 'humbucking' pick-ups Gibson had used since 1957) lent itself to the new vogue for overdriven, distorted sustain, and also because Gibson had discontinued the Les Paul line in 1960, owing to a combination of declining sales and various disputes with Les Paul himself. All the trendsetting guitarists – Eric Clapton, Jeff Beck, Peter Green, Michael Bloomfield – used them, and you had to be a pretty cool dude even to *have* one, let alone know what to do with it.

During his chitlin circuit years, Hendrix had used whatever guitars he could afford; Fender Jazzmasters and Duo-Sonics, Epiphone Coronets and Wilshires and assorted others. He had had to pawn or sell too many guitars in times of economic hardship to get too hung up on any one instrument, but the Stratocaster had been his preference ever since his days with the Isley Brothers. Though he was left-handed, he had grown accustomed to conventional, right-handed models which he would then restring and modify to suit his particular requirements; he removed the nut, replacing it upside-down, and readjusted the string height and intonation at the bridge. Unlike Bobby Womack, Otis Rush, Albert King and Defunkt's Ronnie Drayton, he chose to retain conventional chord and scale constructions rather than create new patterns to play on a right-hand-strung guitar, and he seldom bothered with special left-hand models, both because right-handed guitars were more plentiful and easier to obtain, and because – with a touchingly American faith in mass-production – he believed that they were likely to be manufactured to a higher standard. He also had little time for any snobbery concerning 'vintage' guitars. Leo Fender had sold his company to CBS in 1965 and Fender's new corporate bosses ramped up production and cut quality corners, ultimately leading to a fetishization of the guitars produced under the *ancien régime* and a growing demand for 'vintage' guitars. The older Strats were distinguished by a smaller and more elegant headstock design than the bulbous monstrosity introduced by the new management because it permitted them to display a larger version of the company logo. During his first UK sojourn, Hendrix played 'pre-CBS' Strats, not necessarily because he preferred them, but because as older models they would be more readily available on the second-hand market than the spanking-new 'CBS' big-head Strats. Once he had achieved American superstardom, he could have as many brand-new Strats as he wanted, so he used exclusively late-model versions, which presumably he found perfectly satisfactory. The double cutaway allowed him to reach almost all the top frets, especially since he had exceptionally long fingers.

Inevitably, his modifications gave the instrument a slightly different sound. The pick-ups were set to provide what Fender considered optimum response from each string, but of course, Hendrix's reverse-stringing meant that the strings weren't in the positions they were supposed to occupy. Furthermore, the bridge pick-up was angled so that it 'heard' the treble strings closer to the bridge than the basses; for Hendrix the reverse was true. The single-sided headstock was designed so that the string tension was heaviest on the bass E and lightest on the treble E, but again, for Hendrix it worked the opposite way. The results he achieved with his jury-rigged set-up were so spectacular that, for a while, some right-handed guitarists – Steve Miller was one example – began buying left-handed Stratocasters and having them strung and set up right-handed. 'Reverse staggered' pick-ups can be bought from various accessory companies; Stevie Ray Vaughan's favourite Stratocaster, on which Fender's SRV signature model was based, was fitted with a left-handed tremolo system, and for a hot eighties minute reverse headstocks were intensely fashionable. All these devices are supposed to bring the guitarist a silly millimetre nearer to Hendrix's own sound.

The Stratocaster didn't lend itself to distortion with anywhere near the ease of the Les Paul, but Hendrix turned this, too, to his advantage. The unmodified Fender sound has a clean, sharp high-frequency response which the Gibson cannot match, but the various distortion-inducing floor-pedals he used – 'fuzz-box' was the generic term of the era – could garbage up his sound until it matched anything a Gibson could produce. End result: an unparalleled palette of guitar sounds unavailable elsewhere.

Second only in importance to Hendrix's Stratocaster was his acquisition – almost immediately after its arrival in Britain – of the brand-new Marshall 100-watt 'stack'. It was the creation of Jim Marshall, a former big-band drummer and drum tutor (Mitch Mitchell was among his pupils) who had opened a hugely successful instrument shop in Ealing. As musicians demanded more power and volume than could be delivered by the exceedingly rare and expensive Fender amplifiers or by Vox, the leading domestic brand beloved of The Shadows, The Beatles and their admirers, Marshall grew sick of having to repair them, and – egged on by Eric Clapton and The Who – set about building something sturdier. Once Marshall had developed the 100-watt head, Pete Townshend insisted on a monster cabinet containing eight 12″ speakers, but faced with a potential roadies' strike, he settled for the more manageable arrangement of two stackable cabinets containing four speakers each. This rapidly became the industry standard it remains today, and the 'wall of Marshalls' was institutionalized as a trademark of the Second British Invasion. (Townshend is still vaguely niggled that Hendrix carted his Marshalls to the Monterey Pop Festival while The Who had to make do with rented Fenders; not only did these amps not produce the sound to which The Who were accustomed, but they weren't allowed to smash them for their grand finale.)

Marshalls weren't just louder than anything that had come before, they were also more sensitive; their preamps sucked up more of the sound of the guitar's pick-ups than Fenders or Voxes. For Hendrix, this meant that the guitar was, literally, 'alive' all over; he could produce sounds by lightly tapping the instrument's neck or body (or, of course, by banging them as hard as he could), generating his unique onomatopoeic guitar language without playing an actual note. At high volumes, the impacts would jar the guitar into feedback (the sound of the amplifier's speakers reintroduced into the pick-ups, instantly transformed into a hum or a scream), creating tones which sounded more like a synthesizer than a guitar. The resulting pitch could then be raised or lowered with the tremolo, giving Hendrix access to sounds unobtainable by anybody else before the introduction of affordable synthesizer technology. (As an example, the multi-overdubbed studio version of 'The Star Spangled Banner' originally issued on the posthumous *Rainbow Bridge* and resurrected on the *Jimi Hendrix Experience* boxed set was actually created with a sixteen-track multiplicity of feedback guitars further modified with variable tape-speed.)

Habitually, Hendrix would run his Marshalls with all tone and volume controls turned full up to 10, adjusting the levels directly from the guitar. From years of experience, he would be able to position his body and his guitar relative to the amplifier's speaker cabinets so that the resulting feedback would modulate to the precise tone he wanted: a high harmonic, a low fundamental or a tone transitional between the two. For crash-and-burn extravaganzas like the climax of 'Machine Gun' or the intro to the Monterey version of 'Wild Thing', he would summon up a raw explosion of sound by clouting the guitar, 'select' the required frequency by moving back and forth until it emerged from the *mêlée*, move it up or down by raising or lowering the tremolo arm, and 'interrupt' it or make it 'flutter' by interposing his body between the guitar's pick-ups and the amplifier's speakers. When he wanted to return to conventional playing, he could do so by turning the guitar's volume down to manageable levels, and then moving out of feedback range.

As soon as he got the money to indulge himself, Hendrix rapidly became an ardent technophile. He ran up colossal bills at prestigious New York music shops, buying every new gadget as it came on the market; his Electric Lady recording studio was designed to be the most modern, the most luxurious and the best-equipped in the world. That his work as both a recording and performing musician now seems like a shining testament to what can be achieved with 'old' or 'low' technology is simply a manifestation of historical irony; he used the most advanced stuff he could lay his hands on at the time, from the custom floor-pedals like the Octavia and the Univibe which he commissioned from Roger Mayer, to be the then-futuristic gadgetry he installed at Electric Lady. Hendrix would not only have been utterly at home in the digital world of Synclaviers, Pro Tools and Akai samplers, but he would probably – if he had survived – have been among the first to adopt them as basic, workaday tools.

Alan Douglas, who supervised many of Hendrix's later recording sessions, has said that no one could produce Hendrix's records; all a producer could do was to help him produce himself. Though this may well have been true by 1969 – when they first started to record together – the statement seems more like a dig at Chas Chandler than an objective assessment of Hendrix's recording career. As a producer, Hendrix's forte was the creation of weird and wonderful new sounds and effects; the more orthodox and mundane task of recording straight, basic instrumental sounds probably seemed a trivial one to him. *Electric Ladyland* (1968) was the first album on which he assumed production credits (even though a few of the songs had been recorded the previous year under the Chandler administration), and it admirably highlights this dichotomy. The bass and drums on – for example – 'Voodoo Chile (Slight Return)' are, even on CD, appallingly muzzy and indistinct; not a patch on the clear, punchy rhythm tracks on George Martin's Beatles records, the Stax soul hits or even his own early Experience records, all of which were recorded on far more primitive gear than that used on *Ladyland*. More than a few of his later records – many of which were, admittedly, mixed and completed by others after his death – are chaotic and disorienting, with eccentric balance levels and stereo imaging. By contrast, his near-contemporary and fellow guitarist-producer Jimmy Page built his multi-platinum-selling Led Zeppelin records on thunderously tight and clear bass and drum foundations, 'professionalizing' hard-rock recording just as the megawatt PA systems the group used for their live performances 'professionalized' stadium rock shows. Again, the deluge of live Hendrix recordings issued in the last couple of decades demonstrates clearly how his voice – hardly the sturdiest vocal instrument at the best of times – suffered for the lack of effective stage monitoring, when the awesomely concussive levels of amplification he used rendered it almost impossible for him to hear what he was singing. (His tendency to forget lyrics on stage didn't help, it must be admitted.)

Nevertheless, *Electric Ladyland*'s two longest pieces – 'Voodoo Chile' on side one and '1983/A Merman I Should Turn to Be' on side three – effectively demonstrate the extremes of his approach as a producer/ musician. 'Voodoo Chile' is a jam: a straight extension of venerable Delta blues themes performed more or less spontaneously by Hendrix with Mitch Mitchell on drums, Jefferson Airplane's Jack Casady on bass and Stevie Winwood behind the organ. Here we find Hendrix wrestling with wood and wires, creating on his feet in a form where inspiration is all. (A blues jam without genuine feeling or a constant flow of ideas achieves levels of tedium unknown outside double-glazing sales conferences.) Recorded 'live in the studio', it is 'hands-on' music-making of the most traditional, lo-tech variety, a lengthy four-way conversation which was probably utterly unrepeatable. '1983', by contrast, is a lengthy studio fantasia which collages a variety of performances; embellished with sound effects and constructed on tape in a manner as unreproducible in live performance as The Beatles' *Sgt Pepper* was at the time. The final 'performance' was not by the band; it was by Hendrix and his engineer Eddie Kramer, and the 'instrument' was a mixing desk. There is nothing like it anywhere else in pop; it steers a supremely sure-footed path between the fumbling abstractions of contemporary Pink Floyd records and the art-deco cartooning of The Beatles. It is rock's premier work of science fiction; Hendrix was the music's first and funkiest cyberpunk.

As a guitarist, he remains imitated but unassimilated. Eddie Van Halen, by far the most influential hard and heavy guitarist of the eighties, borrowed the Hendrix vocabulary – tremolo tricks and all – in order to say very little, while defiantly citing Eric Clapton (whom he resembled about as much as I do Tom Cruise) as his primary influence. Prince, with equal perversity, names Carlos Santana as his guitar guru, even as he unleashes patently Hendrix-derived flourishes as both theatrical device and sound effect – though he has gone on record as suggesting that mastering 'The Star Spangled Banner' is an essential rite of passage for any tyro electric guitarist. Meanwhile, Hendrix fetishism continues unabated among the guitar fraternity. During the seventies and eighties, many of the most valuable contributions to Hendrixology came from magazines like *Guitar Player* and *Guitar World* (the latter magazine devoted two special issues entirely to Hendrix in the eighties), and he appears, from the grave, to endorse as many products as most living guitar stars.

During the eighties, the 'Hendrix Strats' advertised by UK Fender dealers represented unofficial collectors' shorthand rather than an authorized signature model like Fender's Eric Clapton and Jeff Beck Stratocasters, but Hendrix's name and image do appear on Jim Dunlop's special-edition reissues of the old Dallas–Arbiter Fuzz Face distortion box and Vox Cry Baby wah-wah pedal he favoured. In the late eighties, I bought a 'Jimi Hendrix' wah-wah (Model JH-1) – purely in the interests of research, of course – and found, on its base, a logo depicting a silhouette of Hendrix, a discography of recommended albums (including the posthumous cut-and-paste *Crash Landing*, which does not often figure in such lists), and a stern warning to the effect that 'any use of the Jimi Hendrix name with effects pedals without the consent of the Hendrix Estate Management and Dunlop Mfg Co is prohibited by law.'

There's nothing wrong with all of this – after all, Hendrix did use these particular gizmos, and the reissues are made to the exact specifications of the originals – but the most specious 'posthumous endorsement' came in 1985, when Schecter, the US guitar and accessory company, announced their Jimi Hendrix Model, a right-handed Strat clone with a left-handed neck and 'Jimi Hendrix Signature Model' reverse-staggered pick-ups, complete with a scrawled 'Jimi Hendrix' on the scratchplate, though it was not a facsimile of Hendrix's actual signature. Duran Duran's original guitarist Andy Taylor appeared in the company's ads under the legend, 'Hendrix has inspired a whole generation of guitarists. Now he's inspired a guitar.' The ad presumably inspired a terse communication from the

Hendrix estate's lawyers: the Jimi Hendrix Model rapidly disappeared from Schecter's catalogue, to be replaced by an instrument known as the H Series, identical in all respects except for the presence of the 'signature'.

These post-millennial days, Fender will be happy to sell you either their 'regular' mirror-image Hendrix Strat or a left-handed-neck-on-right-handed-body Jimi Hendrix 'Voodoo' model. Alternatively, their Custom Shop facility would be more than willing to run you up an exact reproduction, hand-painted decorations and all, of the early-sixties Strat Hendrix smashed and burned at Monterey, a white big-head 'Woodstock' Strat or, indeed, anything your little heart and big wallet desire.

As in all apects of life under late capitalism, you pays as much money as you can afford, and you takes as much choice as you can get.

Discography

Part One: Foreground

Though it was, as Sam Cooke might have put it, a long time comin', the current state of the Hendrix catalogue is a miracle of clarity compared to the mixed-up confusion of times past. All of Hendrix's currently available significant recordings (apart from the prehistoric Jungle Records items) are released by Experience Hendrix via Universal/MCA and should be awaiting you at any full-service record store.

Are You Experienced (1967)

Hendrix as superstar-in-waiting, UK-style. Rough, raw, crunchy, funky and designed for maximum impact, this was the first Jimi Hendrix Experience album, and it's still the most immediate and accessible item in the Hendrix catalogue. It arrived in the summer of 1967 on the back of three consecutive hit singles and hit the British market hard enough not to be eclipsed by The Beatles' *Sergeant Pepper*, released less than a month later. The first deluxe edition, as supervised by Alan Douglas, combined most of the contents of both the US version and the original UK release, including those first three British singles ('Hey Joe', 'Purple Haze' and 'The Wind Cries Mary', and their respective B-sides, 'Stone Free', '51st Anniversary' and 'Highway Chile') as a curtain-raiser before zooming into the album itself with track 7, the devastating 'Foxy Lady'. Inexpensively recorded in four-track studios, *Are You Experienced* brings you hard rock, deep blues, thermonuclear soul, psychedelic soundscapes, pretty songs and science-fiction guitar-2-die-4; everything you need is here, and Jimi hadn't even bought his first wah-wah pedal yet. The one departure from the original tracklisting was the substitution of the unfocused and heavily flanged 'US' version of Jimi's groovy slow blues 'Red House' for the drier, grittier rendering released in the UK.

The current family-authorized edition improves on the previous regime's release by including the 'British' 'Red House' (from the original vinyl album) rather than the over-FXed 'American' version (from the US edition of the *Smash Hits* compilation). The bad news is that, in order to differentiate itself from the Douglas version, it moves the A- and B-sides of Hendrix's first three UK singles from the beginning of the CD to the end, which makes neither aesthetic nor historical sense. If you own a programmable CD player, however, you can improve the 'experience' immensely by reshuffling the running order to bring the singles back to the front.

Jimi Plays Monterey (recorded 1967. Some of these performances were released in 1970 on one side of an album shared with Otis Redding. First full release 1986. Though it is unavailable at the time of writing, Experience Hendrix should be bringing this back to the stores in the near future. When they do . . . buy it.)
Hendrix as superstar-in-waiting, US-style. Once again, this is Hendrix going for impact, getting as far into your face as possible, down to kill on-stage at the Monterey International Pop Festival with around 45 minutes to make the audience forget everything they'd just seen, including The Who at their demolition-derby best. *Monterey* is, more or less, *Are You Experienced* live, concentrating on the most stage-friendly material and interspersing the hits with a few well-chosen covers ranging from Howlin' Wolf's 'Killing Floor' to The Troggs' 'Wild Thing' via B. B. King's 'Rock Me Baby' and Bob Dylan's 'Like a Rolling Stone'. The CD is wonderful, but if your Hendrix budget is limited and your TV is stereo-capable, we recommend the DVD or video version, especially if you fancy grooving on the insolent ease with which he wrenches those astonishing sounds out of his Fenders and Marshalls . . . and watching that handpainted pink Strat go up in flames.

Axis: Bold as Love (1967)
Hendrix as songwriter. By late 1967, Hendrix had made his point: he was firmly established as rock royalty in Britain, Europe and the States and therefore could afford to turn down the firepower and reveal a few of the musical cards he'd been keeping up his embroidered sleeves. This second studio album is lighter, subtler and more varied than its blockbusting predecessor, with less concentration on stunt-guitar soloing and more emphasis on texture, humour and lyricism. The climactic title track shows off his grandest psychedelic vision thus far; 'You Got Me Floating' was the hit-single-for-the-asking that no one bothered to release; the airy, swinging 'Up from the Skies' showcases his newly acquired wah-wah pedal as well as Mitch Mitchell's swinging, graceful brushed drums; 'Little Wing', 'Castles Made of Sand' and 'One Rainy Wish' unveil the softer, sweeter sides of his personality; Noel Redding's 'She's So Fine' finds the Experience having Big Fun with some of The Who's patented mannerisms; and – just in case anyone thought Hendrix had suddenly forgotten how to rock – there was 'Spanish Castle Magic'. The connoisseurs' Hendrix album, *Axis: Bold as Love* is a masterclass in song construction and creative rhythm guitar accompaniment. And for those who care about such things, the solos are pretty good, too.

The BBC Sessions (recorded 1967–8, first released in condensed form by Rykodisc as *Radio One*, 1989)
Hendrix as get-down rocker. Consider this a live album without an audience. Cut on the fly for various BBC radio and TV shows, these 1967–8 sessions alternate excerpts from the standard Hendrix repertoire of the time – 'Fire', 'Hey Joe', 'Purple Haze', 'Foxy Lady', 'Spanish Castle Magic', an early version of 'Hear My

Discography

Train A-Comin'", 'Burning of the Midnight Lamp' and so forth – with just-for-the-hell-of-it covers, including Elvis Presley's 'Hound Dog', Muddy Waters' 'Catfish Blues' and 'Hoochie Coochie Man', Howlin' Wolf's 'Killing Floor' and The Beatles' 'Day Tripper'. We also get a triple helping of Hendrix's Curtis Knight-era instrumental feature 'Drivin' South' and a complete audio replay of his epically disruptive appearance on Lulu's BBC TV show, performing an impromptu 'Sunshine of Your Love' as a tribute to the recently disbanded Cream. Rough, ready and exuberant, this is the sound of a genius having fun. And if the liner-notes debunk the wonderful myth that the backing vocals on Hendrix's version of The Beatles' 'Day Tripper' were actually by John Lennon (rather than Noel Redding), that's a small price to pay for the hi-octane pleasures contained herein. Big Fun for Hendrix freaks, but a second-line purchase best appreciated by those already familiar with the front-rank Hendrix basics. Like . . .

Electric Ladyland (1968)
Hendrix as studio dreamwaver and master soundscaper. Originally a vinyl double-album, this ambitious, sweated-over studio concoction emerged in 1968 with the credit 'Produced and Directed by Jimi Hendrix' after the artiste took over the studio reins from manager/producer Chas Chandler less than halfway through the proceedings. The original Experience were augmented (and, in some cases, supplanted) by guest musicians including Steve Winwood, Al Kooper and Mike Finnegan (keyboards), Jack Casady (bass), Buddy Miles (drums) and Dave Mason (acoustic guitar) and – though early reviews suggested that the album was sprawling and incoherent, and that its author had overreached himself – it's now unquestionably accepted as a masterpiece. (Come to think of it, the same criticisms were initially levelled at the Stones' ultimate triumph, *Exile on Main Street*, another 'difficult' double-album which needs a little time to settle down in listeners' minds.) Here's where you find 'All Along the Watchtower' with its three *perfect* solos ('straight', slide and wah), 'Crosstown Traffic', both versions of 'Voodoo Chile' (chattery wah-wah funk-rocker, and Delta-goes-to-cyberspace blues workout) and the science-fiction *tour de force* '1983/Moon, Turn the Tides'. Plus some funk, some soul, some jazzy jams, some love songs, some death-before-dishonour rock and roll . . . you know, the usual. Usual for Hendrix, that is. Don't ask. Buy.

Live at Winterland (recorded 1968, released by Rykodisc 1987. Again, currently unavailable, but hopefully on its way back.)
Hendrix as populist hero. This 1968 San Francisco show finds him with the Experience burning down the house – opening up, appropriately enough, with 'Fire' – with a post-Monterey, pre-*Ladyland* repertoire primarily derived from *Are You Experienced*, plus a few diversions like Cream's 'Sunshine of Your Love', eight minutes' worth of the grinding instrumental 'Tax Free', a sizzling 'Killing Floor' with Jefferson Airplane's Jack Casady sitting in on bass, and *Axis*'s 'Spanish Castle

Magic'. Deeply cool and richly endowed with whomp–factor–five attack, it's no Monterey, but then again it ain't the Isle of Wight, either. For which relief, much thanks.

Live at Woodstock (recorded 1969; extracts appeared on *Woodstock* and *Woodstock II* [1970/71]. Single-disc twelve-song version released 1994; repackaged two-CD sixteen-song expansion released 1999.)

Hendrix as hippie figurehead. By the early autumn of 1969, Hendrix had disbanded the Experience, replacing them with a larger band still including Mitch Mitchell on drums, but with Billy Cox replacing Noel Redding on bass, and experimenting with new sounds, new styles and new sidemen. He'd originally been scheduled to climax the Woodstock festival by topping the bill on the Sunday night, but since the festival overran drastically, he ended up playing on the Monday morning, by which time most of the audience had had to go home, returning to whatever passed for their 'normal' lives. They missed a spacier, groovier, more cooled-out Hendrix, working his way, with rhythm guitar and percussion filling out the sound, through a few hits, a few jams, a few works-in-progress (including, yep, 'Hear My Train A-Comin") and the awesome 'Star Spangled Banner', which entitles him to a place on the same improvisatory pedestal as John Coltrane (just ask Vernon Reid). Like *Monterey*, this is also available as a DVD or video, which every guitarist with a yen to learn from the master should view at least once, but if you don't have the CD version of 'The Star Spangled Banner', you're missing out. Prince used to say that no one who couldn't play this was entitled to call themselves an electric guitarist, and that ain't the *half* of it.

Band of Gypsys (1970)/*Live at the Fillmore East* (1999)

Hendrix as funkmeister. To buy off a former manager who had paper on him from before he went to London, Hendrix rounded up Billy Cox and Buddy Miles and booked himself into New York's Fillmore East over the New Year's Eve of 1969/70, performing four shows spread over two nights in order to cut a live album. Whereas the Experience records often sound as if Hendrix and Mitchell are zooming off towards the horizon dragging Noel Redding along behind them, this particular rhythm section blow up a phat phunk groove and Hendrix sits on them, playing fractionally behind the beat instead of fractionally in front of it. That gives the eight-minute 'Who Knows' a hellaciously sexy bounce marred only by Buddy Miles' thankfully brief scat-vocal cameo, and *Band of Gypsys* thus showcases a side of Hendrix's playing you can't hear anywhere else; no wonder this was Miles Davis's favourite Hendrix album. The star turn, though, is the incendiary 'Machine Gun', which ranks alongside 'The Star Spangled Banner' both as a textbook of Hendrix's mastery as a shaper of outrageous sonic textures and as a scarifying glimpse into the mind of a thoughtful African/Native American in a nation at war with both a foreign land and within itself. Not one of the best-known Hendrix albums – despite high initial sales which ranked it second only to *Are You Experienced* during Hendrix's lifetime – but one of the deepest.

If more is required, the two-CD set *Live at the Fillmore East* provides an extra-large second helping, containing all of the usable outtakes from the Gypsys' four concerts: alternate versions of all the selections from the original album, including two fresh renditions of 'Machine Gun', plus Gypsys tilts at Experience standards like 'Stone Free', 'Voodoo Chile (Slight Return)', 'Hear My Train A-Comin'' and 'Wild Thing'. It's clear why Hendrix programmed the original album as he did, choosing takes on the basis of the quality of his vocal performance rather than guitar stuff, as demonstrated by the 'Machine Gun' alternates, where the guitar is even more staggering than on the familiar *Band of Gypsys* version.

Blues (recorded 1966–70; compilation first released 1994, reissued with revised packaging 1998)
Hendrix as rootsman. Most of these pieces – some associated with the likes of Albert King, Muddy Waters and Elmore James, some built by Hendrix himself out of certified traditional ingredients both ancient and modern – are impromptu: jams, goofs and live recordings not originally intended for release. However, they tell you all you need to know about Hendrix's relationship with his most vital source of inspiration. You get Hendrix's only acoustic country blues performance: the album opens with a solo rendition of, you guessed it, 'Hear My Train A-Comin'' played on a twelve-string, and it closes with a mammoth 12-minute live version of the same song, the latter unfortunately flawed by the Cox/Mitchell rhythm section's entry, which slows the funky groove Hendrix set up with his solo intro down to a sludgy crawl. There are also two versions of 'Red House' (including, yippee, the original UK *Are You Experienced* cut) and a jaw-dropping wander through the outer suburbs of Albert King's 'Born Under a Bad Sign'. Like *Woodstock*, *Monterey* and *The BBC Sessions*, this is definitely an item for the experienced Hendrix buff rather than the novice, but the better you know your Jimi – and the better you know your blues – the more you'll love it.

First Rays of the New Rising Sun (recorded 1969–70; this compilation 1997)
Hendrix as ghost. At the time of his death in 1970, Hendrix had been working on a double-album provisionally entitled *First Rays of the New Rising Sun*, but what he left behind was an immense stash of studio tapes in widely varying degrees of completion. Engineer Eddie Kramer and drummer Mitch Mitchell slid nervously into the production chair and set about the nigh-impossible task of second-guessing the master's wishes: the first fruits of their labours were two intriguing but ultimately incoherent albums, *The Cry of Love* and the movie soundtrack *Rainbow Bridge*, the latter being the only legit Hendrix release never to be released on CD. Other tracks from the same stockpile subsequently appeared, with ill-considered overdubs from studio musicians who had never worked with

Hendrix himself, on the posthumous early seventies issues *Crash Landing*, *Midnight Lightning* and *Loose Ends*.

Cry of Love was first replaced by 1995's *Voodoo Soup*, a cleaned-up (souped-up?) retread with twenty-odd years' worth of added hindsight. It lost two tracks and gained seven, mostly from *Rainbow Bridge*, plus everything benefited from both a new digital clarity and the removal of a bunch of extraneous studio effects. Sounding more authentically Jimian than ever, it kicked off with a previously unreleased instrumental entitled 'New Rising Sun', as well as scooping up the cream of Hendrix's post-*Ladyland* studio work, bringing 'Angel', 'Room Full of Mirrors', 'Peace in Mississippi', 'Drifting', 'Message to Love' and 'Steppin' Stone' together on to one album for the first time, and more than earning its place in the pantheon of great Hendrix albums. True, it wasn't *First Rays* (in the absence of the author, how could it be?) but it brought the Hendrix studio quartet – finally! – to a reasonably satisfactory completion.

Voodoo Soup was itself superceded by the current *New Rising Sun*, trumpeted as 'Hendrix as you never heard him before.' Actually, it's a straight-up remastered reissue of *Cry of Love*, plus a few tracks drawn mainly from *Rainbow Bridge*, containing none of *Soup*'s 'new' material and featuring nothing not available on vinyl twenty-five years ago. As a selection of crucial Hendrix material for those unfamiliar with these particular sides, it's bulletproof; as a revelation for hardcore fans, it's a dud.

The Ultimate Experience (recorded 1966–70; this compilation 1997)
Hendrix as pop star. Replacing the now-obsolete collection *Smash Hits*, *The Ultimate Experience* is heavily weighted towards Hendrix's brief period as a radio-friendly singles' artist, pulling the 'Greatest Hits' – 'Hey Joe', 'Foxy Lady', 'Purple Haze', 'All Along the Watchtower', 'Red House' (British version!), 'Little Wing', 'Voodoo Chile (Slight Return)' and the like – off the first three studio albums, with only 'Angel' and the Woodstock 'Star Spangled Banner' to represent his post-*Ladyland* music. If you can only afford one single CD and you want to cop some Hendrix flavour – some early Hendrix flavour, anyway – *The Ultimate Experience* represents serious value. Be warned, though – once you've heard it, you're gonna want more.

South Saturn Delta (recorded 1967–70; compilation released 1997)
Hendrix as ghost (slight return). Herewith the new management of Planet Hendrix took its first steps into the marginal, semi-canonical hinterlands of the Great Man's recorded legacy and returned with 65-or-so minutes' worth of rare Jimi groove, including restorations of pieces previously disfigured by the *ancien régime*'s questionable overdubs; edits rescued from the semi-dodgy posthumous albums *War Heroes*, *Loose Ends* and *Rainbow Bridge* (not to mention the now-deleted blink-and-you-missed-it *Voodoo Soup*); some alternate mixes of familiar

tracks; plus several items salvaged from what would have been the fourth Experience album if they hadn't broken up in 1969.

'Look Over Yonder' and 'Pali Gap' were rescued from *Rainbow Bridge*. 'Power of Soul' (with Billy Cox and Buddy Miles) has been heard twice before: in a storming live version on the *Band of Gypsys* album, and as a ludicrous mutilation of the original studio cut, which now appears here lovingly restored as the funkiest hallucination you'll have all month. Another *Gypsys* special, 'Message to Love', shows up here as 'Message to the Universe', performed by Hendrix's percussion-heavy Woodstock line-up. Then two heavy-duty Experience instrumentals: 'Midnight' and 'Tax Free'. A couple of demos: a very early guitar-and-drums backing-track sketch for 'Little Wing' and an equally preliminary version of 'Angel'; and a searing version of Dylan's 'Drifter's Escape'; but the prizes are the title track – off-centre jazz-funk supercharged by some horn-section charts highly evocative of the Gil Evans arrangement of 'Crosstown Traffic' – the lovely solo version of 'Midnight Lightning' which ends the album, and Chas Chandler's original mix of 'All Along the Watchtower'.

Footnotes, of course, but fascinating ones – Hendrix nerds will have cause for discreet celebrations: still on the 'missing' list are *Voodoo Soup*'s fabulous instrumentals 'Peace in Mississippi' and 'New Rising Sun', but there's always tomorrow. Isn't there?

The Jimi Hendrix Experience (four-CD boxed set, recorded 1966–70; released 2000)
In the tradition of The Beatles' *Anthology* series, a multiple-CD boxed set, handsomely caparisoned in purple 'velvet' and featuring a treasure chest of outtakes, remixes, jams, demos, works in progress and other ephemera. The key fact is this: we never got enough of Jimi Hendrix or of his music. Despite the *Let It Be* débâcle, The Beatles were able to wind up their musical affairs in a relatively orderly manner – though their personal and business relationships were a very different matter – and when their *Anthology* series emerged, it was very much a series of footnotes to, and sidelights on, what was an essentially 'finished' body of work. Moreover, The Beatles were essentially 'master builders' rather than improvisers, and the material featured in their *Anthology* series was made up of sketches, works in progress, stages in the creative process leading up to the final results familiar to us all from the records released during their creative lifetime. Fascinating though that material is, it essentially functions as a study aid for those of us intrigued by how those finished results were achieved. In terms of listening for pure pleasure, the original releases remain the first port of call.

By contrast, Bob Dylan, who allowed us to rummage through his back pages under the rubric of *The Bootleg Series*, offered a more contradictory bill of fare. It was mind-boggling to discover that Dylan, Kooper, Bloomfield *et al.* first attempted 'Like a Rolling Stone' as a waltz, but even more so that Dylan could sit on a piece as magnificent as 'Blind Willie McTell' for as long as he did.

In this respect, *The Jimi Hendrix Experience* follows the Dylan rather than Beatles model. There are plenty of illuminating study aids – the Trekkie dialogue ('Starfleet to scout ship, please give your position') from 'Third Stone from the Sun' presented unedited and unprocessed; an extremely early 'Hey Joe' with lyrics blown all over the place; an in-progress 'Purple Haze' minus the final layers of guitar overdubs; the first harpsichord experiment for what eventually became 'Burning of the Midnight Lamp'; a take of 'Foxy Lady' discarded because of audible amp hum; and more – but the emphasis is overwhelmingly on stuff you can listen to rather than simply make notes on.

Such, such are the joys: some magnificent live performances, a few previously familiar from the long-deleted *Hendrix in the West*, but most fresh out of the can. The real collectors' wet dream as far as the live stuff is concerned is a one-two combo of 'Killing Floor' and 'Hey Joe' cut in Paris during the Experience's first fortnight as a unit. As far as anyone knows, these are the band's earliest recordings. 'Hey Joe' is muted and oddly sinister, with an extremely tentative intro, an abrupt ending and Mitch Mitchell going for it BIG TIME during the guitar solo.

The studio offcuts are no less rewarding. A 1969 remake of 'Stone Free', discarded because Reprise preferred to issue the original 1966 version on *Smash Hits*, demonstrates just how much more sophisticated the Experience had grown; and later recordings with Billy Cox, plus either Buddy Miles or Mitchell, provide a far richer and clearer portrait of Hendrix's later studio work than we've had thus far. Then there's the new stuff. 'Country Blues' is a deluxe jam based on a riff not dissimilar to Howlin' Wolf's '44'; 'Takin' Care of No Business' is a fine, sardonic variant on the 'Brother Can You Spare a Dime' chord changes: 'I'm so broke I couldn't even pay attention,' Hendrix drawls. The funky reflective minor blues 'Somewhere' is bookended by the Hookeresque soliloquy 'It's Too Bad'.

And, thank the Lord, there's 'Cherokee Mist'. Not to mention the reappearance of two items out of print for so long that they might as well be brand new: the gorgeous solo–guitar sketch of 'Electric Ladyland', which represents the absolute peak of Hendrix's mastery of Curtis Mayfield's sweet arpeggiated funk, and the studio version of 'Star Spangled Banner' in which Hendrix, let loose on a sixteen-track desk for the first time, creates a masterpiece of demented grandeur in which a chorale of speeded-up and slowed-down guitars generate textures inaccessible to all other humans until the arrival of the polyphonic synthesizer.

This is pure treasure. Not just because it affords us a voyeuristic glimpse into the creative processes which produced the work that redrew the map of popular culture in the late sixties, but because so much of it is simply great music in its own right. If nothing from the original, orthodox, official Hendrix canon had ever been heard or released, if the world had never known an *Electric Ladyland* or an *Are You Experienced*, then what's in this box would still be more than enough to earn Hendrix his keys to the kingdom.

Discography

Drivin' South (Jungle Records, UK)
Knock Yourself Out (Jungle Records, UK) (recorded 1965; these compilations released 2000)

Back in the vinyl era, the Hendrix section of the record racks was clogged up with seriously dubious 'prehistoric' Hendrix recordings, i.e. those cut for Ed Chalpin and others prior to Hendrix's relocation to the UK. *Drivin' South* is a live recording, cut on Boxing Day 1965, some seven months before Hendrix upped and split to London, at a club in Hackensack, New Jersey. It finds our hero with Curtis Knight & the Squires working out on a variety of blues and soul standards, mostly sung by Hendrix himself, and drawn from the repertoires of B. B. King ('Sweet Little Angel'), Albert King ('Travellin' to California'), Jimmy Reed ('Baby What You Want Me to Do', 'Bright Lights Big City'), Howlin' Wolf ('Killing Floor'), Muddy Waters/Bo Diddley ('I'm a Man'), Elmore James ('Bleeding Heart'), The Mar-Keys ('Last Night'), Lee Dorsey ('Get Out My Life, Woman') and Ray Charles ('What'd I Say'), and kicking off with Hendrix's signature 'Driving South'. Recording quality is strictly amateur hour and the band are never less, but rarely more, than adequate, but it demonstrates that even if Hendrix had been content to remain an orthodox bluesman, he would still have been easily a match for such highly lauded white counterparts as Eric Clapton, Michael Bloomfield or Peter Green.

Knock Yourself Out, also with Curtis Knight & the Squires, is a lot less fun. Mostly studio-recorded and featuring Knight as lead singer throughout, the heavily Booker T & the MGs-derived instrumentals are the most listenable tracks, though Knight's 'Like a Rolling Stone'-alike protest song 'How Would You Feel' has a certain period charm. Among the poorly recorded live tracks we find borrowings from The Four Tops ('I Can't Help Myself'), the Stones ('Satisfaction'), James Brown ('I Feel Good'), Otis Redding ('Mr Pitiful') and Barratt Strong ('Money'). Of academic interest only: approach with extreme caution.

Part Two: Background

Any comprehensive guide to the musics which influenced Hendrix, and which were in turn influenced by him, could well occupy a full-length book of its own. The following selections therefore merely scratch the surface, but should provide a rough map of the terrain and a few pointers for further exploration.

Caveat: to nominate, for example, one album by Bo Diddley as opposed to three by Stanley Clarke does not necessarily mean that Clarke's work is three times as important as Bo's; simply that the one album includes a fair proportion of the most influential Bo Diddley stuff, whereas the vital Clarke tracks may be spread over three different records.

It's also worth stating that the artists cited are not necessarily the only distinguished or worthwhile ones in their respective fields, and that the records listed are not necessarily the *best* work of the artist in question in terms of any quantifiable absolute (including the author's personal taste); they are the ones most relevant to the text.

(i) The Blues: Robert Johnson and after
Robert Johnson
   The Complete Recordings (Columbia, 1990)
   Beg, Borrow and Steal (Catfish UK, 1998)
Son House
   Father of the Delta Blues (Columbia, 1992)
Muddy Waters
   The Chess Box (Chess, 1992)
   Hoochie Coochie Man (Epic, 1988)
Howlin' Wolf
   The Genuine Article (Chess, 1994)
   The London Howlin' Wolf Sessions (Chess, 1972)
John Lee Hooker
   The Ultimate Collection (Rhino, 1991)
   The Best of Friends (PointBlank, 1998)
B. B. King
   The Best of B. B. King Vols 1 & 2 (Ace, 1986)
   Blues Is King (See for Miles, 1966)
   His Definitive Greatest Hits (Universal, 1999)
Albert King
   King of the Blues Guitar (Atlantic, 1973)
   Blues Power (Stax, 1968)
   I Wanna Get Funky (Stax, 1977)
   Albert Live (Utopia, 1977)
Albert Collins
   Ice Pickin' (Alligator, 1979)
Albert Collins, Robert Cray & Johnny Copeland
   Showdown! (Alligator, 1985)
Ike Turner
   Rockin' Blues (UK Stateside, 1986)
Johnny Guitar Watson
   Gangster of Love (UK Red Lightnin', 1976)
Buddy Guy
   The Very Best of Buddy Guy (Rhino, 1992)
   Buddy's Baddest (Silvertone, 1999)
Buddy Guy & Junior Wells
   Buddy Guy & Junior Wells Play the Blues (Atco, 1972)
   Drinkin' TNT and Smokin' Dynamite (Red Lightnin', 1981)

Junior Wells
  It's My Life, Baby! (Vanguard, 1964)
Various Artists
  The New Bluebloods (Alligator, 1987)
  Blues Guitar Blasters (UK Ace, 1988)
Robert Cray
  Strong Persuader (Mercury, 1987)

(ii) The inevitable Beatles and Dylan
  Rubber Soul (UK Parlophone, 1965)
  Revolver (UK Parlophone, 1966)
  Sgt Pepper's Lonely Hearts Club Band (US Capitol/UK Parlophone, 1967)
  Magical Mystery Tour (US Capitol/UK Parlophone, 1967)
  The Beatles (a.k.a. The White Album) (Apple, 1968)
  Abbey Road (Apple, 1969)

  Bringing It All Back Home (Columbia, 1965)
  Highway 61 Revisited (Columbia, 1965)
  Blonde on Blonde (Columbia, 1966)
  John Wesley Harding (Columbia, 1968)
  Before the Flood (Columbia, 1974)

(iii) Blues-rock, white R&B, hard rock and suchlike
The Rolling Stones
  The Rolling Stones (London, 1964)
  Let it Bleed (London, 1969)
The Yardbirds
  Five Live Yardbirds (UK Columbia, 1964)
  Roger the Engineer (Demon, 1965)
  Over Under Sideways Down (Raven, 1990)
The Who
  My Generation (UK Brunswick/US Decca, 1965)
  Live at Leeds (Polydor, 1970)
  Thirty Years of Maximum R&B (Polydor, 1994)
The Animals
  The Animals (UK Columbia, 1964)
John Mayall with Eric Clapton
  Blues Breakers (London, 1966)
The Paul Butterfield Blues Band
  Paul Butterfield Blues Band (Elektra, 1965)
  East-West (Elektra, 1966)
John Hammond
  So Many Roads (Vanguard, 1965)

Cream
  Disraeli Gears (Polydor, 1967)
  Wheels of Fire (Polydor, 1968)
  Very Best of (Polydor, 1995)
Electric Flag
  A Long Time Comin' (Columbia, 1967)
Mike Bloomfield, Al Kooper & Steve Stills
  Super Session (Columbia, 1968)
Jeff Beck Group
  Truth (Epic, 1968)
Johnny Winter
  Second Winter (Columbia, 1970)
Led Zeppelin
  Led Zeppelin (Atlantic, 1969)
  Led Zeppelin II (Atlantic, 1970)
  Led Zeppelin IV (Atlantic, 1972)
Dr Feelgood
  Malpractice (UK United Artists/US Columbia, 1976)
Fabulous Thunderbirds
  Portfolio (Chrysalis, 1987)
  Tuff Enuff (Epic, 1986)
Stevie Ray Vaughan
  Couldn't Stand the Weather (Epic, 1984)
  Soul to Soul (Epic, 1985)
  In Step (Epic, 1989)
ZZ Top
  The Best of ZZ Top (Warner Bros, 1977)
  Deguello (Warner Bros, 1979)
  Eliminator (Warner Bros, 1983)
Jeff Beck
  Beckology (Epic, 1991)
  You Had It Coming (Epic, 2001)
Van Halen
  Van Halen (Warner Bros, 1978)
Jeff Healey
  See the Light (Arista, 1988)

(iv) Soul music
Ray Charles
  The Birth of Soul (Atlantic, 1991)
  Ray Charles at Newport (Atlantic, 1959)

James Brown
    Star Time (Polydor, 1991)
    Live and Lowdown at the Apollo Vols 1 & 2 (Polydor, 1962)
Various Artists
    Atlantic Rhythm & Blues (Atlantic, 1987)
Otis Redding
    The Otis Redding Story (Atlantic, 1988)
    Otis Blue (Atco, 1965)
Otis Redding & Jimi Hendrix
    Monterey International Pop Festival (Reprise, 1970)
Wilson Pickett
    Wilson Pickett's Greatest Hits (Atlantic, 1973)
Stevie Wonder
    Anthology (Motown, 1971)
Aretha Franklin
    20 Greatest Hits (Atlantic, 1985)
Sam & Dave
    The Best of Sam & Dave (Atlantic, 1972)
Booker T & the MGs
    The Best of Booker T & theMGs (Stax, 1968)
The Impressions
    Big Sixteen (ABC, 1965)
Ike & Tina Turner
    Tough Enough (Liberty, 1984)
    Nice 'N' Rough (Liberty, 1984)

(v) Black rock & psychedelic soul
Bo Diddley
    Got My Own Bag of Tricks (Chess, 1973)
Chuck Berry
    Golden Decade Vols 1 & 2 (Chess, 1973)
Little Richard
    His Greatest Recordings (UK Ace, 1984)
The Isley Brothers
    The Isley Brothers Do Their Thing (US Sunset, undated)
    It's Our Thing (T-Neck, undated)
    Timeless (T-Neck, 1978)
    3+3 (US T-Neck/UK Epic, 1977)
The Chambers Brothers
    The Time Has Come (Epic, 1967)
    A New Time – A New Day (Epic, 1968)

Buddy Miles Express
  Expressway to Your Skull (Mercury, 1969)
Sly & the Family Stone
  Greatest Hits (Epic, 1970)
  There's a Riot Goin' on (Epic, 1971)
The Temptations
  Anthology (Motown, 1974)
  All Directions (Motown, 1972)
Jackson 5
  Greatest Hits (Motown, 1971)
Isaac Hayes
  Isaac's Moods – The Best of Isaac Hayes (Stax, 1988)
Marvin Gaye
  What's Going on (Motown, 1971)
Stevie Wonder
  Music of My Mind (Motown, 1972)
  Talking Book (Motown, 1972)
  Innervisions (Motown, 1973)
  Original Musiquarium (Motown, 1982)
Curtis Mayfield
  Curtis Live (Curtom, 1971)
  Superfly (Curtom, 1972)
  America Today (Curtom, 1975)
Parliament
  Up for the Down Stroke (Casablanca, 1974)
  Chocolate City (Casablanca, 1975)
  Mothership Connection (Casablanca, 1976)
Funkadelic
  Maggot Brain (Westbound, 1971)
  Funkadelic's Greatest Hits (Westbound, 1975)
  Hardcore Jollies (Warner Bros, 1976)
  One Nation under a Groove (Warner Bros, 1978)
Bootsy's Rubber Band
  Stretchin' Out (Warner Bros, 1976)
Graham Central Station
  Graham Central Station (Warner Bros, 1974)
  My Radio Sure Sounds Good to Me (Warner Bros, 1978)
Prince
  The Hits / The B-Sides (Paisley Park, 1993)
Cameo
  Alligator Woman (Chocolate City, 1982)
  She's Strange (US Atlanta Artists/UK Club, 1984)

Discography

Michael Jackson
  Thriller (Epic, 1982)
Trouble Funk
  In Times of Trouble (D.E.T.T., 1983)
  Say What! (Island, 1986)
Defunkt
  Thermonuclear Sweat (Hannibal, 1983)
  In America (Island, 1988)
Stanley Clarke Band
  Look Out! (Epic, 1985)
Run–DMC
  Raisin' Hell (Profile, 1986)
LL Cool J
  Bigger and Deffer (Def Jam, 1987)
Public Enemy
  Yo! Bum Rush the Show (Def Jam, 1987)
  It Takes a Nation of Millions to Hold Us Back (Def Jam, 1988)
  Fear of a Black Planet (Def Jam, 1992)
Sonny Sharrock Band
  Seize the Rainbow (Enemy, 1987)
Living Colour
  Vivid (Epic, 1988)
Black Rock Coalition
  The History of Our Future (Rykodisc, 1991)
Body Count
  Body Count (Sire, 1992)
Little Axe
  The Wolf That House Built (Wired, 1996)
  Slow Fuse (Wired, 1996)
Rage Against the Machine
  Rage Against the Machine (Epic, 1992)
  Renegades (Epic, 2000)

(vi) Jazz: from Charlie Christian to *Bitches' Brew*
Charlie Christian
  Solo Flight (US Columbia/UK CBS, 1972)
  With the Benny Goodman Sextet (UK CBS Realm, undated)
  Live 1939/1941 (Jazz Anthology, undated)
  1941 Live Sessions (Jazz Legacy, 1982)
Duke Ellington
  The Blanton-Webster Band (Bluebird, 1986)

Charlie Parker
Bird (Verve, 1988)
Charles Mingus
Better Git It in Your Soul (US Columbia, 1977)
Pithecanthropus Erectus (Atlantic, 1956)
Blues and Roots (Atlantic, 1962)
Jimmy Smith
Prayer Meetin' (Blue Note, undated)
The Organ Grinder Swing (Verve, 1965)
Jimmy Smith's Greatest Hits (Verve, 1966)
Wes Montgomery
Yesterdays (Milestone, 1980)
Midnight Guitarist (Jazz Masterworks, 1985)
The Small Group Recordings (Verve, 1975)
Miles Davis with John Coltrane
Kind of Blue (Columbia, 1959)
Miles Davis with Gil Evans
Porgy and Bess (Columbia, 1959)
Sketches of Spain (Columbia, 1960)
Miles Ahead (Columbia, 1958)
Miles Davis at Carnegie Hall (US Columbia/UK CBS, 1961)
John Coltrane
Giant Steps (Atlantic, 1960)
Live at the Village Vanguard (Impulse, 1961)
A Love Supreme (Impulse, 1964)
Ascension (Impulse, 1965)
Om (Impulse, 1965)
Live at the Village Vanguard Again! (Impulse, 1966)
Ornette Coleman
Tomorrow Is the Question (US Contemporary/UK Boplicity, 1959)
The Shape of Jazz to Come (Atlantic, 1960)
Free Jazz (Atlantic, 1961)
Roland Kirk
The Inflated Tear (Atlantic, 1968)
The Best of Rahsaan Roland Kirk (Atlantic, 1971)
Blacknuss (Atlantic, 1972)
Pharoah Sanders
Tauhid (Impulse, 1966)
Albert Ayler
Re-evaluations: the Impulse Years (Impulse, 1973)
Carla Bley/Gary Burton Quartet
A Genuine Tong Funeral (RCA, 1967)

Discography

Archie Shepp
 Yasmina, a Black Woman (UK Affinity, 1969)
Sonny Sharrock
 Monkey-Pockie-Boo (UK Affinity, 1970)
Miles Davis
 In a Silent Way (US Columbia/UK CBS, 1969)

(vii) Fusion
Miles Davis
 Bitches' Brew (Columbia, 1970)
 Music from Jack Johnson (Columbia, 1971)
 Agharta (Columbia, 1975)
 We Want Miles (Columbia, 1982)
 Panthalassa (Columbia, 1998)
John McLaughlin
 Devotion (Douglas, 1970)
Lifetime
 Emergency! (Polydor, 1969)
 Turn it Over (Polydor, 1970)
Mahavishnu Orchestra
 The Inner Mounting Flame (Columbia, 1971)
Herbie Hancock
 Headhunters (Columbia, 1973)
Jeff Beck
 Blow by Blow (Epic, 1975)
 Wired (Epic, 1976)
Weather Report
 Heavy Weather (Epic, 1977)
 8:30 (US Columbia/UK CBS, 1979)
 The Jaco Years (Columbia Legacy, 1998)
Jaco Pastorius
 Jaco Pastorius (Epic, 1976)
 Invitation (Warner Bros, 1983)
Stanley Clarke
 Stanley Clarke (Atlantic, 1974)
 School Days (Nemperor, 1976)

(viii) The harmolodic conspiracy (and fellow travellers)
Ornette Coleman
 Dancing in Your Head (US Horizon/UK A&M, 1979)
 Of Human Feelings (Antilles, 1982)
 Ornette Opens the Caravan of Dreams (Caravan of Dreams, 1985)

Virgin Beauty (Portrait, 1988)
Ornette Coleman & Pat Metheny
Song X (Geffen, 1986)
Ronald Shannon Jackson & Decoding Society
Nasty (Moers, 1981)
Mandance (Antilles, 1982)
Barbecue Dog (Antilles, 1983)
Decode Yourself (Antilles, 1985)
James Blood Ulmer
Tales of Captain Black (Artists House, 1979)
Are You Happy to Be in America? (Rough Trade, 1980)
Free Lancing (Columbia, 1981)
Black Rock (Columbia, 1982)
America – Do You Remember the Love? (Blue Note, 1987)
Sonny Sharrock
Guitar (Enemy, 1987)
Last Exit
Iron Path (Venture, 1989)
Power Tools
Strange Meeting (Antilles, 1988)

Part Three: The Music of Jimi Hendrix

It is a measure of the depth and breadth of Hendrix's work that artists from so many musical disciplines have attempted to find some aspect of themselves by gazing into the ocean of his music. Pride of place amongst Hendrix interpretations must of course go to *The Gil Evans Orchestra Plays the Music of Jimi Hendrix* (RCA, 1974), a gorgeously tantalizing vision of one of the many possible futures Hendrix's music could have explored. Intriguing, but ultimately unsatisfactory, *The Kennedy Experience* (Sony Classical, 1999) in which The Artist Formerly Known as Nigel Kennedy – the violinist now uses only his surname, and if your first name is Nigel you should probably consider doing the same – presents a full programme of Hendrix's compositions, contains a few wonderful moments; unfortunately, too few. A failure, but by no means a dishonourable one.

However, there are a few other notable variations on some of his themes. Including . . .

The Kronos Quartet
'Purple Haze', from *Sculthorpe / Sallinen / Glass / Nancarrow / Hendrix* (Nonesuch, 1986)
Derek & the Dominoes
'Little Wing', from *Layla & Other Assorted Love Songs* (Polydor, 1970)

Rod Stewart
  'Angel', from *Never a Dull Moment* (Mercury, 1972)
Wilson Pickett
  'Hey Joe',* from *Wilson Pickett Vol 2* (Atlantic, 1981)
Pretenders
  'Room Full of Mirrors', from *Get Close* (UK Real/US Sire, 1986)
Stevie Ray Vaughan
  'Voodoo Chile', from *Couldn't Stand the Weather* (Epic, 1984)
The Cure
  'Foxy Lady', from *Three Imaginary Boys* (Fiction, 1978)
The Isley Brothers
  'Machine Gun', from *Timeless* (T-Neck, 1978)
Sting (with Gil Evans)
  'Little Wing', from *Nothing Like the Sun* (A&M, 1987)
Stanley Jordan
  'Angel', from *Magic Touch* (Blue Note, 1986)
The Red Hot Chili Peppers
  'Fire', 12″ single (EMI, 1987)
Soft Cell
  'Hey Joe'*/'Purple Haze', 12″ single supplied with *The Art of Falling Apart* (Some Bizarre, 1983)
Jeff Healey
  'All Along the Watchtower',* limited edition CD single (Arista, 1989)
Eugene Chadbourne
  'House Burning Down', from *LSDC&W* (Fundamental, undated)

Incidentally, 'Let Jimi Take Over' by STP23 (Mr Moto/W.A.V. Recordings, 1989) is the first house single thus far to be constructed around Hendrix samples . . . but it's fairly certain not to be the last.

And the Tributes . . .
Revenge: A Tribute to Jimi Hendrix (Gravity, 1995)
In which a whole heap of existing Hendrix covers by the likes of Iggy Pop, Ben Harper, The Shamen, Living Colour, Stevie Ray Vaughan, John Lee Hooker, Rod Stewart, Frank Zappa, Gil Evans and more are gathered together in one place. Rickie Lee Jones takes a skittishly sexy acoustic swing through 'Up from the Skies'; Vaughan replicates rather than reinvents Hendrix's 'slight return' version of 'Voodoo Chile'; Stewart carouses through a slightly inebriated in-concert 'Angel'; Red Hot Chili Peppers and Iggy Pop inject 'Fire' and 'Foxy Lady' with punk-rock slam; a heavy dub vibe infuses Living Colour's 'Midnight Lamp', Ras Kente & the Take No Prisoner Posse's 'Hey Joe' and both the

*I know these aren't Hendrix's own compositions . . . but it's the thought that counts.

Frank Zappa and Phenomenum takes on 'Purple Haze', whilst The Shamen's 'Haze' samples the hell out of Hendrix's original. With Booker T. Jones backing him up at the Hammond organ, John Lee magisterially Hookerizes 'Red House' (though not as radically as on the subsequent version he cut for his 1997 album *Don't Look Back*). Sadly, the Gil Evans album is represented by its most rockoid and least successful track: a medley of 'Crosstown Traffic' and 'Little Miss Lover' which sounds like Blood, Sweat & Tears at their lumpiest.

Stone Free: A Tribute to Jimi Hendrix (Reprise, 1993)
In which it is eloquently demonstrated both that Hendrix is still a contemporary artist in a way that few of the other late-greats and baby-boom icons of his era could be, and that his music is sufficiently rich to yield different facets to different suitors. Thereby, in this original anthology supervised by Eddie Kramer, The Cure and PM Dawn find the psychedelic adventurer; Buddy Guy the blustering bluesman; Eric Clapton (fronting Chic) the repressed free spirit; The Pretenders the humble seeker; Living Colour and Spin Doctors the arrogant rocker; and Body Count (with Ice-T at the mic) the sullen menace. Belly explore his sensuality, and Seal & Jeff Beck and Slash & Paul Rodgers (the latter pair backed by Hendrix's old Band of Gypsys rhythm section) his rage. The most unusual performances, however, come from avant-jazz guitarist Pat Metheny, whose 'Third Stone from the Sun' is a drily hallucinatory desert ride driven by a haunting bass line which, thanks to the wonders of sampling, enables the late Jaco Pastorius to make a posthumous contribution; and violinist Nigel Kennedy, exploding 'Fire' into a wildly exotic Balkan hoedown. Mind you, 'Move over, Rover, and let Nigel take over' doesn't quite have the same ring.

Jimi Hendrix on Video

The Best . . .

Jimi Hendrix (1973, Warner Home Video, 98 minutes)

Joe Boyd's biographical documentary collage of performance and interview footage takes an inevitable 'greatest hits' approach to Hendrix's life and work, but even though it misses or trivializes many of the undercurrents, it certainly hits most of the high-spots. The interview subjects include Mick Jagger, Lou Reed, Little Richard, Eric Clapton, Pete Townshend, Al Hendrix, Linda Keith, Fayne Pridgeon, and Arthur and Albert Allen, but the most insightful is Germaine Greer, and the most moving is the elfish Mitch Mitchell; the loving light that shines in Mitchell's eyes as he reminisces about his association with Hendrix is a testament all by itself. Hendrix gets to speak, albeit somewhat cryptically, for himself; the performances include an alternate edit of the *Woodstock* 'Star Spangled Banner' (this time with the cameras on Hendrix instead of on muddy hippies picking up garbage), the inevitable Monterey 'Wild Thing', some blurry black-and-white film of the epochal Band of Gypsys' 'Machine Gun', the charming acoustic 'Hear My Train A-comin'' (from Peter Neal's 1968 *Experience*), and some rather dispirited performances from the Isle of Wight. Flawed, but indispensable; unfortunately, it gains little from transfer to DVD.

Jimi Plays Monterey (1987, Virgin Music Video, 50 minutes)

Hendrix's breakthrough performance captured in its entirety (well, almost: D. A. Pennebaker dropped his camera a third of the way through 'Purple Haze' and missed 'Can You See Me' while repairing it). The film is padded – though not unpleasantly so – with the woozy reminiscences of 'Papa' John Phillips (composer-in-chief of The Mamas and The Papas, one of the Festival's organizers and the man who proved that you don't have to say 'no' to drugs if you can say 'sorry' afterwards in a lucrative memoir), an intro in which an artist splatter-paints a wall with a portrait of Hendrix to the accompaniment of 'Can You See Me', and some footage of Hendrix at the 'Christmas on Earth Continued' London concert in December 1967. In the latter sequence, Hendrix performs a truncated 'Sgt Pepper's Lonely Hearts Club Band' and prefaces 'Wild Thing' with an extraordinary impression of a bagpipe band. Eric Burdon's 'Monterey' is set to a montage of proto-hippies arriving at the show and glimpses of the rest of the Festival's cast; by the time the Experience take the stage, the viewer's appetite is thoroughly whetted. 'All we had going for us was our act,' says Pete Townshend, who had the dubious honour of immediately preceding Hendrix. 'What he had was his genius.' *Jimi Plays Monterey* is the most graphic example available of the kind of performances on which Hendrix's legend was built.

Jimi Plays Berkeley (1971, Palace Video, 50 minutes)
In sharp contrast to the glowing lysergic euphoria of *Jimi Plays Monterey*, the mood of this February 1970 Moratorium Day show at Berkeley Community Centre is appropriately tough and confrontational. A savage performance of 'Machine Gun' is intercut with news footage of a riot sparked by police breaking up an anti-war march; a Vietnam vet turned activist argues with pool-hall red-necks, and a complacent little hippie girl who needs a good clip round the ear demands to be admitted free to a showing of the *Woodstock* movie. Accompanied by Mitch Mitchell and Billy Cox, an impassive, clean-shaven Hendrix roars through a devastating set, including the frequently-quoted 'Johnny B. Goode', an electrifying 'Hear My Train A-comin'' and a 'Star Spangled Banner' which almost cuts the Woodstock one. The tongue-waggling and acrobatics seem almost by rote; here Hendrix is more interested in playing than showboating. There are more blacks in the crowd than one is accustomed to seeing at Hendrix shows; with deliberate emphasis, he tells the audience, 'Thank you for showing up *together*.'

. . . and the Rest . . .
Jimi Hendrix Experience (1968, Palace Video, 33 minutes)
This odd little film was made by director Peter Neale in late 1967 and early 1968. It includes interview material both jivey and thoughtful, and some interesting juxtapositions of Hendrix's music with scenes of Indian massacres extracted from old Westerns, and with sublime, gliding parachute sequences. There's also a gratuitous sequence set to 'Foxy Lady' where a Swinging London dolly-bird in a big white fur coat is chased all over town by a menacing camera P.O.V. which subliminally suggests that a sexually provocative woman is just *asking* for sexual assault. Best bits: Hendrix being 'interviewed' by Mitch Mitchell and Noel Redding, and the acoustic 'Hear My Train A-comin'', which also appears, arguably to better effect, in the Joe Boyd documentary.

Rainbow Bridge (1971, Hendring, 72 minutes)
An astonishing farrago of acid-addled drivel produced by Mike Jeffery and sponsored by Warner Bros, this 'documentary' of Hendrix's visit to a hippie colony on the Hawaiian island of Maui was directed by one Chuck Wein, whose major achievement was to lose the original sound recording of the open-air concert which is the only reason anybody would voluntarily watch the movie in the first place. New-age drongos ride horses, meditate, babble about 'rilly getting it

together' and 'getting ready for the space people', smoke killer weed smuggled inside surfboards and – just as you're getting ready to leave – discuss reincarnation with Hendrix, who saunters into shot appearing rather more bombed than the East End of London during the Second World War. The performance – when it finally arrives – is not one of Hendrix's most memorable; the only reason why *Rainbow Bridge* deserves to survive is as an awful warning of the possible consequences of a hippie revival.

Johnny B. Goode (1985, Virgin Music Video, 26 minutes)
The term 'rip-off' is, of course, a relative one (not to mention an actionable one), so I will content myself with enumerating the contents of this slender programme: 'Are You Experienced' is a nice, if inconsequential, scratch-mix of existing Hendrix footage used as an MTV video to promote the *Kiss the Sky* compilation; the Berkeley 'Johnny B. Goode' is just fine, but preferable in the contexts where it has already appeared; 'All Along the Watchtower' (from the Atlanta Pop Festival) is – to put it mildly – somewhat lacklustre, especially since Hendrix forgets most of the lyrics; 'Art Attack' is the action-painting sequence from *Jimi Plays Monterey*, only set to different music; 'The Star Spangled Banner' (also from Atlanta) is not an improvement on either Woodstock or Berkeley; and 'Voodoo Chile' blends performance film with a painted dance troupe performing a heavily thematic 'modern' 'ballet'. This is the sort of stuff that gives Alan Douglas and the Hendrix Estate a bad name.

Bibliography

Enough books and magazines were consulted during the writing of the original edition of *Crosstown Traffic* to fill a small room; in fact, they *did* fill a small room. Not all of them were directly quoted in the text; the listing here is a representative selection. The editions cited are not necessarily either the first or the most recent. Occasionally, they are revisions or updates of the versions originally published; in such cases, the revised date is given.

Not surprisingly, the basic sources were the following:

David Henderson, *'Scuse Me While I Kiss the Sky*, Bantam, 1981
Jerry Hopkins, *Hit and Run*, Perigee, 1983
Curtis Knight, *Jimi: An Intimate Biography of Jimi Hendrix*, Star Books, 1974
Roger St Pierre (ed.), *Jimi Hendrix: Recorded Poems*, International Music Publications, 1986
Victor Sampson, *Hendrix: An Illustrated Biography*, Proteus, 1984
Steve Tarshis, *Original Hendrix: An Annotated Guide to the Guitar Technique of Jimi Hendrix*, Wise Publications, 1982
Chris Welch, *Hendrix: A Biography*, Ocean Books, 1972

These have since been joined by:

Stuart Nicholson, *Jazz-Rock: A History*, Canongate, 1998. Issues debated in chapters of the current work, amplified
Harry Shapiro & Caesar Glebeek, *Jimi Hendrix: Electric Gypsy*, St Martins Press, 1992. Though I disagree strongly with many of its judgements and conclusions, its status as the reference biography – where you go to look things up – is impregnable
Ricky Vincent, *Funk*, St Martins Griffin, 1995

No less valuable were the Hendrix special issues of *Guitar Player* (September 1975) and *Guitar World* (September 1985, March 1988); as well as numerous other articles which have appeared over the years in both publications. I have also drawn on features and reviews from *Guitarist*, *Musician*, *Down Beat*, *Rolling Stone*, *Q*, *New Musical Express* and *Melody Maker*. Particularly to the point was Bill Milkowski's 'Jimi Hendrix: The Jazz Connection', which appeared in the October 1982 edition of *Down Beat*.

Bibliography

The rest of the bookshelf looks something like this:

Gordon W. Allport, *The Nature of Prejudice*, Doubleday Anchor, 1958
James Baldwin,
– *Notes of a Native Son*, Corgi, 1964
– *Nobody Knows My Name*, Corgi, 1964
– *The Fire Next Time*, Penguin, 1964
Whitney Balliet, *The Sound of Surprise*, Pelican, 1963
Michael Bane, *White Boy Singin' the Blues*, Penguin, 1982
Joachim E. Berendt, *The Jazz Book*, Paladin, 1984
Chuck Berry, *The Autobiography*, Faber & Faber, 1987
Hugh Brogan, *The Pelican History of the United States of America*, Pelican, 1986
James Brown (with Bruce Tucker), *James Brown: The Godfather of Soul*, Fontana, 1986
Eric Burdon, *I Used to Be an Animal but I'm All Right Now*, Faber & Faber, 1986
Ian Carr, *Miles Davis: A Critical Biography*, Paladin, 1984
Ian Chambers, *Urban Rhythms*, Macmillan, 1985
Ray Charles & David Ritz, *Brother Ray*, Futura, 1978
Samuel Charters,
– *The Poetry of the Blues*, Avon, 1963
– *Robert Johnson*, Oak Publications, 1973
Robert Christgau, *Christgau's Guide: Rock Albums of the '70s*, Vermilion, 1982
Eldridge Cleaver, *Soul on Ice*, Panther, 1968
Nik Cohn,
– *Awopbopaloobopalopbamboom*, Paladin, 1969
– *Ball the Wall*, Picador, 1989
Bill Cole, *John Coltrane*, Schirmer Books, 1976
Ray Coleman, *Survivor: The Authorized Biography of Eric Clapton*, Sidgwick & Jackson, 1986
James Lincoln Collier, *The Making of Jazz*, Delta, 1978
Stephen Davis,
– *Bob Marley*, Arthur Barker, 1983
– *Hammer of the Gods*, Sidgwick & Jackson, 1985
Bob Dylan, *Lyrics 1962–1985*, Paladin, 1988
Jonathan Eisen (ed.), *The Age of Rock*, Vintage, 1969
Evan Eisenberg, *The Recording Angel*, Picador, 1988
Jenny Fabian, *Groupie*, Mayflower 1970
Julio Finn, *The Bluesman*, Quartet, 1986
Paul Garon, *Blues and the Poetic Spirit*, Eddison Bluesbooks, 1975
Nelson George,
– *Where Did Our Love Go?*, Omnibus, 1985
– *The Death of Rhythm & Blues*, Omnibus, 1988
Charlie Gillett, *The Sound of the City*, Souvenir Press, 1983

Ralph J. Gleason, *The Jefferson Airplane and the San Francisco Sound*, Ballantine, 1969

Richard Goldstein, *Goldstein's Greatest Hits*, Tower, 1970

Jonathon Green (ed.),
– *The Book of Rock Quotes*, Onmibus, 1977
– *A Dictionary of Contemporary Quotations*, David & Charles, 1982
– *Days in the Life*, William Heinemann; 1988

Alan Greenberg, *Love in Vain: The Life and Legend of Robert Johnson*, Doubleday Dolphin, 1983

Germaine Greer, *The Madwoman's Underclothes*, Picador, 1986

Guitar Player (eds.), *The Guitar Player Book*, Grove Press, 1983

Peter Guralnick,
– *The Listener's Guide to the Blues*, Blandford, 1982
– *Sweet Soul Music*, Virgin Books, 1986
– *Lost Highway*, Vintage, 1982
– *Feel Like Goin' Home*, Omnibus, 1971

John Hammond (with Irving Townsend), *John Hammond on Record*, Penguin, 1977

Michael Harambulos, *Right on: From Soul to Blues in Black America*, Eddison Bluesbooks, 1974

Phil Hardy & Dave Laing (eds.), *The Encyclopedia of Rock, Vols 1–3*, Panther, 1976

Sheldon Harris, *Blues Who's Who*, Arlington House, 1979

David Hatch & Stephen Millward, *From Blues to Rock*, Manchester University Press, 1987

Nat Hentoff, *The Jazz Life*, Panther, 1964

Nat Hentoff & Nat Shapiro, *Hear Me Talkin' to Ya*, Penguin, 1962

Calvin C. Hernton, *Sex and Racism*, Paladin, 1970

Michael Herr, *Dispatches*, Picador, 1978

Germ Hershey, *Nowhere to Run*, Times Books, 1984

Dave Hill, *Prince: A Pop Life*, Faber & Faber, 1988

Ian Hoare (ed.), *The Soul Book*, Methuen, 1975

Billie Holiday (with William Duffy), *Lady Sings the Blues*, Abacus, 1973

Barney Hoskyns,
– *Prince: Imp of the Perverse*, Virgin Books, 1988
– *Say It One More Time for the Brokenhearted*, Fontana, 1988

Arthur Jacobs, *A Short History of Western Music*, Pelican, 1981

Maxim Jakubowski (ed.), *The Wit and Wisdom of Rock and Roll*, Unwin, 1983

Leroi Jones,
– *Blues People*, Quill, 1963
– *Black Music*, Quill, 1967

Charles Keil, *Urban Blues*, University of Chicago Press, 1966

Bibliography

Bernard Levin, *The Pendulum Years*, Pan, 1970

Michael Lydon, *Boogie Lightning*, Da Capo, 1974

Craig McGregor,

– *Bob Dylan, A Retrospective*, Picador, 1975

– *Pop Goes the Culture*, Pluto Press, 1984

Michael MacLear, *Vietnam: The Ten Thousand Day War*, Thames Methuen, 1981

Norman Mailer,

– *The Armies of the Night*, Signet, 1968

– *Advertisements for Myself*, Panther, 1961

– *The Presidential Papers*, Corgi, 1965

– *Miami and the Siege of Chicago*, Penguin, 1969

Greil Marcus, *Mystery Train*, Omnibus, 1977

Dave Marsh,

– *Before I Get Old*, St Martins Press, 1983

– *Trapped: Michael Jackson & the Crossover Dream*, Bantam, 1985

George Melly, *Revolt into Style*, Penguin, 1970

Jim Miller (ed.), *The Rolling Stone Illustrated History of Rock & Roll*, Rolling Stone Press/Random House, 1976

Robert Neff & Anthony Connor, *Blues*, Latimer, 1976

A. X. Nicholas (ed.), *The Poetry of Soul*, Bantam, 1971

Eric Nisenson, *'Round About Midnight*, Dial Press, 1982

Lynda Rosen Obst, *The Sixties*, Random House/Rolling Stone, 1977

P. J. O'Rourke, *Republican Party Reptile*, Picador, 1987

Harry Oster, *Living Country Blues*, Minerva Press, 1975

Robert Palmer, *Deep Blues*, Papermac, 1981

John Phillips (with Jim Jerome), *Papa John*, Virgin Books, 1986

Brian Priestley, *Mingus: A Critical Biography*, Paladin, 1982

David Ritz, *Divided Soul*, Grafton, 1986

John Rockwell, *All American Music*, Kahn & Averill, 1985

Rolling Stone (eds.),

– *The Rolling Stone Interviews*, Paperback Library, 1971

– *The Rolling Stone Interviews Vol 2*, Warner Paperback Library, 1973

– *The Rolling Stone Record Review*, Pocket Books, 1971

– *The Rolling Stone Record Review Vol 2*, Pocket Books, 1974

– *The Rolling Stone Rock 'n' Roll Reader*, Bantam, 1974

– *The Rolling Stone Rock Almanac*, Rolling Stone Press, 1983

Mike Rowe, *Chicago Breakdown*, Eddison Bluesbooks, 1973

Lillian B. Rubin, *Quiet Rage*, Faber & Faber, 1987

James Sallis, *The Guitar Players*, Quill, 1982

James Sallis (ed.), *Jazz Guitars*, Quill, 1984

Gene Santoro (ed.), *The Guitar: the History, the Music, the Players*, Columbus, 1984

Charles Sawyer, *B. B. King: The Authorized Biography*, Blandford, 1980

Bobby Seale, *Seize the Time*, Arrow, 1970

Nat Shapiro (ed.), *An Encyclopedia of Quotations about Music*, David & Charles, 1978

Robert Shelton, *No Direction Home: The Life and Music of Bob Dylan*, Penguin, 1987

Ben Sidran, *Black Talk*, Da Capo, 1981

Robert Somina (ed.), *No one Waved Goodbye*, Charisma, 1973

George Steiner, *Language and Silence*, Faber & Faber, 1985

David A. Stockman, *The Triumph of Politics*, Coronet, 1986

John Swenson, *Stevie Wonder*, Plexus, 1986

J. C. Thomas, *Chasin' the Trane*, Da Capo, 1976

Alice Walker, *You Can't Keep a Good Woman Down*, Women's Press, 1982

Ed Ward, *Michael Bloomfield: The Rise and Fall of an American Guitar Hero*, Cherry Lane, 1983

Ed Ward, Geoffrey Stokes & Ken Tucker, *Rock of Ages: The Rolling Stone History of Rock & Roll*, Penguin, 1987

Tom Wheeler,

– *The Guitar Book*, Macdonald, 1981

– *American Guitars*, Harper & Row, 1982

Francis Wheen, *The Sixties*, Century/Channel Four, 1982

Charles White, *The Life and Times of Little Richard, the Quasar of Rock*, Pan, 1985

Timothy White, *Catch a Fire: The Life of Bob Marley*, Elm Tree, 1983

Garry Wills, *Reagan's America*, William Heinemann, 1988

Valerie Wilmer, *As Serious as Your Life*, Quartet, 1977

Tom Wolfe,

– *The Electric Kool-Aid Acid Test*, Bantam, 1968

– *Radical Chic & Mau-mauing the Flak-Catchers*, Bantam, 1970

– *Mauve Gloves and Madmen, Clutter and Vine*, Bantam, 1977

Malcolm X with Alex Haley, *The Autobiography of Malcolm X*, Penguin, 1965

Jimi Hendrix also moonlights as a character in fiction: he can be found in Michael Moorcock's 1974 novella 'The Dead Singer' (collected in *Moorcock's Book of Martyrs*, Quartet, 1976), in Lewis Shiner's novel *Deserted Cities of the Heart* (Abacus, 1987), and also in David Dalton's *Been Here and Gone: A Memoir of the Blues* (Methuen, 2000). Not to mention a few pages further on in this book.

Gratefully Undead

A quick visit to the universe next door

An interview with Jimi Hendrix is, in itself, a major event. Now fifty-eight years old, the one-time 'wild man of rock' rarely leaves his Hawaiian retreat, where he lives with his second wife and seven children, composing film scores and electronic blues symphonies in what is probably the best-equipped 'home studio' in the world, downloading his work via an ISDN line to the Internet.

Following his narrow escape from death after an accidental barbiturate overdose in 1970, Hendrix released the classic *First Rays of the New Rising Sun*, which remained in the Top 50 for almost two years, before retreating from the hard-rock wars. He maintained homes and studios in Manhattan and London – where he opened the second Electric Lady studio in 1973 – forging firm and lasting friendships and musical collaborations with Miles Davis and Stevie Wonder, recording and jamming with a floating pool of musicians – foremost amongst whom were, of course, his old sidekicks Mitch Mitchell and Billy Cox – without forming another permanent band. He performed memorably with Wonder on *Music of My Mind* and *Talking Book*, and with Miles on *On the Corner*, but released nothing new under his own name for over five years. Including tracks recorded at Channel One in Jamaica with Sly Dunbar and Robbie Shakespeare as rhythm section and Lee Perry manning the board, *Black Gold* was the eagerly awaited follow-up to *First Rays*, but with disco on the rise and punk waiting in the wings, the grandiose concept album received a frostily baffled critical reception. However, the unexpected breakout of the 'Rainbow Warrior' hit single took the album into the charts and it was eventually reassessed as a triumph, though ultimately it failed to match the sales success of *First Rays of the New Rising Sun*.

Relocating to Los Angeles in the early eighties to maintain closer contacts with the film industry following his first ventures into soundtrack work, he was tempted by young admirers in the heavy-metal fraternity to cut the ill-judged *Back to Gitcha*. The playing was as dazzling as ever, but the context sounded contrived: a ham-fisted attempt to recreate the early Experience sound. Worse, he started to dabble with serious drugs, and many observers believe that, if the album hadn't been a failure, he would have been sucked back into the hard-rock lifestyle. His decision not to tour behind the album was undoubtedly a wise one. The movie work then took precedence: his soundtrack for the Arnold Schwarzenegger showcase *Predator* generated the spin-off US No. 1 single 'The Jungle Came Alive' (featuring a rap from the then-little-known KRS-1), which reinvigorated interest in his back catalogue as well as a major reassessment of *Black Gold*.

In 1991 he retreated to Hawaii, where he numbers Todd Rundgren and Steely Dan's Walter Becker amongst his friends and neighbours. On his occasional excursions into the outside world he sometimes pops up jamming in small clubs with friends like Buddy Guy or Prince, but his only major public appearances over the last couple of decades have been at global spectacles like Live Aid – where he reunited the original Experience for a blazing return to early glories – or the Nelson Mandela concerts, where he shared the stage with Stevie Wonder.

To mark the release in autumn 2000 of *The Jimi Hendrix Experience*, the first volume of a boxed-set 'Anthology'-style peek into the back pages of the first four years of his career, he granted this exclusive interview to his biographer, Charles Shaar Murray.

The new boxed set is fantastic . . .
Uh, thank you. It's like the first one of a series. This one goes up to *First Rays of the New Rising Sun*, which was like a great place to draw a line. Because look what went down around that time. Janis passed. Jim Morrison passed. That cat in Canned Heat with, like, the big thick eye-glasses passed. The Beatles broke up. The, uh, US National Guard shot all those student kids at Kent State for protestin' the war. All of the main guys in the Black Panther Party got shot up by the police or, like, locked down for ninety-nine years or had to split the country and so forth. It was like, *whoah*! That whole time was like . . . a whole new era of music was gonna be startin' up and I knew I had to be there. Not 'cause I was so *important* or nothin' . . . it wasn't like I was goin' [*in pompous voice*], 'Aw shit, they can't get along without me . . .' [*laughs*] . . . but I realized [*laughs*] . . . I *real eyes*ed that everything had to change.

That was when you nearly died, wasn't it?
Yeah, right . . . I was, uh, in this chick's apartment in London and there was all kinds of bullshit goin' on, like with the management and contracts and money and blah-blah, and 'cause of that we was playin' all these shows in, uh, Europe and Sweden and Germany and so forth when we should have been back in New York finishin' up the album, and Bill Cox was all messed up 'cause some cat spiked him with some bad acid, so he was all freaked . . . I just wanted to chill and get some rest so I did a few of these sleeping pills that she had around. What I didn't know was that these German pills were like twice as strong as the ones I was used to, and the next thing I know is that I'm wakin' up in hospital with, uh, Mitch and Keith Moon and Ginger Baker all playin' in my head at the same time, and I had this sore throat from all the, uh, tubes they put down me to pump my stomach. Oh, *man* . . . it was *rough*.

But like in a certain way it was the best thing that could possibly have happened. I knew if things had been just a little bit different I could'a died right there and then, with all the biz stuff in a mess and the album not finished . . . oh man, the thought of *First Rays* not comin' out just the way I had it planned, now that would have, ah . . . *killed* me all by itself. So I got rid of the, uh, managers, and I got a good accountant to straighten everything out, finished up the record . . .

And you had the biggest album of your career to date . . .
And then I thought now it was time to step back, take a break. Five years, man, non-stop. I wasn't burned out, but I was gettin' close to runnin' on empty. [*in pretentious English voice*] My *reech* was ex*cee*ding my *grarsp*. I didn't even want to have a regular band no more. I wanted to play with some different cats I could learn some new shit from . . .

So you did the records with Miles and Gil Evans . . .
Yeah, Gil, man. He was incredible. He got all these great cats together to play my songs and it was, like, *whoah*, man. Suddenly everything was Technicolor. It was like he heard in those songs everything that I heard when I was writing them and *tryin'* [*laughs*] . . . tryin' to play 'em. And Miles was scary. The first time we tried to get it together he wanted $50,000 just to walk in the studio . . . but we talked him down. Instead of bein' my record with him playin', it was *his* record with *me* playin'. *On the Corner*, man . . . you know he was cuttin' *Bitches' Brew* while we was playin' Woodstock. All this new shit comin' together. He was like this Zen guy. He wouldn't tell you nothin' about the tune: he'd just hit some chords on the, uh, piano and give the drummer a beat and then . . . you'd kinda be on your own, but you wasn't on your own 'cause you'd be with him. And Mitch was there, and you know Mitch always brought the jazz, so in that way it was easy. And Miles always said to forget about jazz . . . and don't even think about rock . . . just play music, you know? Forget about what you want. Just find out what the music wants and, uh, play that.

And then Stevie Wonder came to Electric Lady to make *Music of My Mind* . . .
[*Laughs*] Yeah, Stevie. Stevie's a trip. I love Stevie. We met him in London in '67 and did some jammin' and stuff. So I was just hangin' out and watchin' him doin' all this stuff with the synthesizers and so forth, and he had these cats Robert Margoulieff and Malcolm Cecil . . . Tonto's Expanding Head Band, they were called. And the Expanding Head Band was cool. I always wanted me [*laughs*] one of those, man, 'cause my head [*laughs*] . . . naw, man, we won't talk about that. So there was me tryin' to get the guitar together all these years, and, uh, suddenly there was all these sounds on this Starship Enterprise thing. And I thought, oh, man, now I got to learn me some keyboards so I could get this shit together . . . or maybe I can put the guitar through the Moog and play it that way.

So I played a little bit on Stevie's record, and I did a little jammin' with various cats here and there, but really, man, I hardly touched the guitar for two or three years. I bought the Moog and the ARP and blah-blah-woof-woof . . . Pete Townshend had some of that stuff too, so we was talkin' about what we was doin'. I mean, man, all that [*does mouth impression of the sequencer parts from 'Baba O'Reilly' and 'Won't Get Fooled Again'*] was . . . a different world. And I worked with all the synths but guess what, man . . . [*laughs*] I wasn't no keyboard player, though I learned some stuff since.

But it was great to be away from the, uh, battlefield. All that whole hard-rock shit had just gotten so crazy, with Led Zeppelin and all that, and Black Sabbath. It was like this arms race or something: who was faster, who was louder, who could solo for longest, who had more smoke bombs and dry ice and so forth . . . it wasn't just that we couldn't win, it was like no one could win. Just like the real arms race, you know? So it just got to be time to say, like, 'Later for that.' [*Laughs*] 'See ya. Bye-bye.'

So later when Eddie Van Halen came along . . .
[*Laughs*] Whoah, man, now that was scary. [*Laughs*] Dwiddley-dwiddley-dwiddley-wheeeee-graaaaowwwwwwww! It was like some old, like, cowboy movie, you know. The doors of the saloon swing open and some cat walks in and comes right up to you [*drops into deep, drawly Robert Mitchum-type voice*]: 'Hey, stranger . . . they tell me you're fast.'

It was so amazing when you put the original Experience back together for Live Aid . . .
[*Laughs*] Whoah, man . . . now that was sort of funny. I mean, you should have seen the rehearsal. Me and Noel was friends again, sort of, but he'd been playing guitar all those years back in Ireland and it took a while for him to find his groove again on the, uh, basso profundo. And then it was like, 'What do we play?' We thought two of the old songs and maybe jam on something like some old R&B or rock-and-roll thing. So okay, we do 'Fire', no problem; we do 'Purple Haze' [*laughs, parodies his own singing*] . . . you know, uh, pupple heeeeeyyyyyyzzzzz . . . no problem. Then we go, okay, what else? Someone else's song, right? Noel wants to do some like Jerry Lee Lewis-type thing. Mitch is holding out for us doin' something of our own, like 'Angel', 'cept that back in the day we did that with Billy and Noel doesn't know it . . . and I'm thinkin' maybe we could try something by Stevie, like 'Superstition', or maybe like, you know, 'Get Up Stand Up' by Bob Marley . . . and it was just like the old days . . . you know, arguing.

Then we got there and everything was running late, and the sound was weird and it was like real old-time, like the, uh, package shows like with The Walker Brothers or the R&B revues in the real, real, real old days, like with Little Richard or Sam Cooke and them. That conveyor-belt thing, you know: 'Get 'em on the stage!' Three songs. 'Get 'em off the stage! They're over-running by, uh, thirteen and one-eighth of a second! They're screwing things up for the, uh, television!' Blah–blah woof-woof, all this, you know. So everything is runnin' overtime and all these cats with like, uh, the ear-goggles and the walkie-talkies and the clipboards are goin' nuts and Bob Geldof is screamin' at everybody, you know, fockin' this an' fockin' that . . . and then we only get to do two songs after all.

And guess what? We had like this rerun of Monterey because, uh, The Who were there, and it was great seein' Pete again an' all, but it was right back to, 'Uh-uh, I ain't goin' on after you guys' . . . 'Well, we ain't goin' on after you.' And then we both started laughin', because now we all grown up [*laughs*] we don't be havin' to be provin' shit no more. We was all like kids back then, you know: like me-me-me-me-me all of the time. Now we seen them glam bands and punk bands and New Romantic bands and heavy metal bands all come and go . . .

What did you think of all those different styles?
It was like . . . pop music, you know? It was cool for what it was and where it was, but I felt like now I was someplace else. Roxy Music had somethin' goin' on, with Eno and all his sounds . . . and David Bowie was, like . . . I mean [*laughs*] I had ''Scuse me while I kiss this guy,' [*laughs*] but he was, like, him and his guitar player was like ''Scuse me while I blow this guy' [*laughs*].

What about punk?
It was real, you know? It was rough [*laughs*] . . . but it was real. Like some raggedy little dog goin' row-row-row all in your face and so forth. Chained up, barkin'. Just straight-up angry shit. I mean, it wasn't like me and Pete didn't know about feelin' like smashin' shit up. It's part how you feel, and part . . . drama.

What was it like sitting in with The Clash?
Well [*laughs*] . . . it was different. The reggae thing helped, 'cause Stevie turned me on to Bob Marley and them. A different groove, you know? But them New Romantics . . . it was like when I was a kid back in the fifties you had all them Fabians and Bobbys in white socks and luminous teeth and plastic eyelashes. Those cats will always be around. It's just the names and the faces that change.

You got very heavily into dub at one point, didn't you?
[*Laughs*] I-I-I-I-I sure did-did-did-did! [*Laughs*] They had all these raggedy-ass desks and boards with all wires and cables hangin' down everywhichwhere, but, man, I couldn't believe the sounds those cats in Jamaica were getting! And, you know, I thought I knew what to do with an echo! Me and The Beatles and, ah, Pink Floyd and so forth . . . we were amateurs, man. Lee Perry just got to come from the same planet as Sun Ra and George Clinton . . .

And you?
[*Laughs*] And me! And, uh, Beefheart . . .

So you cut those *Black Gold* sessions with Sly & Robbie . . .
Yeah . . . I needed that different groove for two or three of those songs, and I wanted to cut 'em with Carlie and Family Man from The Wailers, but Bob was out on tour at the time . . . Sly and Robbie weren't as tech as they got later on with

Black Uhuru, but they already had it goin' on [*laughs*] big time. That album freaked everybody out in America and, ah, Europe, but the dub plates of 'Rainbow Warrior' that we got Scratch to mix jus' [*laughs*] mash up de soun' system-dem backayard. Jus' mash it up, mon [*laughs*]. Mash it up inna Brixton, mash it up inna Brooklyn, mash it up inna Tivoli Gardens . . . [*laughs*] Yah, mon. Jah protect an' guide, seen?

Seen I. What kind of music do your kids like?
Rap, rap and rap [*laughs*], and just for a change, a little bit of hip-hop. Jaco, the oldest, he's starting to check out some jazz, but he got it from, you know, Gang Starr and Digable Planets and all this. You know how it is. They're real hardcore about not bein' into whatever the old man's into. The kind of rap I can dig is more like, you know, De La Soul or PM Dawn. Or The Fugees or The Roots. More inner space than in-your-face [*laughs*]. We've been talkin' about maybe doing some things with The Roots next year.

What's the weirdest gig you ever did?
[*Laughs*] Ooohhh, man . . . I guess it would have to be this show we did in Santa Monica with, ah, Frank Zappa and Captain Beefheart. That was like fallin' down the, uh, rabbit hole like in *Alice in Wonderland*. I mean, Don [*laughs*] is really out in space . . . if I'm the Alpha Quadrant he's like the Gamma Quadrant. And Frank was such a control freak . . . but then you're from England and you got Tony, uh, Blair [*laughs*], so you know all about that.

Is the tape of that show ever gonna get released?
Not [*laughs*] . . . while I'm alive!

What's the biggest mistake you ever made?
[*Laughs*] Man . . . you got all week?

How about *Back to Gitcha*?
[*Groans*] What's that? Never heard of it! Uh, naw, man. That was so not a good idea. I just had all these young guys from, uh, Poison and Guns 'N' Roses and so forth . . . Slash was practically livin' at my house and sayin', 'Hey, you gotta come back and show everybody how it's done,' and there was all this powder around . . . so I got back into gettin' high and next thing I know I'm playin' this guitar looks like an, uh, electric can-opener. Had to pull the plug on that shit real quick, but by then the record was done. That was like it for, uh . . . ear-bleed.

Your last outside work was sessions with John Lee Hooker and Ice-T . . .
[*Laughs*] Old Johnny Lee. He's amazing. What is he now, eighty-some years old? He's an inspiration to all of us, man. What joins him up with Ice-T is that they're both storytellers. They just tell different kinds of stories.

Yeah, but Ice ain't exactly a singer.
Hmmmmm [*laughs*] . . . I remember someone else they useta say that about. Bob

Dylan, maybe, or Johnny Rotten or [*laughs*] . . . some other cat whose name I can't remember right now [*laughs*].

How did you feel when The Beatles broke up?
Like there was a little bit less magic in the world.

Would you have wanted them to get back together?
Not unless they felt the magic was back. It was like . . . lots of folks wanted the old Experience, and they were sad when we broke up, and they would have been so happy, man, if we'd put it back together, but . . . Noel left when the magic was gone. We could still play a show, but we couldn't make new music together. Now Mitch and me was different: we got something new almost every time we sat down. And if you can't create together, man, then you shouldn't be in a band. John was still John, and Paul was still Paul, but the John-and-Paul thing wasn't there no more.

You were still living in New York when John Lennon got shot, weren't you?
[*Coughs*] Well, you know, I had an apartment in Manhattan, but I was actually on the West Coast to talk about some movie thing when it happened. Caught the first plane back East, went to Central Park with the people, tried to figure it all out . . . see, we always thought that if one of us ever got shot it would be on-stage, and it would be like Mick or David Bowie, or someone like that . . . see, we live our own lives: you know, get up, have some orange juice, read the paper, play with the kids, go to the studio, try to make some music, have dinner, talk to Carlos or Stevie or John Lee on the phone, go to bed . . . like, life, you know? Daily stuff. But we also got these other lives we don't know nothin' about, and those lives are in other people's heads. Now John had just made this new record, but he'd stayed home for like seven years or something, so the life he was leadin' was . . . quiet, y'know? And he had control over his life. But he got killed because of something that went down in whatever life he was livin' in that other cat's head . . . and you don't got no control over that life. You don't even know about all those other lives you livin'. So it would have been like scary shit, man, even if I didn't know the cat from back in the day. You know, London. Early days. I mean, I lived in Ringo's pad in London for a while, and Paul made them hire me for Monterey, and we played a lotta shows at the Savile Theatre, which was owned by Brian Epstein . . . so we had this connection.

How'd you get into the movie work?
I did a little thing for Francis Coppola which he stuck into *Apocalypse Now*, but the first main thing was Ridley Scott, man. I always loved all that science-fiction and other worlds and future stuff, you know? And he knew about that. He had this thing happening with *Blade Runner*, so he got in touch and we did that. I'd spent all this money on Fairlights and Synclaviers and all this [*laughs*] and the only guys who had that stuff were Stevie and Zappa and Pete and some Greek cat . . . and

me. So I had to do something with it, right? OK, so we do the movie and, wow, that was a trip. I'd be sittin' there in the studio watchin' all this stuff on a big monitor and kinda jammin' to it on the guitar, and then goin' back over it and the guitar would be, like, Harrison Ford and then all the stuff on the Synclavier would be, like, the world around Harrison Ford. And then we'd hook it all up to the videotape and sync it, you know, get the SMPTE codes all nice and tight, and then we'd watch it and say, 'Does this work?' and if it did we'd keep it and move on to the next part. It was cool because, like, all my life I'd be seein' pictures in my [*laughs*] expanding head band and tryin' to paint those pictures with music, and now we have some other cat's pictures and then make the sounds which those pictures like create and generate. But if the pictures ain't happenin' then there ain't no music . . . there was one time where I tried to make some music for a picture that wasn't happening and . . . [*groans*] . . . whoah, man. Ain't never doin' that again. [*Laughs*] Not even for Arnie. *Eraser*? Man, that shoulda been [*laughs*] . . . erased.

So anyway, after *Blade Runner*, James, uh, Cameron called me up to do *Terminator* . . . and it sort of went from there, with Spielberg and Quincy on the, uh, movie of *The Color Purple*. Purple, man, how could I say no? [*Laughs*] And nobody says no to Quincy . . . [*laughs*] 'cept Michael Jackson. And that was all old-timey stuff – no electric guitar or nothin'. I said, 'Get Taj [Mahal] or Ry Cooder,' but Q just twisted my arm [*laughs*] . . . like he does. What else? We got the *Batman* movie – I said, 'Get Prince,' but Tim Burton wouldn't take no 'No' [*laughs*] for no answer – and all of that. So we did it together. George Lucas said he was kickin' himself back in the day for not getting me to do some stuff for *Star Wars*, but I told him that orchestra stuff was right first time. Right now I'm foolin' around with a script based on the old '1983' song . . . but let's wait and see where that goes.

What kind of guitars you playing now? Still with the Parker Fly, I see . . .
You know ol' Pop Staples turned me on to that? And he's even older than John Lee! Yeah, the Fly is cool. I ain't even started figuring out some of the things you can do with the, uh, plastic-acoustic sound, like mixed with the electric and into the Synclavier and all through your molecules and chromosomes and stuff. So I got a few of them, and a Roland-Ready Strat for playing like trumpets and violins in the distance . . . and some real old Strats and some new old-type Strats for blues and stuff.

You've tried a lot of guitars over the years, haven't you?
Yeah, well [*laughs*]. You know how I am, I got to try everything that's out there. Back in the old days I got so sick of the, uh, Strat trem puttin' everything all out of tune whenever I went [*laughs*] like out there, I got into some Ibanez and Jackson guitars with those Floyd Rose and Kahler locking-type trems when we were doin' that record I, uh . . . [*laughs*] can't remember, but they had problems too.

Like all those nuts and bolts and knobbles and metal lumpy things stickin' all into your hand when you went to muting. And puttin' them things on a guitar means you got to cut out a big old chunk of the wood which makes your sound go all thin and puny, and then you got to pump it back up again with all kinds of processors and mutilators and, you know, implements of torture. And then I saw the Steinberger and it was like, whoo man, what is that? It was like playing [*laughs*] air guitar but still gettin' a sound, which was kind of cool, but I like to, you know, wrestle with the guitar a little bit. Like when you're makin' love, you need to feel like there's someone there, you know? [*Laughs*] Like if there ain't anybody there, you ain't makin' love. You're doin' [*laughs*] . . . somethin' else.

And like next I went to the Paul Reed Smith, which was like luxury. Too much luxury. Too smooth. Too, like, sweet. Like I love to listen to Carlos [Santana] playin' one of those, because bein' smooth and sweet is his thing and it's beautiful, but I need like a sharper sound. I might go back to the Strat full-time if I can get them to make me some kind of special Strat with a little of that Fly thing built into it. They've been chasin' me for the longest time to do a deal for a signature-type Jimi Hendrix model, and I've always said I just want a good Strat that I can buy anywhere and that anybody else can buy, and maybe this time I'm'a gonna do it. It's like no matter how long I stay away from playin' blues, I always got to come back . . . and I can't stay away from the Strat, either.

Did you check out the SynthAxe?
[*Laughs*] Awwwww . . . [*laughs*]. Don't even go there, man!

How about amps?
Well, it used to be Marshall, Fender, Marshall, Fender, Marshall, Marshall and, uh . . . [*laughs*] Marshall. Jeff Beck has this thing where he'll wire together a couple of Marshall stacks for that big grrrraaaaoooooooowww thing and a Fender Twin for that clear, sharp, high end all at once. And Stevie Ray, rest his soul, would have this whole big raggedy pile of every kind of amp you could think of all hooked up together. If your crew don't like love you to death, man, there's no way you can keep all that shit workin'. Some of them new ones . . . I mean, there's so many buttons to push it's like *Star Trek*. Phasers on stun, ready photon torpedoes, divert auxiliary power to forward thrusters, ready transporter room three, blah-blah woof-woof . . . it was like in the studio you can do all that stuff, you can take for ever checkin' stuff out, gettin' every single thing just right. In fact, that's why Chas got pee-oh-ed with me when we were doing *Electric Ladyland* and it was part of why Noel got pissed off. But live, man, you just want it to be like there so all you have to think about is . . . you know, remembering the words and hitting the right notes [*laughs*]. Well, some of 'em, anyway. So now I got me this Roland thing for the studio which is, like, every amp in the world [*laughs*] . . . and a few that ain't.

You know one thing that was cool? When we got monitors. We had so many live recordings where the band was sounding great but it was all so loud that I couldn't hear myself singing and . . . I never had the biggest voice in the world, you know, and when we would hear the tapes back the singing was like . . . oh, terrible, man. And I would say, 'Oh, man, promise me this'll never come out,' and, you know, if I'd'a died back then in 1970 you know it would'a come out. But then the PA systems got better and you had monitors and you could hear every note you were singin' so nice and clear . . . made me wish we'd had all that back in the sixties. I tell you, man, if we had those back then I'd'a done 'Spanish Castle Magic' live a lot more often. And all the pretty ballads. But since I don't do them big tours no more, all I need is right here. If I jam, I take a Twin or a Bassman and some of Roger Mayer's stomp-boxes, or I just plug into what's there. When I was a kid, I didn't have no money for nothin' fancy . . . couldn't even keep my guitar outta the pawnshop sometimes . . . so I learned to play anything. Any kind of amp, any kind of guitar, right-hand, left-hand, I can work with it.

What are you working on now?

You know, it's funny, man. Listening to all that stuff on the boxed set, and the stuff for the second one which we'll be puttin' out next year . . . for 2001 [*hums* 'Also Sprach Zarathustra'] made me think about, you know, songs. So maybe I'll do a record of songs next year. Call up Mitch and Bill again. Just like the old days. [*Laughs*] Well, no. Not like the old days. But kinda.

Do you miss those old crazy days?

[*Laughs*] No, man. I do not miss that stuff at all. I mean, whatever there was to do, I did it, and it was fun, but that life nearly killed me once [*laughs*] and after LA I decided it wasn't gonna get no second chance. I'm just glad I made it through and got to be [*laughs*] . . . an old man. You know, like old John Lee says, you never get out of these blues alive? Well, I feel like I did. I'm just grateful, man. Gratefully . . . [*laughs*] . . . undead.

The author would like to thank Ian MacDonald, author of the definitive Beatles study *Revolution in the Head*, for additional research.

1963: A Merman I Should Turn to Be

Gypsy Boy sits shivering in the bar of the abandoned motel by the shore, waiting for Nightbird, obsessively picking at his unamplified guitar as if it were a scab, burning the midnight lamp. The power lines had been down for over a week, and the oil-fired generator in the shed out back functioned only intermittently, so most of the time he was dependent for light on torches powered by batteries scavenged from the gift shop, and for heat on odd items of busted furniture that he burned on what used to be the stage. Sometimes he was careful not to risk torching the entire building; sometimes, after a few drinks from the bar's remaining bottles, he didn't care whether he burned it down or not. So far, he hadn't.

Later, when he attempted to recollect the time he spent there, it seemed to have lasted little longer than a single night: a sweaty, hallucinatory, toss-and-turn, damp-pillowed fever-dream of a night, but a single night nevertheless. At the time, though, it felt as though he'd never been anywhere else and never *would* be anywhere else.

Two nights before the war finally broke out, Gypsy Boy came to the Cherokee Inn, soaking wet from the blizzard raging outside. He'd hitch-hiked from the Greyhound station carrying only a Stratocaster with one spare set of strings, a Twin Reverb amp with a loose output valve and a couple of missing control knobs, just under $300 in limp, torn bills, and a single suitcase stuffed with crumpled, sweat-stained stage clothes and scraps of paper covered with illegible scrawlings which he claimed were poems and song lyrics. He checked into the cheapest room they had, telling the bored Puerto Rican boy behind the reception desk that, if a Miss Bird arrived or called, he wanted to know immediately, day or night, but that if a Miss Dagger inquired after him they must under no circumstances admit that he was there or even that they'd ever heard of him. The boy yawned, scribbled something next to his name on the register and handed him his key. He hauled his suitcase, amplifier and guitar across the courtyard, past the filthy swimming pool, and let himself into his room. He surveyed the stained wallpaper, the threadbare blankets, the worn-out TV, the fly-blown mirror, the cracked toilet seat and the dusty bath. The tubercular grinding of the heater just about masked the pounding rain and the howling wind battering the walls of the room, but it couldn't drown out the sounds of the couple fighting next door. He crawled between the sheets and eventually drifted into a troubled sleep which was only fractionally more restful than no sleep at all.

Nightbird didn't call. Conserving his money, Gypsy Boy haunted the motel like some disconsolate ghost with post-adolescent acne and a raggedy, half-grown-out process. Occasionally he'd appear in the coffee shop, pushing the watery scrambled eggs around his plate and nursing the same cup of coffee for hours on end, but most of the time he stayed in his room, watching TV, following the news around the dial, hearing the President attempting, over and over, to reassure the country that the war would easily be won, no matter what kind of weapons the enemy were using. The occasional Cassandras who warned that the use of dirty weapons, anywhere in the world, would eventually render the entire planetary surface uninhabitable were mocked both by official spokesmen and by the smiling, self-assured television anchors. The Cassandras insisted that it didn't matter who was fighting or where, but what they were fighting *with*. The anchors smiled, the President reassured, the networks cut to commercials whenever a Cassandra looked like he or she was about to win the argument.

Once, towards the end of the second week, Gypsy Boy attempted to spin out his decreasing funds by sitting in with the band who played Thursday, Friday and Saturday nights in the bar, but after the first set they told him he played too loud and sounded too weird and was scaring the customers, all seven of them. As he lugged his guitar and amplifier back to his room, he thought he heard the sax player mutter something about *goddam crazy niggers*, and the rest of the band, huddled round a table near the stage with their cigarettes and beers and shots of Black Jack, erupted into cawing laughter which he fancied he could still hear even when he was back in his room, sprawled out on his bed watching Huntley and Brinkley. The worn-out picture tube enveloped them in fuzzy, garish reds and blues which blended, when the winds jarred the aerial, into a sickly mauve halo.

Sometimes, he would reread the tattered comic book he'd found in the coffee shop one morning after breakfast. It was issue 352 of *Astro Man*, one of his childhood favourites, and in the lead story, Astro Man, patrolling a distant sector of the galaxy, landed on an idyllic planet populated by gentle, peaceful people living a pastoral tribal lifestyle, kind of like Native Americans. Astro Man fell in love with a beautiful maiden there and promised to return on his next swing through that sector, but on his next stop, he became ensnared by a seductive sorceress who almost succeeded in trapping him in her world for ever. After his escape, he returned to the Indian planet, but found it devastated by nuclear war with the remains of its formerly peaceful people fighting over the ruins. Apparently time moved much faster there: the few weeks he'd been away had been the equivalent of a thousand of their years, and the girl he loved was long dead. The comic-book company had hired some new artists since the last time he'd read *Astro Man*, and all the characters looked different. Now Astro Man looked a little like him, the lovely tribal maiden like Nightbird, and the evil sorceress like Dolly. He read the story over and over to distract himself from the news, but somehow it failed to cheer him up. Nightbird still didn't call, but then neither did Dolly.

By the beginning of his third week, Gypsy Boy was out of money. He'd tried to save money by only eating once a day and allowing himself only three cigarettes a day and a couple of beers each weekend, but eventually he'd had to go to the desk and confess to the Puerto Rican boy that he was broke. The boy had sucked his teeth contemptuously and gone to get the manager, a doughy woman in a stained overall, with brassy bottle-blonde hair and eyes like pale-blue marbles. In the end they cut a deal: he handed over his amp and in exchange was allowed to keep the room for another five days.

By now, the tone of the war news had shifted. The President wasn't quite so reassuring, the anchors' smiles weren't quite so self-assured, and the Cassandras were getting a rather more respectful hearing. The winds were steadily increasing in strength, and a cloud of death was blowing from the warzone towards the coast. The word 'evacuation' began to be heard more and more frequently, and it was suggested that the President had a master plan to save the population, though no one was prepared to state exactly what that plan might be. A friendly chamber-maid who occasionally sneaked him a hamburger or a pack of cigarettes told him that her brother was in the military and was claiming that a fleet of giant space shuttles was going to fly millions of people to safety under an airtight dome on Mars. A tabloid newspaper suggested that the answer was an undersea colony capable of sheltering Americans until the planet was habitable again, fit for them to inherit. However, since the same paper also claimed that the President was having a passionate affair with the movies' favourite blonde, Gypsy Boy didn't take that one too seriously.

At the end of the week, he still hadn't heard from Nightbird. He went back to the desk, gave the doughy woman his guitar, returned to the room and reread the *Astro Man* book, dividing his attention between the garish four-colour figures on the page and the mauve blurs on the TV screen. They were talking evacuation again, this time within the next forty-eight hours. Apparently the tabloid had been right after all: huge submarines were already massing offshore to take the population down to their new home on the ocean floor.

Everybody packed up and moved out, including the doughy woman, the chambermaid and the Puerto Rican. Gypsy Boy decided to stay. With a sidelong grin, the doughy woman flipped him the master keys to the Cherokee Inn. The first thing he did was to retrieve his guitar and amp from under her desk in the back office, haul them down to the bar, and plug in. The red light on the amp's front panel glowed reassuringly at him, and the loose output valve buzzed and hummed. He kicked in the front of the cigarette machine, retrieved a pack of Marlboros, lit up, turned everything up to 10 and wailed 'til his fingers bled. He fell asleep sitting on the stage, the amp still humming to him throughout the long, stormy night. When he awoke, the power had gone, and the phones were dead.

Exploring the motel's storage rooms, he found torches, lanterns and a freezer full of gently defrosting hamburgers and eggs. In the back yard, a derelict shed contained an ancient generator which, with much cursing and a couple of ripped fingernails, he managed to start up. He left the amp permanently switched on so that its hum and its red light would tell him whether the electricity was flowing or not. Occasionally he went outside, but the air was growing steadily fouler, and he felt sick and weak when he breathed it.

The woman found him curled up on the stage, his guitar clasped in his arms, huddling for warmth next to the embers of a small fire he'd built from the last bar stool. She shook him gently by the shoulder. As he awoke, his gummy eyes at first refusing to focus, she appeared to him, wreathed in the mauve haze he remembered from the TV set in his old room. He seemed to see two shifting figures, sometimes standing side by side, sometimes blurring into one. The woman on the left was tall, African-featured, with broad shoulders and heavy breasts; the one on the right was small, lithe, impish, Cherokee.

He hauled himself up on one elbow, rubbed his eyes and stared up at Dolly and Nightbird as they smiled down at him. His eyes finally settled into focus, and now there was but one woman, with Dolly's height and strength and Nightbird's elfin smile and liquid grace. The halo still surrounded her, but it was no longer the sickly hue he had seen on the TV screen. Instead, it was now a healing purple aura of boundless depth, richness and compassion. She helped him gently to his feet and held him close. As her purple aura enveloped him, the air was chilly and foul no more; now it was warm and fresh and sweet. He felt strength returning to his limbs and a new clarity augmenting his vision. Even his hearing was different: the world seemed to vibrate harmoniously, and in the distance he could hear one huge, all-encompassing chord, in which every note he could imagine, and a few of which he could never even have dreamed, happily co-existed. With that part of his mind which was still Gypsy Boy, he reflected that he had never quite understood what 'harmony' was before that moment.

Protected by the purple glow, Astro Man and the Angel flew towards the shore without even a single glance back at the ruins of the Cherokee Inn. They plunged into the ocean and dived down, past the fleet of submarines, past the huge plastic domes which bubbled the ocean floor. Not a single drop of water touched their bodies as they hurtled along the coast. Slowing to a comfortable drift, they rolled over and over until they could see, reaching down to them through the swelling murky waters, what appeared to be the first rays of a new rising sun.

New York drowned as they held hands.

[For J. G. Ballard and Michael Moorcock]

Index

Index

Bridges, Jeff, 254
'Bright Lights, Big City', 210, 275
Broonzy, Big Bill, 140, 145–6, 166, 192, 193
Brotzmann, Peter, 252
Brown, Bobby, 124
Brown, Clarence 'Gatemouth', 161
Brown, H. Rap, 212
Brown, James, 37, 47, 98, 110, 123, 195, 204,
    207–9, 212, 222–3, 241
  as bandleader, 49, 199–200, 208–9
  and George Clinton, 208–9, 224
  and Miles Davis, 248
  and Hendrix, 224n
  and Jackson 5, 218
  and Miles Davis, 67
  as performer, 207, 208
  and pop, 116, 117, 178, 212
  and Prince, 126
  and Sly Stone, 215
  and Norman Whitfield, 218
Brown, Oliver, 192
Brown, Ray, 237
Brown, Tony, 72
Brown, Willie, 133, 134, 136, 137
Bruce, Jack, 56, 67, 69, 241, 244, 245
Buddy Miles Express, 65, 200, 219
Burchill, Julie, 85
Burdon, Eric, 57, 63, 102, 170, 181n
  and Hendrix, 59, 61, 63, 71, 72, 102, 114–15
Burgess, Anthony, 226
Burke, Solomon, 36, 50, 168, 193, 204, 205, 211
Burks, John, 236
Burnett, Chester, *see* Howlin' Wolf
'Burning of the Midnight Lamp', 92, 269, 274
Burrell, Kenny, 235
Burton, Gary, 243
Bush, George H. W., 33, 130
Butler, Jerry, 232
Butterfield, Paul, 55, 165, 219, 232
Byrds, The, 58, 61, 233, 241

'California Night', 179
California, Randy, 54
Calloway, Cab, 157
Cameo, 127
Cameron, James, 123
Campbell, Jeff, 247
Canned Heat, 172
Capitol Records, 63, 220
Capote, Truman, 86
Capricorn Records, 117
Captain Beefheart, 36, 242

Carey, Mariah, 124
Carmichael, Stokely, 73, 98
Carr, James, 205
Carr, Leroy, 143
Carter, Amy, 33
Carter, Calvin, 162
Carter, Ron, 241, 244
Casady, Jack, 65, 181, 264, 269
'Castles Made of Sand', 210, 247, 268
Casuals, The, 48
'Catfish Blues', 180–1, 269
CBS, 28, 123, 213, 249, 260
Chalpin, Ed
  and Public Enemy, 122
  recording deal with Hendrix, 53, 55, 63, 65,
    67, 68–9, 71, 122, 219–20
  recordings of Hendrix, 63, 64, 65, 115, 170–1
Chambers Brothers, 212, 213
Chandler, Chas, 11, 55, 64, 214, 263
  and The Animals, 55, 63
  and Hendrix, 4, 10, 31, 55–60, 62, 63, 64, 65,
    70, 72, 182, 214
  and Soft Machine, 63, 112, 242
Chandler, Raymond, 184
Charles, Ray, 42n, 47, 103, 178, 192–4, 195, 199,
    204, 228, 232
  and The Beatles, 104, 196
  and Hendrix, 164, 210
  and race issues, 107
Cheech & Chong, 51
'Cherokee Mist', 274
Cherokee music, 185, 238
Cherry, Don, 232, 234
Chess Records, 164, 165, 166, 168
Chic, 12
Chicago (Chicago Transit Authority), 242–3, 249
Chicago blues, 140, 145–6, 161, 165, 167
Chicago Plastercasters, 88
Chicken Shack, 170
chitlin circuit, the, 49, 106
Chong, Tommy, 51
chords, 156, 157, 173, 227–8, 230, 238
Christgau, Robert, 101, 215, 250
Christian, Charlie, 1, 132, 149–59, 228, 235
  death, 158
  guitars, 151
  influence, 150, 173
  recordings, 153–4, 155, 156–7
Christian, Clarence, 150
Christian, Edward, 150, 151
'Christmas on Earth Continued', 9
Chuck D, 122

311

Index

Index

Index